THE LIBERAL PERSUASION

ARTHUR SCHLESINGER, JR., AND THE CHALLENGE OF THE AMERICAN PAST

EDITED BY
JOHN PATRICK DIGGINS

PRINCETON UNIVERSITY PRESS

PRINCETON, NEW JERSEY

Library of Congress Cataloging-in-Publication Data

The liberal persuasion : Arthur Schlesinger, Jr., and the challenge of
the American past / edited by John Patrick Diggins.

p.   cm.

Includes index.

ISBN 0-691-04829-0 (cl : alk. paper)

1. Schlesinger, Arthur Meier, 1917–.   2. Liberalism—United
States—History—20th century.   3. United States—Historiography.
4. Historians—United States.   5. United States—Foreign
relations—1945–1989.   6. United States—Foreign relations—1989–.
I. Diggins, John P.

E175.5.S38L53   1997   973'.072—dc21   97-18920   CIP

This book has been composed in Berkely Book Modified

Princeton University Press books are printed
on acid-free paper and meet the guidelines for
permanence and durability of the Committee on
Production Guidelines for Book Longevity
of the Council on Library Resources

http://pup.princeton.edu

Printed in the United States of America

10   9   8   7   6   5   4   3   2   1

CONTENTS

THE LIBERAL PERSUASION

Introduction

THE VITAL HISTORIAN

JOHN PATRICK DIGGINS AND MICHAEL LIND

ONE MORNING in January 1961, newly elected president John F. Kennedy walked into the Oval Office to meet with Arthur Schlesinger, Jr., then on leave from Harvard University and recently appointed presidential assistant. After the historian shook hands with his new boss, he said, "I'm not sure what I'm supposed to be doing here." "Neither am I," the president confided.[1]

In retrospect Schlesinger's presence at the beginning of the "thousand days" of the Kennedy administration seems appropriate, almost inevitable. In his dual capacity as scholar and public intellectual, Schlesinger has been present, indeed prominent, at critical episodes during the evolution of mid-twentieth-century American liberalism. As a young historian he had provided FDR's America with what Van Wyck Brooks has taught us to call "a usable past," finding the nineteenth-century headwaters of New Deal liberalism in Jacksonian democracy. As an eminent public intellectual he joined Reinhold Niebuhr and others in the early years of the Cold War in defending a tough-minded anticommunist liberalism against "the children of light," those who were as naive about human nature as they were about the Soviet Union. There was no reason to be surprised, then, that Schlesinger, the spokesman and chronicler of a certain brand of American liberalism, was to be found where history was being made by one of the last leaders in the tradition that Schlesinger had both shaped and recorded. While American politics has meandered erratically, Arthur Schlesinger, Jr., from the beginning of his long and productive career, has almost always been found at the "vital center."

Born and raised in the small town of Xenia, Ohio in 1917, Arthur Schlesinger, Jr., left his rural roots at age seven when his father took a position at Harvard University; it was Cambridge, Massachusetts, that offered an intellectual milieu for the young son. A passion for history ran through the family. His father, Arthur Schlesinger, Sr., was one of the first scholars to teach social history and to advocate investigating the role of women in America's past, and his mother, Elizabeth Bancroft Schlesinger, descended from an illustrious ancestor, the most influential historian of the pre–Civil War era, George Bancroft.[2]

At sixteen Schlesinger started at Harvard and graduated *summa cum laude* in 1938 (two years ahead of his contemporary, John F. Kennedy). After a year at

Peterhouse College, Cambridge, where Schlesinger completed and published his senior thesis, *Orestes Brownson: A Pilgrim's Progress* (1939), he returned to Harvard as a member of its Society of Fellows, a select few who were free to follow their curiosities without taking postgraduate seminars and examinations. Pearl Harbor interrupted the scholarly life and Schlesinger spent the World War II years working for the Office of War Information (OWI) and the OSS (Office of Strategic Services). In an army private's uniform he served in London and Paris and, after Germany's collapse, Wiesbaden.

Before going overseas, Schlesinger had completed the manuscript of *The Age of Jackson.* He added a foreword in May 1944, and the book was published in September 1945. It received a remarkable reception from the general public as well as professional historians, winning the twenty-eight-year-old author a Pulitzer Prize. The following year Schlesinger returned to Harvard and began teaching American intellectual history just when the Cold War in Europe was breaking out and communism replaced fascism as the ideological menace of the twentieth century.

Schlesinger's *The Vital Center* (1949) takes its epigrammatic title from the poet W. B. Yeats's insight that in times of turmoil and fear, the "centre cannot hold" if "the best have lost all conviction / and the worst are full of passionate intensity." In the opening phase of the Cold War, some of the best minds in America had a failure of nerve and would soon join the Progressive Party of Henry Wallace, who in 1948 repudiated the Truman Doctrine and advocated what came close to appeasement of the Soviet Union. Schlesinger had no patience with fellow travelers who had allowed themselves to be taken in by apologists for Stalin's totalitarian system. As a scholar he fought the Cold War with the intellectual weapons of American history: Nathaniel Hawthorne's insight that idealism can mask the egotism of power; William James's philosophy of pragmatism that sees all knowledge as tentative and contingent; and, above all, Reinhold Niebuhr's theology of existentialism that calls upon men and women to struggle for an impossible victory and be ready to accept an inevitable defeat. With such mentors counseling skepticism and finitude, Schlesinger could effectively challenge the Marxist prophecy that the whole complex world was inevitably marching to a single destiny.

During the fifties, Schlesinger finished three volumes of his magisterial *The Age of Roosevelt,* which narrated the story of Franklin D. Roosevelt and the New Deal from the 1920s, when the Republican Party and Herbert Hoover presided over the coming of the Great Depression and felt the "crisis of the old order," to 1938, when the Democratic Party began to encounter setbacks in congressional elections. Schlesinger put aside the Roosevelt history when President Kennedy called him to Washington in 1961, though he had no intention of exploiting his time in the White House to write an "Age of Kennedy." The assassination made such a book inevitable, however, and Schlesinger's *A Thousand Days: John F. Kennedy in the White House* (1965), which won both the

National Book Award and the Pulitzer Prize, reminded an America still recovering from mourning what it takes to have a calling for politics. With the assassination of Robert Kennedy in 1968, Schlesinger again drew on his talents as a scholar to pay similar tribute in *Robert Kennedy and His Times* (1978).

Leaving Washington in 1964, Schlesinger accepted a new appointment as the Albert Schweitzer Professor of Humanities at the Graduate School of the City University of New York. By a quirk of professional fate, Schlesinger once again found himself upholding "the vital center": he had as colleagues two distinguished professors, Herbert Gutman on his left and Gertrude Himmelfarb on his right. Schlesinger retired in 1993; he is currently at work on his memoirs.

To study Schlesinger's writings, as both a scholar and a polemicist, is to study the great movements in American politics and thought of which he has been perhaps the most consistent and articulate exponent. In *The Vital Center* Schlesinger wrote, "Mid-twentieth century liberalism, I believe, has . . . been fundamentally reshaped by the hope of the New Deal, by the exposure of the Soviet Union, and by the deepening of our knowledge of man." As the Old Left was succeeded by the New Left, Schlesinger has added a critique of multiculturalism and identity politics to his liberal critique of communism. The enterprise of vital-center liberalism, then, might be restated as a rejection of the dogmas of the reactionary right and the radical left from the perspective of a liberalism sobered by knowledge of the dangers of hubris and the limits to human understanding.

Mid-century American liberalism was concerned, first and foremost, with "the hope of the New Deal," with defending the intervention of the national government in the economy to preserve and raise the living standards of ordinary Americans. The mid-century liberal critique of the economic dogmas of the right now seems more urgent and relevant than it has for half a century. This comes as something of a surprise. From the 1940s to the 1980s, liberals of Schlesinger's school aimed most of their fusillades at the radical left in its call for a collectivized economy. In the 1990s, however, the socialist left, both anticommunists and anti-anticommunists, is demoralized, disoriented, powerless, and intellectually exhausted. Identity politics, which provided so much of the energy for multiculturalism and affirmative action, from the sixties to the nineties, now seems to have more critics than supporters.

The crack-up of socialism and the controversy over multiculturalism have been accompanied, since the seventies and more particularly since the end of the Cold War, by an astonishing renaissance of laissez-faire conservatism. Leaders of the new Republican majority in Congress speak openly of rolling back the New Deal and restoring an imagined Golden Age of minimal government and cornucopian capitalism. Not since the 1930s have mainstream Republicans (and not just the party's right wing) been so willing to reject the principles as well as the programs of the New Deal. And not merely the New Deal—the revival of the states' rights "compact theory" of the U.S. constitution by Clarence Thomas and other conservatives on the Supreme Court suggests that the nationalist legacy of Lincoln as well as that of FDR is now open to question. While the practice of Republican politicians is likely to be more moderate than their rhetoric, nevertheless, it is clear that the greatest challenge to mainstream liberalism today is coming from the right.

Ironically, at the very time that conservative intellectuals and polemicists have been pressing the attack against liberalism in the name of the unfettered free market, that market has been failing to fulfill the promises of its champions. For a generation, productivity growth in the western industrial democracies has been much lower than it was during the postwar period of 1945–1973. Although in recent years the American economy has outperformed those of Germany and Japan, wages and incomes have stagnated for the majority of workers in the United States for two decades, while the top fifth has reaped almost all of the gains from economic growth. Some blame this economic condition on high levels of government spending, rather than on low levels of public investment, or on the ease with which employers can relocate jobs or drive down wages in what increasingly is a global pool of mostly poor and non-unionized labor. To date, the alternative to the conservative cure for the ills of capitalism—more capitalism—has taken the form of sporadic and superficial populist or nationalist protest movements, like those opposed to the NAFTA and GATT treaties. With the industrial world in the midst of what some have called a "soft depression," with 1930s rhetoric of opponents of the New Deal revived as the conventional wisdom of the majority in Congress, and with the rise of anti-system candidates from Patrick Buchanan on the right to Jerry Brown on the left, the struggles and debates of New Deal liberalism seem far more relevant than they did only a few years ago.

The New Deal liberalism with which Schlesinger is identified was a product of the economic grievances and insecurities of the last era of worldwide crisis in capitalism. For Schlesinger, writing as a chronicler of the New Deal, government became a vehicle through which a great leader like Roosevelt could guide the country out of depression by some measure of national planning and control. The economic effects of the New Deal were arguably less important than its role in restoring confidence that representative government could deal with an unprecedented crisis. Roosevelt was sworn into office in March 1933, two months after Adolf Hitler became chancellor of Germany and took his first step toward assuming dictatorial powers. In the United States, writers on the left and the extreme right agreed that liberal government was doomed—a cheerful prospect for those who aroused their followers with one or another combination of strong-arm rule and utopian panaceas. As the decade drew to a close and war broke out in Europe, fewer Americans had faith in their inherited political and economic systems. Schlesinger, a student at Harvard during these years, heard professors and intellectuals speak of "revolution" and what would later be called the myth of the false alternative: either America would collectivize the mode of production and begin the transition to communism, or the country would succumb to the forces of fascism. This apocalyptic atmosphere, incredible as it seems today, persuaded many intelligent people to reject democracy as obsolete or impossible. "Wherever we find a state," declared the Marxist philosopher Sidney Hook, "there we find a dictatorship."[3] Surely Schlesinger is correct in holding up Roosevelt as the supreme embodiment of crisis leadership and political inspiration, whose achievement restored faith in democratic government.

"For Roosevelt, the technique of liberal government was pragmatism," Schlesinger wrote, describing FDR's experimental sensibility, trial-and-error method, impatience with systems and abstractions, avoidance of dogma and doctrinaire solutions, and a willingness to compromise in order to steer "a middle road."[4] Roosevelt's pragmatic approach, however, suggests why the New Deal lacked an enduring legacy to which America would commit itself. If the New Deal was a pragmatic adaptation to existing conditions, what would sustain it once those conditions changed? The rejection of grand political and economic theory in favor of improvisation by New Deal liberals, moreover, has arguably left them at a disadvantage in political debates with those who possess concrete programs for change.

An even deeper problem confronting the pragmatic liberalism Schlesinger is identified with might be called the Tom Paine problem in American history— the fact that liberals and conservatives alike, for the first two centuries of U.S. history, tended to identify with the vision of Tom Paine (shared also by Thomas Jefferson) of a self-regulating, harmonious society threatened by an intrusive government. The problem is compounded in our era, inasmuch as Paine is the hero both of Ronald Reagan and his critics, of the conservative president who told Americans that government was not the solution but the problem, and the radical intellectual who insists that the state necessarily protects the interests of the social elite. The Paine-Jefferson theory of democracy has blinded Americans from seeing that an atomized society without political authority is prey to the pressure of organized interest groups and particularly to the rule of oligopolistic capitalism.

The rapprochement of American liberalism and a modest sort of statism dates from Herbert Croly's *The Promise of American Life* (1909), a book that influenced Theodore Roosevelt's idea of "the New Nationalism" with its notion of pursuing Jeffersonian goals by Hamiltonian means. For Croly and Roosevelt, a strong government was necessary to protect the public against predatory "malefactors of wealth." In *The Age of Jackson,* Schlesinger sought a historical precedent for the Progressive and New Deal concern with the abuses of concentrated wealth. Schlesinger's Andrew Jackson moves away from a lingering Jeffersonian antistatism toward identifying democracy with the aspirations of urban workers and with the authority of national government over irresponsible and monopolistic capital, in the form of the Second Bank of the United States. Critics have argued that Schlesinger's Jackson looks more like a prototype of FDR than an antebellum southern politician. Schlesinger himself notes that, although Jackson twice triumphed at the polls to defeat the impulses of localism and sectionalism, the Jacksonian democrats failed to "codify" a philosophy of government, with the result that the country lapsed back into the influence of the Jeffersonian ethos, with its two dicta: "That government is best, which governs least," and "The world is too much governed."[5]

An economic philosophy of pragmatism, and a version of American history that placed the New Deal firmly in the line of descent of popular heroes like Thomas Jefferson and Andrew Jackson, shielded New Deal liberalism from conservative charges that it was an alien, "Bolshevik" or "fascist" transplant into the American body politic—at least from FDR to Kennedy and Johnson. Since Johnson, however, every president—Democrats such as Carter and Clinton, no less than Republicans—has run against "big government." The hostility of American voters to the national state is somewhat illusory; voters hate taxes and like receiving checks from the government; most Americans are opposed only to entitlements going to other Americans. Still, the atheoretical pragmatism of New Deal liberalism may have made it more difficult for conscientious liberals to make a reasoned case against unprincipled expansion of entitlements—while the continued strength of the Paine-Jeffersonian vision of American society and history has made it easy for conservatives to revive fifty-year-old claims that the New Deal, far from being the goal of American history, was a detour from the path of libertarian virtue. Liberals in the years ahead, in defending and updating the New Deal, may have to put forth a more rigorous and principled defense of the role of the state in the economy than the New Dealers themselves provided. At the same time, while following Schlesinger in seeking a "usable past" for a union of liberalism and strong national government, the liberal historians of the future may find Jeffersonian southerners like Andrew Jackson less plausible as ancestors than nationalistic Whigs whom the Democratic historian may have underrated, such as Daniel Webster, Henry Clay, and John Quincy Adams.

After "the hope of the New Deal," the most important aspect of Schlesinger's version of liberalism has been its rejection of the dogmas and illusions of the radical left, old and young: the pro-Soviet Old Left and the multicultural New Left have constituted two distinct movements, each with its own tempting dangers to pluralist, vital-center liberalism.

In the winter of 1947, Schlesinger and Niebuhr led anticommunist liberals in transforming the old Union for Democratic Action into Americans for Democratic Action (ADA). The ADA, resolute in its opposition to communism, struggled to win the mantle of the New Deal with the Progressive Citizens of America (PCA), a group of Henry Wallace progressives who saw no conflict between American ideals and Soviet realities. Schlesinger's position, both anti-Stalinist and anti-McCarthyite, rejected the idea of a significant internal communist conspiracy and supported George Kennan's doctrine of containment of the Soviet Union and its satellites. For Schlesinger, as for Niebuhr, opposition to totalitarianism abroad did not mean support for reaction at home. In *The Vital Center,* Schlesinger wrote: "We must commit ourselves to . . . the struggle within the world against Communism and fascism; the struggle within our country against oppression and stagnation; the struggle within ourselves against pride and corruption; nor can engagement in one dimension exclude responsibility for another."

Two decades later, some would claim that anticommunist liberalism had been discredited by the debacle of the war in Vietnam, and find utopias in Ho's North Vietnam, Mao's China, or Castro's Cuba, as their progressive predecessors had once discovered the land of the future in the Soviet Union. New Leftists of the sixties would travel to Hanoi and return home to sing the praises of "rice roots democracy."[6] In *The Bitter Heritage* (1966), Schlesinger warned against such infantile delusions:

> It is important not to become romantic about the Viet Cong. They did not simply represent a movement of rural organization and uplift. They extended their power as much by the fear they incited as by the hope they inspired. And the systematic murder of village headmen—half a dozen a day by 1960–could be an effective weapon, especially when the people of the countryside had been given little reason to prefer the government in Saigon to their own survival. It was warfare in the shadows, ambush and assassination and torture, leaving behind a trail of burned villages, shattered families, and weeping women.[7]

Few leftist activists of the sixties listened to Schlesinger. Yet the "anti-anticommunist" position that became so politically correct during the Vietnam War, and that led a younger generation to dismiss Schlesinger as a "cold war intellectual," has received, at last, the judgment of history in the aftermath of 1989. The containment strategy of "cold war liberalism" has been vindicated against the two alternatives: the progressive strategy of appeasement and the right's dangerous strategy of "rolling back" communism by force in Eastern Europe and elsewhere.

Half a century separates Schlesinger's struggles with the Marxists from his recent confrontations with the multiculturalists. As Schlesinger saw it, the Old Left of the thirties emerged from the radical Depression years weighed down with "ideology," a fixed, doctrinal point of view. Schlesinger has been fond of citing Sir Isaiah Berlin's distinction between the "hedgehog" that knows one big thing and the "fox" that holds many small ideas and also holds fleeting perspectives. The Marxists, for Schlesinger, were among the "hedgehogs throughout American history who have attempted to endow America with an all-inclusive creed, to translate Americanism into a set of binding propositions, and to construe the national tradition in terms of one or another ultimate, ranging from Natural Law to the Class Struggle."[8]

The debate over multiculturalism has placed Schlesinger in what at first appears to be an awkward stance in defense of a defense of "Americanism" and a rigid view of "the national tradition." Schlesinger has no quarrel with revising historiography to include the formerly excluded: "The republic has at last begun to give long-overdue recognition to the role and achievements of groups subordinated and ignored during the high noon of male Anglo-Saxon dominance—women, Americans of South and East European ancestry, black Americans, Indians, Hispanics, Asians." Outside the academy, however, multiculturalism leads to a politics that is more divisive than inclusive. In contrast to New Deal liberalism, which united Americans of different classes and regions by means of universal entitlements and reforms, multicultural politics galvanizes groups whose demands, based as they are in affirmations of identity, are frequently non-negotiable and shun coalitions. Indeed, identity-based groups often bypass political parties altogether and function as direct pressure groups seeking to influence the courts or the bureaucracy. The New Deal's politics of hope based on democracy has given way to a new politics of complaint based on diversity.

Faced with the political fragmentation of American society among rival subcultures—a fragmentation that finds its image and justification in the separate histories of each "culture," each a tale of woe and victimhood—Schlesinger has stressed the need for a national consensus. Has he repudiated the liberal pluralism he once espoused? Has he become the hedgehog of hegemony? Schlesinger's project in *The Disuniting of America* (1991) is not to be mistaken for the myth of pre-ethnic purity. The alternative to multiculturalism is not a stodgy "canonical" nativism, but a revised and enriched liberal pluralism:

> The cult of ethnicity, pressed too far, exacts costs. It may even portend a new turn in American life. Instead of a transformative nation with an identity all its own, America increasingly sees itself as preservative of old identities. Instead of a nation composed of individuals making their own free choices, America increasingly sees itself as composed of groups more or less indelible in their ethnic character. The national ideal had once been *e pluribus unum.* Are we now to belittle *unum* and glorify *pluribus?* Will the center hold? or will the melting pot yield to the Tower of Babel?[9]

In his inaugural address, John F. Kennedy spoke of the assumption of power by "a new generation . . . , tempered by war, disciplined by a hard and bitter peace, proud of our ancient heritage."[10] Liberals of Kennedy's generation believed in government as a potential force for good. The "deepening of our knowledge of man" of which Schlesinger wrote gave his generation of mid-century liberals both a suspicion of power and a willingness, even a desire, to wield it.

A desire to exercise a power that one distrusts may seem like a paradox, but it would have seemed perfectly comprehensible to the leading spirits among the Founding Fathers, who, like mid-century pragmatic liberals, were revolutionaries without illusions. Liberals in the FDR-Truman-Kennedy-Johnson tradition revolutionized the relationship of Americans to their national government, helped great masses of hitherto-excluded Americans to share the nation's prosperity and—in an effort that ultimately helped shatter the New Deal coalition—tore down the four-century-old structure of American apartheid.

In Schlesinger's view, not only are there shifts back and forth between liberal and conservative cycles in American history, but liberalism itself depends upon the presence of important thinkers and great leaders. Significantly, except for his occasional collected essays or tracts written in response to a reigning controversy, all of Schlesinger's books are inspired by great figures of thought or action: the reformer-theologian Orestes Brownson, presidents Andrew Jackson, Franklin D. Roosevelt, and John F. Kennedy, and attorney general, senator, and presidential candidate Robert Kennedy. Schlesinger may not go as far as Emerson and declare that there is no history, only biography; but clearly he would agree with Emerson that history requires heroes as "representative men" (and women!), leaders of courage and conviction, even the superior "genius" whose achievements are recognized not because they surpass democratic norms but rather because they reflect and incarnate human aspiration.[11]

The dangers of excessive regard for power and of hero worship are so often stressed that it is easy to confuse virtue with incompetence and a free society with a feeble government. This, in turn, can lead to a reaction in the form of a deliberately anti-intellectual activism, a tough-mindedness that is really little more than mindlessness. The politician, Max Weber advised, "works with the striving for power as an unavoidable means. Therefore, the 'power instinct,' as is usually said, belongs indeed to his normal activities. The sin against the lofty spirit of his vocation, however, begins when this striving for power ceases to be *objective* and becomes purely personal self-intoxication, instead of exclusively entering the service of 'the cause.'" Without a commitment to a cause, the politician is "constantly in danger of becoming an actor" interested only in "impressions," and thus the "mere 'power politician' may get strong effects, but actually his work leads nowhere and is senseless." Power without principle results in "vanity," the "occupational disease" of democratic politics. In his novel *Democracy,* Henry Adams (a predecessor of Schlesinger as both historian and public philosopher) writes of a senator: "He had very little sympathy for thin moralizing, and a statesman-like contempt for philosophical politics. He loved power, and he meant to be President. That was enough."[12]

That would never have been enough for Adams, or for Schlesinger. Throughout his career Schlesinger has sought to join intellect to power in order to elevate it to the moral authority political office should convey. In the mid-sixties he was featured on the cover of *Time,* a familiar figure in the former Kennedy administration with his horn-rimmed glasses and playful bow tie. His association with those in power indicated that the public problems of democracy are worthy of thought and reflection, even if Schlesinger remained more optimistic than Adams. Yet his participation in the politics of the Democratic Party raises questions about the tension between scholarly objectivity and partisan commitments. Part One of the present anthology, "History as a Vocation," addresses this issue.

The first chapter, William E. Leuchtenberg's presidential address to the American Historical Association in 1991, recounts Schlesinger's experience as a political activist as well as a scholar; Leuchtenberg concludes, in agreement with Schlesinger, that historians need not avoid subjects of controversy and deepest concern. Sir Hugh Thomas, writing from a neoconservative perspective, describes his experience as an advisor to Prime Minister Margaret Thatcher. Thomas likens Thatcher's reliance on think tanks and scholars to FDR's Brain Trust, but the dictum he draws from Lord Salisbury—that government must be "just but not generous"—would perhaps lead Schlesinger to reach for his first volume on the Depression and the New Deal, the Herbert Hoover years when government seemed to be neither.

The next three essays in Part One are also by Schlesinger's close friends and admirers. Historian and former ambassador George Kennan assesses Schlesinger's book *The Cycles of American History,* addressing such issues as the realistic vision of the Founding Fathers, foreign policy and the cold war, and the quandaries that must be faced in bringing the American tradition to bear upon human rights. Economist John Kenneth Galbraith, ambassador to India in the Kennedy administration, writes an affectionate memoir of Schlesinger and suggests why the historian must not only write history but try to help make it. Historian John Morton Blum, describing Schlesinger as a "Tory Democrat," notes the way in which he combines democratic sentiments with aristocratic sensibilities to call for an "affirmative state" headed by leaders of civic dedication and ethical responsibility.

Jacksonian democracy, the topic of Part Two, has long been a subject of controversy among American historians. Anti-bank and pro-entrepreneurial, democratic and racist, egalitarian and sexist, radically aggressive and conservatively possessive—it seems a study in contradictions. Robert Remini describes the impact Schlesinger's *Age of Jackson* had on his generation of the 1940s and how it revised previous interpretations of Frederick Jackson Turner and Charles Beard. Recently historians have been uncovering the extent of the racism that characterized the Democratic Party of the Jackson era, an issue addressed by historian Sean Wilentz, who demonstrates how one working-class leader, William Leggett, came out in favor of the abolition of slavery. The age of Jackson was also an age of romantic individualism that made the concept of the self almost sacred and autonomous. Jean V. Matthews demonstrates how the women's rights movement and the protests of free blacks both stuck out against the sting of gender humiliation and racial discrimination in the name of liberty as "self-development." One wonders whether the disputed origins of modern American feminism may be now traced back to the overmasculinized age of Andrew Jackson.

Part Three, "Modern Liberalism and the Challenge of Governance," brings the reader into the twentieth century. In the eighteenth century Alexander Hamilton had worried that America would become a nation without a nation-state. Alan Brinkley's examination of the attitudes of Americans toward the role of government during and after the two world wars would indicate that Hamilton's worries would still be justified. In both instances the concentration of authority in the national government indicated that it was possible to bring some rational order to the economy, even to the point of bringing business leaders into the government, the dream of Hamilton looking to the "rich, well-born, and able." But for reasons that Brinkley uncovers, the liberal state remained weak and ill-defined in the postwar years of both generations. Nevertheless, the idea of the welfare state always contained the ideas of care and compassion. Kathleen McCarthy's essay indicates that some of the origins of twentieth-century welfare policies may be located in nineteenth-century women's philanthropic activities.

The three essays that complete this section on domestic politics go far toward explaining the decline of American liberalism. Fred Siegel indicates how Ronald Reagan ran off with FDR's fatherly image and at the same time repudiated everything his predecessor stood for, even to the point of threatening to go after social security until he felt the wrath of the elderly. Meanwhile, as Siegel demonstrates, students and intellects of both the New Left and the Old Right, the generations of the sixties and the thirties, echoed one another in their criticism of the American state as oppressive. Always at war with liberalism, the New Left denounced the New Deal as creeping corporatism that turned Americans into passive consumers instead of active citizens. The election of Jimmy Carter in 1976 signaled the beginning of the end of the older liberalism. As Leo Ribuffo points out, Carter was the first Democratic president to refuse to consider expanding the welfare state; instead, he sought to promote economic efficiency at the expense of social equality. Although Carter never used the word "malaise" in the very speech with which it has been forever associated, a common impression emerged that the president was reflecting the brooding analysis of Christopher Lasch's *Culture of Narcissism,* an impression that Ribuffo corrects. The historian Lasch, who died in 1994, was one of liberalism's brightest and severest critics; some of his misinterpretations of Schlesinger are dealt with in a subsequent chapter.

It has often been said of American liberalism that it seeks to include the excluded. But from the age of Jackson up to the era of Roosevelt, inclusion of black Americans was resisted by two constituencies upon which the Democratic Party depended: workers and white southerners. Not until the civil rights movement of the post–World War II years did liberalism become emphatically identified with the cause of America's black minority. The plight of black Americans is analyzed by the urban historian Richard Wade, who draws comparisons between the immigrant ghetto and the black ghetto to dramatize the difference between assimilation and opportunity and confinement and frustration. Once again liberalism looks disadvantage in the face and searches to fulfill its goals of justice and equality.

Part Four, "America and the World," deals with the beginnings of the Cold War, its sudden end, and its consequences for American foreign policy. Betty M. Unterberger, a specialist on American–East European relations, notes how the Russian people still believe that America's deployment of soldiers in Vladivostok in 1918 signified a desperate counterrevolutionary attempt to restore the old order, when in fact Woodrow Wilson was attempting to help Russians realize American ideals of freedom and self-determination. But the history of this tragic misunderstanding is complex, as Unterberger's archival research indicates. Ronald Steel analyzes how the collapse of Soviet communism at the end of the 1980s meant not simply an end to the rivalry of the two superpowers, but an end to the rationale that had for half a century justified American global interventionism. Having lost its traditional mission, what should be the new foundations of an American foreign policy?

Part Five, "Ideological Controversies," registers the tensions that have rocked the academy in recent years. Ever since the 1965 publication of his *New Radicalism in America,* the late Christopher Lasch was one of Schlesinger's foremost critics. Louis Menand points out the instances in which Lasch's criticisms of Schlesinger in particular and of liberalism in general miss the mark. Historian Eugene D. Genovese, an authority on slavery and long a supporter of Black American Studies, discusses both the promises and the problems faced by Black Studies in the academy, some of which relate to Schlesinger's *Disuniting of America.*

Part Six, "Intellectual Heroes," is a set of analyses and portraits of figures who have influenced Schlesinger's outlook. George Cotkin shows how William James's philosophy of pragmatism helped shape modern liberalism and deepened Schlesinger's commitment to pluralism and diversity. Distinguishing the intellectual from the scholar, Neil Jumonville draws comparisons between the careers of Schlesinger and Henry Steele Commager, both of whom sought to relate the study of history to politics and public policy. Finally, the treat of treats, Sir Isaiah Berlin recollects his encounters with Edmund Wilson at Oxford in the fifties. Listening in on a conversation between Berlin and Wilson is like visiting intellectual history in the making.

• • • • •

The editor wishes to thank the authors for their contributions to this collection of essays in honor of Arthur Schlesinger, Jr. I am particularly indebted to Michael Lind, to Fred Siegel for helpful comments, to Peter Dougherty for his advice, and to Eric David Schramm for editorial assistance.

NOTES

1. Schlesinger mentioned this wonderful exchange at an evening commemorating the Kennedy administration held at New York's Century Club in 1993.

2. For the biographical details of Schlesinger's life, and an excellent analysis of his scholarship, see Marcus Cunliffe, "Arthur Schlesinger, Jr.," in *Pastmasters: Some Essays on American Historians,* ed. Marcus Cunliffe and Robin W. Winks (New York: Harper and Row, 1969), 345–74.

3. Sidney Hook, *Toward an Understanding of Karl Marx: A Revolutionary Interpretation* (New York: John Day, 1993).

4. Arthur Schlesinger, Jr., *The Politics of Upheaval,* Vol. 3, *The Age of Roosevelt* (Boston: Houghton Mifflin, 1960), 649.

5. Arthur Schlesinger, Jr., *The Age of Jackson* (Boston: Little, Brown, 1945), 505–23.

6. The expression was invoked by Students for a Democratic Society (SDS) leader Tom Hayden upon returning from Hanoi; quoted in John Patrick Diggins, *The Rise and Fall of the American Left* (New York: Norton, 1992), 241.

7. Arthur Schlesinger, Jr., *The Bitter Heritage: Vietnam and American Democracy, 1941–1966* (Boston: Houghton Mifflin, 1967), 36.

8. Arthur Schlesinger, Jr., "The One against the Many," in *Paths of American Thought,* ed. Arthur Schlesinger, Jr., and Morton White (Boston: Houghton Mifflin, 1963), 533.

9. Arthur Schlesinger, Jr., *The Disuniting of America* (Knoxville: Whittle, 1991), 2.

10. Quoted in Arthur Schlesinger, Jr., *A Thousand Days: John F. Kennedy in the White House* (Boston: Houghton Mifflin, 1965), 4.

11. On the reconciliation of heroic excellence and egalitarian democracy, the thesis of Emerson's *Representative Men,* see Perry Miller, "Emersonian Genius and American Democracy," in *Nature's Nation* (Cambridge: Harvard University Press, 1967), 163–74.

12. Max Weber, "Politics as a Vocation," in *From Max Weber: Essays in Sociology,* ed. H. H. Gerth and C. Wright Mills (New York: Oxford University Press, 1946), 116; Henry Adams, *Democracy: An American Novel* (1880; reprint, New York: Airmont, 1968), 50.

PART ONE

HISTORY AS A VOCATION

Chapter 1

THE HISTORIAN AND THE PUBLIC REALM

WILLIAM E. LEUCHTENBURG

OVER THE PAST century no question has more polarized the historical profession than the dispute over what is the appropriate relationship of history to the public realm. Generation after generation, a substantial corps of scholars has insisted that historians should concentrate on contributing to the solution of contemporary problems. Indeed, the conviction that history should cater to the needs of the present goes back to the earliest days of the American Historical Association, when it was voiced by its very first presidents, including Andrew Dickson White and Charles Kendall Adams. A generation later, one of C. Vann Woodward's patrons declared, "If Dr. Johnson were alive today, he would say it was [pure] research which is the last refuge of the scoundrel." On the other hand, more than half a century ago Robert Livingston Schuyler celebrated "the usefulness of useless history," and more recently Theodore S. Hamerow, confronted by "that troublesome question with which historians are constantly assailed: 'What is the use of history?'" replied, "The answer is that history is of no use; it simply is." On only one point have the two sides agreed—that their positions are irreconcilable.[1]

The belief that history should address the urgencies of the day has taken two forms, the first of which is the claim that current needs should be privileged in the writing of history. That notion found classic expression in 1907 when James Harvey Robinson and Charles A. Beard boasted that they had "consistently subordinated the past to the present" in keeping with their "ever-conscious aim to enable the reader to catch up with his own times; to read intelligently the foreign news in the morning paper; to know what was the attitude of Leo XIII toward the social democrats even if he has forgotten that of Innocent III toward the Albigenses."[2]

The emphasis on applicable history has also taken a second form: advocacy of attempts by historians to shape public policy. When Herbert Baxter Adams secured for the AHA the unusual recognition from Congress of a federal charter, he anticipated, in John Higham's words, that he had "opened a channel through which the aristocracy of culture might, in historical matters, exert a vigorous, uplifting influence on national politics." In the Progressive Era, that archetypal figure, Charles A. Beard, who had worked at Hull House when he was a college student and had helped establish a workingman's college at Oxford in his graduate student days, continued, while professor at Columbia, to participate in the activities of civic reform groups such as the National Municipal League and campaigned for a Socialist congressman. Subsequently, he served as an adviser to governments in the Balkans and in Japan. By the time the United States intervened in World War I, it seemed altogether natural for John Franklin Jameson to organize a National Board for Historical Research, put together lectures on history for delivery at U.S. Army training camps, and place the *American Historical Review* in the service of the government by seeking articles establishing German war guilt.[3]

World War II opened further opportunities for historians. Even before Pearl Harbor, the federal government created a board to analyze foreign intelligence under the diplomatic historian James Phinney Baxter III, president of Williams College, and Baxter, in turn, appointed William L. Langer of Harvard to direct research. Out of those beginnings came a new agency, the Office of Strategic Services, with Langer as chief of Research and Analysis, an endeavor that involved some of the most prominent senior historians in the country, including Hajo Halborn and my former teacher, Franz Neumann, as well as a brilliant galaxy of younger men including Franklin Ford, H. Stuart Hughes, Carl Schorske, and Robert Wolff.[4]

When, less than a decade later, the landmark case of *Brown v. Board of Education* was being considered by the Supreme Court, the justices, John Hope Franklin has recalled, raised a number of "searching and quite difficult questions [that] sent legal counsel scurrying not to the history books but to the historians!" In numerous papers prepared for the attorneys, in seminars and conferences conducted for the staff of the NAACP Legal Defense Fund, and in more informal ways, Franklin, C. Vann Woodward, and other scholars made it possible for counsel for black pupils to parry the argument that the framers of the Fourteenth Amendment did not intend it to empower the national government to desegregate schools. Though the Court's decision in *Brown* could not be shown to have turned on the evidence adduced by the historians, it could be said, as Franklin observes, that historians "had answered the call to participate in an important public policy issue; and it would seem that their participation had been effective."[5]

In the nearly four decades since Franklin and his associates helped to bring about the demise of Jim Crow, historians have made their mark in the public realm in countless ways. History professors such as Mike Mansfield have performed with distinction in Congress, and Eric Goldman served in the Johnson White House. During the Vietnam War, petitions published in the *New York Times* in 1967 with the message "Mr. President: Stop the Bombing!" bore the signatures of 184 historians. Robert Kelley, J. Morgan Kousser, Peyton McCrary, Allan Lichtman, and several others have been employed as expert witnesses in litigation ranging from environmental policy to voting rights, and historians recently assisted in the brief of a significant abortion suit, *William L. Webster, et al. v. Reproductive Health Services, et al.* After the Supreme Court in a 1980 ruling announced that it required historical evidence of discriminatory intent in voting rights cases, the Justice Department, the NAACP Legal Defense Fund, and other plaintiffs "had little choice," as Kousser noted, "but to *call in the historians.*" In fact, it has been said that "some cases have been decided primarily because the courts have placed credence in testimony by historians."[6]

The past generation has seen, too, the burgeoning field of public history come into its own. Large numbers of historians have found jobs in government agencies, national and local, as well as in the private sector, and the United States Senate, the House of Representatives, and the Federal Judicial Center have set up historical offices that have proven to be of inestimable value both to those institutions and to historians. With startling swiftness, the field grew large enough to make possible the birth of a National Council on Public History, two new professional journals, and, at the University of California at Santa Barbara, an undergraduate major in the history of public policy. Implicit in these developments has been an assumption about what role the historical guild should perform. Peter N. Stearns and Joel A. Tarr, directors of a program in "applied history" at Carnegie-Mellon University, have lauded historians who, by "applying historical thinking to the making of public policy," thereby "depart from the discipline's narcissism."[7]

Vigorous though these manifestations of public activity have been, they have run up against a considerably stronger contrary emphasis, given its most unequivocal expression by Julien Benda. In his widely noted 1928 volume, *La trahison des clercs* (The treason of the intellectuals), Benda deplored "contempt for the man who shuts himself up with art or science and takes no interest in the passions of the State." The modern intellectual, he complained, was "violently on the side of Michelangelo crying shame upon Leonardo da Vinci for his indifference to the misfortunes of Florence, and against the master of the Last Supper when he replied that indeed the study of beauty occupied his whole heart." Benda applauded the example of Goethe, who said, "Let us leave politics to diplomats and the soldiers," and who in *Dichtung und Wahrheit* reported his response and that of his friends to the French Revolution: "In our circle, we took no notice of news and newspapers; our object was to know Man; as for men, we left them to do as they chose." Benda demonstrated that he accepted that counsel literally when in 1941, at a time when Nazi troops were occupying France, he wrote Andre Gide, "L'inactuel, mon vrai domaine." As the German scholar Wolf Lepenies has commented, "For Benda, avoiding being up-to-date was, for the intellectual, an important virtue that had almost been destroyed by the Dreyfus Affair and its aftermath. The treason of the intellectuals consisted mainly in their attempt to enter politics and thereby exert an influence on the issues of the day."[8]

Though few would go as far as Benda, many historians share his discomfort with the effort to be timely. In postwar America, the progressive school of history associated with Charles Beard fell out of favor, and, as John Higham remarked, "the label *present-minded* now loomed up as an epithet." Oscar Handlin warned against promising that history "would equip citizens with the nostrums to dissolve current and future problems," for "other, more flexible departments of knowledge could always outbid it in a marketplace geared to relevance." Handlin extolled instead the examples of "clerks in the Dark Ages who . . . by retiring from an alien world to a hidden monastic refuge" managed to "maintain a true record . . . [that] informed the future of what had transpired in their day."[9]

Historians surveying the state of the discipline have reported pervasive sentiment for disengagement. In 1964, J. H. Plumb observed that "fewer and fewer historians believe that their art has any social purpose; any function as a coordinator of human endeavour or human thought." Considerably more emphatic was Theodore Hamerow. In a book published as recently as 1987, he found "growing recognition that scholarship can offer no guarantees for the solution of social problems," and that "we have had to recognize that history in this sense is 'irrelevant.'" He wrote of historians today:

> Now, after all the bold ventures and exciting experiments in historical investigation of the last generation, they are less certain than ever of the importance of history for the education of the citizen, the conduct of the government, or the guidance of the community. These doubts are so profound and persistent as to suggest a grave crisis, the gravest perhaps since the emergence of history as an organized profession about a hundred years ago.[10]

When I contemplate this predication of "crisis," I do so, inevitably, from the perspective of a historian who has been engrossed in the public realm for more than half a century. So compelling did political concerns seem to me when I was young that for a time I abandoned graduate studies to pursue them. In the years that I was in and out of graduate school, I served as Queens County Director, then State Youth Director, of the Liberal Party; as Assistant Editor of publications of the American Labor Conference on International Affairs, designed to provide material on foreign policy to the labor press; as New England Field Representative for a civil rights lobby, the National Council for a Permanent FEPC headed by A. Philip Randolph; as upstate New York petition canvasser for Governor Herbert Lehman and Senator James Mead; as National Executive Secretary of Students for Democratic Action; and as Rocky Mountain organizer for Americans for Democratic Action. Subsequently, I became ADA's representative on the staff of Richard Bolling in Kansas City in his first campaign for Congress in 1948 and then State Director of its Massachusetts chapter, where I also functioned as a speech writer for the governor, testified before legislative panels, chaired the United Labor Committee, and organized Boston's first citywide committee against racial discrimination.

I drifted back into the Ph.D. program at Columbia on the understanding that I could write a dissertation that was congruent with my political interests, and when, simultaneously, I moved from my ADA office on Beacon Street to a teaching job in Northampton, it was not in history but in political science. While teaching at Smith, I spent summers on the staff of the CIO Textile Workers giving courses in current affairs and political action to shop stewards, and was appointed campaign manager for a union leader in Holyoke who won the Democratic nomination for Congress. (I might add that so sharply honed were my political skills by then that Anna Sullivan became the worst defeated candidate in the history of western Massachusetts.)

My teaching and writing have dovetailed with my political interests. At Harvard, where I held my first college teaching job in history, I invented a course called "The Progressive Tradition in American Politics," and I have written almost exclusively in the field of recent U.S. history so that I could keep one foot in the present, where I continued to be politically active. In the process of moving from Harvard to Columbia in the summer of 1952, I took a post as Western Field Representative for a presidential candidate in Utah and Wyoming, and at the 1952 Democratic national convention in Chicago worked, along with the pollster Louis Harris, as "delegate analyst" in charge of estimating how each state would vote on the first and succeeding ballots. Shortly after arriving at Columbia, I was elected Democratic county committeeman in Westchester County, and I consumed my first sabbatical as New York State chairman of Americans for Democratic Action.

I can only suggest the range of public activities in which I have been engaged since that time. I spent several November nights writing presidential election analysis for NBC, first for Chet Huntley and David Brinkley, then for John Chancellor; took part with other historians on the final day of the Montgomery march with Martin Luther King; sued Richard Nixon to deny him the right to destroy the Watergate tapes, and, again in league with other scholars and journalists, sued Henry Kissinger to prevent him from sequestering his transcripts of official telephone conversations; commuted to Washington for two years as the American Historical Association's representative on the National Study Commission on Records and Documents of Federal Officials chaired by the former Attorney General of the United States, Herbert Brownell; gave a featured talk to the Democratic Leadership Council on the vitality of liberalism (a message I very much doubt they wanted to hear); testified before the Senate Judiciary Committee against confirmation of Robert H. Bork to the Supreme Court; served on an Advisory Committee on Oral History headed by Robert F. Kennedy; participated in any number of secondary school programs and on the Bradley Commission on History in Schools; honored the memory of Eleanor Roosevelt at ceremonies at Vassar College and elsewhere; entered into a discussion on whether the presidency was in crisis with Jimmy Carter at the Wilson Center; gave literally thousands of newspaper interviews—for example, to the *Baltimore Sun* about Reagan's place in history, to the *Detroit Free Press* on morality and politics, and to the *Wall Street Journal* on the relation of private behavior to public performance in the White House; was consultant for a good number of documentary films, including "The Civil War"; spoke in the French Senate at the centennial of France's gift of the Statue of Liberty to the United States; joined with William Chafe, John Hope Franklin, and Anne Firor Scott in raising many thousands of dollars from historians for Harvey Gantt's campaign to unseat Jesse Helms; was heard on scores of radio programs in cities in this country such as Charleston and Cincinnati and abroad in cities from Vancouver to Melbourne; appeared on a great many television programs including the *CBS Evening News with Dan Rather*, ABC's *Nightline*, an NBC special, Walter Cronkite's *CBS Reports*, and programs on the BBC and Norwegian television; worked with Bill Moyers as a member of the CBS team covering the 1985 inauguration and with Paul Duke of "Washington Week in Review" on the PBS team assigned to the 1989 inauguration; and reminded members of the House of Representatives at the home of my former student, Congressman Stephen J. Solarz, of the shameful failure of the American government headed by Franklin D. Roosevelt to provide a haven for European Jews, millions of whom would be murdered by the Hitler government in the Holocaust.[11]

More recently, I have talked to a gathering of United States senators, was interviewed by the *New York Times*, the Associated Press, the *Atlanta Constitution*, the *Los Angeles Times*, the *New York Daily News*, the *Kansas City Star*, the *Washington Post*, the *Baltimore Sun*, and *USA Today*, spoke on NPR's *All Things Considered*, was consulted by one of Mario Cuomo's advisers on how FDR managed to run for president while in the midst of a budget crisis in Albany, sent memos to Ken Burns for his documentary film on the history of baseball, published an article in the popular history journal *American Heritage*, delivered the keynote address at the annual conference of the National Council on Public History and covered both of Clinton's inaugurations, the first with Dan Rather and Charles Kuralt for CBS and the second with Brian Lamb for C-SPAN.[12]

How then does someone with this background respond to the assertion that writing history is justifiable wholly apart from any utility to the public realm? I unequivocally agree. When Professor Hamerow states that "the importance of history is essentially intrinsic; it lies in the interest in the past which human beings instinctively feel as part of their humanity," and that "the life of the community cannot continue without it," I readily concur. For millennia, people have found history indispensable to comprehending who they are, and I anticipate that they always will. "A people without history," say the Lakota tribe, "is like wind upon the buffalo grass." Moreover, insofar as history is an art form, which the best historical writing surely is, it no more needs justification by good works than does a sonnet or a sonata.[13]

Those who insist that history is worthwhile only when it offers solutions to current problems reveal a hostility to the very nature of the historical enterprise. In the famous passage obliterating the Albigenses in the Robinson and Beard book, the fundamental objection was, as the philosopher Morton White has pointed out, that "the medievalist was interested in explaining medieval events when he should have been trying to illuminate modern events," a judgment that suggests a passion for contemporaneity run amok. It would be hard to imagine anything more ill-advised than for all historians, including those in medieval history, to tailor their research to the morning's headlines. The humanities, asserted the philosopher Charles Frankel, "have usually been at their best and most vital . . . when they have had a sense of engagement with issues of public concern," and he demonstrated that belief by taking leave from Columbia to become Assistant Secretary of State for Educational and Cultural Affairs. Yet Frankel also declared, "Scholarship cannot and should not be shackled to problem solving. It must be free to follow crooked paths to unexpected conclusions."[14]

Despite a lifetime of civic engagement, I also find totally repugnant any aeffort to politicize scholarly associations or to impose favored orthodoxies on the classroom. Indeed, it is precisely those who have been most involved in public affairs who have been most resistant to such attempts. At Columbia in 1968, those who were most vocal against the assault on the university were the historians and political scientists who had been working for two years against the Vietnam War under the leadership of Fritz Stern, a circumstance that accounts for our being known as "the Stern gang." President Reagan's intervention in Nicaragua appalled me, but when, while I was president of the Organization of American Historians, a resolution was introduced to put the OAH on record in opposition, I cast the lone vote on the executive board against it, because I thought it an abuse of our authority. And though in 1990 I was outspoken in denouncing President Bush's actions in the Persian Gulf, I also insisted that the AHA should not take a stand, for I would no more want to inflict my views on others than have views inflicted on me, nor did I wish to see the organization torn apart by factional fights over such issues.

I hope never again to witness a night like the one at the AHA convention some thirty years ago when historians grappled with one another for control of the microphone during the bitter debate over resolutions on Vietnam and civil rights with Vann Woodward, in the words of the *New Republic*, "presid[ing] over the cacophony with the puzzled air of a kindly Southern judge at a hearing for psychiatric commitment."[15] One memory of that turbulent night that sticks in my mind is of the man standing next to me in the crowded hall: my colleague, Orest Ranum, whose years of research notes were deliberately incinerated in the Columbia uprising of 1968.

I saw all too painfully at Columbia that year, when I was a member of the faculty committee that ran the university after the chaos of the spring, and in later years what "politicization" could mean: the paralysis of a great university, the trashing of classrooms by hit-and-run marauders, and physical assaults on professors. Elsewhere, the consequences were sometimes worse, resulting even in death.

Historians long involved in the public realm have also been among the most forthright in underscoring the perils of such involvement for scholarship. When I first arrived at Columbia to teach in the fall of 1952, Richard Hofstadter was seeking to deny the president of the university, Dwight Eisenhower, the opportunity to become president of the United States, and years later we worked side by side in the "Stern gang." Nonetheless, Hofstadter warned, "The activist historian who thinks he is deriving his policy from his history may in fact be deriving his history from his policy, and may be driven to commit the cardinal sin of the historical writer: he may lose his respect for the integrity, the independence, the pastness, of the past."[16]

In his searching analysis of the progressive historians, Hofstadter wrote of the most prominent of them: "Today [Charles A.] Beard's reputation stands like an imposing ruin in the landscape of American historiography. What was once the grandest house in the province is now a ravaged survival." What had gone wrong? Beard had risked too much on "a daring gamble," Hofstadter maintained, for "he had never been content with the role of the historian or the academic alone; he had always hoped to be politically relevant, had always aspired to become a public force. . . . And yet any man who makes written commitments year after year on difficult public questions will live to find some of his views evanescent and embarrassing." Moreover, "Beard took a further and more gratuitous risk; he finally geared his reputation as a historian so closely to his political interests and passions that the two were bound to share the same fate," and that fate was disaster. "In proposing not just to draw general moral lessons about the direction and meaning of history but to forge specific recommendations for policy upon which he believed the life and death of American democracy depended," Beard, Hofstadter concluded, "became our supreme tragic example of the activist mind in history."[17]

The conviction that a greater role for scholars in the state would be advantageous rests on the assumption that they are more farsighted and more humane than those in power. Sometimes they are. We would do well to remember, though, that it was not so long ago that most members of the AHA sanctioned the institutions of white supremacy that emerged out of Reconstruction and an even shorter time ago that not a few historians were apologists for Stalin's despotic regime, though it stifled freedom of expression, sent dissenters to vile prison camps, and was responsible for millions of deaths. In the past generation, we have had reason enough to know that the country's fate is not always secure in the hands of "the best and the brightest." Furthermore, the reputation of historians for prescience has recently taken a bad battering. The pace of change in Eastern Europe caught almost everyone unprepared, and after the massacre at Tiananmen Square, one scholar confessed: "I am a chastened China watcher, as are many of my colleagues in universities and think tanks. Not since the Iranian revolution have the analysts been so surprised." He added that "no China specialist—in or out of the government— foresaw the massive setback that occurred."[18]

Scholars in turn have often been disappointed by their encounters with government. When Charles Frankel accepted a post at the State Department, John Kenneth Galbraith told him, "You'll find that it's the kind of organization which, though it does some big things badly, does small things badly too." Politicians are infinitely more likely to ask historians for confirmation of views they already hold than for examples from history that might lead them to change their opinions. Wielders of power, Otis Graham has pointed out, do not ignore history—indeed, they are historians of a sort themselves, though "quite poor ones"—but they are intent on "using the past mostly to reinforce bias and strengthen advocacy positions." As the 1966 midterm elections approached, I was asked by the Johnson White House to prepare a memo drawing comparisons to the 1942 off-year contest, and I complied with a document pointing to the vulnerability of the administration so long as it persisted in the Vietnam War. I need not tell you that, predictably, it had absolutely no effect.[19]

Even when the viewpoints of scholars and officials are absolutely congruent, unanticipated consequences may ensue. In 1974, John Doar, chief counsel of the congressional inquiry into the impeachment of Richard Nixon, commissioned Vann Woodward to prepare a report on allegations of wrongdoing by American presidents throughout our history, and Woodward in turn called on me to supervise the twentieth-century section. We had only a few weeks to complete this large task, and I recruited four of my former graduate students who I knew could be counted on to do work of high quality in a hurry. In the final hours, they overran my Connecticut house and barn, but we met the deadline, as did all the others. So intent were we on seeing Nixon deposed that we sacrificed all our own projects to that end. Some have concluded that the final report was, in the words of one historian, "a major salvo in the assault on

Richard Milhous Nixon," for it suggested how much more monstrous were Nixon's deeds than those of his predecessors, as indeed they were. But I have always thought that, so thoroughgoing and fairminded were the historians in revealing the many instances of wrongdoing in the past, that, if Nixon had actually stood trial, the document, in its total effect, would better have served him than the prosecution.[20]

The appearance of historians in the courts, either as expert witnesses or as advisers, has also been problematic. In 1962, one of the historians who assisted the NAACP in the *Brown* case created embarrassment when, in an address at the AHA's annual convention that *U.S. News & World Report* spread over three pages, he confessed that "we were . . . sliding off facts, quietly ignoring facts, and above all, interpreting facts in a way to do what [Thurgood] Marshall said we had to do—'get by those boys down there.'" Nearly three decades later, counsel in the *Webster* case (which featured a brief signed by more than four hundred historians) admitted afterward that "factors constrained our ability to 'tell the truth,'" in particular the "tension between truth-telling and advocacy." The impression that historians are objective scholars who can certify the facts of the past much like scientists reporting on the contents of a test tube proved illusory when, in a water rights case, one historian gave expert testimony for the plaintiff while another testified for the defense; and in the highly publicized *Sears* case, two prominent historians took opposite sides over the disposition of women to aspire to specialized job opportunities. In an important South Carolina voting-rights case, a historian who has worked intensively on southern politics told the court that history revealed an intent by officials to discriminate racially, only to be flatly contradicted by the co-author of the country's leading textbook in Constitutional history, who denied that the historical evidence supported such a conclusion. Critics have accused scholars of cooking evidence, and one authority has even charged, with exquisitely delicate phrasing, "Expert witnesses are whores."[21]

Expert witnesses, though, have vigorously refuted the charge that they are no more than hired guns for litigants. J. Morgan Kousser, who has maintained that testifying in court and before a congressional committee on behalf of voting rights permitted him "*to tell the truth and do good at the same time*," has declared, "Social scientists' virtue is no more at stake as they walk down the dark alleys of policy relevance than it is on the brightly-lit streets of the campus." Similarly, Peyton McCrary has affirmed that "the courtroom helps keep the academics honest," for "if experts do not testify fully, logically, convincingly, and honestly, then the process of cross-examination by skillful attorneys is likely to expose their faults." "The standards of the courtroom," he deduced from his own experience, "are as high as those of academe." Despite, or more likely because of, the bitter experience of the *Sears* case, a Conference on Women's History and Public Policy in 1989 explored "mechanisms for enhancing communication between historians of women and those in the political arena and in the courts."[22]

Few historians of his generation have so encapsulated the tension between the historian as scholar and the historian as public participant as has Arthur Schlesinger, Jr. He burst on the scholarly world like a comet. His biography of Orestes Brownson (1939) appeared when he was only twenty-one, his bestseller *The Age of Jackson* (1945) only six years later. In these same years, he was establishing himself as a conspicuous public figure. When I traveled through New England in 1946 as regional agent for the FEPC lobby, I was told that the person to see in Cambridge was Schlesinger, and when I first met him, at the founding convention of Americans for Democratic Action in Washington more than fifty years ago, he was already a mover and shaker in the new organization. "For a man so young, Arthur Schlesinger, Jr. has exerted a remarkable influence on the body politic," conceded a rightwing polemicist as early as 1953 in a nasty piece in the *American Mercury*. "His presence on forums and at other occasions where the elite meet to bleat is ubiquitous."[23]

His public career has ranged over half a century. In World War II, he worked for both the Office of War Information and the Office of Strategic Services, and in the 1950s, he twice served on the presidential campaign staff of Adlai Stevenson and, in addition, was elected national chairman of ADA. From 1961 to 1963, he had a significant national role as special assistant to President Kennedy at the White House. His public activities, though, have not been limited to politics and government. He has been a member of the board of directors of the Harry S. Truman Library and a trustee of the Twentieth Century Fund. In addition, he has developed an independent career as a film critic. In 1964, he was invited to be on the jury of the Cannes Film Festival. In short, as one writer has stated, in "his triple career as historian, liberal political commentator, and active Democrat," Schlesinger has "played an important part in shaping the new liberalism and in defending political commitment as a proper role for intellectuals."[24]

Yet despite this lengthy experience, Schlesinger has not regarded massive commitment by scholars to politics as either likely or desirable. In a collection of essays published in 1969, he wrote: "Public affairs will never involve more than a small minority of intellectuals, and rightly so, for the vitality of intellectual life depends on the endless diversity of intellectual roles and interests. Since most governments will pursue more or less hopeless policies, most intellectuals will continue to criticize them."

Intellectuals, he cautioned, would "influence government most effectively not by learning the art of public relations, not by transforming themselves into publicists or hucksters, not by organizing pressure groups and marches on Washington but by thinking hard about basic problems and coming up with basic answers. Thinkers are most powerful when they think." Five years later, he was of the same mind. Confronted by Ernest May's proposition that "if history is to be better used in government, nothing is more important than that professional historians discover means of addressing directly, succinctly, and promptly the needs of people who govern," Schlesinger retorted, "It may well be more important for professional historians to write the best professional history they can and trust to the multiplier effect."[25]

Unlike many other activists, Schlesinger has questioned the assumption that the world would be a better place if politicians paid heed to historians, who had ready answers for them. "Far from unveiling the secret of things to come," he has written, "history bestows a different gift: it makes us—or should make us—understand the extreme difficulty, the intellectual peril, the moral arrogance of supposing that the future will yield itself so easily to us." Indeed, he has asserted:

> History . . . can answer questions, after a fashion, at long range. It cannot answer questions with confidence or certainty at short range. Alas, policy makers are rarely interested in the long run—"in the long run," as Keynes used to say, "we are all dead"—and the questions they put to history are thus most often the questions which history is least qualified to answer.
>
> Far from offering a short cut to clairvoyance, history teaches us that the future is full of surprises and outwits all our certitudes.[26]

Even when government officials do appear to draw upon historians, Schlesinger has found the lines of influence less clear than they seem. "As one who is by profession an historian and has been by occasion a government official," he has stated, "I have long been fascinated and perplexed by the interaction between history and public decision: fascinated because . . . past history becomes an active partner in the making of new history; perplexed because the role of history in this partnership remains both elusive and tricky." He explained:

> The problem is tricky because, when explicit historical judgments intervene, one immediately encounters a question which is, in the abstract, insoluble: Is the history invoked really the source of policies, or is it the source of arguments designed to vindicate policies adopted for antecedent reasons? Moreover, even when history is in some sense the source of policies, the lessons of history are generally so ambiguous that the antecedent reasons often determine the choice between alternative historical interpretations. Thus, in France between the wars Reynaud and Mandel drew one set of conclusions from the First World War, Bonnet and Laval another. Yet one cannot, on the other hand, reduce the function of history in public policy to that of mere rationalization, for historical models acquire a life of their own. Once a statesman begins to identify the present with the past, he may in time be carried further than he intends by the bewitchment of analogy.[27]

If, then, Schlesinger has contended, one cannot assume that the state is so malleable that it can easily be manipulated by intellectuals, neither should one accept the gloomy conclusion that involvement by scholars in public affairs is bound to be ineffective. "Historical generalizations," he has written, "will enlarge the wisdom of the statesman, giving his responses to the crises of the moment perspective, depth and an instinct for the direction and flow of events." Furthermore, he has suggested, public service may be of value to historians too. In 1949, more than a decade before he entered the Kennedy White House, he told an interviewer: "American historians spend too much time writing about events which the whole nature of their lives prevents them from understanding. Their life is defined by universities, libraries and seminars. . . . I gained more insight into history from being in the war and working for the government than I did from my academic training."[28]

Schlesinger has also discounted the claim that scholars who become immersed in the public realm inevitably compromise themselves. In an exchange with a New Left historian, he noted that his critic appeared "to hold that scholars should never work for the state lest they become corrupted by partisanship and power." He riposted:

> Does he really wish the management of affairs to be handed over exclusively to lawyers, bankers, businessmen and generals? He must be kidding. . . . Compromise is involved in every activity of life, not in government alone. It is entirely possible to deal with practical realities without yielding inner convictions; it is entirely possible to compromise in program and action without compromising in ideas and values. . . . My own impression is that academic politics is fully as devious, mean, dishonest, and corrupting as the politics of the state.

On another occasion, he maintained:

> The assumption that power will inexorably subvert intelligence exhibits a fatal lack of confidence in the force of facts, ideas and reason. Over the longer run, it may become evident that intelligence may begin to subvert power. Though the state does its best to employ the intellectual as a technician and keep him in the back room, it cannot forever escape him as a carrier of general ideas. The habit of thought is infectious; and, as it begins to infiltrate government, it may affect government as much as government affects it.[29]

The premise that scholars should take part in public affairs has an ancient lineage, Schlesinger has observed. "In classical Asian civilizations, men of ideas were often part of the world of power as a natural course," he has written. "The Brahmans constituted one of the highest castes in India; China recruited its literati by competitive examination and commissioned them to run the state as civil servants." Similarly, Western intellectuals in the eighteenth century, "from Turgot, Voltaire and Struensee to Franklin, Adams and Jefferson, assumed collaboration with power as the natural order of things."[30]

That observation pertained especially to America's founding fathers. "The men who organized the struggle for independence and created the new republic were politician-intellectuals, capable at the same time of the most realistic political maneuver and of the most recondite intellectual analysis," he declared. When the republic was young, "politicians invoked ideas without embarrassment, and intellectuals entered politics with no sense that they were doing anything but what was expected of thinkers in their society and their time. The assumption of the age was that intellect and responsibility marched together—that the world of thought naturally and inevitably interpenetrated the world of power."[31]

Schlesinger, though acknowledging that history should imbue statesmen with "a profound and humbling sense of human frailty," has denied both that the state can do nothing to ameliorate the condition of humankind and that scholars must abstain from involvement in the public realm. He has not doubted the capacity of the state, as well as of intellectuals, for mischief. It was he and Kenneth Jackson, the pioneering head both of the Bradley Commission and of the National Council for History Education, who offered an eloquent remonstrance against New York State's unwise plan to warp the curriculum. Yet he has identified himself, too, with the conviction "that history never stands still, that social change can better the quality of people's lives and happiness, and that the margin of human gain, however limited, is worth the effort." Above all, he has concluded, "we are never relieved, despite the limits of our knowledge and the darkness of our understanding, from the necessity of meeting our obligations."[32]

Like Arthur Schlesinger, while heeding all the warning signals, I am not persuaded that historians should eschew subjects of contemporary concern or avoid the political arena; nor is that the conclusion of a number of other scholars who have warned of the dangers of engagement. Asked how, after "three decades of controversy, criticism, and misunderstanding," he now felt about venturing to write *The Strange Career of Jim Crow*, Woodward responded: "Pressed for an answer, I would confess to feeling somewhat chastened and perhaps a bit wiser for the experience, but on the whole quite unrepentant. . . . Since the historian lives in the present he has obligations to the present as well as to the past he studies." History, he said on another occasion, should not be conceived of as "a sort of verbal museum to preserve and display worthy relics of the past" or "confined to a passive role," for "the fate of ideologies, empires, and rulers hangs on historical revelations and revisions."[33]

Granted that their capacities are not unbounded, history professors do not have to remain immured behind campus walls. They can reach out to their colleagues not only in national but in state and local governments, as well as in the private sector; they can collaborate with teachers in elementary and secondary schools doing the indispensable work of instructing the young in understanding the past; and they can, in the tradition of Macaulay and Parkman, write not just for one another but for a literate public.

Such an obvious agenda, though, does not begin to encompass what is expected of us. As John Hope Franklin has pointed out:

> Let a person move into a group of people and be introduced as an historian; and someone will raise a question that he knows is at least as profound as any that Socrates ever raised. To the historian it will sound like "Please, Sir, say something historical!" The actual words, carefully articulated, will be, "Please, Sir, tell me what the next four years will provide in the way of history." It is no use to reply, "I am not a soothsayer; I am an historian." For the reply is likely to be, "That is precisely why I put the question to you and not to someone else."[34]

Making an effort to meet such expectations—if not as prophets then as guides to comprehending the sources of the predicaments of our time—may conceivably be of value not just to the nation but to scholars as well. "The vast majority of academics in traditional arts and science disciplines rarely venture forth to confront, enlighten, or change the world," observed a historian who has taken a different course. "Monasticism does have its shortcomings. It contributes to excessively narrow specialization; it impedes teaching by making it too removed from the world most students hope to occupy; it denies the practical world the benefit of academic knowledge and thought; and it denies professors the benefit of having their work tested in the world of practice."[35]

In a presidential address to the American Historical Association a third of a century ago, Allan Nevins, taking note of the question whether "the political historian who has never testified before a congressional committee, or written a speech for a governor or mayor, or haunted the city hall for a year, is not handicapped as compared with the man who has," recalled Macaulay's remarks on Gibbon, who had been a militia officer and a member of Parliament:

> We have not the smallest doubt that his campaigns, though he never saw an enemy, and his parliamentary attendance, though he never made a speech, were of far more use to him than years of study and retirement would have been. If the time he spent on parade and at mess in Hampshire, or on the treasury bench and at Brooks's, during the storms which overthrew Lord North and Lord Shelburne, had been passed in the Bodleian library, he might have avoided some inaccuracies; he might have enriched his notes with a greater number of references; but he could never have produced so lively a picture of the court, the camp, and the senate house.[36]

Quite apart from such considerations, scholars need to embrace an active role in national affairs because they have a vital professional stake in doing so. I would hate to think of what might have happened over the past several years if the AHA had not joined in the National Coordinating Committee for the Promotion of History, an umbrella organization of fifty-one groups, which was able to achieve legislation requiring the State Department to set up a systematic program to declassify documents, and to plan legislative strategy on bills before Congress of paramount significance for scholars, including a measure reauthorizing the National Historical Publications and Records Commission's grant. The Committee emphasized, in particular, the need to mobilize to advance legislation clarifying "fair use" of unpublished copyrighted material, thereby modifying a recent court decision that, as Anne Firor Scott has said, was "a time bomb waiting to blow up all our work in primary sources."[37]

Charles Frankel once put this matter in a larger frame. "The right not simply to dissent but, if one pleases to be indifferent; the right to be private; the right to be useless from every respectable point of view; the right to be irreverent about what is officially sanctified—when have these rights ever been safe from the crowd?" he asked. "When have they been safe even from other intellectuals?" Frankel continued:

> It may once have been possible for scholars to guard their independence by keeping their distance from power. It may be possible for individual scholars to do that still. But it is not possible for the scholarly community as such to maintain its independence by running away from government. For key decisions that affect scholarly independence will be made in any event. And if they are made without the participation of men and women who know something about the nature and necessary conditions of scholarly and intellectual life, they cannot be expected to be the right decisions.[38]

My conviction that historians have something to contribute to decision making rests on an even more elementary proposition: that movers and shakers act in part because of the history they carry around in their heads. In 1947, Secretary of State George Marshall declared, "I doubt seriously whether a man can think with full wisdom . . . regarding certain of the basic international issues today who has not at least reviewed in his mind the period of the Peloponnesian War and the Fall of Athens." The president under whom Marshall served had a cruder notion of the past. "The oligarchy in Russia," Harry Truman wrote his daughter, "is no different from the Czars, Louis XIV, Napoleon, Charles I and Cromwell. It is a Frankenstein dictatorship worse than any of the others, Hitler included." Still more notorious was Lyndon Johnson's preoccupation with historical analogy. The lesson Johnson applied in Southeast Asia came from what he had absorbed from the 1938 Munich crisis—that if leaders shirked their responsibilities abroad, they only postponed their problems, which wound up being worse. "We're not," he vowed, "going to have any men with any umbrellas."[39]

It does not seem too much to suppose that historians, sensitive to the nuances of metaphor, can better that record. We ought to take on such assignments with full recognition that history is not an exact science and that historians are not seers. Still, as Carl Degler has asserted, "A recourse to history may well save governments and other agencies from ill-considered acts of policy, even if a knowledge of the past cannot tell us what action to take." Though historians have shown themselves to be fallible, and can be counted on to be so again, Joseph Strayer has said of history: "We may go wrong in following the clues which it offers, but we would be lost without them. . . . History at its best gives us a real chance of reacting sensibly to a new situation. It does not guarantee the correctness of our response, but it should improve the quality of our judgment." Strayer reasoned: "A rough parallel may be found in certain card games. There is almost no chance that one distribution of cards will be repeated in a subsequent deal in bridge. Yet a man who has played several thousand hands of bridge should be able to make intelligent decisions and predictions even though every deal presents a new situation." Furthermore, as Alan Brinkley has said, "Illuminating the past is a way of protecting individuals and society from the glib and self-serving analogies that politicians routinely use to justify their own interests," and "a knowledge of history arms one to consider critically the claims of political figures."[40]

The issue, I believe, is less whether historians should intervene than whether they can do so more effectively. Ernest May and Richard Neustadt have offered a manual on how policymakers can avoid the trap of beguiling historical analogies that has opened up a debate on that vexing matter, and at the Georgia Institute of Technology Robert McMath has introduced a course, taught at the Carter Library, on "The Uses of History for Policy-Makers" that could be a model for others. More than a decade ago, twenty-one prominent historians led by Robert Kelley urged President Carter to institutionalize a historical presence in the federal government, perhaps on the model of the Council of Economic Advisers. It will be objected that history is not as technically refined a subject as economics and that historians diverge widely in their views, but it has also been said that if all the economists in the world were laid end to end, they still would reach no conclusion; yet the CEA has proven to be a constructive innovation. The notion has some pitfalls—notably the possibility that historians in such an agency might become captives of the reigning administration—and it might well prove preferable to adopt the proposal in a more modest form. But it deserves more scrutiny than it has received. Governments might well benefit from an enhanced role for historians not because they are good predictors but because they are men and women skilled in retaining institutional memories, perceiving the complexity of problems, and placing events in the stream of time.[41]

In sum, in considering the long warfare between historians who favor engagement and those who oppose it, I would join issue on the one point on which they agree—that their positions are irreconcilable. Instead, I see a creative tension between the two attitudes. Scholars would do well to give a respectful hearing to both groups, for neither holds a monopoly of the truth. One can agree that history has value wholly apart from any utilitarian end it serves without accepting the conclusion that historians must refrain from public involvement, and one can acknowledge that historians have an obligation to their community without dismissing the sage admonitions that the skeptics raise.

The historians who reject involvement might well ask themselves if they truly believe that, devoting their lives as they do to the study of history, they have nothing to contribute to the compelling public concerns of their only time on earth. For all his criticism of the progressive school, Richard Hofstadter generously conceded that "at their best, the interpretive historians have gone to the past with some passionate concern for the future," and even Julien Benda endorsed certain public actions by intellectuals: "When Gerson entered the pulpit of Notre Dame to denounce the murderers of Louis d'Orleans; when Spinoza, at the peril of his life, went and wrote the words 'Ultimi barbarorum' on the gate of those who had murdered the de Witts; when Voltaire fought for the Calas family; when Zola and Duclaux came forward to take part in . . . the Dreyfus affair."[42]

On the other hand, those of us who do take part in public affairs need constantly to remind ourselves that we are not omniscient, and that we must never, no matter how worthy the cause, compromise our commitment to, in John Higham's words, "the simple axiom that history is basically an effort to tell the truth about the past." We who are professors ought to remember that there are advantages, not only for ourselves but for society, to the detachment the campus affords us, and that unceasing involvement may diminish our capacity to see the world more clearly. When we do speak out, and we should choose those times wisely, we must take care to distinguish between doing so as historians and doing so simply as politically active citizens. Above all, we should take care not to create an atmosphere in the classroom in which views that diverge from our own cannot freely be voiced, and we should respect the rights of others in the profession to express beliefs contrary to our own or to remain silent.[43]

The intellectual, Charles Frankel wrote, "may and should take sides in the political struggles of his time, but there is likely to be an edge of irony or regret in his attitude when he does so." It seems inevitable that historians will always feel this tension—"caught," in Hofstadter's words, "between their desire to count in the world and their desire to understand it." Their "passion for understanding" moves them toward "detachment" and "neutrality," but "the terrible urgency of our political problems . . . plays upon . . . their desire to get out of history some lessons that will be of use in the world." For my own part, I would commend the message Emerson left us in his celebrated Phi Beta Kappa oration, "The American Scholar"—that "action is with the scholar subordinate, but it is essential," and that "there can be no scholar without the heroic mind."[44]

NOTES

This essay derives from the presidential address to the American Historical Association I delivered in Chicago on December 28, 1991. For this festschrift, I have augmented the essay by delineating the seminal contribution that Arthur Schlesinger has made to this question. I have also emended the text slightly to bring it up to date. I am grateful to Allan Brandt, Alan Brinkley, Jean Anne Leuchtenburg, and Edwin M. Yoder, Jr., for insightful comments and am appreciative of materials sent to me by Leon Fink, Otis L. Graham, Jr., Michael Hunt, Robert Kelley, J. Morgan Kousser, David E. Kyvig, Peyton McCrary, Page Putnam Miller, and Raymond Wolters.

1. Herman Ausubel, *Historians and Their Craft: A Study of the Presidential Addresses of the American Historical Association, 1884–1945* (reprint, New York, 1965), 24; John Herbert Roper, *C. Vann Woodward, Southerner* (Athens, Ga., 1987), 4, quoting the dean of the graduate school at Louisiana State University, Charles Wooten Pipkin; Robert Livingston Schuyler, "The Usefulness of Useless History," *Political Science Quarterly* 16 (1941): 23–37; Theodore S. Hamerow, *Reflections on History and Historians* (Madison, 1987), 33. For the wide divergence of views on the proper role for the historian, see Norman Graebner, "The State of Diplomatic History," *Society for Historians of American Foreign Relations Newsletter* (March 1973): 2–12.

2. James Harvey Robinson and Charles A. Beard, *The Development of Modern Europe: An Introduction to the Study of Modern Europe,* 2 vols. (Boston, 1907–8), 1: iii. For especially ardent espousal of history geared to contemporary issues, see Robert S. Lynd, *Knowledge for What? The Place of Social Science in American Culture* (Princeton, 1939), 133, and Howard Zinn, *The Politics of History,* second edition (Urbana, 1990), 309.

3. John Higham, *History: Professional Scholarship in America* (Baltimore, 1989), 14, 124. For Jameson, see Morey Rothberg and Jacqueline Goggin, eds., *John Franklin Jameson and the Development of Humanistic Scholarship in America, Volume I: Selected Essays* (Athens, Ga., 1992). I wrote a foreword for this volume. For the role of scholars in the World War I era, especially valuable are George T. Blakely, *Historians on the Homefront* (Lexington, Ky., 1970); Carol S. Gruber, *Mars and Minerva* (Baton Rouge, 1976); and Lawrence E. Gelfand, *The Inquiry* (New Haven, 1963).

4. William L. Langer, *In and Out of the Ivory Tower: The Autobiography of William L. Langer* (New York, 1977), 180–93.

5. John Hope Franklin, "The Historian and the Public Policy," in Franklin, *Race and History: Selected Essays, 1938–1988* (Baton Rouge, 1989), 312–14.

6. Everett Carl Ladd, Jr., "American University Teachers and Opposition to the Vietnam War," *Minerva* 8 (October 1970): 545; Robert Kelley, *Battling the Inland Sea: American Political Culture, Public Policy and the Sacramento Valley, 1850–1986* (Berkeley, 1989), xviii; J. Morgan Kousser, "Are Expert Witnesses Whores? Reflections on Objectivity in Scholarship and Expert Witnessing," *Public Historian* 6 (Winter 1984): 11; *City of Mobile v. Bolden,* 446 U.S. 55 (1980); Peyton McCrary and J. Gerald Hebert, "Keeping the Courts Honest: The Role of Historians as Expert Witnesses in Southern Voting Rights Cases," *Southern University Law Review* 16 (Spring 1989): 101, citing decisions such as *Bolden v. City of Mobile,* 542 F. Supp. 1050 (S. D. Ala. 1982); Peyton McCrary, "Racially Polarized Voting in the South: Quantitative Evidence from the Courtroom,"

Social Science History 14 (Winter 1990): 507–31; Chandler Davidson, ed., *Minority Vote Dilution* (Washington, D.C., 1984).

7. Kelley, *Battling the Inland Sea,* 339–40; Kelley, "Public History: Its Origins, Nature, and Prospects," *Public Historian* 1 (Fall 1978): 21–22; Barbara J. Howe and Emory L. Kemp, eds., *Public History: An Introduction* (Malabar, Fla., 1986); Susan Porter Benson, Stephen Brier, and Roy Rosenzweig, eds., *Presenting the Past: Essays on History and the Public* (Philadelphia, 1986); David F. Trask, "The State of Public History in the Washington Area," *Public Historian* 1 (Fall 1978): 37–41; *New York Times,* June 7, 1980. "Public history" is often treated as a modern-day upstart, but as the chairman of the National Council on Public History pointed out, "History has been practiced outside the academy for generations." Michael C. Scardaville, "Looking Backward Toward the Future: An Assessment of the Public History Movement," *Public Historian* 9 (Fall 1987): 37.

8. Julien Benda, *The Treason of the Intellectuals,* trans. Richard Aldington. (New York, 1928), 46–47, 81; National Humanities Center, *Newsletter* 12 (Fall-Winter 1990–91): 8.

9. Higham, *History,* 132; Oscar Handlin, *Truth in History* (Cambridge, Mass., 1979), 415. See, too, "Academy Compromised by Political Commitment," *Woodrow Wilson Center Report* (Cambridge, Mass., 1979), 415.

10. J. H. Plumb, "The Historian's Dilemma," in Plumb, ed., *Crisis in the Humanities* (Baltimore, 1964), 25–26; Hamerow, *Reflections,* 12, 3.

11. William E. Leuchtenburg, *Flood Control Politics: The Connecticut River Valley Problem, 1927–1950* (Cambridge, Mass., 1953); Leuchtenburg, "The Montgomery March," *American Heritage* 40 (December 1989): 66–68; *New York Times,* February 11, 1977; Woodrow Wilson International Center for Scholars, *Jimmy Carter on the Presidency: A Wilson Center Conversation, March 5, 1984* (Washington, D.C., 1984). In an account of the Montgomery march, Walter Johnson noted: "At one point the bus driver, to avoid a huge truck, drove off onto the shoulder of the road. As he did so, Hofstadter remarked that the 'liberal interpretation of American history had just nearly been wiped out.' A younger historian commented that if all the full professors were wiped out 'the mobility in the profession would be extraordinary.'" "Historians Join the March on Montgomery," *South Atlantic Quarterly* 79 (Spring 1980): 165.

12. *Senate History* (Fall 1991): 1; William E. Leuchtenburg, "The Conversion of Harry Truman," *American Heritage* 42 (November 1991): 55–68.

13. Hamerow, *Reflections,* 12, 33; Peter N. Carroll, *Keeping Time: Memory, Nostalgia, and the Art of History* (Athens, Ga., 1990), 178, quoted in David E. Kyvig, "Public or Perish: Thoughts on Historians' Responsibilities," *Public Historian* 13 (Fall 1991): 13. See, too, Carl N. Degler, "Remaking American History," *Journal of American History* 67 (June 1980): 23.

14. Morton G. White, *Social Thought in America: The Revolt against Formalism* (New York, 1952), 50; *New York Times,* July 2, 1978.

15. C. Vann Woodward, *The Future of the Past* (New York, 1989), 4.

16. Richard Hofstadter, *The Progressive Historians: Turner, Beard, Parrington* (New York, 1968), 464–65. For examples of how political commitments may affect scholarly writing, see Harry Elmer Barnes, *In Quest of Truth and Justice: De-Bunking the War Guilt Myth* (Chicago, 1928); Conyers Read, "The Social Responsibilities of the Historian,"

American Historical Review 55 (January 1950): 283–84; Michael A. Bernstein, "American Economic Expertise from the Great War to the Cold War: Some Initial Observations," *Journal of Economic History* 50 (June 1990): 408. C. Vann Woodward has confessed that in his eagerness to develop the theme of *The Strange Career of Jim Crow* he overlooked the fact that, prior to segregation, blacks had no public space at all. "The oversight illustrates the dangers of allowing present-day issues to shape or define historical investigation," he has written. Woodward, *Thinking Back: The Perils of Writing History* (Baton Rouge, 1986), 96–97. One writer had no qualms about stating that "the public historian . . . may have to bend the findings to the whims of the project design that the client has in mind." Lawrence De Graaf, "Summary: An Academic Perspective," *Public Historian* 2 (Spring 1980): 69. Public historians, however, have given considerably more sustained attention to ethical problems than have academic historians. See, for example, Ronald C. Tobey, "The Public Historian as Advocate: Is Special Attention to Professional Ethics Necessary?" *Public Historian* 8 (Winter 1986): 21–30.

17. Hofstadter, *Progressive Historians,* 344–45, 464.

18. David Halberstam, *The Best and the Brightest* (Greenwich, Conn., 1973); Michel Oksenberg, "Confession of a China Watcher: Why No One Predicted the Bloodbath in Beijing," *Newsweek,* June 19, 1989: 30. See, too, W. R. Connor's illuminating essay, "Why Were We Surprised?" *American Scholar* 60 (Spring 1991): 175–84.

19. Charles Frankel, *High on Foggy Bottom: An Outsider's Inside View* (New York, 1969), 11; Otis L. Graham, Jr., "The Uses and Misuses of History: Roles in Policymaking," *Public Historian* 5 (Spring 1983): 7; William E. Leuchtenburg to Hayes Redmon, May 1966; *Washington Post,* July 20, 1984. My views on Vietnam were stated more forcefully in a letter to Redmon on July 6, 1966.

20. C. Vann Woodward, ed., *Responses of the Presidents to Charges of Misconduct* (New York, 1974); Roper, *Woodward,* 5. The four students were John W. Chambers, Robert P. Ingalls, James Boylan, and Mark I. Gelfand. The other two supervisors were Merrill D. Peterson and William S. McFeely. For the experience of one of the other historians on the project, see James K. Banner, Jr., "Historians and the Impeachment Inquiry: A Brief History and Prospectus," *Reviews in American History* 4 (June 1976): 140–49. For the "unease" of a "resident historian" on a project with the most worthwhile aims, see John Demos, "History and the Formation of Social Policy toward Children: A Case Study," in David Rothman and Staton Wheeler, eds., *Social History and Social Policy* (New York, 1981), 301–24. Demos concluded: "Historical inquiry and policy formation made a new, awkward, and necessarily uncertain tandem. But practice may yet bring greater synchrony and increasingly substantial results." Ibid., 324.

21. Alfred H. Kelly, "An Inside Story: When the Supreme Court Ordered Desegregation," *U.S. News & World Report,* February 5, 1962: 88; Sylvia A. Law, "Conversations Between Historians and the Constitution," *Public Historian* 12 (Summer 1990): 14. I was one of the historians whose name appeared on the brief. For the water rights case, see Carl M. Becker, "Professor for the Plaintiff: Classroom to Courtroom," *Public History* 4 (Summer 1982): 69–77; Leland R. Johnson, "Public Historian for the Defendant," ibid., 5 (Summer 1983): 69–77. For the South Carolina case, see McCrary and Hebert, "Keeping the Courts Honest," 115–18. McCrary was the historian who found a discriminatory motive; Herman Belz testified for the defense. In the immense literature on

the *Sears* case, see Equal Opportunity Commission v. Sears, Roebuck and Co., 428 F. Supp. 1264, 1308–1312 (N.D. Ill., 1986), affirmed 839 F. 2d 302 (1988); Joan C. Williams, "Clio Meets Portia: Objectivity in the Courtroom and the Classroom," in Theodore J. Karamanski, ed., *Ethics and Public History: An Anthology* (Malabar, Fla., 1990), 45–56; Peter Novick, *That Noble Dream: The "Objectivity Question" and the American Historical Profession* (Cambridge, 1988), 502–10; Thomas Haskell and Sanford Levinson, "Academic Freedom and Expert Witnessing: Historians and the *Sears* Case,"*Texas Law Review,* 66 (1988): 1629; *New York Times,* June 6, 1986; Karen J. Winkler, "Two Scholars' Conflict in Sears Sex-Bias Case Sets Off War in Women's History," *Chronicle of Higher Education,* February 5, 1986: 1, 8; Ruth Milkman, "Women's History and the Sears Case," *Feminist Studies* 12 (Summer 1986): 375–400; Alice Kessler-Harris, "Equal Opportunity Employment Commission v. Sears, Roebuck and Company: A Personal Account," *Radical History Review* 35 (1986): 57–79; Rosalind Rosenberg, letter to editor, *Chronicle of Higher Education,* July 2, 1986: 22. Harold Green, director of the Law, Science, and Technology Program at George Washington University, is the source of the gibe about "whores" quoted in Kousser, "Are Expert Witnesses Whores?": 5. See, too, Eleanor P. Wolf, *Trial and Error: The Detroit School Desegregation Case* (Detroit, 1981); Raymond Wolters, "Advocacy, Ideology, and Objectivity: Scholars as Expert Witnesses for the Plaintiffs in School Desegregation Cases," unpublished paper. A professor of law has asserted that the efforts of Supreme Court justices "to ground today's decisions in historians' history are fundamentally misguided." Mark Tushnet, "Should Historians Accept the Supreme Court's Invitation?" *OAH Newsletter* (November 1987): 12.

22. Kousser, "Are Expert Witnesses Whores?": 7, 19; McCrary and Hebert, "Keeping the Courts Honest," 128; Alice Kessler-Harris and Amy Swerdlow, "Report on the First Conference on Women's History and Public Policy," *Perspectives* 28 (May-June 1990): 10; Final Report to the Ford Foundation on the Conference on Women's History and Public Policy, June 15–17, 1989, Sarah Lawrence College, Bronxville, N.Y. I am indebted to Professor Swerdlow for a copy of this report. Despite misgivings, the historians involved in the *Webster* case reaffirmed their belief that they had taken the right course. There is an excellent discussion in *Public Historian* 12 (Summer 1990). See, too, Allan M. Brandt, "Writing Policy-Directed History," unpublished paper presented at the History of Science Society meeting, Madison, Wisconsin, November 3, 1991.

23. Arthur Schlesinger, Jr., *Orestes A. Brownson: A Pilgrim's Progress* (Boston, 1939); idem, *The Age of Jackson* (Boston, 1945); Ralph de Toledano, "Junior's Misses," *American Mercury* 77 (November 1953): 5.

24. Carroll Engelhardt, "Man in the Middle: Arthur M. Schlesinger, Jr., and Postwar American Liberalism," *South Atlantic Quarterly* 80 (Spring 1981), 119. I have reversed the order of quotes in Engelhardt's essay.

25. Arthur Schlesinger, Jr., *The Crisis of Confidence: Ideas, Power and Violence in America* (Boston, 1969), 96–97; idem, review of *"Lessons" of the Past, Journal of American History* 61 (September 1974): 444.

26. Arthur Schlesinger, Jr., "On the Inscrutability of History," *Encounter* 27 (November 1966): 17; idem, *The Bitter Heritage: Vietnam and American Democracy, 1941–1966* (Boston, 1966), 93. One scholar has referred to "Schlesinger's own continuing, contrapuntal themes of the indelibly flawed nature of man, the inherent intractability of

institutions, and the consequent limits of politics." James A. Nuechterlein, "Arthur M. Schlesinger, Jr., and the Discontents of Postwar American Liberalism," *Review of Politics* 29 (January 1977): 38.

27. Schlesinger, *Bitter Heritage,* 80–81.

28. Ibid., 83; *New York Times Book Review,* September 18, 1949, quoted in Ronald Radosh, "Historian in the Service of Power," *Nation,* August 6, 1977: 104.

29. "An Exchange of Views: Arthur Schlesinger Jr. and Ronald Radosh: The Historian and Power," *Nation,* August 20, 1977: 148; Schlesinger, *Crisis of Confidence,* 95.

30. Schlesinger, *Crisis of Confidence,* 54, 60.

31. Ibid., 60–61.

32. Arthur Schlesinger, Jr., *The Politics of Hope* (Boston, 1962), 67; idem, "On the Inscrutability of History," 17.

33. C. Vann Woodward, *The Strange Career of Jim Crow* (New York, 1974); idem, *Thinking Back,* 98; idem, *Future of the Past,* xi.

34. Franklin, "The Historian and the Public Policy": 309. One scholar has concluded, "In America, at least, although the pursuit of learning may well be its own reward, it cannot for long among the otherwise occupied citizens be its own justification." Robert A. McCaughey, *International Studies and Academic Enterprise: A Chapter in the Enclosure of American Learning* (New York, 1984), 255. For the observation that "in the nineteenth century more than the twentieth, history was written for and read by large numbers of people other than academics," see Mary O. Furner, *Advocacy & Objectivity: A Crisis in the Professionalization of American Social Science, 1865–1905* (Lexington, Ky., 1975), 297.

35. Carl Brauer, "More Scholars Should Venture Forth to Confront, Enlighten, or Change the World," *Chronicle of Higher Education,* March 14, 1990: B2. The former chairman of a state committee for the humanities urged greater collaboration between the academy and the public, not least because "it is through such engagements that scholars can discover whether the insights gained in their research are really communicable, pertinent, and lively." Ron Perrin, "Humanists Must Forge Links between Their Work and the Public," *Chronicle of Higher Education,* September 27, 1989: A56.

36. Allan Nevins, "Not Capulets, Not Montagus," *American Historical Review* 65 (January 1960): 264–65.

37. Anne Firor Scott to "Dear Colleague," November 1991.

38. Charles Frankel, "The Political Responsibility of the Intellectual," in Paul Kurtz, ed., *Moral Problems in Contemporary Society: Essays in Humanistic Ethics* (Buffalo, 1973), 174–75. For Frankel's views, see William E. Leuchtenburg, "Charles Frankel: The Humanist as Citizen," in John Agresto and Peter Riesenberg, eds., *The Humanist as Citizen* (Research Triangle Park, N.C., 1981), 228–54.

39. W. Robert Connor, *Thucydides* (Princeton, N.J., 1984), 3; Harry S Truman to Margaret Truman, March 3, 1948, quoted in Margaret Truman, *Harry S Truman* (New York, 1973), 360. Hugh Sidey, *A Very Personal Presidency: Lyndon Johnson in the White House* (New York, 1968), 218. Senator J. William Fulbright replied to Johnson's insistence that the situation in Vietnam corresponded to that at Munich by saying, "The treatment of slight and superficial resemblances as if they were full-blooded analogies—as instances of history 'repeating itself'—is a substitute for thinking and a misuse of history." Alfred Steinberg, *Sam Johnson's Boy: A Close-Up of the President from*

Texas (New York, 1968), 788. See, too, Chalmers Roberts Oral History, Lyndon B. Johnson Library, Austin, Texas. For the Supreme Court's misuse of history, see Alfred H. Kelly, "Clio and the Court: An Illicit Love Affair," *Supreme Court Review* (1965): 119–58.

40. Carl N. Degler, "Is the New Social History Threatening Clio?" *OAH Newsletter*16 (August 1988): 5; Joseph R. Strayer, "Introduction," in Strayer, ed., *The Interpretation of History* (Princeton, 1943): 14–15; Alan Brinkley to the author, January 13, 1992.

41. Richard E. Neustadt and Ernest R. May, *Thinking in Time: The Uses of History for Decision-Makers* (New York, 1986); Gordon Wright et al. to Jimmy Carter, November 3, 1976. See, too, *OAH Newsletter* (January 1977): 4. At Kelley's behest, the Executive Board of the Organization of American Historians sent a similar communication to President Ronald Reagan. Executive Board Minutes, April 1, 1981; Richard Kirkendall, "Executive Secretary's Report," *OAH Newsletter* (July 1981): 11. I am indebted to Kirkendall, Arnita Jones, and Sharon Caughill for locating these materials for me. For a similar recommendation, see Ernest R. May, *"Lessons" of the Past: The Use and Misuse of History in American Foreign Policy* (New York, 1973), 172. One critic has objected, "A History Office in the West Wing . . . would be 'on the team,' with the inevitable narrowing of vision and independence." Graham, "Uses and Misuses of History": 13. Graham, though, has shown the potentialities as well as the limitations of the role of historians in policymaking in "Intellectual Standards in the Humanities," in Daniel Callahan, Arthur L. Caplan, and Bruce Jennings, eds., *Applying the Humanities* (New York, 1985), 261–69, and he has provided an example of sophisticated analysis of a policy question by a historian in *Losing Time: The Industrial Policy Debate* (Cambridge, Mass., 1992). I have also found informative Page Putnam Miller, "History in Government and Public Policy," unpublished paper. For the difficulties but also the opportunities historians encounter when they try to predict, see Louis Gottschalk, *Understanding History: A Primer of Historical Method* (New York, 1951), 264–71. One study of economists found that on nineteen occasions when they forecast the future of Treasury bond rates, they got the direction wrong fourteen times. *New York Times,* September 28, 1991.

42. Hofstadter, *Progressive Historians,* 465; Benda, *Treason of the Intellectuals,* 50. For the responsibility of the scholarly community, see George McT. Kahin, "A Polarization of Knowledge: Specialization on Contemporary Asia in the United States, *Journal of Asian Studies,* 33 (August 1974): 515–22.

43. Higham, *History,* 132.

44. Charles Frankel, "Definition of the True Egghead," *New York Times Magazine,* October 21, 1956: 62; Hofstadter, *Progressive Historians,* 464; *The Collected Works of Ralph Waldo Emerson* (Cambridge, Mass., 1971), 1: 59. C. Vann Woodward's biographer has written that "Woodward's life would be taken up with a continuing effort to find a proper balance between the competing masters of political causes and of disinterested scholarship. All scholars who seek societal reform ultimately face the dilemma posed by the contradictions between the two impulses. . . . Scholarship requires a degree of detachment from the concerns of the moment, while genuine activism permits little time for reflection on events and characters of the past 'irrelevant' to contemporary causes." Roper, *Woodward,* 59–60. For the travail of one historian who sought to combine scholarship with involvement in public affairs, see Paul M. Evans, *John Fairbank and the American Understanding of Modern China* (New York, 1988).

Chapter 2

THE HISTORIAN AS POLITICAL ADVISOR

Hugh Thomas

> "A State just and not generous"
> (*A definition of the state's function*
> *by Lord Salisbury, c. 1890*)

ONE OF GIBBON'S most famous comments about himself was when, in his autobiography, he reflected that his experiences as a lieutenant in the Hampshire regiment had not been "of no value" to the historian of the legions. Other historians have found themselves citing that reference, either in relation to themselves or to others, when caught up in some active political or military undertaking. Surely the historian of Franklin Roosevelt thought of the sentence when he served in President Kennedy's White House. I myself occasionally remembered it when, between 1979 and 1990, I worked indirectly but all the same a good deal for Margaret Thatcher when she was prime minister. I remember a year ago regretting to a friend that I had spent so much time in politics, and that I had thereby delayed coming to terms, in connection with a book that I was writing about the conquest of Mexico, with the nature of Charles V's imperial policies. The friend, a Frenchman with a deep knowledge of history, thought that I must have learned much from the experience to my long-term benefit as a historian: "When you talked to Mrs. Thatcher, did you not gain some knowledge which was of incomparable value to you in judging Charles V?" he asked. I wondered. I know that Arthur Schlesinger has wondered about his own experiences in politics and their impact on his historical studies. In this essay I shall note a few of my experiences and speculate about their usefulness to a historian to a modest extent. Only to that extent, for I am still too close to the events described.

I had a more undefined position in the political scene in Britain than Arthur Schlesinger had in the United States, being chairman of a think tank, the Centre for Policy Studies, which Margaret Thatcher used when she was in power. I was not inside the machinery of government. Thatcher had, however, founded this think tank herself, with Keith Joseph, in the mid-1970s to act as an alternative, largely free-market, source of advice for policy making, different from, and to some extent opposed to, the more middle-of-the-road Conservative Research department.

Thatcher maintained this think tank, and continued to use its services, after she attained power for several reasons. First, because she genuinely thought that the advice which she would be getting from civil servants might be too conventional. Second, because there were people already in the think tank whose advice she enjoyed but might be difficult to fit into the Whitehall structure.

This compromise of continuing to use this think tank for advice but to keep it outside the government machinery contained within it the seeds of difficulties. For example, the Centre had always had a small program of publications and those continued after May 1979, the date of Thatcher's victory. The civil service, and several ministers who suddenly found their departments being castigated for doing or not doing something which they did not previously know about, naturally were suspicious. Second, some of those in the think tank, knowing that they still had the ear of Thatcher, but at the same time finding her more remote than she had been before she got into power, began to feel persecuted. I did not feel that way myself, first because I had only begun to do odd jobs for Thatcher a year or so before she won her election; second because I had been briefly inside the civil service in the 1950s and could well imagine how those distinguished public servants must have felt when the prime minister seemed to rely on outsiders—that experience in the civil service had also taught me not to be too much in awe of government departments ("Once one's been inside one can never quite take them seriously again, can one?" Percy Lubbock amiably said to me, recalling his own brief time in the Home Office in 1904).

Third, I remembered Lord Lothian's advice as British ambassador to Washington: "If you want to know what is happening in the court of FDR, you much read Saint Simon," having in mind the circle of intellectuals known as the "Brain Trust." Margaret Thatcher's court was no doubt less elaborate than the White House had been in 1940 but all the same it was a court. It was a court which to begin with seemed exhilarating. In 1979 Thatcher seemed to have achieved a miraculous victory and, for a few months, everything seemed possible. For different reasons this mood was not what all my colleagues in the Centre recall of the time (they thought of "betrayal," for instance); and it was obviously not the mood which many Conservative grandees had. But for a political innocent such as myself, parachuted into a position of influence if not power, the time was intoxicating. There were many heady moments: I remember at a Christmas party in one of the secretary's rooms in Downing Street assuring Lady Guinevere, who then advised the prime minister on sartorial matters, that Britain always did well in the eighties of a century: in the 1880s, the African empire; the 1780s, the Industrial Revolution; the 1680s, the Glorous Revolution; and so on (I got stuck in the 1380s). The Falklands crisis made things seem even more exalted: is it my imagination or did Michael Howard, at a dinner which I had organized, assure the prime minister that "not since Agincourt" had British losses been so few in comparison with those of the enemy? I remember saying to David Wolfson, "Well, it's the first victory the West has had since the war." "Rather a pity it was against the West as well," was his astute reply.

Though I later differed from Thatcher over her European policy, I shall always be most grateful to her for allowing me to see how all this worked. Usefulness for historical understanding? I am less certain of that. All courts no doubt have something in common, and the people desirous of favor must have much in common too: one or two people who sought me out and told me that "if I happened to be talking to Margaret and the subject of honors were to come up," they thought that a knighthood or a peerage might really be quite a suitable prize for them. Of course they had their equivalents in Rome as in the court of Louis XIV. More important was the psychological dependence of everyone on the prime minister, their realization that their view of Horseguards parade was her gift to them. Perhaps there was also something different there in 1979; as in quite different circumstances in both 1940 and 1945, there were in Downing Street and its suburbs, among which I include the Centre for Policy Studies, a group of people (particularly Sir John Hoskyns and his tiny Policy Unit) who really knew that they were where they were to do something quite new: regenerate the country or turn back the frontiers of the state, or whatever other phrase seemed most suitable.

It took some years before the difficulties between the Centre and the government were resolved. Early on I received a telephone call one morning from Lord Thorneycroft, then chairman of the Conservative Party. He said to me: "Hugh, I have this very day had five separate cabinet ministers ringing me up to complain about one or other of your publications."

In the end, I contrived, with of course the full support of Thatcher, to make the Centre something which, though independent in its financing, free to use journalists, dons, or businessmen as sources of ideas in a way which was less possible for the civil service, and independent in its approach, had to respect the position of the prime minister; and, where there seemed a clash of interests, the prime minister's interest (as expressed through her admirable chief of staff, the serene figure of David Wolfson, or the noble figure of the late Ian Gow[1]) would be accepted as paramount.

How else could the thing have worked? The interest for me was to work for the prime minister, not to create a pressure group for new policies independent of her, such as existed in good measure elsewhere (the Institute for Economic Affairs, for example). Later I thought I knew the prime minister's mind well enough to be able to anticipate what she thought and sometimes I did catch myself saying, "The prime minister would not like that" in a firm voice, and the statement would be accepted.

This did not mean that the Centre had, blindly, to accept government policy. For example, one of our study groups in 1984 wrote a fine paper, entitled "Making it Work," on Britain's relations with the European Community. This document included two recommendations which caused a frisson of anxiety in the Conservative Central Office just before the European elections of that year: support for Britain's membership of the Exchange Rate Mechanism of the European Monetary System; and an acceptance (as of course was later agreed) that there should be a wide extension of qualified majority voting in the European Council.

There were other instances of such departures from government policies. For example, I had assembled a group of Russian specialists: they included such now, alas, dead masters of their subject as Leonard Schapiro and Hugh Seton-Watson, but also younger men, such as Dominic Lieven, and the brilliant Antony Polonsky, with my loyal friend George Urban acting as rapporteur. This group proposed policies toward the Soviet Union—we were still in the age of Andropov—of a quite unremitting harshness. "Why not", Leonard Schapiro asked, "have a complete trade boycott of the Soviet Union? It is the kind of thing they understand." The plan had a breathtaking simplicity and, for a moment, I thought that the prime minister was interested, but it was an idea so harsh as to make the Foreign Office decide that we were a gang of dangerous academic wild men. In the summer of 1984 they took some very careful defensive action, leading to Thatcher's friendly reception (as my friends, at the time, thought far too friendly) of Gorbachev before he was in power.

There were, however, occasions when it seemed politic to me to prohibit a publication which would have seemed admirable were it not being published under our auspices. For example, the late Elie Kedourie wrote a really brilliant critique of government policy toward higher education. But it was couched in the form of an *ad hominem* attack on the minister responsible, Robert Jackson. How could we, an institute concerned to assist the government, publish such a paper? There was a similar occasion when a director and benefactor of the Centre, Sir Cyril Taylor, who had had a long experience in London local government, wrote an essay arguing that the great cities of Britain, above all London, needed some kind of focal centre, even if it were considered essential to abolish most metropolitan counties. The minister responsible (I think it was William Waldegrave) telephoned to say, in his usual persuasive tones, that it was surely wrong for us, an institution held to be friendly to the government, to publish such a paper when the Cabinet had already made up its mind on the matter, and when we were about to enter a long argument on the subject with the opposition. I accepted this point of view, though in retrospect I think that Taylor was absolutely right in his prescription and that we should have gone ahead and published.

We were not all the time inclined to be what at the time seemed to the right of the prime minister. In the course of the Falklands war, for example, I maintained a constant private contact by telephone with the Prime Minister Manuel Ulloa of Peru, whom I knew and who desired to be a go-between for Britain and Argentina. At that time he was traveling around Europe in the hope of being able to make a peacemaking journey to England but, for his own political reasons, he did not want to be in London at the moment the British landed on the islands. In fact he never reached London. But on the telephone he was full of interesting information and ideas, being a close friend of then-Argentine Foreign Minister Costa Mendes, whom he often telephoned immediately before he talked to me. I passed on everything to Thatcher, also by telephone, so I have no doubt that Ulloa's information was not exactly private. "How does he know Argentina so well?" Thatcher asked me. "Surely the two countries are a long way apart." "All successful Peruvians marry Argentinian girls as their second wife," I replied, without adding, though, that Ulloa (who did marry an Argentinian on his second time) was well into his third marriage by then.

One day, the American minister, Ed Streater, rang up and asked if he could come and see me. I saw him immediately, and, without beating around the bush, he asked: "What the hell are you doing with the Peruvians?" I expect that was a question Francis Pym, the British foreign secretary, would also have like to put, but perhaps he was, as usual, too polite to do so. I asked Streater how he knew that I was doing anything. "Well," he said, "we are a global power, you know."

On one occasion, Ulloa told me that his plans for coming to London might have to be delayed a bit because of the sinking of the *Belgrano*. I passed on this tragic and to me, extraordinary news, not to Thatcher but to someone else in No. 10 (I think her private secretary, Clive Whitmore), who said, "Well, it's news to us that she's actually gone down. Could you ring your friend back to make sure?" My conversations with Ulloa continued for another two weeks after that—a fact which proves the falseness of the argument of Tam Dalyell, the persistent Labour MP who for years insisted that the sinking of the *Belgrano* ruined the chance of a Peruvian peace plan being achieved.

So far as history is concerned, I could see that a serious crisis such as the Falklands, constituted for several weeks, caused conventional procedures to break down. No one objected to what I was "up to" with Ulloa, because perhaps something positive, as I of course hoped (for example, preserving Britain's relations with Latin America), might come of it. Ordinary procedures in peacetime is less tolerant of such private action, as I discovered a year later, when, on the suggestion of George Jellicoe, I made a personal peace bid with the Argentines through the then-head of the Argentine Foreign Office. Thatcher's foreign office private secretary was very dubious about the benefits of any such adventure, though I thought that the prime minister herself wanted the discussions which I had initiated to go on. Peace was later pursued very successfully, though, through the same charming individual, by Sir Crispin Tickell.

One thing which I found myself doing for Thatcher was writing drafts of speeches. I had begun to do this at the end of 1977 before she came to power, and the last time that she asked me for a contribution was in August 1990, when she went to Houston in the early days of the Persian Gulf crisis. So I was involved for a long time, if much more at the beginning than at the end. This activity had an importance which I found quite unexpected. There was a regular pattern of procedure, at least in the early days. I would be asked to go and see the prime minister at Downing Street, and would talk with her on the most diverse themes for half an hour or so, perhaps more. Since the speeches, or lectures, with which I was involved were usually on the subject of foreign policy, there would be present the Foreign Office private secretary in Number 10 (to begin with, Michael Alexander, a most independent and interesting man, who was later allowed to resign from the Foreign Service after he was ambassador to NATO: a waste of a great talent). I would then go home and write a draft which would try to take into account what the prime minister had implied was on her mind, but which often would reflect my own feelings, and would be laced with comments deriving from my own reading. I once in 1979 managed to persuade the prime minister to quote Baudelaire's line, "Je regrette l'Europe aux anciens parapets . . ." from *Le Bateau Ivre*. I am sure that whoever said that a speechwriter is a politician *manqué* (it was *à propos* of a president of the United States) is quite right, for I often found myself putting things into the draft which I would have liked to have said myself. A special interest of mine in those days was European defense and I often tried to get the prime minister to support the concept of a European defense community (EDC). This idea was at that time unacceptable for a host of reasons. Basically, the idea was thought to risk breaking the link with the United States. But, I would say, what about Mr. Dulles's support for the first EDC? No one seemed to know anything about that, and the suggestion would somehow vanish.

That kind of covert policy making played a part in the minds of all the speech writers, and indeed it was important in its own right, because a major speech was an occasion when a policy or a new approach was commonly launched. "The Speech" was thus a statement to be endlessly discussed and redrafted. There would, at least in the early days of Thatcher's administration, be several meetings about these drafts, many lasting for a quite inordinate amount of time, during which each word, each comma even, of the draft would be discussed with an astonishing attention. Thatcher may not have often written her speeches herself (her off-the-cuff speeches were very effective, though), but her interest in finding the right word, the right anecdote, the right quotation for a speech was remarkable. Her patience was phenomenal. She has often been reproached for having a sharp tongue, or for being rude to colleagues, foreign statesmen, and civil servants, but in those very long conversations I never saw that side of her. She was always, in my experience, courteous, interested, generous, agreeable, and sometimes reminiscent about a whole variety of things. It was through these lengthy discussions, in her sitting room in Downing Street, sometimes in the absurdly small flat which prime ministers have to live in on top of that house, sometimes at Chequers, and occasionally in the great conference hotels (the Grand at Brighton, the Metropole in Blackpool) that I came to know the prime minister rather well. Her memory for detail was excellent. Once she had placed something in her brain, she retained it there. I do not think that I ever recovered my standing after I made two historical howlers in half an hour. "When was Simon de Montfort's parliament, Hugh?" she asked, in order to prove some point which had come up about the longevity of English liberty. "1258," I replied firmly. "Wasn't it 1265? I am sure I remember the anniversary; we celebrated it soon after I came to the House of Commons." "No, Prime Minister, it was 1258." Some assistant gladly found an encyclopedia. I was of course wrong. A little later, the conversation turned to Alexander the Great. I made a few trite remarks about Philip of Macedon, which the prime minister wrote down. Then came another question: "What was Philip's number as a king of Macedon?" "The Fifth," I replied, with an unerring air. "I could have sworn he was the Second," said Thatcher. The same secretary who had destroyed me over Simon de Montfort was happy enough to confirm, from a quick look at the Britannica, that once again I was wrong.

Very often these meetings occurred very late at night, a really Spanish hour. On at least two occasions I saw the eyes of two advisers glazing over with sleep, one of them actually at the table where she, he, and I were sitting. Once the admirable, loyal, and tireless appointments secretary, Caroline Ryder, came in and said firmly, "Mrs. Thatcher, you are tired; you ought to go to bed immediately and you will be fresher in the morning." But Thatcher knew that the question of whether, in an as yet undecided sentence of next week's speech, one should say "supine" or "prone" had to be decided first. By the end of the night, it often seemed as if expression and word were more important than content.

Many ministers and others thought that the time devoted to the preparation of these speeches were extravagant. Lord Carrington once came up to me in the corridors of the Metropole Hotel in Blackpool and said, "Do please get the prime minister to stop working on the Melbourne lecture. It's excellent, it was excellent six hours ago, and she ought to be doing far more important things." But Thatcher probably found these long sessions a therapy, a relaxation, a way of getting her own thoughts straight on a variety of things.

Statesmen in the past made fewer speeches than they do now, but I don't think that there is much new in the idea of a leader having a speech written by a friend or collague. Charles V's major speech at the Cortes of Santiago de Compostela in 1520 was written by an appointee of his, the Flemish bishop of Tuy.

Thatcher seemed in those days to have a keen interest in history and, whenever an international crisis occurred, she went to some trouble to talk (sometimes through me) to historians who knew about the country concerned. I once introduced to her Malcolm Deas of St. Antony's College, Oxford, at a party. "So you teach history," she said looking at him enviously, and added, "When I am finished with all this, I should like to come and study under you." Deas's face flushed, with alarm or pleasure I never quite knew. In this respect the prime minister was showing herself like many other statesmen who have come around to the idea that only history really can give both the knowledge and the perspective which is necessary for good judgment in politics. Polybius said: "For it is history alone which, without involving us in actual danger, will mature our judgment and prepare us to take the right views." (That was the kind of quotation which I was often trying to insert into drafts of the prime minister's speeches, sometimes with success.)

Thatcher differed from most of her predecessors in that she needed and sought an ideology. Perhaps that was because she had been a scientist—the first trained scientist ever to be prime minister of Britain, in fact—and therefore assumed that problems have a solution. Perhaps it was because she had once been influenced by an ex-Marxist who saw most things in ideological terms. More likely, though, she simply thought that the postwar conservatives had been too acquiescent. Had not Evelyn Waugh said that the Conservative Party's trouble was that they had never put the clock back even five minutes? At all events, she looked for a general theory by which she could test her politics. This approach was utterly different from the usual attitude of British conservatives, and much resented by many of them, particularly the so-called "wets." The fact that the prime minister was a woman also riled some people ("Rab" Butler was quite virulent to me about that aspect of the thing, and I have often thought how odd it should have been that his memorial service was held in Westminster Abbey the very day that the Falklands fleet set off). But even more disagreeable, there was the fact that Britain was being seen as an experiment as to how a certain philosophy might work. That absolutely infuriated many survivors of old Conservative governments.

I had something to do with the refinement of this philosophy, I think. Having myself become "an emigré from socialism" (the words of Keith Joseph), after Labour's disastrous turn to the left in the 1970s, I wanted myself some kind of explanation of how politics should be managed. I was also at the time writing my *Unfinished History of the World,* which gave me an excuse to read or reread various works on political thought which I had not looked at since Cambridge. Thus I was myself browsing through Tocqueville, Popper, Hayek, and Friedman about the time that I met Thatcher. She too was looking at these and similar books, perhaps for the first time. Keith Joseph had, in the early years of her party leadership, after 1975, given her extensive reading lists, which included works by all those writers but also Adam Smith ("*The Theory of the Moral Sentiments,* Hugh, not *The Wealth of Nations*"). The first time I wrote a speech for Thatcher, perhaps in late 1977, I produced a document entitled "Politics of the Open Society," or something like it. It was what I myself thought at the time. To my amazement, Thatcher decided to use the text almost in full, without much change. I waited with fascination for the day when she was going to deliver this (in my opinion) admirably succinct statement of democratic beliefs. Appropriately, from my point of view, the speech was going to be at the Royal Commonwealth Society, in Northumberland Avenue, a club of which my mother had been long a member. It was at noon one day in March 1978. I had to go to lunch on a barge in the Thames of Cheyne Walk. "What news, what news?" I asked my hostess, Harriet Berry, when we arrived. "Oh, no news," she said, "just Mrs. Thatcher banging on." "But what did she say?" I spluttered. "Oh, the same old stuff," said Harriet. This speech received absolutely no attention at the time; and, to my knowledge, that fine statement has never been reprinted in any collection of speeches.

But this free market ideology, Hayekian Popperism, or Friedmanist Hayekism, had to be given some roots in the British conservative past. That was not at all easy. Chamberlain and Baldwin were capitalists, but it was hard to find anything which they had said which was interestingly pro-capitalist. Anyway, to revive those particular names in public memory was, even in the 1970s, a sure way of committing political suicide. Harold Macmillan, though an active businessman for much of his life, and though still very much alive, was seen by Thatcher as the fount of all the nation's troubles. For the only real philosopher among her predecessors, Balfour, she had a special disdain: I remember her pleasure when I told her the story of AJB in Londonderry House, unable to decide which of two identical flights of stairs he was going to descend. The only predecessors for whom Thatcher had real respect seem to me (I may have forgotten some friendly words about Bonar Law) to have been Churchill and Lord Salisbury. Of "Winston," for anyone of Thatcher's generation (and mine too), it was then next to impossible to make any criticism. He might have been in domestic politics (at least after 1945) a "wet" of the very deepest water, to use the rough language of the 1980s, but his humor, his prose, and his war leadership were so inspiring that it seemed churlish to mention that. Lord Salisbury was a different matter. Not long before I met Thatcher, she had read the early essays of Lord Salisbury, in a new edition of Dr. Sola Pinto, and she knew his views rather well. She certainly knew them better than I did and, on several occasions, pointed out some fine sentence which summed up some still surviving point of conflict—Ireland, or national security, for example.

My memory is hazy about the details of my Salisburian conversations with Thatcher, though I caught a whiff of what must have gone on when, by chance, I recently looked up the entry on Salisbury in the Dictionary of National Biography. I notice that in it, I had marked, surely in those early Thatcherian days, a passage where the marquis is described as wanting to see the state "just and not generous." The sentence not only sums up well that era of pure Thatcherism, it might now be said, but it probably must have seemed a bridge by which Thatcherians, apparently so far from the *grandes lignes* of conservative theory, might at least make a connection with that old tradition.

My copy of the DNB also gives another documentary hint of past, and to me as certainly to Thatcher, forgotten conversations: for example, in the entry for Adam Smith, I find another sidelining, of a passage where Smith is said to have met Edmund Burke when, in 1784, the latter was passing through Edinburgh on the way to being installed as Lord Rector of the University of Glasgow. Burke, Smith is recorded as having said, "is the only man who thinks on economic subjects exactly as I do, without any previous communication having passed between us." So there! Smith's ideas were not to be dismissed as those of a libertarian ideologue; he was a man who thought as the great Burke did. There comes back to me the memory of a Sunday evening in Downing Street, when I pointed out to Thatcher some very Smithian passages in Burke's *Thoughts on Scarcity* (indicating the difficulties which occurred when the state enters the marketplace as a customer or a seller), to enable her to make some riposte to Ian Gilmour who, though still I think in the cabinet, had been deploring, in a somewhat masked fashion, that the new conservativism of Thatcher was far from the great Burkean tradition.

These conscious searches for a theory to explain her actions must make Thatcher an unusual person in modern politics. In some ways, though the theory pursued was quite different, she must be closer to Franklin Roosevelt than to most U.S. presidents. In respect for her desire for interesting outside and unconventional advice, the Brains Trusts of both FDR and Kennedy were obvious precedents. My own experience was certainly deepened by working for her, but I now have some irritation, at myself, that I stayed so long working in the periphery of politics rather than in the mainstream of history. But perhaps that is the kind of regret which always occurs when one grows older. Arthur Schlesinger, though I think appalled at my political trajectory (I had met him in Washington in the days of the New Frontier, when I was a keen Gaitskellite), remained a firm friend throughout the period of my life I have discussed here, and if he is I think closer now than then, it is because he has seen that I have absorbed what I learned in that epoch and indeed never allude to it (this is the first occasion that I have brought myself to talk about such matters as are here discussed), while happily reentering the world of historical writing with pleasure and satisfaction.

It is obvious from the above that I have much respect for Thatcher personally. This is not the occasion to review her place in history. She certainly transformed the position of the British state by reducing the stranglehold over its operations that the trade unions had gained in the 1960s and 1970s. She thereby strengthened the state. She liberated the state from its managerial role in the economy, and reduced the dependence on it of much subsidized private industry. She began the astonishing, basically benign, process of privatization, and I can remember her talking of her dislike of that word, though of course supporting the thing itself. By remaining firm in the face of a nervous, over-valued, and therefore aggressive Soviet Union, she helped to make possible the fall of the Soviet empire—a phrase which now everyone uses but few dared to in the early 1980s, except for Hugh Seton-Watson. At the same time I think that she made a mistake in supposing that standards of profit and loss should be applied to education. Her patriotism was in the end too strong for her to see clearly Britain's opportunities in Europe, and she far preferred the apparent cosiness of a strengthened "special relationship" with the United States of Ronald Reagan to a collaboration with the European leaders. This preference in the end destroyed her, and the relation between Britain and Europe remains an open wound.

NOTE

1. Ian Gow was assassinated by the IRA outside his own house in Eastbourne in 1990.

Chapter 3

THE HISTORIAN AND THE CYCLES OF HISTORY

GEORGE F. KENNAN

ARTHUR SCHLESINGER, JR., historian, essayist, lifelong student of American political institutions, has written a provocative book, a series of fifteen essays drawn mainly from articles published by the same author at various times in recent years, but revised or reedited or in various other ways reinforced by the author's present views. What emerges in *The Cycles of American History* is a series of mature reflections on a number of serious questions to which the author has, over the course of the years, given much study and thought. These questions are viewed historically, as they all deserve to be; and the author's treatment of them is enriched not only by his superb knowledge of American political history but also by a fine literary style which adds to both the readability and the force of the thoughts brought forward.

It is never easy to review a work composed of a number of different articles, bearing on different subjects. Particularly is this true when certain of the articles, as is the case here, are of such weight and quality as to merit full-length reviews in their own right. The diversity is further heightened, in this instance, by the fact that the essays are almost evenly divided between those that deal with America's domestic-political institutions and customs and those that relate, at least by implication, to the position of this country as a member of the world community.

Let us begin with the second of these two categories.

Schlesinger sees two profoundly rooted but conflicting strains in the way Americans view themselves—in the role, that is, in which they cast themselves—as a nation among other nations. Sometimes these two strains do battle with each other in the same American breast; more often large segments of opinion lean decisively one way or another, with the result that each of the strains has had its period, or periods, of ascendancy in American public life.

One of these views, strong initially among the Founding Fathers themselves, saw Americans as essentially no different from the general run of human beings: subject to the same limitations; affected by the same restrictions

Editor's note: This article originally appeared in the *New York Review of Books* on November 6, 1986, as a review of *The Cycles of American History.*

of vision; tainted by the same original sin or, in a more secular view, by the same inner conflicts between flesh and spirit, between self-love and charity. This view, in its original eighteenth-century form, was also informed by the recognition that history had had, to that time, few examples to show of a solid and enduring republic, whereas one could point to a number of examples of empires and monarchies that answered reasonably well to this description. Against this background of perception, the Founding Fathers tended, for the most part, to see the establishment of the national independence and unity of the United States as an experiment—not an easy one, not one whose success was automatically assured—rather, as Schlesinger describes it, one "undertaken in defiance of history, fraught with risk, problematic in outcome." With this question mark lying across its future, the fledgling republic could obviously not appear as a guide or teacher to the rest of humanity. Its first duty was to itself. The best it could ask of its international environment was to be left alone to develop its institutions in its own way and to prove, if it could, that a nation thus conceived and thus dedicated could, as Lincoln put it, "long endure."

In the opposite strain of perception Americans were seen not as conducting and enacting a great experiment but as fulfilling a predetermined destiny. This view had its origins in the religious convictions of many of the early New England colonists. They saw in the very fact of their removal to this continent the influence of "a wonder-working Providence"—a "journey of the elect," as Schlesinger describes it, "to salvation beyond history." From this it was only a step to the belief that Americans had taken over from the old-testamentary model the quality of the chosen race. Schlesinger cites several striking examples of the intensity of this feeling among prominent figures of the early decades of the republic.

With time, of course, this view became secularized. Nationalistic fervor, that contagious hysteria of all nineteenth-century Western society, gave it a far wider currency than it had ever before enjoyed. Strength was lent to it by the nation's survival of the Civil War, which to many appeared as evidence that the "experiment" of American nationhood had been successfully completed. What remained then was a widespread impression, supported by patriotic emotion, that the Almighty, in Schlesinger's words, "had contrived a nation unique in its virtue and magnanimity, exempt from the motives that governed all other states."

Of central importance, in this dichotomy of view, was the relationship to a sense of history. The old concept of America as experiment had been embedded in profound historical consciousness. It was as part of an unbroken historical continuity, partially inscrutable but still man's greatest aid to self-understanding, that the "experiment" was seen to have its existence.

Not so for those who saw America as destiny. Essential to their outlook was "a narcissistic withdrawal from history"—a phenomenon which, as Schlesinger correctly observes, reached its apotheosis in the recent postwar decades. "For all the preservation of landmarks and the show biz of bicentennials," he writes,

> we have become, so far as interest and knowledge are concerned, an essentially historyless people. The young no longer study history. Academics turn their back on history in the enthusiasm for the historical behavioral "sciences." As American historical consciousness has thinned out, the messianic hope has flowed into the vacuum.

At this point, Schlesinger leans heavily on the brilliant insights of Reinhold Niebuhr's *The Irony of American History* to challenge directly the validity of the messianic approach. He describes this as an illusion: "No nation is sacred and unique. . . . All nations are immediate to God. America, like every country, has interests real and fictious, concerns generous and selfish, motives honorable and squalid. Providence has not set Americans apart from lesser breeds. We too are part of history's seamless web."

In the essay on "Foreign Policy and the American Character" Schlesinger traces the effect of this deep dichotomy on the recent and current conduct of American foreign policy. Here, the two poles have acquired, justifiably, a different semantic clothing: realism vs. ideology. Admitting that in the mentality of most political leaders of this century the division between these two outlooks was never a complete one (so powerful were the two strains in mass opinion that the practical politician has had no choice but to try to appeal simultaneously to both), Schlesinger nevertheless sees the Reagan administration as representing "a mighty comeback of messianism in foreign policy." He draws attention, in particular, to the way this affects outlooks toward the Soviet Union. Realism sees in that political entity "a weary, dreary country filled with cynicism and corruption, beset by insuperable problems at home and abroad, lurching uncertainly from crisis to crisis." Ideology, on the other hand,

> withdraws problems from the turbulent stream of change and treats them in abstraction from the whirl and contingency of life. So ideology portrays the Soviet Union as an unalterable monolith, immune to historical vicissitude and permutation, its behavior determined by immutable logic, the same yesterday, today and tomorrow. . . . We are forever in 1950, with a dictator in the Kremlin commanding an obedient network of communist parties and agents around the planet. In the light of ideology, the Soviet Union appears as a fanatic state carrying out with implacable zeal and cunning a master plan for world dominion.

These observations provide the point of departure for a vigorous attack on the Reagan foreign policy. Drawing attention to the contradictions even in the handling of the East–West confrontation ("a long twilight struggle between bark and bite"), this polemic runs the gamut from Central America to the arms race. It comes down hard on the irony of the simultaneous and symbiotic prospering of the Pentagon and the Soviet Defense Ministry. "There is no greater racket in the world today than generals claiming the other side is ahead in order to get bigger budgets for themselves. This tacit collusion, based on a common vested interest in crisis, remains a major obstacle in the search for peace."

And the conclusions are uncompromising:

> Ideology is the curse of public affairs because it converts politics into a branch of theology and sacrifices human beings on the altar of dogma. . . . In the end [it] is out of character for Americans. . . . [They] would do well to sober up from the ideological binge and return to the cold, gray realism of the Founding Fathers; men who lucidly understood the role of interest and force in a dangerous world and thought that saving America was enough without trying to save all humanity as well.

Similarly related to the choice between realism and ideology is the next of the essays, addressed to the respective roles of moral absolutes and national interest in foreign policy. The discussion gains in significance by virtue of the pervasive bewilderment that prevails today in academic, journalistic, and governmental circles over precisely this question. Schlesinger takes as his point of departure the wholly sound observation, already recognized by thinkers as far apart in time as Alexander Hamilton and Niebuhr, that morality is not the same thing for an individual, responsible only to himself, as it is for a government, trustee for the interests of others and bound to represent those interests as it sees them, rather than to obey its own moral impulses. But Schlesinger also recognizes that the concept of national interest, essential as it is as a foundation for national policy, is a poorly defined term, varying greatly with circumstances and vulnerable to serious error and distortion both in understanding and in application. A democracy, he notes, presents particularly ample possibilities for just this sort of confusion and error. As a guide to policy, the concept requires, for this reason, a certain sort of disciplinary restraint; and this he finds in the observance of the values of prudence, of proportionality (that action should bear a reasonable relationship to its presumed consequences), and of international law.

With these modifications, Schlesinger finds national interest "an indispensable magnetic compass for policy," without which "there would be no order or predictability in international affairs." And he ends his discussion with a conclusion, firmly rooted in Federalist thinking, which could scarcely have been better expressed. Moral values, he concludes, "do have a fundamental role in the conduct of foreign affairs." But this role is not to provide abstract and universal principles for foreign policy decisions. "It is rather to illuminate and control conceptions of national interest." The beginning of a true state morality lies, in his view, in "the assumption that other nations have legitimate traditions, interests, values and rights of their own." Thus: "National interest, informed by prudence, by law, by scrupulous respect for the equal interests of other nations and above all by rigorous fidelity to one's own sense of honor and decency, seems more likely than the trumpeting of moral absolutes to bring about restraint, justice and peace among nations."

These considerations lead into the next of the essays, "Human Rights and the American Tradition." Here, perhaps inevitably, the sharpness of vision is somewhat dimmed—inevitably, for the problem at hand is one of great and baffling complexity. Schlesinger gives us as balanced an appraisal of this problem as any this reviewer has seen. He does full justice to the many sober voices out of the American past warning us that political practices in other countries are best influenced by the power of example rather than by preaching and exhortation. He recognizes the disadvantages that rest on direct efforts by our government to bring pressure on other governments for the correction of human rights abuses. He feels that the greater part of this burden should be assumed by nongovernmental associations and, to the extent we can persuade them to do it, by the United Nations and other international agencies. But he also recognizes, and approves, what he calls "the profound and admirably uncontrollable American impulse to exhibit sympathy for victims of despotism in other lands." He notes (and one supposes with agreement) that Franklin Roosevelt, although never doubting that foreign policy must be founded on national interest, considered ideals "an indispensable constituent of American power." He admits that the American pressures for the observance of human rights elsewhere will never make such rights forever secure; but it will, he thinks, "make tyranny insecure for a while to come."

Perhaps, perhaps. But even the most sober discussion of the human rights problem in this country fails, in the judgment of this reviewer, to probe the depths of this complex subject. There is the general failure to distinguish between personal rights (protection against the abuse of person and the invasion of property) on the one hand, and civil, largely electoral, rights on the other. The one can exist without the other, and has done so many times. But to demand the first, and less intrusive, of the two without demanding the other (as seems to be the case when we approach the Soviet Union) raises the unanswered question whether we are saying that we would be satisfied with a species of benevolent despotism. Beyond this, there is the common failure to take into consideration the possible or probable consequences of what we are demanding—a particularly weighty omission, since it is others, not we, who will have to live with those consequences. Nothing in the vast historical record justifies the common American assumption that anyone who opposes oppression would, if he were to succeed in overthrowing it, invariably govern more humanely himself. Too many past efforts to overthrow a given tyranny have been motivated not by a desire to do away with tyranny altogether but by a desperate determination to replace one tyranny by another of one's own making.

What we are faced with here is, in many instances, not just the need for persuading a given ruling group to behave more humanely but rather the problem of changing an entire political culture; and this is not accomplished simply by urging a given ruling group to behave more humanely. Demands that this or that regime should concede more in the way of "human rights" to its citizens raise, in other words, questions both of national custom and of political philosophy which we ourselves, at least in our collective capacity, are unlikely to have thought through; and without the answers to them our efforts are only too likely to be fumbling and confusing. This reviewer remains of the opinion that the best way we—and particularly our government—can influence the political practices of other governments is to apply our ax vigorously to some of the failures and evils of our own society, letting the chips fall where they may. This fallout, we may be sure, will not be ignored.

These observations will have sufficed only to give some idea of the general direction of those of Schlesinger's essays that touch on foreign policy. The ones that deal with purely national affairs strike a different note. There are six of them, all richly informed by Schlesinger's familiarity with American political history, all interesting and deserving of the sort of detailed critical comment that cannot be given within this space. But three of them—one on the questionable fate of American political parties, another on the past, present, and future of the presidency (and who could be better qualified to write on this subject than the author of major works on the age of Andrew Jackson and on the life of Franklin Roosevelt?), and a third on the vice-presidential office—go to the heart of some of the country's greatest present concerns.

By virtue of party and organizational connections and his views on specific national questions, Arthur Schlesinger rates as a liberal. But what emerges from these highly interesting papers is a very conservative outlook. Despite all its faults and its declining fortunes, Schlesinger wants to see the party system preserved. This, despite what he terms "the devastating and conceivably fatal impact" of television and the computerized public opinion polls on that system. "Without the stabilizing influence of parties," he says, "American politics would grow angrier, wilder and more irresponsible."

He rejects, similarly, the various suggestions for the reform of the presidential office. He recognizes the multitudinous deficiencies of the existing system, but fears that to change it would produce even greater ones. He rejects the proposals for a single six-year presidential term. He disagrees with those who would introduce into our system the essential features of the British and Canadian parliamentary ones, centering on the establishment of a relationship of mutual responsibility between executive and legislative organs. He rejects, on balance, the proposals for abolishing the electoral college in favor of direct presidential elections; though he favors the so-called National Bonus Plan, under which a pool of 102 electoral votes would be conceded, within the

College, to the winner of the popular vote. He favors a further shortening of the interregnum between successive presidential administrations. But in general he is against structural surgery. "If the political will exists in Congress and the citizenry," he thinks, such surgery "will not be necessary. If the will does not exist, it will make little difference."

With respect to the vice-presidency, Schlesinger's view is less conservative. He joins many others in the conclusion that the vice-presidential office, as we now have it, is an anomaly and sometimes even an absurd one. He deplores the Twenty-fifth Amendment, giving to a one-time vice-president who has succeeded to the presidency the power to appoint his successor with the confirmation of both houses of Congress. He would prefer to see the vice-presidency, as such, abolished, and replaced by an arrangement under which the decision on succession to the presidency, in case of the death or disability of an incumbent, would be at once submitted to the will of the voters in a special election—an arrangement that would meet the principle that no one should come to occupy the highest office in the land other than by decision of the voters themselves.

These views, argued in the book with a comprehensiveness and historical authority to which this summary can do no justice, come before the public at a peculiarly appropriate moment. In less than a year the two-hundredth anniversary of the Constitution will be upon us. One can well agree with Schlesinger that one should approach only with the greatest skepticism and caution suggestions for the amendment of a document that for over two centuries has served its purpose as well as has the American Constitution. The fact remains that our present federal system is simply not working well—not well enough, in any case, to meet obvious national needs—in a number of areas of decision where the entire future of the country may be at stake. These concern, in the main, matters that require the long view: environmental protection, immigration, drug control, public finance, and, above all, nuclear arms control. In all of these matters the failures are evident; in some of them the Congress even confesses its helplessness. It is idle to shrug these failures off with the comforting reflection that our institutions have worked well enough in the past. So great have been the changes in the physical and technological environment of our lives in this present century that there can be no assurance that what was adequate to the past will continue to be adequate to the future.

There are two thoughts to which, in the mind of this reviewer, these gloomy perceptions conduce. The first is the question whether, if the traditional political institutions of the country cannot be usefully altered by constitutional amendment, they might not be usefully supplemented with something that does not now exist: namely, some sort of an advisory body, advisory both to president and to Congress, but standing outside them, and made up of persons remote from participation in partisan political activity but qualified by training, experience, and temperament to look deeply into present trends and possible remedies and to tell both the legislative and executive branches of the government of the things they *must* do, whether they like it or not, to head off some of the worst eventualities that seem now to be, almost unhindered, in the making. The constitutionally created institutions of government would of course have to remain the seats of final decision; but the existence of a sober and deliberate outside voice of this nature might conceivably serve to remove from the bull-pit of partisan contention questions to which, while the imperative need for solutions is everywhere evident, partisan politics can find no answers.

In a body of this nature scientific authority would be prominently represented, as would distinguished previous experience in public affairs; but the accent, in the determination of its composition, would have to be on character rather than on smartness, and on wisdom rather than on narrow expertise, on knowledge of the past as well as a sense of the future. Such a body might provide much of the answer to a demand that has recently been raised with growing insistence: the demand for a better use of our great fund of acquired experience in public life—for a better use, that is, of the "elder statesmen" who are to be found in such abundance in our society but whose experience, as things now stand, goes largely wasted.

This leads to the second thought. If no more imaginative effort is undertaken, is there not a danger that the celebration of the two-hundredth anniversary of the Constitution may exhaust itself in what Schlesinger calls "show biz"—the sort of parades, costumes, outward replicas, and reenactments that characterized the anniversaries of the Declaration of Independence and of the Statue of Liberty?

Should not the President and former Chief Justice put their heads together and arrange for the convocation, by official invitation, of a small gathering of historians, authorities on constitutional law, and other qualified persons (no more in number than those who deliberated on the Constitution two hundred years ago) to examine the adequacy of that document at the distance of two hundred years (as the authors of the document hoped and expected would occasionally be done)? Such a group could not only confront collectively the questions Arthur Schlesinger has raised in this book, but also assess the soundness and suitability of the habits and traditions that have grown up in these two past centuries around the institutional framework the Constitution has provided. Again, the findings of such a body could of course be no more than advisory; but they might serve an educational purpose for the public at large; and they might point the way, as nothing else could, to the improvement of an institutional and traditional framework whose evident inadequacy to the challenges now before us threatens in many ways the continuity and intactness of our national life.

Chapter 4

THE LESSONS OF AN HISTORIAN

John Kenneth Galbraith

IN ANY REASONABLY learned conversation or writing on the political and economic position or problems of the United States in our time, the view most likely to be cited, the name most certain to be mentioned, is that of Arthur Schlesinger, Jr. It will be called into support of the speaker or author, or as the best reflection of what is being opposed. No one else in our time and Republic quite enjoys such prestige as both an ally and an opponent, and, no doubt, especially the former. Many who hold different views are known to choose their opponents more carefully.

The basis of the Schlesinger esteem and prestige as a social commentator and critic is not simple, not one-dimensional. There are in the world varying degrees of mental competence, much as we may regret it. All women and men are not, in this respect, born equal. By natural endowment Schlesinger is high among the mentally fortunate.

There is also the matter of diligence, particularly important as regards one who has spent his years in academic precincts. Here the Schlesinger lesson and example are of special relevance. In the academic culture diligence is a greatly important and greatly unmentioned attribute. At any given time a far from negligible proportion of all professors are resting their minds and often even their bodies in preparation for the next intellectual orgy. They are eloquent on the book they are about to begin. Leisure is closely intertwined with academic freedom.

In my younger days at Harvard I was deeply impressed by an older colleague, also a historian, who spoke frequently and impressively of the truly significant work he had under way. We listened with admiration and continued to listen over the years. He retired and died with the book unwritten and, I believe, not yet started. At his memorial service there was, however, grave mention of what the world was now denied. A well-known economics professor of an earlier generation studied Massachusetts town finance. After completing work on one town, a task that could have been accomplished in a week or two but to which he devoted at least a year, he moved on to contemplate another town. He was thus occupied for a lifetime. Only one book ever emerged, and that went forever unread.

It was in my earlier days in Cambridge that I was instructed in this matter of academic toil and its avoidance by Arthur Schlesinger; it was over the wall that separated his house from mine. We were both afflicted by colleagues who, looking at the too evidently excessive flow of books and papers coming from our respective desks, would say: "Arthur [or Ken], aren't you working too hard? I think you are pressing yourself too much." Sometimes there would be an added question: "Seriously, what about your health?"

To this, at Schlesinger's suggestion, we agreed we would make reply: "Not at all. The trouble with you is that you're lazy."

Alas, I never had the courage to carry out this agreement. Nor, quite possibly, did my neighbor.

That was too bad, for it would have identified a major truth as to academic life. Along with intelligence, diligence is a prime requisite, and it too, as I've said, is a Schlesinger hallmark.

But these are lesser matters perhaps. A larger Schlesinger lesson is of the importance not only of intelligence and diligence but of the way one retrieves from past experience what is needed for present guidance. One can be rather blunt about this: no one can speak with effect on any current problem who isn't versed in the previous experience. It is not that history repeats itself; it is not that those who fail to see the errors of the past are doomed to repeat them. A small core of truth lies back of both these aphorisms, but the matter is both more general and more fundamental. To be fully informed and effective on any current matter Schlesinger has shown that one must have a knowledge of the behavior patterns that have governed response to similar circumstance in the past. I turn for illustration and affirmation, not surprisingly, to economics.

As I write, the United States, as also its trading partners, is suffering a serious recession. There have been many recessions before; in American history they have been called panics, crises, and depressions, the designation changing as succeeding generations have sought a milder, less frightening term to characterize the current misfortune and distress: not a panic, only a crisis; not really a crisis, only a depression; not a depression, only a recession; not really a recession, only a growth adjustment.

It is not the fact that we have had recessions (or growth adjustments) before that is important. Rather, it is that we see what is common as to motivation and reaction to previous experience. Seeing this deeper behavior pattern, the Schlesinger lesson, we have a full appreciation of what is now taking place.

Thus, when President George Bush said confidently in the late summer of 1990, a year and a half ago as I write, that the recession would be short and quickly over, anyone guided by Schlesinger was immediately alert. Sometimes, as in the early 1980s, recessions *are* short; sometimes, as in the 1930s, they are anything but short. What one can rely on is the established political response. That, in the absence of other seemingly available or politically convenient action, is a resort to the rhetoric of reassurance. So it was with Herbert Hoover, who, in March 1930, said the worst effect on employment of the recession would be over in sixty days; who, in May, said, "We have now passed the worst and with continued unity of effort shall rapidly recover"; who, a little later, said that business would be normal by fall. In those days he sternly rebuked a delegation calling on him to ask for action against the depression. They were too late, he told them; the depression had ended several weeks earlier.

I repeat: it is not for exact or even approximate parallels in historical experience that Schlesinger has taught us to look: it is for the common elements in human, social, and, notably, political motivation.

I could go on. I have been fascinated all of my academic life by the phenomenon of the great speculative boom (and its aftermath), going back to the Tulipomania in Holland in 1637. It was Schlesinger who, by example, urged upon me not only the modern relevance of this experience but more particularly the need again to see the common threads in human motivation. These, when looked for, appeared and reappeared with a wonderful consistency. Whether of tulip bulbs, of John Law's Louisiana promotions, of the stock of the South Seas Company or of RCA, the great speculative favorite in the stock market boom of the late 1920s, or of the deeply redundant real estate developments in the 1980s, prices were going up. The mentally vulnerable, of whom there is always a more than adequate reserve, were attracted and responded. Their response caused prices to go up more; this price rise then confirmed them in their superior wisdom and foresight. They and others bought more; prices went up more; the process now had a life of its own, which continued until the current stockpile of financial and mental decrepits was exhausted. Then prices faltered, and there came the rush to get out, the crash. One reliable aspect of such an event is the enthusiasm that will have led some of the participants beyond the law. The drama, if such it may be called, almost always ends in public indignation, the courts, suicide, or assignment to relatively comfortable places of detention.

The lesson, however, is not that any particular history repeats itself. Rather, it is that deeper tendencies in human behavior, once identified, have a high consistency in effect. One looks beyond or below the event to those deeper forces.

I have dwelt, as I say inevitably, on economics; there are, of course, other matters on which Schlesinger, drawing on the great constants in human motivation, is one's guide.

Over the last seventy-five years and more, for example, there have been the recurrent lapses into political paranoia. There was the threat of foreign radicals and the Palmer raids after World War I. And the McCarthy frenzy after World War II. And in their time, the lesser moments of Huey Long, Gerald L. K.

Smith, Father Coughlin, and the Townshend Plan. And in recent days there have been the assertive claims of religious fundamentalism, the pressure for prayer and oaths of allegiance in the schools, the threat from flag burning and now, as I write, to common decency from David Duke and Pat Buchanan. At a deeper level are the assertive claims of ethnic groups on the school and college curricula that challenge the once proud claim of the Republic to social assimilation and common national identity—the attack on the slightly less than graceful metaphor of the melting pot.

On all these aberrations Arthur Schlesinger has been, I do not exaggerate, our most consistent and our most effective voice for reason. This too stems from his understanding of the sources and manifestations of human motivation. More than anyone else he has kept them in perspective.

Thus, while Schlesinger calls for resistance, his is never the voice of despair. He knows that the motivating forces are less than durable. The Gerald L. K. Smiths and the David Dukes are regional and temporary; they cultivate their own opposition. So do those who now would surrender education to ethnic history and lore. It is, indeed, the duty of the citizen and especially the scholar to resist. But out of the deeper experience Schlesinger also provides a substantial measure of reassurance.

I have sometimes thought that I have here learned from Schlesinger too well. I rather welcome an outbreak of mental disengagement and oratory, as, for example, over flag burning. It gives voice to people who, on any important matter, would not be able to speak and certainly would not be heard; there is also a certain enjoyment in the social idiocy of it all. It is the lesson of Schlesinger that the motivating force is temporary and will soon subside. In retrospect, it will merely seem foolish.

I was brought up in Canada where prayer in school is a commonplace. We prayed every morning. I cannot think that it affected me deeply, though it did leave me in some doubt as to its practical efficacy, particularly on such matters, vital in our farming community, as a request for rain. It is Schlesinger, no doubt, who reassured me, who caused me not to search my inner being for the deeper damage.

Finally, there is the most important Schlesinger lesson of all. That is to go beyond history, as required, to personal involvement and action. Again I speak from firsthand experience.

In the early 1950s, seeking the continuation of the Roosevelt spirit and the social commitment of the New Deal, he joined Adlai Stevenson in his campaign for the presidency and served as a central figure in that notable effort. He and George Ball, in turn, drafted me into service. I use the word "draft" advisedly; Schlesinger did not allow me the option of refusing.

Later in the decade he was one of the first of the academic community to align himself with John F. Kennedy, and he served in the latter's administration as a voice of quiet restraint among the many of more adventurous mood. Again here the lessons from past behavior and particularly a knowledge of the hubris that comes from wonderfully and, as it seems, righteously achieved power.

In the mid-1960s, convinced of the shaping disaster in Vietnam, Schlesinger joined a small group of us at lunch one day to urge that we spend all available hours in the months and years ahead organizing and guiding responsible political opposition to the war. So we did. Out of the resulting effort and, needless to say, that of many others came the Eugene McCarthy campaign, the decisive Chicago convention, and the resulting clear conclusion that the war could not go on.

Here, perhaps, was the greatest of the Schlesinger lessons. The good historian does not stop with the history. As the situation requires and compels, he goes on to making it.

Chapter 5

ARTHUR SCHLESINGER, JR.: TORY DEMOCRAT

JOHN MORTON BLUM

ONE OF THE EMINENT historians of the century, Arthur Schlesinger, Jr., in his *Age of Jackson* (1945) and three-volume *Age of Roosevelt* (1957–60) set the terms of the historical debates that have since ensued about Jacksonian democracy and the New Deal. That extraordinary achievement has sometimes seemed *sui generis,* but it was not quite that. For Schlesinger approached the writing of history under the significant influences of his times and of his mentors. In his first book, *Orestes A. Brownson: A Pilgrim's Progress* (1939), Schlesinger struck an introductory note applicable also to his later work. "The measure of what is historically important," he wrote, "is set by the generation that writes the history, not by the one that makes it. No historian can entirely escape judging by the standards of his day; in some sense he must always superimpose one set of values on another." And, Schlesinger might have added, one set of insights. For as he later wrote: "The passage of time, the knowledge of consequences, the illumination of hindsight . . . give problems of the past new form and perplexity."

The values and insights of Schlesinger's generation derived from a special set of circumstances. It is the generation of Americans, to indulge in paraphrase, "born in this century," exposed to the Great Depression, inspired by the New Deal, "tempered by war, disciplined by a hard and bitter peace, proud of our ancient heritage." The temper of those times marked the consciousness of all Americans born about 1917 but did not shape their minds.

For the shaping required more than a common and concurrent exposure to public events. Consider the difference between Arthur Schlesinger and Caspar Weinberger. Not even the further common experience of Harvard College made those two alumni spiritual or intellectual companions. But there were identifiable intellectual forces at Harvard during the 1930s that played on the attitudes Schlesinger brought to history. As he has said himself, he was "profoundly indebted" to his father "for his wise counsel and keen criticism," and to his mother for her understanding of the American past, the Middle Period especially. They were remarkable people who filled their lives with remarkable friends. The senior Schlesingers, dedicated and involved democrats, supported the great liberal causes of Arthur's youth, among them the League of Nations, justice for Sacco and Vanzetti, religious tolerance, women's rights.

And at Sunday tea, while his mother poured, Schlesinger could listen in his parents' living room to Cambridge luminaries, among them Felix Frankfurter, herald of the Second New Deal. Schlesinger's cycle of American liberalism began at home.

It was a liberalism tempered by a view of the nature of man that ran counter to the usual American liberal creed. Again the introduction to the Brownson volume speaks to the question where Schlesinger acknowledges a "principal obligation to Perry Miller." In 1939, as always, Miller radiated a learned interest in ideas and their social implications. With incomparable range over time—he addressed with equal trenchancy Cotton Mather, Ralph Waldo Emerson, and Thorstein Veblen—Perry Miller was an outstanding intellectual historian not the least because he was a committed intellectual. So also Schlesinger. And Schlesinger, like Miller and the Puritans Miller understood so well, recognized that man was never free of sin or evil. So Schlesinger could naturally see man through Brownson's eyes. Brownson in Schlesinger's account was born twice. "Faith in the people," Schlesinger wrote of the innocent Brownson, "had meant to him what faith in God meant to most men— properly so, because he regarded people as visible manifestations of the spirit of God." But after the election of 1840, when the people chose a Whig, Brownson was born again, now stripped of his innocence. The people, as Schlesinger put it, "could not be close to Him, they must therefore be divorced from Him; they could not be basically virtuous, they must therefore be basically corrupt." That understanding proceeded also of course from Schlesinger's times, as he observed in *The Vital Center*. His generation, he wrote, as a result of the rise of fascism and the exposure of the Soviet Union, discovered—or in Niebuhr's good phrase rediscovered—a "dimension of experience—the dimension of anxiety, guilt and corruption."

A democratic faith in the people, coupled with a conviction about the corruptibility of man, characterized the young historian of the Jackson era, as also did his pride in his ancient heritage—the American heritage and its European roots. That pride reflected both the beliefs of his parents and the influence of older friends, surely of Bernard DeVoto with his loving sense of the majestic sweep of the American continent and the American past. Schlesinger and DeVoto stood together at the ending of World War II in the long telegrams they published then. Those separate but similar essays read the Civil War as a conflict unavoidable because of the issue of slavery and its moral as well as its political vectors. They went on to view the emerging conflict between the United States and the Soviet Union, between freedom and repression, in an identical light. So Schlesinger was present, in Dean Acheson's metaphor, not just at the Creation but also at the expulsion from Eden.

The foregoing speculations point to an interpretive bias that Schlesinger openly confessed in his bicentennary essay, a bias for seeing history through the lenses of Augustine and Calvin and their secular successors. Their Calvinist ethos, as Schlesinger has written, "was suffused with convictions of the depravity of man, of the awful precariousness of human existence . . . of the nakedness of the human condition." Those beliefs argued against American exceptionalism. They also turned "all life into an endless and implacable process of testing." Thus Schlesinger's deep respect for the American Constitution which did not assume the innocence of man, and by not so doing, looked to the separation of powers to check the corruptibility of the executive. From the same ethos there followed Schlesinger's belief, with the Founding Fathers, in the necessity of experimentation "in defiance of history," precisely of the American experiment with a democratic republic and, recurrently, with means for assuring its uncertain survival. Thus Schlesinger's tributes to both William James and Reinhold Niebuhr, and to FDR and JFK.

With Franklin Roosevelt, Schlesinger also realized that there was "no magic in Democracy that does away with the need for leadership." Roosevelt, as Schlesinger described him and agreed with him, conceived of "the President as the *leader* of the nation, so truly interpreting the unspoken needs and wishes of the people that he could count on their support in great tasks." In his analyses of leaders to whom he has given heroic stature, Schlesinger revealed his related beliefs about the qualities appropriate for high democratic office. "Who was General Jackson," Schlesinger asked, and as part of his answer he wrote that Jackson "normally acted with the landholding aristocracy, both against the financial aristocracy and the canebrake democracy." No "border savage," Jackson entered the presidency "a man of great urbanity and distinction of manner," in Martin Van Buren's words, "free from conceit," in the perception of Thomas Hart Benton, "vigorous" in thought and judgment "with . . . almost intuitive perception," and in Schlesinger's own phrase, with "a deep natural understanding of the people." Jackson, then, was a democrat with a keen political intelligence and the urbanity and manner of a natural aristocrat, spiritually for the people, instinctively against the plutocrats. Like *The Age of Jackson, The Age of Roosevelt* took its name from a president concerned for the people, inimical to the plutocracy who felt the same way about him, "intuitive rather than logical," patrician in manner as well as in birth, the very model of noblesse oblige.

So also with Adlai Stevenson and John F. Kennedy, as Schlesinger has noted. In spite of their differences in temperament, "they had affinities in background and taste . . . the same sort of spacious, tranquil country house; the same patrician ease of manners; . . . the same . . . humor; the same style of gossip." Fittingly, so Schlesinger continued, Kennedy was the heir and executor of the Stevenson revolution, but Kennedy assumed power "in the school of Roosevelt." Kennedy, Schlesinger went on, was "the young Lord Salisbury"— like others Schlesinger praised a man of virtue, a natural aristocrat, and in the English usage, a Tory Radical; in Schlesinger's phrasing, a Tory Democrat. Those labels applied also to Winston Churchill and Walter Lippmann, a statesman and an observer of statesmen for whom Schlesinger has expressed special admiration.

The natural aristocrat, the Tory Democrat brought a touch of Plato to the worthy experiments in statecraft of the American republic. For as a function of his temperament and beliefs, the natural aristocrat carried in his person an inherent check against the corruption of the power he acquired. The Tory Democrat sought power for use in behalf of the people with whom he resonated, sought power out of conscience rather than self-aggrandizement or greed. He used power boldly on those very accounts, but used it with the recognition that it belonged to the people to whom he would return it soon. The Tory Democrat exemplifed in his self the moral and intellectual equivalents of the Constitution's checks and balances. So in his hands, the right hands, power was safer than in the possession of the demagogue or arriviste, the Huey Long or Richard Nixon. And the virtuous man in the White House staffed government with others dedicated, as he was, to public service. Even Joe Kennedy was one of those. When Ray Moley asked Kennedy whether anything in his somewhat notorious career could embarrass FDR if Roosevelt made him first chairman of the SEC—so Moley reported, and so Schlesinger quoted Moley—Kennedy "with a burst of profanity defied any one to question his devotion to the public interest. . . . What was more he would give his critics . . . an administration of the SEC that would be a credit to the country, the President, himself and his family." Joe Kennedy believed in public service and in his family. He warned his boys about the businessmen he knew—"sons of bitches," so John F. Kennedy recalled his father saying when the CEO of U.S. Steel broke his promise to the White House.

In *The Imperial Presidency* Schlesinger spelled out his message. Especially in foreign policy, the republic needed a powerful leader, a powerful chief executive. Consequently Congress had to protect its constitutional role, had to keep the president accountable. Otherwise it risked corrupt use of swollen presidential power. Even with a vigilant Congress, presidents had reached beyond their prescribed authority. So the wise exercise of executive power depended not only on the accountability of the president to Congress but also on the president's self-restraint, on the personal checks and balances he brought to his office. Schlesinger's natural aristocrat had, as Justice Holmes said of Franklin Roosevelt, a "first-class temperament."

That temperament—intuitive, experimental, and controlled—rejected the ideologies of the right and left because they were rigid and deterministic. Conversely, that temperament gladly mobilized what Schlesinger has called the "affirmative state." The affirmative state had precedents as old as the republic itself, specifically in the vision of Alexander Hamilton who saw the federal government as the agency for the promotion of national growth and strength. Hamilton set out to use the state to affect a "release of energy"— Schlesinger's phrase—by encouraging the endeavors of rich and enterprising

men. A generation later, in Andrew Jackson's time, the release of energy required the abolition of privilege, of political privilege in access to the ballot, of
economic privilege in access to incorporation. The affirmative state then attacked the power of the plutocracy by encouraging competition which monopoly had constrained. Other times called for other remedies.

The affirmative state of the New Deal, refurbishing ideas of the Progressive
Era, became the compensatory state that Walter Lippmann commended in his
Method of Freedom (1934). That book, in Schlesinger's judgment, was "in some
respects . . . Lippmann's most brilliant and prophetic work." Laissez-faire had
failed, Lippmann argued, but the centrally planned and regimented economy
of the totalitarian state violated the freedom of the individual. In contrast, "the
Compensated Economy," so Schlesinger rephrased Lippmann, "retained private initiative and decision so far as possible but committed the state to act
when necessary to 'redress the balance of private action by compensating public action'—by fiscal and monetary policy, by social insurance, by business
regulation, by the establishment of minimum economic levels below which no
members of the community should be allowed to fall." Keynesian in its macro-
economic policy, the compensatory state, as Schlesinger envisaged it, had a
symmetrical social obligation. In the 1960s, especially in the programs sponsored by Robert Kennedy, the state provided a compensatory force for black
Americans, and for other proscribed and minority groups, by forbidding discrimination and its injustices, and by empowering those groups politically to
elect candidates who would help them help themselves.

The affirmative state had received an earlier definition from Lippmann's
fellow progressive, Herbert Croly, who characterized it as using Hamiltonian
means for Jeffersonian ends. Croly's *Promise of American Life* (1909) impressed
Schlesinger, who provided an incisive introduction for a reprint in 1965. He
had already used Croly's characterization in the opening chapters of *The Age of
Jackson*. As Schlesinger observed in his introduction, Croly drew from George
Santayana his concern for men of virtue as national leaders, and from William
James his insistence on "the importance of experiment as the test of meaning
and truth." James and Santayana played a similar role in Schlesinger's own
political formulations. Croly also, so Schlesinger noted, brought to his argument "his masterful conception of the American past as a drama of ideas embodied in personalities," just the technique Schlesinger used so admirably
himself. So also, Schlesinger, like Croly, was striking in his "interweaving of
the ideas of nationalism and democracy in the fabric of American history."

Those characteristics found spectacular expression in *The Age of Roosevelt*.
The structure of the second volume particularly sets Hamiltonians against
Jeffersonians in creative tension. But the cast in *The Coming of the New Deal*
exceeds by far the cast in Croly's work. Schlesinger's commanding narrative of
men and their ideas encompasses two generations. His New Dealers absorbed
the lessons taught by the foremost progressive antagonists, Theodore Roose-

velt and Woodrow Wilson, whose separate views of political economy, as Schlesinger explains them, had offsetting protagonists in Herbert Croly and Louis Brandeis, in George Perkins and William McAdoo. The successors of those protagonists, arranged again in competing pairs, advised FDR—Rex Tugwell aligned against Felix Frankfurter, Chester Davis against Jerome Frank, Arthur Morgan against David Lilienthal. The architecture of the book—the symmetry of the pairings, the careful layering of ideas and men— has a strength and beauty that matches the strength and beauty of the prose.

Elsewhere in recounting the American past, Schlesinger, as Croly had, weaves nationalism together with democracy. They march together in the closing chapters of *The Age of Jackson,* chapters that anticipate the merging of nation and freedom in the person of Abraham Lincoln. They will surely march together again in the volumes of *The Age of Roosevelt* devoted to the coming and the meaning of American engagement in the second World War. And they are embodied together in the personalities, as Schlesinger renders them, of the Kennedy brothers. Together they inform Schlesinger's sense of community and his consequent concerns, as he has expressed them recently, in his *Disuniting of America.*

Yet as the foregoing analysis had attempted to indicate, American nationalism and democracy, in Schlesinger's estimation, are not destined automatically to prosper, or even automatically to survive, for national existence is as precarious as human existence. Schlesinger's realism rests on that perception. Jacqueline Kennedy was incidentally describing Schlesinger when she characterized her husband as an idealist without illusions. So constituted, during the Age of Schlesinger, Arthur has sustained a quality he ascribed to Franklin Roosevelt, a quality of inestimable importance to the history Schlesinger has written and the country he has served, a "deep and unquestioning confidence in the energy and inventiveness of free society." And so armed, Schlesinger continues serenely to rediscover the American past.

PART TWO

THE ERA OF ANDREW JACKSON

Chapter 6

THE AGE OF JACKSON AND ITS IMPACT

ROBERT REMINI

F OR THE White House the new year began in gloom. The President's wife
spent a sleepless and painful night, and Mr. Adams, waking at daybreak,
found the dawn overcast, the skies heavy and sullen. He prayed briefly, then
fumbled for his Bible and turned to the Book of Psalms, reading slowly by the yellow
light of his shaded oil lamp. "Blessed is the man that walketh not in the counsel of
the ungodly, nor standeth in the way of sinners, nor sitteth in the seat of the scorn-
ful." On he read to the ultimate assurance. "For the Lord knoweth the way of the
righteous: but the way of the ungodly shall perish."

The familiar words assuaged disappointments of four years. To an Adams, the first
psalm seemed almost a personal pledge. "It affirms that the righteous man is, and
promises that he shall be, blessed," he noted with precise gratification in his journal,
and went to his desk for his usual early-morning work. As his pen began to scratch
across the paper, the lamp, its oil low, flared for a moment, then flickered out. Mr.
Adams sat in the gray light.[1]

Those words and the words that followed changed my life. It was sometime
in 1947 and I can remember vividly sitting in Butler Library at Columbia
University reading what Arthur Schlesinger had written on the first page of his
celebratory *The Age of Jackson,* and sensing the gloom in the White House on
January 1, 1829, and feeling Adams's bleakness of spirit over the terrible rejection he had recently suffered from the American electorate. In reading Schlesinger's book I began to lose my New York provincialism and eventually abandoned the twentieth century in favor of the Jacksonian era, writing my
doctoral dissertation on Martin Van Buren. Richard H. Brown, who also wrote
his dissertation on Van Buren, told me recently that after reading *The Age of
Jackson* he decided against becoming a lawyer. Today he is the academic vice
president at the Newberry Library.

Brown and I were not alone. That book had a tremendous impact on the
entire academic world of historians. The two fixtures of the American historical profession right after World War II were the powerfully influential Progressive historians Frederick Jackson Turner and Charles Beard. (To some extent
Vernon Louis Parrington was also a fixture—at least at Columbia in those

days.) All interpretive matters, it seemed, began and ended with those two worthies. The frontier thesis and economic causality answered every need and problem. Students at Columbia, and I daresay at other graduate schools around the country, argued and debated the Turnerian and Beardian ideas. And in most of our initial attempts at writing history we jammed Turner and/or Beard into our interpretations whether they fit or not.

But now, with the publication of *The Age of Jackson,* we had a third figure to add to this pantheon. The Schlesinger thesis offered something new and exciting, something profoundly illuminating. In addition, it was written in superb prose that captured and recreated on the printed page a period of American history that was dynamic and wildly exciting, prose that sprang characters to life in full dimension. To this day I remember one line in the book when Schlesinger described Henry Clay's physical appearance. It's a description I've used many times myself, and that description reads like this: "Henry Clay's sardonic and somewhat sensual mouth was like a line cut straight across his face." Every time I looked at Clay's picture when writing his biography I kept remembering how apt, how accurate, how revealing Schlesinger's description was. And to think that this masterpiece of historical writing was accomplished by a young man in his early twenties.

The Schlesinger thesis posited the belief that "more can be understood about Jacksonian Democracy if it is regarded as a problem not of sections but of classes."[2] It was not the existence of the frontier and the kind of lives pursued by the settlers of the west that best explained Jacksonian Democracy. Eastern urban workers constituted the most solid core of support for the Jacksonian movement. Schlesinger examined the economic difficulties of the 1820s and discovered that the East and the workingmen comprised the most critical mass of the Jacksonian coalition.

And Jackson himself, said Schlesinger, was deeply sympathetic to the plight of urban workers. Indeed, in my own research over many years I have found that basic argument to be essentially sound. To cite one example: in writing Jackson's biography I came across a document describing how laborers in the Philadelphia Navy Yard in the summer of 1836 complained about working more than ten hours a day. They appealed to Jackson for relief and he immediately directed the secretary of the navy to issue the necessary orders to redress the grievance. He "left upon the minds of all who have conversed with him," said the writer, "a deep impression of his solicitude to see the laboring class of the country" freed from the burdens imposed by a business aristocracy. "His motto is, Let labor have security, prosperity will follow—all other interests rest upon it, and must flourish if it flourishes."

According to Schlesinger, the ideology of Jacksonianism evolved from the conflict between classes and best expressed its goals and purposes in the problems and needs facing urban workers.[3] The essential meaning of Jacksonian Democracy can be found, Schlesinger said, in its economic rather than its political objectives. To understand the movement one must first study and evaluate the Bank War. If Schlesinger did nothing else he awakened historians to the centrality of the Bank War in understanding the Jacksonian phenomenon. What he did, therefore, and what historians instantly responded to, was that he had provided a clearer definition of Jacksonianism and a more precise explanation of its origins than had been available heretofore.

Moreover, Jackson's exercise of federal powers to check the power and influence of corporate wealth in the affairs of government moved the Democratic Party (and liberals, I might add) away from its earlier Jeffersonian antistatist assumptions to an acceptance of the concepts of positive government, something FDR would later pursue with a vengeance.

But historians need to be reminded, especially today, that Schlesinger did not ground his interpretation exclusively on class. He is too much a pluralist to confine himself narrowly to monistic and simplistic causation. He emphasized strongly the intellectual and moral factors that operate in history. And he did not eschew completely the entrepreneurial elements in Jacksonian Democracy, particularly among Westerners.

Another fascinating aspect of *The Age of Jackson,* and one that came in for some sharp criticism, was Schlesinger's argument that there were striking similarities between the forces behind Jackson and those who supported Franklin Delano Roosevelt. Both the Jacksonian and New Deal phenomena were led by two rather well-to-do, charismatic men, both idols of the poor and humble, who put together coalitions that won the support of laborers and farmers, intellectuals and creative artists.[4] Both Jackson and Roosevelt were strong leaders advocating human rights over property rights; and they were denounced by an aristocracy of wealth as dictators; they were denounced for their ignorance of economics, for their contempt of constitutional limitations to their power, and for their egregious attacks upon the reputation and authority of the Supreme Court.

The popular reaction to *The Age of Jackson* brought its author instantaneous fame. Here a young Harvard professor had awakened America to a clearer understanding and recognition of one of the most important and debated problems in American history, to a concern that still troubles us today. "The crucial question," wrote Schlesinger, "is not, Is there 'too much' government? but, Does the government promote 'too much' the interests of a single group? In liberal capitalist society this question has ordinarily become in practice, Is the government serving the interests of the business community to the detriment of the nation as a whole? This has been the irrepressible conflict of capitalism: the struggle on the part of the business community to dominate the state, and on the part of the rest of society, under the leadership of 'liberals,' to check the political ambitions of business."[5]

We need only think about recent history to substantiate the truth of that statement. During the Reagan and Bush administrations Washington became, in the words of William Greider, a "Grand Bazaar" where moneyed interest groups regularly bought influence and power from public officials, betraying American democracy in the process.[6]

The publication of *The Age of Jackson* also provoked one of the most heated and continuing scholarly controversies to hit the profession since the publication of Charles Beard's *Economic Interpretation of the Constitution*. Schlesinger stirred up quite a storm. It is not an exaggeration to say that responding in print to Schlesinger and his ideas became a minor industry. Over the next two decades his book induced, by my estimate, over 300 books and articles and an untold number of doctoral dissertations. Every historian who followed him has had to deal, directly or indirectly, with the issues raised by Arthur Schlesinger.

Bray Hammond was probably the first to attack *The Age of Jackson*.[7] He served as assistant secretary of the Board of Governors of the Federal Reserve System and argued that the Jacksonians were no less drawn to filthy "lucre," to use his word, than conservatives, even more so. "They had no greater concern for human rights," he declared, "than the people who had what they were trying to get."[8] He chided Schlesinger for not appreciating the services provided by the central bank and claimed that Jacksonians were just as business oriented as the men they attacked.

A most important outcry of protest came from the faculty and graduate students of Columbia University. Professor Joseph Dorfman criticized Schlesinger's identification of workingmen, insisting that the term was readily applied to anyone engaged in production, be he banker, merchant, carpenter, or bricklayer, thus cutting across all classes.[9] Arthur Schlesinger himself responded to this "wage earner" thesis in a letter to the editor of the *American Historical Review*—and it is the only time I know of that he publicly responded to any criticism of his book. In the letter Schlesinger stated, "Of course many businessmen were pro-Jackson," just as they were for FDR, but he insisted that such information hardly refuted the main thesis of his book that more can be understood about Jacksonian Democracy when viewed as a problem of classes, not sections, and that liberalism in America has been the movement of other groups of society to restrain the power of the business community.[10]

Professor Richard Morris of Columbia University then published an article entitled "Andrew Jackson, Strikebreaker," documenting that Jackson used federal troops to put down a strike of Irish canal workers in Maryland.[11] (It seems to me that in 1946 Harry Truman—everybody's favorite president these days—threatened to use the army to settle a railroad strike and then asked the Congress for legislation to draft the strikers into the army, thereby breaking the strike.) Two of Morris's graduate students, William A. Sullivan and Edward Pessen, analyzed voting patterns in Philadelphia and Boston, respectively, and concluded that workers did not vote for Jackson in those cities.[12] But other scholars later disputed these findings, and, to be fair to Pessen, he himself eventually backed off somewhat from his original position.[13] Charles Sellers, in an essay entitled "Andrew Jackson versus the Historians," concluded that the attempt "to demonstrate that workingmen did not vote for Jackson" had met "with questionable success."[14]

Other scholars, most notably Richard Hofstadter, put forward an alternative thesis, namely that no class conflict or ideological difference existed in our history; rather he suggested that there was a basic consensus on middle-class values, "a common climate of American opinion." He argued that the leading Jacksonians were not champions of urban workers or of small farmers, but "cold-blooded political entrepreneurs"[15] principally concerned with advancing their own economic and political advantage.[16] And not infrequently, he said, they were captains of great wealth, an interpretation that Bray Hammond in his *Banks and Politics in America* readily endorsed.[17]

Another Columbia student, Marvin Meyers, in a much admired work, *The Jacksonian Persuasion,* added an interesting twist to the entrepreneurial thesis by contending that the Jacksonians did not appeal so much to the ambitions of a rising laissez-faire capitalism but to a restoration of the old republican way of life.[18]

But perhaps the most important and provocative expression of the liberal consensus school regarding Jacksonian Democracy appeared nearly two decades after the publication of *The Age of Jackson.* Lee Benson's *The Concept of Jacksonian Democracy: New York as a Test Case* offered an innovative methodology, namely the use of quantification to discover what he called scientific evidence about voting behavior and political rhetoric. He called for the development of techniques of "multi-variate analysis," capable of amassing all the different determinants that he believed went into deciding voting behavior.[19] After employing his more sophisticated approach to historical data he concluded from his study of New York that the Jacksonians "attacked rather than sponsored the Whig idea of the positive liberal state." They "opposed political programs that required the state to act positively to foster democratic egalitarianism, economic democracy, social and humanitarian reform." The Whigs, not the Democrats, he said, were more like modern New Dealers. Moreover, he went on, the Jacksonians' strongest support came from relatively high-status socioeconomic groups in the eastern counties, and relatively low-status ethnocultural and religious groups in all sections of New York.[20] Ethnicity and religion, he argued, played a more important role than economics in determining how a person voted or which party won his allegiance. He regarded the Jacksonian rhetoric about democracy and the rights of the people as just so much "claptrap" and insisted that local issues in elections meant much more to the voters than national issues. Benson agreed with Hofstadter and other consensus advocates by claiming that in New York both the Democrats and the Whigs endorsed not only political democracy for white men but liberal capitalism as well.

This consensus school, or the homogenization of American history, as John Higham called it, had numerous advocates for a time,[21] but did not remain fashionable for very long because of sharp attack,[22] especially from social historians who derided the revisionists' concepts of class and culture and pointed out the limitations and biases of voting studies.[23] Other historians, like Richard L. McCormick, warned that ethnoculturalists concluded far more from voting patterns than was warranted and were in the process of substituting one determinism with another.[24] And Frank Otto Gatell, in several thoroughly researched articles, found that class differences and conflict did intrude into the politics of the Jacksonian era.[25]

Although Benson's call for "multivariate analysis" and other techniques of quantification has been heeded by a number of historians and has become an important new research tool, and although his emphasis on ethnicity and religion added to our understanding of individual behavior, by the beginning of the 1980s this ethnocultural approach had been somewhat discarded by historians. There has been a new demand that scholarly studies of the past should reflect race, gender, *and* class in any discussion of historical movements or events. Today many historians seek to describe or portray what might be called a "political culture" for the period. They contend that the electorate normally develops a wide set of values based on many factors, including class, religion, nationality, family, residence, employment, age, and such negative reference factors as nativism and racism, and then invariably vote to safeguard those values as they perceive them. Several of these historians have demonstrated rather convincingly that national issues did in fact matter a great deal in general elections.

So, after nearly fifty years since the publication of *The Age of Jackson,* and after all this scholarship, where are we? Well, we do have a more sophisticated understanding of class and social relationships during the antebellum period. Many scholarly studies of voting and social and economic conditions have illuminated important aspects of the age of Jackson. Important issues such as slavery and Indian removal have been integrated more completely and with more sophistication into this era, issues that Schlesinger himself did not address directly. But we come back to the old questions: Who were these Jacksonians? Did the Bank War really pit "the humble members of society—the farmers, mechanics, and laborers," as Jackson called them in his Bank veto, against the "rich and powerful" who were bent on using the government for their own "selfish purposes"? Were the Jacksonians true populists, or were they liberal capitalists out to increase their wealth and social status by feeding the electorate a lot of political "claptrap"?

There are still some critics out there who insist that what distinguishes the Jacksonians, besides being men-on-the-make, was that they were the defenders of slavery and the murderers of American Indians, and not particularly enlightened about the gender question, either. According to Jackson's most hostile critics, most of the Old Hero's followers were hardly more than a gang of right-wing, red-neck, states'-rights conservatives. Members of the Whig Party, on the other hand, were advocates of moral reform, reforms that included women's rights and abolition. They were not greedy capitalists. Moreover, through selective tariffs to aid developing manufactures, a public works program to improve transportation across the country, and a central banking system to provide sound credit and currency, the Whigs have been credited with the "vision thing" (to use President Bush's term) of how the United States might develop into an industrial superpower that would benefit all classes of Americans. They were heralded as more modern and forward-looking than Democrats, and as having recognized not only the economic realities of their existing circumstances but the obsolescence of the old order. They had faith in the future. They encouraged the new technology. They welcomed a modern, an industrial, a dynamic society. Democrats, on the other hand, especially the most conservative, were committed to an "old fashioned" society and looked back with nostalgia on their virtuous and uncorrupted past.

The most recent works on the antebellum period do not deny that Jacksonian democracy had some unlovely aspects, especially its more racist overtones—overtones, I might remind you, that one finds almost universally in the antebellum era, be the individuals Democrats, Whigs, abolitionists, hodcarriers, or bankers. But the Jacksonians cannot be identified and characterized simply as anti-black, anti-Indian, or anti-female. Basically they were, as Schlesinger insisted in 1945, anti-privilege and anti–monied interests that sought to use the government for private gain. I think after fifty years we have concluded that Jackson did in fact put together an alliance of laborers, artisans, yeoman farmers, and, yes, slaveholders committed to getting rid of class biases in the government. Jackson repeatedly preached that the people are sovereign, that the majority is to govern.[26] He argued for a policy of rotation—his so-called spoils system—aimed in large measure at ridding the government of entrenched elites. He opposed internal improvements not only because it violated the Constitution and his states'-rights philosophy but because it favored the wealthy in society. He demanded Indian removal not only because of national security and the necessity of getting the Indians out of harm's way and prevent their certain annihilation, but to assist yeoman farmers and planters in the acquisition of cheap land. He also advocated preemption rights to aid farmers. He called for democratic reforms, including the direct election of senators, judges (including justices of the Supreme Court), and the president, and the right of the people to instruct their legislators.[27]

But most of all Jackson initiated the Bank War, in Sean Wilentz's words, to "remove the hands of a few unelected private bankers from the levers of the nation's economy and restore a more democratic commerce of small producers."[28] His hard money policy was aimed at curtailing the power of credit- and paper-manipulating bankers and speculators who would corrupt the democracy and thereby threaten individual liberty. Jacksonians felt it incumbent upon themselves to keep one eye peeled for the danger of corporate power in government affairs and the other eye alert for the threat of over-centralized governmental power.

The great contribution of Jacksonianism to our history is that to a considerable extent it squashed the most enduring forms of political deference and tried to address the institutional bases of economic and political privilege by which the monied few take advantage of the producing many. "Deference" and "privilege" were the two things they hated most in American society. They valued equality, but, as the following essay indicates, the idea was always shadowed by race.

NOTES

1. Arthur M. Schlesinger, Jr., *The Age of Jackson* (Boston, 1946), 3.

2. Ibid., 263. It should be pointed out that Schlesinger's father in an essay on Jacksonian Democracy suggested that both the frontier and eastern labor contributed to the Jacksonian movement. Charles Beard also thought that economic struggles between classes, along with the frontier, should be considered in discussing Jacksonian politics. See Arthur M. Schlesinger, *New Viewpoints in American History* (New York, 1922), and Charles and Mary Beard, *The Rise of American Civilization* (New York, 1927).

3. It should be mentioned that the socialist Algie M. Simons was the first to point out the importance of labor to the Jacksonian movement. See his *Social Forces in American History* (New York, 1911).

4. Thomas P. Abernethy studied Jackson's early career in Tennessee and argued that the Old Hero opposed democratic reform in his state, that he was a frontier aristocrat, and that his later conversion was an act of unprincipled opportunism. See Abernethy, *From Frontier to Plantation in Tennessee* (Chapel Hill, 1932). Schlesinger took note of Abernethy's contention and said, "No amount of inference based on what Jackson was like before 1828 can be a substitute for the facts after 1828" (n. 25, 43–44).

5. Schlesinger, *Age of Jackson*, 514.

6. William Greider, *Who Will Tell the People: The Betrayal of American Democracy* (New York, 1992).

7. Bray Hammond, "Jackson, Biddle and the Bank of the United States," *Journal of Economic History* 7 (May 1947), 1–23. See also his review of *The Age of Jackson* in *Journal of Economic History* 6 (May 1946), 79–84. It is not my intention in this paper to discuss every interpretation advanced to challenge or refine the Schlesinger thesis, but I do hope to cover the major criticisms.

8. Hammond, *Banks and Politics in America* (Princeton, 1957), quoted in Alfred A. Cave, *Jacksonian Democracy and the Historians* (Gainesville, 1964), 80.

9. Joseph Dorfman, "The Jackson Wage-Earner Thesis," *American Historical Review* 54 (October 1948) 296–306, and idem, *The Economic Mind in American Civilization* (New York, 1946).

10. Letter to the editor, *American Historical Review* 54 (October 1948).

11. Morris, "Andrew Jackson, Strikebreaker," *American Historical Review* 55 (October 1949), 54–68.

12. William Sullivan, "Did Labor Support Andrew Jackson?" *Political Science Quarterly* 62 (December 1947); and Edward Pessen, "Did Labor Support Andrew Jackson? The Boston Story," *Political Science Quarterly* 64 (June 1949).

13. Edward Pessen, *Most Uncommon Jacksonians: Radical Leaders of the Early Labor Movement* (Albany, 1967).

14. Robert T. Bower, "Note on 'Did Labor Support Jackson?' The Boston Story," *Political Science Quarterly* 65 (September 1950); Charles G. Sellers, Jr., "Andrew Jackson versus the Historians," *Mississippi Valley Historical Review* 44 (March 1958).

15. Sean Wilentz, "On Class and Politics in Jacksonian America," in Stanley I. Kutler and Stanley N. Katz, eds., *Reviews in American History: The Promise of American History, Progress and Prospects* (Baltimore, 1982), 45.

16. Richard Hofstadter, *The American Political Tradition and the Men Who Made It* (New York, 1948).

17. Bray Hammond, *Banks and Politics in America from the Revolution to the Civil War* (Princeton, 1957).

18. Marvin Meyers, *The Jacksonian Persuasion: Politics and Belief* (Stanford, 1957).

19. This includes such things as ethnicity, religious preference, local habits, traditions, and economic conditions, and negative reference groups such as nativism and racism.

20. Lee Benson, *The Concept of Jacksonian Democracy* (Princeton, 1961), 331–32.

21. See, for example, Louis Hartz, *The Liberal Tradition in America* (New York, 1955), and Daniel Boorstin, *The Genius of American Politics* (Chicago, 1953).

22. Cultural Marxists were among the first to attack the ethnocultural thesis. See Michael A. Lebowitz, "The Significance of Claptrap in American History," and idem, "The Jacksonians: Paradise Lost?" in Barton Bernstein, ed., *Toward a New Past: Dissenting Essays in American History* (New York, 1968), 65–89. Several cultural historians reemphasized class in analyzing voter preference and criticized the ethnoculturalists for distorting social relationships, social consciousness, and the use of political power. See Eric Foner, *Politics and Ideology in the Age of the Civil War* (New York, 1980).

23. James E. Wright, "The Ethno-Cultural Model of Voting: A Behavioral and Historical Critique," *American Behavioral Scientist* 16 (1973), 653–74; James R. Green, "Behavioralism and Class Analysis: A Methodological and Ideological Critique," *Labor History,* 13 (1972), 89–106.

24. Richard L. McCormick, "Ethnocultural Interpretations of Nineteenth-Century American Voting Behavior," *Political Science Quarterly* 89 (1974), 351–77.

25. See, for example, the many articles of Frank Otto Gatell, especially "Money and Party in Jacksonian America: A Quantitative Look at New York's Men of Quality," *Political Science Quarterly* 82 (1967), 235–52.

26. See Sean Wilentz, review of Charles Sellers, *The Market Revolution: Jacksonian America, 1815–1846* (New York, 1992), *The New Republic* (June 1992), 34–38; Robert V. Remini, *The Jackson Legacy: Essays in Democracy, Indian Removal and Slavery* (Baton Rouge, 1990).

27. Remini, *The Jackson Legacy,* 7–42.

28. Wilentz, review of Sellers, *Market Revolution,* 36.

Chapter 7

JACKSONIAN ABOLITIONIST: THE CONVERSION OF

WILLIAM LEGGETT

SEAN WILENTZ

> "I am an abolitionist."
> (*William Leggett, 1838*)

WILLIAM LEGGETT was one of the boldest and most incisive Democratic political writers of the 1830s. Over a brief span at mid-decade, Leggett's editorials in the *New York Evening Post* laid the philosophical foundations for Locofoco egalitarianism—the hard-money, free-trade doctrine that galvanized Manhattan's Jacksonian radicals and later came to dominate the administration of President Martin Van Buren. A polemicist in the tradition of Paine, Cobbett, and William Duane, Leggett intended that his provocations be read as serious exercises in political theory. Better than any other Jacksonian partisan, it was Leggett who seized upon the full implications of the writings of Adam Smith, Thomas Jefferson, and John Taylor and turned them into caustic, systematic attacks on capitalist enterprise, delivered on behalf of the producing classes. He also became a self-declared Jacksonian abolitionist—the Democrat, Arthur Schlesinger, Jr., has observed, "in whom social radicalism and antislavery united most impressively."[1]

Abolitionism of any variety was, of course, anathema in the 1830s, to the major political parties as well as to many of Leggett's fellow defenders of northern labor. Leggett himself, early in his editorial career, dismissed the leading immediatist abolitionists as lunatics, the promoters of "absurd and mad" schemes; and when he later broke with orthodox Democratic anti-abolitionism, he paid a heavy political price for his heresy.[2] Yet Leggett saw his break—and his conversion to what he pointedly called a form of abolitionism—not as departures from his Jacksonian principles but as their fulfillment. His writings on slavery, along with those of a handful of other Democratic dissidents, pioneered a distinctive Jacksonian antislavery viewpoint—one that, though less radical than immediatist abolitionism, was based on fundamental moral and political objections to slavery, and was dedicated to hastening American slavery's utter destruction. In the 1840s and 1850s, the basic precepts of this antislavery Jacksonianism deepened the schism within the northern Democracy that helped prepare the way for the Civil War.

Current appraisals of the abolitionist, antislavery, and Jacksonian movements all but ignore this principled Jacksonian antislavery dissent. The Jacksonians, according to numerous accounts, were "hard" racists who followed an official pro-slavery line; principled white opposition to slavery, so the argument goes, was rooted in a capitalist-evangelical humanitarianism that the Democrats detested; those Jacksonians who eventually drifted into antislavery politics supposedly did so after the mid-1840s, chiefly in order to help keep blacks out of the western territories and thereby guarantee white supremacy. In some recent considerations of the Democrats, the decisive political issues and events of the era before the Civil War have receded completely in favor of an imagined Jacksonian politics of racial identity. Above all else, these accounts assert, the Jacksonians, and especially pro-labor Jacksonians, were driven by the desire to maintain the social and psychological advantages of their "whiteness," a desire inflamed by Democratic Party racism. Schlesinger's unabashedly pro-Democratic contention, that "the group which took the lead in the political stage in combating the slave power were the radical Democrats in the straight Jacksonian tradition," has been buried by the Jacksonians' critics. Instead, we are told that the Jacksonians were intense racists who either supported or tolerated slavery's expansion—while the relatively few Jacksonians who came to oppose slavery's expansion were likewise motivated by antiblack prejudice.[3]

There has thus been little room in recent histories of abolitionism and antislavery for William Leggett—a humanitarian but no capitalist, a Jacksonian who hated slavery and championed black equality.[4] The omission would have galled Leggett's political allies, who honored him as an antislavery martyr—the man who (as John Greenleaf Whittier wrote) had labored more successfully than any other "to bring the practice of American democracy into conformity with its principles."[5] Similarly, the racialist interpretation of Jacksonian antislavery would have surprised the hundreds of thousands of rank-and-file northern Democrats who in the 1840s and 1850s challenged their party's expedient neutrality toward slavery and helped transform a faltering abolitionist cause into a mass antislavery political movement. It was not racism that united these dissident Democrats (although many of them expressed racist sentiments), but rather their moral repugnance at human bondage and their egalitarian hostility to the world the slaveholders made. In trying to check slavery's expansion, they expected not simply to keep the institution from spreading but to hasten its utter destruction—without violating the United States Constitution. Nor did Jacksonian antislavery originate in the territorial debates of the mid-1840s, as many revisionist historians now assume it did. Rather, it began to emerge, intellectually and politically, a full decade earlier—most conspicuously in the work of William Leggett.

Leggett's early opinions about slavery are obscure. As a boy in New York City (where he had been born in 1801), he must have had continual contact with slaves and slaveholders; and his abbreviated residence at Georgetown College, ended by his father's business failure in 1816, brought him face-to-face with southern slavery. In 1819, he moved with his family to rural downstate Illinois, where he would have heard the debates over slavery extension that accompanied the Missouri statehood controversy. But young Leggett's interests ran to literature, not politics. In about 1820, he began writing poems for his local newspaper, the *Edwardsville Spectator,* and in 1822 he arranged for the private publication by a local printer of a brief collection of his verse. Three years later, during an unhappy stint in the United States Navy, Leggett had a second collection of poems, *Leisure Hours at Sea,* published in New York.[6]

In 1826, after he resigned from the Navy, Leggett resettled in Manhattan, an aspiring man of letters, his head full of short stories drawn from his experiences at sea and out west. The critics praised his Illinois stories for their authentic tone—but the New York literary market was overstocked with talented newcomers. A scuffling grub-streeter, Leggett made ends meet as a theater reviewer and (briefly and inauspiciously) as an actor. After an ill-fated effort at editing his own literary weekly, Leggett, who by now had married, was in difficult financial straits. Luckily his Manhattan admirers included William Cullen Bryant, and in 1829, Leggett obtained the assistant editorship of Bryant's prominent, pro-Jackson *Evening Post.* (He would eventually become a part-owner of the paper, thanks to a loan from a well-placed Jacksonian.) When he accepted the position, Leggett asked that he be allowed to limit himself strictly to literature and the theater, as politics remained beyond his interests and understanding. As late as 1830, his views on slavery and related political topics may have been unformed. They are, in any event, unrecorded.[7]

Leggett's published stories, however, revealed a great deal about his thoughts on race. Since the late 1780s, popular New York writing (including plebeian almanacs as well as the more elite magazines) had displayed a special curiosity about black characters and perceived racial differences. Although some of this output included pseudo-scientific ruminations about the origins of African inferiority, most of it, especially in the almanacs, ran to more matter-of-fact dialect vignettes—often satiric, but also sympathetic, suggesting (as the historian Shane White has observed) "an identification, even an empathy with blacks."[8]

Leggett's fictions conformed to these ambiguous conventions. On the surface, they exhibited a fascination (grating to modern readers) with what Leggett called "African peculiarities." At the first mention of a black character,

Leggett would launch into a close description of the character's "flat nose," "ebony cheeks," "woolly head," and so on. Sometimes these passages led to scenes of racial condescension that foreshadowed the mockery of the black minstrel shows. In one of Leggett's sea yarns, black Jake, the ship's jigmaker, chatters on deck with a monkey "as if there existed some means of rational intelligence between them." Caesar, a minor character in another story, is a well-cared-for colored servant who is prone to breaking into "a grotesque and joyful grin," and whose main dramatic contribution is to mistake his employer for a wandering spirit and then to jabber, "Oh misses . . . I'be seen his ghost! I'be seen his ghost!" Leggett's most fully developed black character, the servant Mungo in the story, "The Squatter: A Tale of Illinois," repeatedly turns up as "the honest and affectionate Mungo" or "the devoted Mungo," with the usual paternalist bathos.[9]

Yet Leggett could also portray blacks, including those he appeared to mock, as capable and even noble figures, whose higher qualities went largely unnoticed by their white social superiors—as if the author wished to undermine his readers' racialist presumptions. Jake, the shipmate who converses with a monkey, is also the only hand on board who, unheeded, tries to prevent a near-tragedy from befalling his captain's foolish son. And Mungo, the squatter's servant, mingles his professions of loyalty with an independent spirit and sharp intelligence. Breaking with his usual style, Leggett describes Mungo as a handsome older man with a strapping physique, "every way deserving of [his] 'human face divine.'" A major protagonist in "the Squatter"—arguably, at the story's surprise conclusion, *the* major protagonist—Mungo is brave and inventive as he saves his employer's son from a raging prairie fire and frees the squatter (who has been wrongly convicted of murder) from jail. By the story's end, Leggett leaves the impression that the servant is smarter and more cunning than the white characters are—and far more cunning than they imagine he is. Along the way, Leggett casts a baleful eye on the kind of racism expressed by one angry white man, a boatman, who refers to Mungo as "that cursed piece of Indian ink."[10]

Devoid of explicit political commentary, Leggett's melodramatic stories nevertheless proclaimed his broad humane sympathies with the unfortunate: down-and-out western settlers, hard-bitten sailors, abused black servants. The same sensibility inspired his political writings defending the laboring classes in the 1830s, summed up in his observation that the only real purpose of government is to protect the weak against the strong and place "the property of the rich . . . on the same footing with the labours of the poor."[11] When he had to confront the mounting abolitionist agitation, however, Leggett's sympathies were less certain.

Leggett's first important writings on slavery and abolition date from 1834. Encouraged by his patron, Bryant, he had long since acquired a taste for political writing and begun turning out knowledgeable, spirited pro-Jackson editorials on banking and trade policy. Bryant was sufficiently impressed that when he departed for an indefinite stay in Europe in June 1834, he left Leggett in charge of the *Post*. During Bryant's absence, the newcomer moved the paper toward an even more doctrinaire hard-money position, helping to deepen the divisions between the so-called Bank Democrats and the Jacksonian radicals who led the Locofoco insurgency in 1835.[12]

Coincidentally, abolitionist activities in New York accelerated. Under the spur of the immediatist American Antislavery Society, founded in 1833, Manhattan became the national headquarters for the raising of abolitionist money and the distribution of abolitionist propaganda. Shocked public reaction culminated on July 4, 1834 (two weeks after Bryant's departure) in a mob attack on an integrated meeting at the evangelical Chatham Street Chapel, followed by a week of destructive assaults on the churches and homes of blacks and white abolitionists—the worst racial disorders in New York until the draft riots almost thirty years later. Leading conservative anti-abolitionist newspapers denounced some of the more prominent white abolitionists, indulged in racist caricatures of the blacks, and claimed that Negro gangs had instigated the fighting. Leggett replied in an afternoon editorial on July 8, and then followed up with several more pieces over the next few weeks.[13]

The destruction at the Chatham Street Chapel and elsewhere appalled the young editor. However objectionable the abolitionists' arguments might be, he wrote, there was no justification for attacking their homes and meeting places with brickbats and torches. The assailants—mostly wild boys and criminals, Leggett charged—represented "the very dregs of society," "a motley assemblage of infuriated and besotted ruffians, animated with a hellish spirit." He would spare nothing, including the use of military force, to disperse any future mobs: "Let them be fired upon if they dare to collect again to prosecute their nefarious designs."[14]

The anti-abolitionist editors earned an equal share of Leggett's criticism. Singling out James Watson Webb of the *Courier and Enquirer* and William Leete Stone of the *Commercial Advertiser*—vociferous anti-Jacksonians as well as anti-abolitionists—Leggett lamented "the violent tirades of certain prints," which had set loose "a mad spirit" among the populace. Worse, the conservative editors had persisted in whipping up matters to a hysterical pitch by "painting disgusting portraits of the 'blubber lips and sooty blood of negroes.'" While they condoned violations of other men's rights to free speech, the editors (who liked to pose as gentlemen) spoke dangerously, in ways calculated to excite the basest emotions of the mob.[15]

Yet even while he condemned the rioters and their journalist abettors, Leggett also chastised the abolitionists. Immediatist emancipation plans, he insisted, were "wholly wild and visionary," and needed to be combated. (In contrast, Leggett commended the "rational and practicable" relocation projects of the American Colonization Society—glossing over the irony that his antagonists, Webb and Stone, were among the loudest pro-colonizationist editors in the nation.)[16] At the very least, the abolitionists, with their impractical urgency and the self-righteous tone, would lure free blacks and slaves into entertaining false hopes about rapid emancipation. More ominously, their preachings might lead to black rebellions that would prove more disastrous for the rebels than for their intended victims. Precisely because the abolitionists were fanatics, Leggett observed, there was little use in trying to silence them with force; such suppression would only backfire by solidifying the abolitionists' self-righteousness and by bringing them naïve and unwarranted public sympathy. Far better, Leggett reasoned, to engage and defeat their arguments in open and civil debate.[17]

Seemingly a call to reason, Leggett's musings occasionally expressed deeper, explicitly sexual fears that he shared with angrier anti-abolitionists. As Leonard L. Richards has shown in his close study of anti-abolitionist violence, much of the fury in New York and elsewhere stemmed from the widespread perception, fed by lurid street rumors, that the abolitionists intended to encourage interracial sexual relations (dubbed "mulattoization" or "amalgamation"). Some abolitionists tried flatly to deny the charge, but cries of "No Amalgamation!" appeared regularly in the columns of the *Courier and Enquirer* and *Commercial Advertiser.* Leggett, for all his revulsion at anti-abolitionist racism, likewise assumed that the abolitionists favored "promiscuous intermarriage of the two races," a prospect he deemed "preposterous and revolting alike to common sense and common decency."[18]

Leggett also endorsed the mainstream Democratic argument that abolitionism was actually a cover for upper-class efforts to harm northern wage earners and disrupt the Jacksonian coalition. William Lloyd Garrison and his allies (Leggett wrote seven months after the riots) gained their chief support from the northern "aristocracy"—"that party which has always been in favor of encroaching on the rights of the white labourer in this quarter." The northern laboring classes—"the great mass of the democracy"—shunned Garrison, for they knew that ex-slaves would travel north and try either to raise themselves to the standards of white workers or to "lower the condition of the white labourer by association if not amalgamation." Moreover, the freedmen, once relocated in the North, would depreciate the overall value of labor and throw white men out of their jobs. "Those who employ labour and have an interest in depressing it" would receive the greatest benefit; thus, Leggett's tortured logic ran, it was they who sponsored the abolitionist crusade.[19]

Unlike the most extreme anti-abolitionist Jacksonians (notably his fellow hard-money radical, Theophilus Fisk), Leggett never veered over into proslavery. He even allowed, in one of his milder critiques of the abolitionists, that he shared their "abstract notions" concerning "the subject of the emancipation and equal rights of the blacks." But in his opposition to immediatism,

Leggett was prepared to support the alliance of slaveholders and northern labor that was the core of the Jacksonian national coalition. In a quick sketch of American political history, he noted proudly that "the true democracy of the north has always supported the southern policy," out of "a near affinity of interests and principles." Northern Democrats and southern Democrats opposed "all partial and exclusive legislation," and the elevation of the paper-money aristocracy; northern labor's rights went hand-in-hand with southern slaveholders' power; an attack on one was an attack on the other. Thus, as friends of equality, all northern Democrats, whatever their views about slavery, were duty-bound to oppose abolitionism.[20] Or so Leggett believed through the winter of 1835.

In one of his tributes to Leggett, Whittier claimed that the editor suddenly converted to abolitionism on September 4, 1835, when he at last allowed himself the time to read the abolitionists' program.[21] Although there is some truth to this melodramatic account, Leggett's switch also followed a prolonged reevaluation of his anti-abolitionist views.

His self-questioning began after the Chatham Street riot. Even as he worried about how anti-abolitionist violence would make heroes of the abolitionists, Leggett's prose betrayed sympathy for the mob's victims. Subtly, a more generous, at times sentimental tone crept into his descriptions of abolitionists and blacks. On July 12, 1834, as the unrest subsided, he spoke of how the rioters had directed their rage against "the cabin of the poor negro, and the temples dedicated to the service of a living God." Ten days later came his renunciation of the anti-abolitionists' racism and his allowance that the abolitionists' main goal might be "in itself proper." Confusingly, he continued to attack the abolitionists as promoters of "a species of insanity," while in the same editorials he modulated those attacks and took swipes at anti-abolitionist extremists. However "misguided on a single subject," he allowed a year after the riots, the abolitionists were "not knaves or fools, but men of wealth, education, respectability and intelligence . . . actuated by a sincere desire to promote the welfare of their kind."[22]

The continuing anti-abolitionist repression of 1835 shaped Leggett's thinking more than anything the abolitionists themselves said or did. The notorious decision in July by the Charleston, South Carolina, postmaster to destroy abolitionist pamphlets sent through the mails touched off a typical Leggett explosion, decrying the abrogation of what he deemed constitutionally protected rights to free discussion. (Still opposed to abolitionism, Leggett favored a more egalitarian method to curtail abolitionist propaganda, by revising the postal laws and charging prohibitive rates for "educational" materials.) Leggett's anger deepened when President Jackson's postmaster general, Amos Kendall, refused to condemn the Charleston outrage, and when the Tammany-appointed New York City postmaster, Samuel Gouverneur, announced he would in future decline to forward abolitionist mailings. "He has truckled to the domineering pretensions of the slave-holders," Leggett snapped in one of his pieces on Kendall, and established "a *censorship of the press*, in its worst possible form, by allowing every two-penny postmaster through the country to be judge of what species of intelligence it is proper to circulate."[23]

Events from late July through early September 1835 caused Leggett to sway wildly from continued criticism of the abolitionists to even harsher attacks on their opponents. "We have . . . witnessed the rapid increase of abolition fanaticism with the deepest regret, not unmingled with alarm," he wrote on August 22; "[i]f aught had been in our power to arrest that frantic sect, we should not have stood an inactive spectator to its progress." A week later, replying to Democratic and Whig criticism of his editorials on the postal controversy, he pointedly denied that he was an abolitionist—but the more he asserted them, the more his anti-abolitionist claims lacked conviction. First, in early August, came the word that the Tammany Democrats were suspending all patronage advertising in the *Evening Post,* in retaliation for Leggett's attacks against Kendall and Gouverneur. At the end of the month, a dispatch from Charleston related how a reward of twenty thousand dollars had been posted in New Orleans for the successful kidnapping of the abolitionist leader Arthur Tappan and his delivery to the city levee. The same day, a New York group called an anti-abolitionist meeting, using what Leggett considered "inflammatory phrases" about "imported traveling incendiaries" and "misguided native fanatics"—language not unlike that which Leggett had used about the abolitionists merely weeks earlier.[24]

Finally, on September 3, the *Post* reported that a mob in Haverhill, Massachusetts, had broken up a lecture by the abolitionist Samuel May by threatening the meeting house with a loaded cannon, and throwing stones and firecrackers through the windows. As in his previous editorials, Leggett mocked the notion that "the best mode of correcting error of opinion is to destroy the freedom of speech." Once again he suggested that mob assaults would only strengthen the abolitionist movement. But now his reasoning led in a different direction: "It is a question, which history does not answer altogether to suit the practice of Judge Lynch and his myrmidons, whether the blood so shed sinks into the barren earth, or whether, like that which trickled from Medusa's severed head, it will not engender a brook of serpents which shall entwine themselves around the monster slavery, and crush it in their sinewy folds."

"The monster slavery": with that, Leggett announced that he no longer spoke as a friendly critic of anti-abolitionism but as an antislavery man. The next day he printed an editorial (later cited by Whittier as proof of his sudden conversion) proclaiming that he had read the Antislavery Society's program and that it met almost entirely with his "cordial approval."[25]

The label "abolitionist" carried strong connotations of perfectionist extremism in 1835, and Leggett hesitated for three years before he unequivocally applied the term to himself. Even then, he would never feel entirely comfortable with the more prominent radical abolitionists. The immediatist impulse, shaped by the revivalism of the Second Great Awakening and devoted to self-transformation and the transcendence of sin, made him uneasy. He had little sympathy for the broader evangelical reformism of men like Arthur Tappan, whose campaigns for sabbatarianism and other uplifting crusades he deemed an unhealthy mixture of moralism and government coercion. More than a year after he declared his "cordial approval" of most of the American Antislavery Society's principles, Leggett upbraided the leading immediatist newspapers (citing specifically Garrison's *Liberator*) for their "acrimonious, vindictive, intolerant, and unjust propaganda" and their "exceedingly reprehensible temper." In place of the "sweeping and malignant" charges of the immediatists, Leggett, as ever a man of reason and utility, wanted to defeat slavery with "facts and arguments." Always, he distinguished his practical brand of abolitionism—"abolitionism, in my sense," he called it—from others.[26]

But there was no mistaking the sincerity and moral urgency of Leggett's antislavery stance after September 1835. Later that year, criticism from mainstream Democrats—capped off by what Leggett called his "excommunication" by the quasi-official administration newspaper, the *Washington Globe*—only strengthened his resolve. So did various political developments between 1835 and 1837, above all the struggle in Congress over the gag rule and the accompanying rise in southern defenses of slavery as a positive good. Yet Leggett's basic arguments remained consistent from the time of his conversion onward: slavery was "an opprobrium and a curse, a monstrous and crying evil" to slaves and whites alike; and pragmatic, constitutional steps should be taken to hasten slavery's elimination.

It was, for Leggett, a time of financial insecurity and intense physical suffering. In the autumn of 1835, he fell seriously ill and had to stop working. He only recovered his powers slowly; and when his radical Democratic followers tried to nominate him for mayor in the autumn of 1836, he declined, citing his poor health and financial difficulties. Finally, after a brief stint back at the *Post,* Leggett started up his own newspaper, *The Plaindealer,* in December 1836, followed soon after by a two-penny daily, *The Examiner.* Still in fragile health, he hoped that the new papers would provide him with a livelihood without forcing him to trim his sails "to suit the varying breeze of popular prejudice." But after less than a year, following the Panic of 1837, Leggett's publishers went broke. Leggett, seriously ill once more, abandoned journalism for good and withdrew to New Rochelle.[27]

Throughout his ordeals, Leggett never wavered from his dedication to the Jacksonian cause as well as to antislavery. Conservative Jacksonian newspapers like the "puny" *New York Times* might charge that Leggett's conversion to antislavery meant that he had "deserted the democratic party"; but Leggett denied it. He marked Andrew Jackson's departure from the White House in 1837 with a tribute to "a period that will shine in American history with more inherent and undying lustre, than any other which the chronicler has yet recorded," led by a man of "inflexible honesty . . . intrepid heroism, and the ardent love of country." The Old Hero, the nationalist slaveholder who had stood up to the southern nullifier firebrands, bore no responsibility in Leggett's eyes for the curse of slavery. Likewise, Leggett warmly supported Van Buren, Jackson's hand-picked successor, in his run for the presidency. "Is there a single act alleged against Mr. Van Buren for which he ought to blush?" Leggett asked after Van Buren's nomination in 1835.[28]

Incapable of presenting himself as less than rigorously consistent, Leggett spoke not as a Jacksonian and an abolitionist, but as one whose new-found abolitionism had grown naturally out of his Jacksonian beliefs. Early in his reassessment of the abolitionists, this stance posed few problems, as the most prominent anti-abolitionists in New York City were racist, colonizationist anti-Jacksonians such as James Watson Webb and William Leete Stone. Yet even when hitherto friendly Democratic newspapers began attacking him, Leggett couched his antislavery remarks in an unapologetic Jacksonian idiom, throwing his Democratic critics' own political vocabulary back in their faces.

Leggett's simplest rhetorical turn, especially amid the postal controversy, was to link southern anti-abolitionists and their northern apologists with the nullifiers of 1832–33. "According to the doctrines of the Postmaster General," Leggett remarked sarcastically of Amos Kendall, "all that is required to constitute one a Sydney or a Hampden is to nullify the laws." By allowing local sentiments to hold sway over their federal duties, supposed loyal Jacksonians were in fact preaching "a new species of nullification," every bit as noxious as the original.[29]

Alternatively, Leggett complained of northern Democratic vacillation as a heretical deviation from the Jeffersonian and Jacksonian doctrines of strict construction of the U.S. Constitution. In his inaugural address in 1837, Van Buren stirred Leggett's wrath by stating that, in accordance with the spirit of the Constitution, he would veto any legislation that abolished slavery in the District of Columbia. "Hamilton was guided by the *spirit* in proposing the first federal bank," Leggett retorted, "but Jefferson adhered to the *letter* in his argument against that evil scheme. . . . The internal improvement system, the compromise system, the distribution system, and every other unequal and aristocratic system which has been adopted in our country, all claim to spring from the *spirit* of the Constitution; but Andrew Jackson found in the *letter* of that instrument his rule of conduct, and it was fondly hoped that his successor meant to emulate his example." Jacksonian strict construction (as Leggett would later argue at length) clearly allowed for congressional abolition in the nation's capital. Van Buren, having acted in "a cringing spirit of propitiation to the south," had abandoned the true Democratic path.[30]

For all of their cleverness, these salvos betrayed a certain defensiveness on Leggett's part, which may have led him to dress up his antislavery sentiments in impeccable Jacksonian rhetoric. He may even have been straining to convince himself that he had changed his views less than he actually had. Still, his writings elucidated a singular antislavery logic, quite distinct from that of the more radical immediatists—one that was compatible with his Jacksonian egalitarian radicalism, and that was encapsulated in his belief, as he wrote in 1838, that abolitionism was "a glorious, and necessary part of democracy."[31]

Anticipating many subsequent antislavery Jacksonians, Leggett deemed slavery a threat to the equal rights of the white male citizenry. The idea directly contradicted his original view that the Democratic alliance of southern slaveholders and northern labor was the best defense against the moneyed "aristocracy"; in effect, Leggett removed the planters from the category of honest producers and grouped them together with the moneyed classes as reactionary anti-democrats. The displacement came in stages, coinciding with his mounting objections to the suppression of anti-abolitionist activities.

Even in his earliest editorials in antislavery, Leggett linked his purely tactical misgivings about anti-abolitionist mobs to broader statements about the "absolute" constitutional right to free discussion—a more expansive view of the Bill of Rights than the Marshall Court had affirmed in its important *Barron v. Baltimore* decision in 1833. Anti-abolitionism's escalating ferocity in 1835 pushed him toward a more exact denunciation of southern political leaders, for their "braggart style" and "menacing language." Finally, Leggett identified slavery itself as the source of southern truculence. "Whence comes the hot and imperious temper of southern statesmen," he asked in 1837, "but from their unlimited domination over other men. . . . Whence comes it that the knife and the pistol are so readily resorted to for the adjustment of private quarrels?"[32]

Having discovered slavery's inherent hostility to the rule of law and equal rights, Leggett went on to denounce it as an economic and social evil, "an even greater evil to the whites" than to the blacks. Rehearsing what were fast becoming familiar antislavery arguments, he described the South as a blighted, backward region, characterized by a languishing agriculture, a paralyzed commerce, and primitive mechanical arts. "Slavery withers what it touches," he concluded—and as proof, he offered up a contrast (lifted from Alexis de Tocqueville) between two neighboring states: prosperous rural Ohio, where "the whole land . . . blossoms like a garden," and benighted Kentucky, sunk in "a deadening lethargy." Whereas slavery's defenders slandered the North's "honest and free labourers" as "white slaves," their eulogies of human bondage evaded any discussion of the depressed condition of the great majority of the white South.[33]

Leggett did not confine himself, however, to slavery's harmful effects on whites: "the oppression which our fathers suffered from Great Britain," he insisted, "was nothing in comparison with that which the negroes experience at the hands of the slaveholders." Slavery was preeminently a moral and political evil to Leggett, "erected on the prostrate bodies of three millions of slaves"—a repudiation of "the great fundamental maxim of democratic faith," "the natural equality of rights of all mankind." That blacks as well as whites were entitled to those rights apparently struck him as self-evident; in any case, he did not bother to justify the proposition. Only when the bondsman was free to allow "his enfranchised spirit to roam on the illimitable plain of equal liberty," he declared, would the United States live up to its democratic political creed.[34]

Extending Jacksonian equal rights doctrines to include blacks marked Leggett's furthest departure from the mainstream Jacksonians of the 1830s and from the nearly universal white American assumptions about black inferiority. It also marked how Leggett had transcended his own fears of "amalgamation" and competition from black labor. J. David Greenstone, the most perceptive modern commentator on Leggett's antislavery writings, ascribed this shift to the abstractness of Leggett's political thinking, "his view of individuals as bundles of rights and preferences," which supposed left him "relatively uninterested in racial differences."[35] Yet Leggett's fictional writings attest to his deep curiosity about racial differences; and, as his early editorials against the anti-abolitionists show, Leggett was disgusted when those differences became the subjects of racist diatribes. Rather, Leggett, who even in his burlesques always insisted on the basic humanity of blacks, reached the point where he could no longer excuse black subjugation as a necessary price for Democratic unity. "The often quoted and beautiful saying of the Latin historian, *homo sum—humani nihil a me alienum puto,* we apply to the poor bondsman as well as to his master," he wrote shortly after he endorsed the abolitionists. All who denied as much, or who refused, in the face of black humanity, to grant blacks equal rights, denied democracy itself—just as, he noted, British Tories had once denounced antislavery because it contained "'a leaven of democratical principles'" and "'wild ideas of the rights and natural equality of man.'"[36]

A more conventional Jacksonian than most abolitionists, Leggett was also a more prudent tactician, especially regarding the key antislavery effort of the day, the continuing petition campaign supporting congressional abolition of slavery in the District of Columbia. Although he believed (in contrast to Van Buren and his party's leadership) that the goal was both constitutional and desirable, he cautioned that, on its own, abolition in Washington would be at best a symbolic act, gained at tremendous costs in time and energy. "A spirit of conciliation and compromise should govern the matter, as it did in the formation of our sacred *Magna Charta* [sic]," he continued; although certain that the slavery question was "destined to shake our empire to the center," he did not think it sensible to get bogged down in a "collateral" issue, concerning "a spot of ground which is not a pin's point on the map."[37]

Looking back, it is easy to construe such remarks as evidence of flaws in Leggett's antislavery thinking, caused by his characteristically Jacksonian aversion to any but the most minimal forms of government interference with private interests. Greenstone, for example, argued that although Leggett's individualist liberalism helped him eventually denounce slavery as a moral evil, it also disabled him from allowing morality a political role in attacking such evils—and, in the end, prevented him from proposing any specific action to end slavery.[38] Yet this view slights how, at the time Leggett was writing, antislavery activists in general were unsure about what actions they might propose beyond moral suasion, given what many agreed was the mounting futility of the congressional petition campaign. It also overlooks Leggett's own statements that, except for certain constitutional limitations, he would not refrain from using legislative means to bring about "the speedy and utter annihilation of servitude and chains."[39]

These latter remarks were hardly rationalizations for inaction. Leggett's liberal anti-capitalism never *entirely* precluded forceful government, so long as government's purpose was to protect the weak from the strong—as in the case of suppressing mobs or abolishing slavery. His favorite Jeffersonian maxim—"do not govern too much"—never implied no governing at all. Rather, Leggett regarded the U.S. Constitution with utmost seriousness. Since the 1790s, numerous plebeian democrats had developed a stubborn form of egalitarian constitutionalism, insisting that all extra-constitutional efforts to seek redress of grievances were denials of the American Revolution's legacy and were, in any event, doomed to failure. Whereas some reformers spoke of the imperatives of a higher law of conscience beyond the state and federal constitutions, constitutionalist democrats thought the notion pernicious, a pretext for anarchy and (in time) official repression. It was this respect for the sanctity of the Constitution as the national instrument of democracy that shaped Leggett's approach to the slavery debates.[40]

Leggett never doubted that the Constitution barred direct federal interference with slavery in the states where it existed. A Jacksonian strict constructionist, he found no such power conferred explicitly to Congress in the original document; given the Tenth Amendment's reservation of all powers "not delegated to the United States" to the individual states, the issue, in his mind, was settled. Under the circumstances, Leggett sometimes suggested that emancipation could be won only through moral suasion, "sounded through the ears of the slaveholders, to arouse their humanity, convince their reason, and awaken their fears." In his darker moments, especially during his tortured days at *The Plaindealer,* he despaired that even these efforts would be overwhelmed, and he cried out as bitterly as any Garrisonian that the federal compact recognized "in palpable and outrageous contradiction of the great principle of liberty, the right of one man to hold another as property." More often, however, he scrutinized the Constitution and the revolutionary history that lay behind it, and located antislavery statements and hints that (he believed) southern leaders were trying to expunge.[41]

At the heart of Leggett's antislavery constitutionalism was his belief that the Framers had never intended to make slavery a permanent feature of American life. Quite the opposite, Leggett observed: the Founding Fathers abhorred slavery "as the direst curse inflicted upon our country" and purposely avoided inserting the words "slave" or "slavery" in the Constitution. To be sure, an intersectional compromise had prevailed at Philadelphia, and the Constitution wound up giving the institution some covert recognition. Nevertheless, he insisted, Thomas Jefferson, Patrick Henry, and the other great men of the new republic regarded slavery as abnormal and temporary, and hoped that it would "one day or another be wiped out, and the poor bondsman restored to the condition of equal freedom for which God and nature designed him."[42]

Focusing more closely on the proceedings of 1787–88, Leggett then pronounced that it was "a great mistake" to assume (as many southerners and their northern sympathizers did) that the adoption of the federal Constitution left "the power of the southern states over slavery *and all its incidents*" undiminished. Article I, section IX, on the importation of slaves, certainly reduced that power; beyond that, every other "incident" of slavery that conflicted with any provision of "the supreme law of the confederacy" was likewise reduced. Accordingly, under Article I, section VIII, Congress had the incontrovertible authority to abolish slavery in the District of Columbia without compensation to the district's slaveholders. More generally, the people of the United States enjoyed absolute authority over slavery "so far as it presents a question to be considered in reference to any proposed amendment of the federal constitution." (If, for example, any portion of the citizenry wished to remove by amendment the three-fifths clause, the Constitution was amenable.) Above all, the Constitution guaranteed free and open discussion on any matter pertaining to slavery, regardless of the discussion's perceived threat to the institution.[43]

Leggett's ruminations about congressional power over slavery in the capital also led him to contend that, under the federal Constitution, slavery's legal character was purely local. "The foundation of the right of property in Virginia and Maryland is the law of Virginia and Maryland," he observed; as soon as those states ceded a portion of their territory to another government (that is, the federal government), they relinquished their right of legislation to the absolute power of Congress. Regarding federal property protections, meanwhile, Leggett was emphatic: "The constitution does not recognize slaves as *property,* in an absolute sense." National recognition of slavery extended only so far as it applied to certain rights of masters under state laws; otherwise, the Constitution "nowhere gives any countenance to the idea that slaves are considered *property* in the meaning of the term as used in the fifth article of the amendments."[44]

By divorcing constitutional property rights from the specific right to property in slaves, and by delineating the limits of the Constitution's recognition of slavery, Leggett discovered the elements of a powerful political and legal antislavery argument. Writing in the 1830s, before the great debates over Texas annexation and the Mexican War, Leggett may not have been fully aware how important those elements were. Judging from his editorials, he apparently never considered how his observations pertained to the status of slavery in the territories, the enforcement of existing constitutional fugitive slave provisions or other potentially explosive matters. But by casting the Constitution, with strict construction, as a document with clear antislavery overtones, Leggett rebutted early southern arguments about slavery's constitutional character while elaborating counterarguments in line with Jacksonian precepts. And in this he was not alone.

At the very moment that Leggett changed his mind about abolitionism, various other writers and activists were beginning to piece together their own antislavery readings of the Constitution. The debate surrounding slavery in the nation's capital would generate various legal briefs supporting the immediatist abolitionist position, capped off in 1838 by Theodore Dwight Weld's treatise, *The Power of Congress over the District of Columbia.* More broadly, antislavery reformers—including, most conspicuously, the ex-slaveholder James G. Birney and his fellow Ohioan, the hard-money Jacksonian senator Thomas Morris—were starting to argue that slavery was a purely local institution, created and sustained by state law, which could not exist outside local jurisdiction. This conclusion would lead, in turn, to even wider arguments (formulated with particular effectiveness by the Jacksonian sympathizer, Salmon P. Chase) that in time hastened the rise of political antislavery under the banner of the Liberty Party; namely, that the Founding Fathers opposed slavery, that the Constitution was in essence an antislavery document, that the Fifth Amendment had been designed to prevent the federal government from establishing slavery within its exclusive jurisdiction; and that any slave who departed from a slave state immediately became free. Deprived of the artificial aid and comfort of the federal government and the northern states, restricted to its existing localities, slavery (so the argument ran) would eventually collapse.[45]

How much Leggett knew of this buzz of antislavery inventiveness, and of its resemblance to his own Jacksonian abolitionism, is unclear from his editorials. Too ill to work for part of 1835 and nearly all of 1836, he may have lost touch temporarily with other antislavery work; in any event, his own reflections were less bold than the sorts of things Chase, Birney, and Morris were beginning to discuss. His final important *Plaindealer* editorial concerning slavery was the most despairing he ever wrote on the subject, lashing out at "the emblem of our federal union" as "*a cloak for slavery and a banner devoted to the cause of the most hateful oppression,*" and conjuring up apocalyptic visions of a great slave uprising—one which, were it to come, he could not actively support but would pray "might end in giving freedom to the oppressed." The possibility of a different sort of antislavery politics was conspicuously absent.[46]

A year later, however, Leggett, despite his persistent hardships, was in better spirits—still a hero to the Locofocos, preparing to fight against Tammany conservatives for a congressional nomination and "teach the democracy a lesson" while insisting that his friends not hide his abolitionism. Building an antislavery movement was not simply a possibility in Leggett's mind; it was an idea whose time had come. "See what . . . three short years have done in effecting the anti-monopoly reform," he wrote to an associate, "and depend upon it, that the next three years—or, if not three, say three times three, if you please, will work a greater revolution on the slavery question."[47]

Leggett did not live to see his prediction tested. His refusal to disavow his antislavery views narrowly cost him the congressional nomination in 1838; after that, he declined rapidly. Badly in debt, his body failing, he contemplated suicide. Except for the financial assistance of his friends William Cullen Bryant and Edwin Forrest (the popular Shakespearean actor and Locofoco supporter), Leggett's creditors would have seized his remaining possessions in New Rochelle. Finally, Martin Van Buren stepped in. Despite Leggett's attacks on his accommodation of the South, the president remained indebted to the editor. (Van Buren's announcement of his Independent Treasury plan in September 1837 had been widely viewed as a national triumph for Leggett's economic doctrines.) After he learned of Leggett's plight, Van Buren arranged for him to be posted as a diplomatic agent in Guatemala, where he might recover his health. Shortly before his scheduled departure, however, Leggett succumbed to an attack of what one source called "bilious colic." He died soon after, on May 29, 1839, at the age of thirty-eight.[48]

Safely dead, Leggett became a widely honored Democrat. The Young Men's General Committee of Tammany Hall (chaired by the up-and-coming pol Fernando Wood) declared Leggett's passing a "public calamity" and recanted Tammany's criticism of the editor dating back to the post office controversy. Soon thereafter, a bust of Leggett appeared in the Hall, and the Young Men's Committee arranged to erect a monument over his grave. ("Tammany Hall has come round to the *Evening Post*," the hard-money radical *Democratic Review* commented tartly, "not the *Evening Post* returned to Tammany Hall.") Through the mid-1840s, party regulars continued to feature Leggett's name in their campaign propaganda, honoring him as the man who leavened the great battles of the 1830s against special legislation and gigantic monopolies, while keeping silent about his abolitionism.[49]

The antislavery cause had even more reason to mourn Leggett's passing. No Democrat of the 1830s had surpassed Leggett in his opposition to slavery on democratic grounds; none had equaled his ability to express that opposition in commonsense polemics. At a difficult moment, with abolitionism still identified with unpopular Garrisonian radicals and moralistic evangelicals, and with the abolitionist movement at an impasse about strategy and tactics, Leggett's conversion held out the possibility for an entirely new departure, allying the equal rights radicalism of the Jacksonian left with antislavery. The odds against that departure's success were, to be sure, formidable; and there is no reason to assume that, had Leggett lived, he would have succeeded in pulling it off. Still, without question, Leggett's death severely hampered the growth of antislavery Jacksonianism, robbing it of a skillful voice with an established reputation.[50]

As it happened, Democratic antislavery thinking advanced fitfully in the 1840s, and often fell short of Leggett's inclusive egalitarianism. Some northern Democrats, led by Van Buren, became so infuriated by the growth of southern power in the party that they defected to Free Soilism in 1848, only to return to the Democratic fold thereafter and support the Compromise of 1850. Others, including New York's leading younger Barnburners and David Wilmot of Pennsylvania, took more principled antislavery stands, but without Leggett's insistence on black equality. For these Jacksonians, as Wilmot wrote, "the negro race clearly occupy enough of this continent"; free soilism would preserve the rest of it "for ourselves and our children." They saw no contradiction between their opposition to slavery and making racist appeals to white prejudice, the better to deflect opponents' charges that their only allegiance was with the Negro.[51]

Still the main lines of Democratic dissent lay elsewhere, much closer to Leggett's. Although the men surrounding Van Buren (like the former president) were reluctant protesters, more stalwart antislavery Democrats (including Leggett's old partner, Bryant) were motivated by sincere antislavery convictions. Amid the debates over the Wilmot Proviso, certain antislavery men— Free Soilers of what was called "the radical democratic school," including the editor of the Brooklyn antislavery paper, *The Daily Freeman,* Walt Whitman— would acknowledge Leggett as one of their chief inspirations. And even those Free Soilers who, unlike Leggett, celebrated white men's rights and disparaged blacks made it clear that they morally detested racial slavery— and that by attempting to restrict slavery's expansion they aimed, as Wilmot remarked, to "insure the redemption, at an early day, of the negro from his bondage and chains." Together with the more egalitarian antislavery Democrats, these men fiercely attacked the nation's leading racist institution as repugnant to their humanity and their belief in equal rights—by any measure an important blow against long-standing racialist assumptions. A typical New Hampshire antislavery Democratic editorial explained in 1846: "We regard slavery as a great moral, social, and political evil . . . an evil which must sooner or later be removed; and we believe that not only the cause of humanity, but the interest and permanent prosperity of the south would be advanced by the abolition of slavery." Although divided over how far they might extend free blacks' rights, antislavery Democrats overwhelmingly agreed that black bondage, far from a prop for democracy, was fundamentally undemocratic— "a relic of barbarism which must be necessarily swept away," one Barnburner declared—much as Leggett had explained in the late 1830s. And contrary to various erroneous (if now fashionable) assumptions about northern labor and slavery, much of this upsurge, especially in New England, came from nominally Jacksonian workingmen—as in the premier textile town of Lowell, where Free Soilers and renegade Democrats joined forces to create an antislavery stronghold.[52]

As Democratic antislavery spread in the 1850s, so its proponents developed additional rhetorical forms and substantive arguments almost identical to Leggett's. The South, they argued, was a region degraded by slavery, hostile to free speech as well as free labor, its economy stunted and its politics dominated by a slaveholding oligarchy. Southern Democrats had imposed their will on their fellow Democrats, and injected heretical poison into the party's counsels. ("Democracy," Hannibal Hamlin of Maine asserted in the wake of the Kansas-Nebraska struggle, had come to mean "the nullification doctrines of South Carolina in times gone by.") And from the Free Soilers of the 1840s, as well as from the Independent Democrats and Democrats-turned-Republicans of the 1850s, came extensions of Leggett's antislavery constitutional claims, backed by the proposition that the Constitution had purposefully left slavery as a local institution, with the expectancy that it would eventually die out.[53]

Ultimately, of course, it was southern secession, followed by a revolutionary civil war, that extinguished slavery. As a direct consequence of antislavery politics and the collapse of the Jacksonian coalition, the violent upheaval that Leggett had once feared finally arrived—as did the emancipation that he desired. Yet antislavery Jacksonians played a crucial (if of late, neglected) role in bringing the slavery issue to a head in national affairs. And they did so in line with what they (like Leggett before them) took to be an unswerving adherence to Jacksonianism. In 1854, one ex-Democratic congressman insisted that the original Democratic Party had disbanded "and is now known as the Republican Party." The New Yorker Preston King remarked four years later that "to occupy its present ground, the democratic party has changed its members, its principles, it purposes, its character."[54]

Such declarations must have brought some ironic satisfaction to antislavery veterans like John Greenleaf Whittier, whose abolitionist commitments dated back to Leggett's time, and who remembered how the New York Democracy had "clamored down the bold reformer when, / He pleaded for his captive fellow men." True democrats could be Democrats no longer—so legions of northern Jacksonians understood in the 1850s. Leggett died before he could advance the achievement—but proponents of antislavery Jacksonianism eventually won over enough of the Democratic faithful to help put slavery at the center of American political debates. There it would stay until Emancipation.[55]

NOTES

1. Arthur M. Schlesinger, Jr., *The Age of Jackson* (Boston, 1945), 426. The most perceptive analysis of Leggett's anticapitalist political economy appears in Marvin Meyers, *The Jacksonian Persuasion: Politics and Belief* (Stanford, 1957), 185–205, although Meyers unconvincingly tries to square his specific observations about Leggett's simple order of natural liberty—"sometimes openly hostile" to "expansive laissez-faire capitalism"—with his more general contentions that the deluded Jacksonians "moved their world in the direction of modern capitalism" (p. 11). Meyers's account overturned Richard Hofstadter's tendentious essay, "William Leggett: Spokesman of Jacksonian Democracy," *Political Science Quarterly* 58 (1943), 581–594, which cast Leggett as a bourgeois liberal while glossing over his hard-money stance. Some subsequent scholars have nevertheless resuscitated Hofstadter's arguments and proclaimed Leggett a forerunner of such modern pro-capitalist laissez-faire monetarists as Friedrich Von Hayek and the rest of the Austrian School. See, for example, Steven K. Beckner, "Leggett: 19th Century Libertarian," *Reason* 8 (1977), 32–34; and (for a more scholarly account) Lawrence H. White, "William Leggett: Jacksonian Editorialist as Classical Liberal Political Economist," *History of Political Economy* 18 (1986), 307–24. For a less present-minded yet provocative recent discussion, stronger on Leggett's political liberalism than on his economic views, see J. David Greenstone, *The Lincoln Persuasion: Remaking American Liberalism* (Princeton, 1993), 124–39, about which I will have more to say below. One of the few accurate recent descriptions of Leggett appears in passing in John P. Diggins, *The Lost Soul of American Politics: Virtue, Self-Interest, and the Foundations of Liberalism* (New York, 1984), 146, although Diggins is so busy trying to vindicate the writings of Louis Hartz that he fails to comprehend fully Jacksonian anticapitalists like Leggett. The most important reclamation of Jacksonian anticapitalism is John Ashworth's *"Agrarians" and "Aristocrats": Party Ideology in the United States, 1837–1846* (London, 1983), a study which, unfortunately, is weak on the issues of slavery and race, and which begins just at the point where Leggett started to fade from the scene. On the intellectual background to Leggett's liberal anticapitalism, Michael Merrill, "The Anti-Capitalist Origins of the United States," *Review* 13 (1990), 465–497, is an invigorating place to start.

2. *New York Evening Post,* July 8, 1834. Many of Leggett's most trenchant editorials appear in two valuable collections: Theodore Sedgwick, Jr., ed., *A Collection of the Political Writings of William Leggett,* 2 vols. (New York, 1840) [hereafter PW], and Lawrence H. White, ed., *Democratic Editorials: Essays in Jacksonian Political Economy by William Leggett* (Indianapolis, 1984) [hereafter DE]. Where relevant, I have noted the appropriate references in these works as well as to the newspapers where the editorials originally appeared—as with the above editorials: PW, 1: 28; DE, 191. There has been no shortage of historical debate over how to describe various strands of American antislavery politics. Narrow definitions restrict "abolitionism" after 1830 to those so-called "immediatists" who demanded the immediate commencement of the process of complete emancipation in the United States. By these lights, Leggett might not merit his

own self-description as an abolitionist. Yet it is equally important to distinguish Leggett from those antislavery spokesmen who sought merely to restrict slavery's expansion without any direct reference to southern slavery. As Leggett and others made clear, they believed that restriction of slavery was but a step toward the institution's complete eradication—a belief that drew them closer to abolitionism than many latter-day historians have acknowledged. By describing Leggett as a Jacksonian abolitionist, I wish only to draw attention to the importance of those emancipatory beliefs—what might be called a form of moderate or constitutionalist abolitionism, in contrast to the more radical immediatists.

3. For recent racialist interpretations, see Alexander Saxton, *The Rise and Fall of the White Republic: Class Politics and Mass Culture in Nineteenth-Century America* (London and New York, 1990); and David Roediger, *The Wages of Whiteness: Race and the Making of the American Working Class* (London and New York, 1991). On abolitionism and capitalist humanitarianism, see above all Thomas Haskell's two-parter, "Capitalism and the Origins of the Humanitarian Sensibility," originally published in *The American Historical Review* in 1985, reprinted in Thomas Bender, ed., *The Antislavery Debate: Capitalism and Abolitionism as a Problem in Historical Interpretation* (Berkeley, 1992), 107–60. It has been amusing to watch the racialist interpretations of the Jacksonians win rapid and uncritical acceptance among social and labor historians. For a recent example, see Gary Gerstle, "Working Class Racism: Broaden the Focus," *International Labor and Working-Class History* 44 (1993), 33–40. Such approval (and such alacrity) suggest that these interpretations fill current psychological, cultural, political, and academic needs that are independent of historical labors—a subject for another occasion. For additional reflections on recent interpretations, see Sean Wilentz, "Jacksonian Democracy," in John A. Garraty and Eric Foner, eds., *The Reader's Companion to American History* (Boston, 1992); and idem, in *International Labor and Working-Class History* 42 (1992), 141–43. For informed and detailed appraisals of the Jacksonians, slavery, and racial prejudice, see the conflicting interpretations in Eric Foner, "Racial Attitudes of the New York Free Soilers," *New York History* 46 (1965), 311–29; and Richard H. Sewell, *Ballots for Freedom: Antislavery Politics in the United States, 1837–1860* (New York, 1975). For a more sophisticated (although not entirely unproblematic) assessment of plebeian white racism and its political repercussions, see Eric Lott, *Love and Theft: Blackface Minstrelsy and the American Working Class* (New York, 1993). Schlesinger's remarks appear in *Age of Jackson,* 433.

4. Leggett does not appear once in James Brewer Stewart, *Holy Warriors: The Abolitionists and American Slavery* (New York, 1976); Ronald G. Walters, *American Reformers, 1815–1860* (New York, 1978); Lewis Perry and Michael Fellman, eds., *Antislavery Reconsidered: New Perspectives on the Abolitionists* (Baton Rouge, 1979); Robert William Fogel, *Without Consent or Contract: The Rise and Fall of American Slavery* (New York, 1989); or (a bit more surprisingly), Sewell, *Ballots for Freedom.*

5. John Greenleaf Whittier, *Old Portraits and Modern Sketches* (Boston, 1840), 197.

6. The most informative description of Leggett's early years and initial writings appears in Page S. Procter, Jr., "William Leggett (1801–1839): Journalist and Liberator," *The Papers of the Bibliographical Society of America* 44 (1950), 241, 244–45. See also Lester Harvey Rifkin, "William Leggett: Journalist-Philosopher of American Democracy in New York," *New York History* 32 (1951), 46.

7. William Cullen Bryant III and Thomas G. Voss, *The Letters of William Cullen Bryant* (New York, 1975), 1: 260–61, 281.

8. Shane White, *Somewhat More Independent: The End of Slavery in New York City, 1770–1810* (Athens, Ga., 1991), 75. On later manifestations of these ambiguities as they appeared in blackface minstrelsy, see Lott, *Love and Theft,* esp. 63–88, 111–35.

9. William Leggett, *Tales and Sketches. By A Country Schoolmaster* (New York, 1829), 18, 36, 46, 57, 83, 104; idem, *Naval Stories* (New York, 1834), 117.

10. Leggett, *Tales,* 18, 74; idem, *Naval Stories,* 111–26.

11. *Evening Post,* November 20, 1834; PW, 1:78.

12. Rifkin, "Leggett," 46–53.

13. The most thorough description of the rioting appears in Leonard L. Richards, *"Gentlemen of Property and Standing": Anti-Abolition Mobs in Jacksonian America* (New York, 1970), 113–22, 150–55. See also Sean Wilentz, *Chants Democratic: New York City and the Rise of the American Working Class, 1788–1850* (New York, 1984), 263–66; Paul A. Gilje, *The Road to Mobocracy: Popular Disorder in New York City, 1763–1834* (Chapel Hill, 1987), 162–70.

14. *Evening Post,* July 8, 11, 12, 1834; PW, 1:32, 36.

15. *Evening Post,* July 8, 11, 22, 1834, August 8, 1835; PW, 1:32, 40; DE, 191. On Webb and Stone, see also Richards, *"Gentlemen,"* 27–32, 114–15.

16. *Evening Post,* July 8, 1834; PW, 1:31; DE, 192.

17. *Evening Post,* July 22, 1834; PW, 1:37–40.

18. Richards, *"Gentlemen,"* 30–31, 43, 114–15, 120–22; *Evening Post,* July 8, 1843; PW, 1:30; DE, 192.

19. *Evening Post,* February 10, 1835; DE, 195–96.

20. *Evening Post,* February 10, 1835. On Fisk, see Schlesinger, *Age of Jackson,* 425–26. On other labor radicals who turned to racist appeals, pro-southern politics, or both, see Wilentz, *Chants Democratic,* 329–35, and the works cited therein.

21. Whittier, *Old Portraits,* 226–27.

22. *Evening Post,* July 12, 22, 1834; August 8, 1835; PW, 1:35, 38, 2:9–10; DE, 198.

23. *Evening Post,* August 8, 12, 14, 15, 1835; PW, 2:7–28; DE, 197–204.

24. *Evening Post,* August 22, 26, 29, 1835; PW, 2:30–50; DE, 199–201.

25. *Evening Post,* September 3, 4, 1835; PW, 2:54.

26. *Plaindealer,* April 27, 1837; William Leggett to [Theodore Sedgwick, Jr.], October 24, 1838, PW, 2:297–301, 335; DE, 57. On September 5, 1835, Leggett wrote that if believing slavery was a "deplorable evil and curse" amounted to being an abolitionist, "then we are such, and glory in the name" (*Evening Post,* September 5, 1835; PW, 2:60). On piety, evangelicalism, and reform politics in the 1830s, see Daniel Walker Howe, "The Evangelical Movement and Political Culture in the North During the Second Party System," *Journal of American History* 77 (1991), 1216–39.

27. Rifkin, "Leggett," 52–54; Bryant and Voss, *Letters,* 1:457, 476–86.

28. *Evening Post,* August 22, September 7, 1835; *Plaindealer,* March 4, 1937; PW, 2:30–35, 63, 237.

29. *Evening Post,* August 15, 1835; PW, 2:19.

30. *Plaindealer,* March 11, 1837; PW 2:250–53; DE, 222–23.

31. Leggett to [Sedgwick?], October 24, 1838, PW, 2:335.

32. *Evening Post,* August 15, 1835; *Plaindealer,* February 25, 1837; PW, 2:25, 23. A full history of the concept of free speech (and especially of constitutionally protected free speech) in the nineteenth-century United States has yet to be written. John Wertheimer's important work, "Free-Speech Rights: The Roots of Modern Free-Expression Litigation in the United States" (Ph.D. dissertation, Princeton University, 1992), shows how the principle, in its most precisely legal formulation, did not emerge until the early twentieth century—but plainly the idea that the Constitution protected speech was abroad well before then.

33. *Plaindealer,* February 25, 1837; PW, 2:227–32. Tocqueville's famous observation appears in *Democracy in America* (1835–40; New York, 1945), 1:376–79. On Leggett's high regard for Tocqueville's antislavery views, see *Plaindealer,* March 25, 1837; DE, 51.

34. *Evening Post,* September 4, 1835; *Plaindealer,* April 15, July 29, 1837; PW, 2:54, 290, 328.

35. Greenstone, *Lincoln Persuasion,* 134.

36. *Evening Post,* September 7, 1835; *Plaindealer,* April 15, 1837; PW, 2:63–64, 290; DE, 225.

37. *Evening Post,* June 3, September 4, 1835; PW 2:53–54; DE, 202–3.

38. Greenstone, *Lincoln Persuasion,* 136.

39. *Evening Post,* September 4, 1835; PW, 2:54. On the impasse over abolitionist strategy and tactics, see Sewell, *Ballots,* 3–23; and (for a pro-Garrisonian view), Aileen S. Kraditor, *Means and Ends in American Abolitionism: Garrison and His Critics on Strategy and Tactics* (New York, 1969).

40. *Evening Post,* March 11, 1835; PW, 2:61; DE, 20. On the origins of plebeian constitutionalist democracy in the 1790s, see Michael Merrill and Sean Wilentz, *The Key of Liberty: The Life and Democratic Writings of William Manning, "A Laborer," 1747–1814* (Cambridge, Mass., 1993).

41. *Evening Post,* September 7, 1835; *Plaindealer,* July 29, 1837; PW 2:61, 329; DE, 228–30.

42. *Evening Post,* August 29, September 7, 9, 1835; PW, 2:48, 62–63, 66; DE, 210.

43. *Evening Post,* September 7, 1835; *Plaindealer,* February 25, 1837; PW, 2:62, 232–36.

44. *Plaindealer,* February 25, April 15, 1837; PW, 2:234, 297.

45. [Weld], *The Power of Congress over the District of Columbia* (New York, 1838); Sewell, *Ballots,* 90–92; Eric Foner, *Free Soil, Free Labor, Free Men: The Ideology of the Republican Party Before the Civil War* (New York, 1970), 74–77.

46. *Plaindealer,* July 29, 1837; PW, 2:328; DE, 228–30.

47. Leggett to [Sedgwick?], October 24, 1838, PW, 2:335–36.

48. Rifkin, "Leggett," 54; Procter, "Leggett," 243.

49. Rifkin, "Leggett," 54–55; *United States Magazine and Democratic Review* 6 (1840), 442-43.

50. James J. Benton, ed., *Voices from the Press; A Collection of Sketches, Essays, and Poems, by Practical Printers* (New York, 1850), xix; Whitman quoted in Allan Nevins, *The Evening Post: A Century of Journalism* (New York, 1922), 141. See also the radical Free-Soil *Young America,* September 23, 1848, which featured a quotation from Leggett

on its masthead: "Convince me that a principle is right in the abstract, and I will reduce it to practice, if I can."

51. *Albany Argus,* November 22, 1847. On the Free Soilers, in addition to Sewell, *Ballots,* 170–201, see Foner, "Racial Attitudes," and Joseph G. Rayback, *Free Soil: The Election of 1848* (Lexington, Ky., 1970), 99–112, 171–85, 201–30.

52. *Albany Argus,* November 22, 1847; *New Hampshire Patriot,* September 10, 1846; *Niles' Register,* December 20, 1848, 386–87. On Wilmot, see also Charles B. Goring, *David Wilmot, Free-Soiler* (New York, 1924), 174, 272. For more detailed discussions of the emergence of Jacksonian antislavery, see Sean Wilentz, "Slavery, Antislavery, and Jacksonian Democracy," in Melvyn P. Stokes and Stephen Conway, eds., *The Market Revolution in America: Social, Political, and Religious Expressions, 1800–1880* (Charlottesville, 1996), 202–23; and Jonathan Earle, "The Undaunted Democracy: Jacksonian Antislavery and Free Soil, 1828–1848" (Ph.D. dissertation, Princeton University, 1996).

53. Quotation in Foner, *Free Soil,* 178.

54. Ibid.

55. *The Poetical Works of John Greenleaf Whittier* (Cambridge, Mass., 1892), 111.

Chapter 8

RACE, SEX, AND THE DIMENSIONS OF LIBERTY IN

ANTEBELLUM AMERICA

Jean V. Matthews

T HE WORLD HAS never had a good definition of the word 'liberty,'"
wrote Abraham Lincoln in 1864, "and the American people . . . are
much in the want of one." In antebellum America the continued promi-
nence of revolutionary traditions together with the existence of slavery made it
tempting to *celebrate* liberty rather than probe deeply into its meaning. Yet the
meaning of liberty was being explored, deepened, and extended in this period
as new groups laid claim to inclusion in the republican heritage. Two kinds of
people in particular had reason to grapple with the nature of liberty: free
blacks and white women. As Jane and William Pease have pointed out, free
blacks knew from often bitter experience that freedom was not synonymous
with the legal status of freedman. From the 1830s onward spokesmen for free
blacks in the northern states were giving formal articulation to ideas about
what freedom must mean for them, through state and national conventions,
through a black press, and through individual polemical writings.

Among women, too, much smoldering resentment at their secondary status
as well as real personal and economic suffering was beginning to find expression in polemical writings and organized political demands for property
rights. The involvement of many women in both the temperance and the antislavery movements helped to bring inchoate dissatisfactions to the surface and
provide a vocabulary and a constituency. From the 1848 Seneca Falls Convention onward, women's rights conventions became the focus for a fledgling
feminist movement. The movement coalesced around a number of specific
demands to alleviate women's lot in life, but underlying them all was the
anguished feeling that in the "Land of the Free," women of both races were in
fact "unfree," confined, thwarted, and, in one of the most frequently used
words, "degraded" by that very lack of freedom.[1]

The connection between the two movements lies in a certain overlap of
personnel as well as in the structural similarities of racism and sexism. Not all
feminists were immune from racism, not all black males avoided sexual chau-
vinism, but a significant number of *male* feminists were black men and the
majority of antebellum women feminists had connections and sympathies

with the abolition movement. Though the voices to be discussed here are primarily those of black men and white women, black women were involved in movements for the freedom of their sex as well as for the freedom of their race. It is not necessary to claim that the frustrations felt by white women were in any sense equivalent to the oppression faced by free blacks of both sexes, to note that it was quite natural for participants in both movements and for hostile white men to see certain similarities in their situations. "How did woman first become subject to man as she now is all over the world?" demanded the *New York Herald* in 1852. "By her nature, her sex, just as the negro is and always will be, to the end of time, inferior to the white race, and, therefore, doomed to subjection." There were, of course, many ways in which blacks were deprived of freedom which had no real analogies in the experience of white women. Further, the whole problem of injecting the concept of freedom into the sphere of family relations was a question crucial to women but hardly perceived by black men. However, there were certain things that both groups conceived as vital components of freedom, even if not always in exactly the same ways.[2]

To concentrate on the published words of self-defined radicals means dealing with a few prominent and articulate leaders with a very shadowy following. No doubt there were many unknown blacks and white women who read the reports of these conventions and other polemics in silent assent, but it was very difficult actually to mobilize large numbers of either blacks or women behind the rallying cries of liberty and equality. Few things infuriated feminists quite as much as the numerous women who blithely asserted that they had "all the rights they want," and who were often uncomprehending or hostile at any attempt to translate female concerns into the masculine political language of "rights." Frederick Douglass complained bitterly that a national convention of blacks to assert their rights might draw fifty people, while a black Masonic or Odd-fellows celebration could bring out from four to five thousand at a cost that would have supported several newspapers.[3]

Why was it so hard for these often highly talented and dynamic individuals to transfer their own passionate concern with liberty to a mass following? Isaiah Berlin has pointed out that "the lack of freedom about which men or groups complain amounts, as often as not, to the lack of proper recognition." And, he added, "the only persons who can so recognize me, and thereby give me the sense of being someone, are the members of the society to which, historically, morally, economically, and perhaps ethnically, I feel that I belong." A key phrase here is "*feel* that I belong"; the community to which in some objective sense one belongs, or to which one is assigned by others, may not necessarily be the group with which the individual identifies himself and from which he seeks recognition. American culture increasingly consigned all blacks to the community of an inferior and proscribed caste, and all women to a separate sphere which was at the same time flattered and divorced from public power. Through custom and public opinion as much as law, it operated very powerfully to prevent any black from ever being *not* a black or any woman not a woman.[4]

White women, at least, could find certain compensations in this. Nineteenth century American culture offered women a range of identities, all with a certain status, which were clearly more enticing and satisfying to most women, as well as less risky, than that of equal citizen: the "Republican Mother," for example, or the "lady." Moreover, the various levels of "women's culture," which historians have explored so fully, from communities of female kin to various kinds of benevolent and moral reform associations, probably provided a quite satisfactory recognition, by other women, of talents and status. American culture as a whole did not offer similar prestigious identities to free blacks, but the community itself developed hierarchies and organizations that offered status and recognition by other blacks. While in both cases these developments enhanced self-respect and sometimes offered the opportunity to develop organizational skills, they probably served to deflect their participants from examining their situation in terms of the central American language of liberty and equality.[5]

The antebellum feminists and the black leaders who boldly organized to demand full civil rights, including the franchise, were those who for one reason or another—education, class, personal experience, or personality—had dislocated themselves psychologically from what others considered their "natural" community of race or sex, and instead sought recognition from and status within the world of white males. This is not to say that they were deferential toward contemporary white men—quite the reverse—but that their reference point was western civilization; their standard of achievement was the highest standard held up to white males. Their exclusion from participating fully in this culture, the disabilities that prevented them from achieving in its terms, was felt acutely and personally as deprivation of freedom and as *humiliation.*

Elizabeth Cady Stanton singled out the experience of humiliation as crucial to the experience of both free blacks and white women. She pointed to Robert Purvis, a Philadelphia black man who, wealthy and cultivated, was yet "denied all social communion with his neighbors, equal freedom and opportunity for himself and children, in public amusements, churches, schools, and means of travel because of race." A poor white man, she imagined, might think to himself: "If I were Robert Purvis, with a good bank account, and could live in my own house, ride in my own carriage, and have my children well fed and clothed, I should not care if we were all as black as the ace of spades." But, she added, that man had never experienced the "humiliation of color." Similarly, men could not appreciate the subtle humiliations of women possessed of wealth, education, and genius . . . and yet can any misery be more real than invidious distinctions on the ground of sex in the laws and constitution, in the political, religious, and moral position of those who in nature stand the peers of each other? And not only do such women suffer these ever-recurring indignities in daily life, but the literature of the world proclaims their inferiority and divinely decreed subjection in all history, sacred and profane, in science, philosophy, poetry, and song.[6]

In both her examples it is the exceptional person, in terms of wealth, talent, and cultural background, who feels the sting of discrimination because it is felt to be more unnatural and therefore more unjust than the injuries of class. The disabilities of early nineteenth century women and free black men were felt most acutely by those who knew themselves capable of doing and achieving things which the laws or prejudices, or even the internalized prohibitions, of American society prevented them from doing, or which restrained them from enjoying the influence, status, or comforts to which their talents or wealth entitled them.

John Rock, a black doctor lamented that "there is no field" for the young black man of talent. "You can hardly imagine," he insisted, "the humiliation and contempt a colored lad must feel by graduating first in his class and then being rejected everywhere else because of his color." Caste operated unnaturally to deflect the "normal" operations of class, the accepted sifting mechanisms of free society. Color, complained Charles Remond, protesting the segregated cars on Massachusetts railroads, had the effect of wiping out all distinctions among blacks: "It is said we all look alike. If this is true, it is not true that we all behave alike. There is a marked difference; and we claim a recognition of this difference."[7]

If we accept Stanton's focus on humiliation as central to the subjective experience of these black and feminist leaders, then it is not surprising that they should have conceived of liberty primarily in individualistic terms: as equal access to all aspects of American life and as the career open to talents.

In this they were very much in the intellectual mainstream of America, and, indeed, nineteenth-century Western culture, part of a swelling tide of individual self-assertion and the separation of self out of the group. But it took men and women who had a burning awareness of themselves as individuals unjustly cramped, thwarted, and humiliated because of their membership in a subordinate group to demand that the logic of liberal individualism be applied without consideration of race or sex.[8]

To do so implied that the individual could, in a sense, be abstracted from the accidents of race and sex and be seen as essentially the freehold owner and user of energies and talents. Feminists in particular were drawn to the Romantic versions of individualism which conceived of the individual less as a finished unit than as a bundle of potentialities which required freedom as their essential medium of growth. To deprive the individual of the necessary scope for development was thus the ultimate injustice because it violated the essence of human nature. "The fundamental principle of the Woman's Rights movement," resolved a convention of 1853, "is . . . that every human being, without distinction of sex, has an inviolable right to the full development and free exercise of all energies." Women are human, exclaimed the editor of the feminist paper, *The Una,* "and must have the freedom which an unlimited development demands."[9]

If white women tended to put rather more emphasis on freedom as the medium for individual growth, rather than the access to the economic opportunities and rewards of American life which preoccupied black men, it was partly because they could afford such a luxury. But it was also because freedom for women entailed a domestic dimension absent from the struggles of black men—it meant disentangling oneself from the mesh of domestic relations, being ready to refuse, or at least deal coolly with, the "family claim." "A woman is nobody. A wife is everything," declared a Philadelphia newspaper, horrified at the goings-on at Seneca Falls. That was the problem. The prevailing ideology of true womanhood made self-sacrifice the most womanly of virtues; it was the suppression of her own self in the home which allowed it to be a nurturing place for male selves. Elizabeth Stanton thought that the moral freight attached to female self-sacrifice was one of the hardest things for women to bring themselves to repudiate. "Put it down in capital letters," she told a reporter in later years, "SELF-DEVELOPMENT IS A HIGHER DUTY THAN SELF-SACRIFICE."[10]

When women thought about "rights" or about power, in this period, as Elizabeth Clark has pointed out, it was most fundamentally in the context of self-development: "For what is power in the sense in which it is so often applied to women, but the liberty to employ one's faculties in one's own way unobstructed?" demanded the Women's Rights paper, *The Una* in 1853. Rights, insisted an "Indignant" (and articulate) "Factory Girl," even before the Seneca Falls Declaration, arose not from laws but from human capacities. "So far as [woman] can create a new field of endeavor and hope, she has new rights." The underlying fundamental of all rights "is summed up in one word, the right to be whole."[11]

The yearning for self-development and the doubt that it could be accomplished in the feminine sphere of home was one of the things which drew middle-class women to the idea of work. They saw work outside the home as providing a field in which women could realize those latent selves stifled at the domestic hearth. Nothing could supply the place of work to a woman, said the first American woman doctor, Elizabeth Blackwell: "In all human relations, the woman has to yield, to modify her individuality . . . but true work is perfect freedom, and full satisfaction."

Work offered more than self-development, however; it offered independence. Conceiving of freedom in individualist terms led both feminists and black leaders into an instinctive adherence to the traditional republican horror of dependence. Dependence was degrading and essentially antithetical to liberty. But blacks and feminists interpreted what dependence meant in different ways. To the middle class feminist it meant the inability to be economically self-supporting. The paucity of careers open to women hardly enabled them to live decently without being forced to marry for a home or live uneasily in the home of parents or married siblings. Dependence meant financial dependence on a husband. Feminists took as a particular target the common law rules on the property of married women which reduced the wife, in the words of one female petition, to "a mere pensioner on the bounty of her husband." In a culture that elevated the moral value of work, in which even upper class males continually emphasized the amount of hard work they did, the sensitive woman in a well-to-do household could easily come to feel herself a parasite, enjoying a standard of comfort which she had not "earned." Perhaps most important, feminists came to interpret the status of being "kept" as entailing the same kind of degradation of character which traditional republican theory bestowed upon the dependent male: dependents became servile and underhanded because they had to please a master. "'Rule by obedience and by submission sway,' or in other words study to be a hypocrite," wrote the abolitionist Sarah Grimké contemptuously, "pretend to submit, but gain your point"; that "has been the code of household morality which woman has been taught."[12]

Because of their lack of control over economic resources feminists could see *all* women as in a sense "poor" and degraded, not so much by material hardship, but by the lack of independence and thus self-respect that poverty entailed. There were many women, of course, as feminists recognized, who were literally poor and who did not have the choice of dependence, who had to earn their own living and often that of their children. And few of them earned wages sufficient to provide a decently independent life. Feminists interpreted the problem of the working woman, not in terms of the capitalist economic system, but of the pernicious workings of caste. Male prejudice restricted the number of jobs open to women; women's own internalization of male opinion of their capacities, social conventions of propriety, and the torpor induced by subordination meant that few took the time and trouble to acquire marketable skills. "I know girls who have mechanical genius sufficient to become Arkwrights and Fultons," said one speaker at a woman's rights convention, "but their mothers would not apprentice them. Which of the women at this Convention have sent their daughters as apprentices to a watchmaker?" The result was that women were crowded into a very few lines of work and so continually drove down each other's wages. The feminist solution for both lady and mill girl was wider economic opportunities and the will to use them. "Poverty is essentially slavery," wrote Paulina Davis in *The Una*, "if not legal, yet actual." Women must understand this and "they must *go to work*":

They must press into every avenue, every open door, that custom and the law leave unguarded, aye, and themselves withdraw the bolts and bars from others still closed against them. . . . They *must* purchase themselves out of bondage. . . . For as long as the world stands, its government will go with its cares, services and responsibilities. Children and women, till they can keep themselves, will be kept in pupilage by the same power which supports them.[13]

Several historians have pointed out that abolitionists had no sympathy with the concept of "wage slavery" and refused to see any analogy between the working class in the developing capitalist economy and the slave on the plantation. For feminists too, "wage slavery" might metaphorically describe wretchedly low wages, but not the structure of the employment relationship itself. Men of the revolutionary generation had considered wage-earning, as opposed to freehold farming or self-employment, as a form of dependence, and many American workingmen were still clinging to that conception. But to feminists, for women to be paid a specific cash wage, in return for specific work outside the home, was a step upward and onward from the multiple dependencies of woman's traditional domestic sphere. The impersonal capitalist marketplace, however harsh, offered an escape from the more galling personal dependence on particular men.[14]

Like women, free black men, when employed at all, were crowded into a very few occupations, most of which were not only low paid but of little prestige in the wider culture. In many ways they shared with women the task of "servicing" white males. Black spokesmen like Frederick Douglass and Martin Delany denounced black men for their "dependency," by which they meant this employment in "servile" tasks. Black men were barbers, shoe blacks, and porters, and black women were domestic servants and washerwomen— servicing whites rather than their own families. This denunciation immediately got Douglass and Delany into hot water with many people in the black community and they had to back off somewhat and protest that they accepted any useful and honest labor as worthy of respect. But they would not give way too far: the association of blacks with "menial" work only served to depress the estimation in which the community was held by the larger society. He knew, wrote Delany, that he would offend many blacks by suggesting that to be a servant was degrading: "It is not necessarily degrading; it would not be, to one or a few people of a kind; but a *whole race of servants* are a degradation to that people." Both urged blacks to abandon the servicing of whites and instead take up land and become farmers and apprentice their children to the skilled trades. These were ideal "republican" occupations in which a man was self-employed and independent. One of the attractions of farming, in particular, was that not only did it seem a traditional road to economic independence but, according to one committee report in the black national convention of 1843, it bestowed respectability and "character" and "puts the one farmer, be he whom he may, upon the same level with his neighbors. . . ; his neighbors see him now, not as in other situations they may have done as a servant; but as an independent man; . . . farmers, they respect their own calling, feel themselves independent—they must and will respect his, and feel that he is alike independent." Frederick Douglass put particular faith in the crafts. He urged blacks to get their sons apprenticed in the "blacksmith's shop, the machine shop, the joiner's shop, the wheelwright's shop. . . ," although he acknowledged elsewhere that white prejudice seemed most solidly entrenched among the craftsmen of the skilled trades and that it was almost impossible to persuade a white craftsman to take a nonwhite apprentice. Yet the glamour of the independent craftsman in his own shop, though it might be economically obsolescent, was his status as an independent republican citizen.[15]

In asserting the necessity of being independent, blacks and feminists were linking themselves to an established republican tradition, one of the most strongly held values of Jacksonian America. But for them to appropriate this value as a right for themselves was to court considerable risk. Tolerated in menial positions, blacks invoked the fury of whites when they competed with white workers or asserted a claim to equal rights and dignity. Even well disposed whites preferred blacks as objects of benevolence rather than as equal citizens. Though women were not the targets of mob violence like blacks, their assertion of independence was also dangerous, since to most Americans there was an implicit equation of dependence with femininity. As many commentators on womanhood asserted, it was women's dependence which made men love them, so that to repudiate dependence was to risk not only being unloved but also male retaliation. In several antifeminist polemics there is an only partly veiled assumption that the natural attitude of men toward women is antagonism. Women could deflect this antagonism by deferential and dependent behavior, but if they abandoned that behavior men would turn upon them with the full force of untrammeled aggression and competitiveness. "All the sacred protection of religion, all the generous promptings of chivalry, all the poetry of romantic gallantry, depend upon woman's retaining her place as dependent and defenceless," warned Catherine Beecher. The clergy were particularly quick to warn women that when they assumed "the place and tone of a man" then "we put ourselves in self-defence against her"; if, in a favorite metaphor, the vine sought to emulate the independence of the oak, in the resulting disorganization of society, the vine would be "the first to fall and be trodden under foot."[16]

Their emphasis on individual effort, "elevation," and self-development made the relationship of these black and feminist leaders with the black community and with "womanhood" as a whole deeply ambivalent. On the other hand, feminists and black leaders dissociated themselves from many aspects of the culture of "their" group; yet on the other, their identification with it was so deep that any injury or insult to any black or any woman evoked not merely sympathy, but was felt as a personal humiliation. Further, the attainment of personal freedom for individual members of an identifiable group of inferior status could not in fact be achieved without the elimination of the legal disabilities and the wall of prejudice that hemmed in the whole group.

There was thus a reciprocal relationship between individual and community: the whole must be freed and to some extent "elevated" before the individual could rise above it, but it was also the success of the talented and exceptional individuals who would help to elevate the group. After chastising a meeting of free blacks in Canada for their shortcomings, Frederick Douglass pointed out they must bear in mind "that he is closely linked with them; and in proportion as they ascend in the scale of intellectual and moral improvement, so will he; whereas, if they allow themselves to sink into degradation, he also is dragged down along with them." He deplored the jealousy many blacks displayed toward the few who had risen above the general level. "They see colored people occupy a better position, but they say, 'What has Frederick Douglass done for us?'" Douglass did not specify what he and other black leaders whom he named had done for the average black but he implied that they had raised the reputation of the whole race in the eyes of whites and that by their mere existence they ought to raise the self-respect of every black. Some measure of what J. R. Pole has called "equality of esteem" for the whole race or sex had to be wrung out of American society before individual freedom would be truly possible.[17]

It was partly as a vital symbol of "equality of esteem" that blacks and feminists demanded the vote. Liberty as equal access, self-development, and independence, and liberty as membership in the political body of self-governing citizens are logically distinct, and certainly both blacks and women had reason to doubt any easy equation of freedom with republican institutions, and to ask: "Of what advantage is it to us to live in a Republic?" It became a commonplace among feminists that republics were in fact particularly inimical to female self-expression outside the home and that women, as women, had more access to political power and a wider range of personal freedom in aristocratic societies. Blacks who traveled to Europe as feted guests of British abolitionists returned to report that they had been free to travel without segregation or insult, had been easily accepted by white society, and had generally felt themselves to be much freer than in democratic, republican America.[18]

Even so, feminists and black spokesmen insisted on the right of full citizenship in the American republic as the necessary complement of the more private liberty of self-development. While the vote was not the only measure of liberation for antebellum feminists, it was central to them from the beginning. Similarly, every black convention demanded the vote on equal terms with whites. For blacks the issue of the franchise was particularly galling, since in several states after the late 1820s they were in fact *dis*franchised and deprived of a right that they had once possessed.

By the late 1840s activists in many fields, as Lori Ginzberg has pointed out, were increasingly turning toward "regular" political channels as the most effective medium for social change. Among abolitionists, the Liberty Party seemed to offer faster prospects of success than the slow process of purely "moral suasion," and many black abolition workers turned to it enthusiastically. The 1840s and 1850s were a period of high political excitement and intense interest in elections and politics at the national as well as the state levels. Those blacks who still possessed the franchise seem to have turned out as heavily, if not more heavily, than white men. Women, also, were to an unprecedented degree being involved in the political process, in a symbolic and theatrical way as participants in parades and appreciative audiences for speakers. This kind of involvement, however, only served to accentuate their real marginality to the political process. As many male activists, in temperance, abolition, and the labor movement moved to political activities and solutions, women began to seem increasingly irrelevant, and indeed, their activities in these areas were far less prominent than in the 1830s. Without the vote, women, quite literally, did not count. A Wisconsin legislative committee put it bluntly in 1857: "No man or woman can be regarded as an entity, as a power in society, who has not a direct agency in governing its results. . . . There is no reality in any power that can not be coined in votes."[19]

Thus by the 1840s, to be without direct access to the political process, came to seem particularly bitter. Among women, even those who, like many temperance advocates, had hitherto disdained the corruption of "male" politics, were becoming increasingly frustrated by the apparent imperviousness of society to their moral appeals. While much of what women wanted in terms of dignity and avenues for self-expression could not have been achieved through legislation in the lightly governed America of the early nineteenth century, nonetheless some women were beginning to see political power as the means to obtain substantive goals. The Worcester Women's Rights Convention of 1856 was convinced that once women had the ballot, "all the barbarous, demoralizing, and unequal laws, relating to marriage and property" would speedily "vanish from the statute-book."[20]

But the vote was not only a question of power or efficacy; it was a measure of self-respect. As the "Indignant Factory girl" insisted, women might well not repine over exclusion from the "cares of government," and "the managing of business, . . . were it not that there is a covert degradation in the rejection of her." To be excluded from the central ritual of their nation was to be deprived of that recognition which was necessary to the inner sense of being a free person. For both blacks and white women freedom and power were intertwined; the powerless person was not free and was not respected, and thus could not be self-respecting.[21]

The demand for inclusion in the political community was the most stoutly resisted of all black and feminist demands. White men, too, seem to have regarded political participation through the rituals of party loyalties and elec-toral contests less as a means to practical ends, or even as the exercise of power, than as an affirmation of an essential equality as *men*. A republican polity was a fraternal community. Very few white men were prepared to in-clude black men within that fraternity, and even fewer were ready to acknowl-edge women as brothers.[22] For blacks the symbolic association of suffrage with masculinity made its possession of vital psychological importance. The state of Pennsylvania, claimed a convention of its free black inhabitants, by disfranchising them had "striken a blow at our manhood, and not only ours, but a majority of those who people this globe." A white writer supporting black claims concurred: the vote was "a public recognition of the manhood of the enfranchised man." If women were to claim the attributes of manhood, free and independent individuality, then they too would have to be included in the formal community of such individuals. "In no other way," said a speaker at an Ohio woman's rights convention in 1853, "can we so surely rouse her to the recognition of her individual worth and responsibility, her indepen-dent selfhood, as by securing for her the rights of citizenship, the privileges of free men."[23]

Frederick Douglass in 1865 summed up the reasons why he wanted the vote for black men, in terms with which feminists would have concurred. He wanted it, he said, first because it was a *right,* and men who consented to be deprived of rights were "insulting their own nature." Second, he wanted the vote as a means of educating black people: "Men are so constituted that they derive their conviction of their own possibilities largely from the estimate formed of them by others. . . . By depriving us of suffrage, you affirm our incapacity . . . you declare before the world that we are unfit to exercise the elective franchise, and by this means lead us to undervalue ourselves, to put a low estimate upon ourselves, and to feel that we have no possibilities like other men." If he lived in a monarchy, he continued, he could accept being without the vote, since it would be no "particular deprivation"; but in a nation with "manhood" suffrage "to rule us out is to make us an exception, to brand us with the stigma of inferiority."[24]

Both feminists and black leaders thus saw the ballot not only as an instru-ment for practical ends but as an attribute of individual freedom and self-respect. Its exercise would at the same time affirm personal worth and teach its possessors how to be free. In this way they combined older, classical republi-can ideas of liberty as a function of the participation of equals in the public realm with newer, liberal ideas of individual freedom as a personal possession.

Finally, both blacks and feminists realized that the removal of external con-straints was not sufficient. Freedom, while it was exercised in the society of one's fellow men, began in the head. The worst effect of lack of liberty was that in the long run it unfitted people for the use of freedom. They internalized their oppression, became incapable of even realizing their degraded state, and in the end did, indeed, exhibit the inferiority with which prejudice branded them. Erik Erikson has spoken of that "cold *self*-appraisal in historical terms which no true revolutionary movement can do without." These black and feminist leaders endeavored to force their constituencies into painful self-analysis. Though antebellum feminists did not always escape the alluring notion of female moral superiority, on the whole they had a chastened sense that being oppressed is not particularly good for one's character. They had harsh words for women as they found them: "mawkish, and treacherous, and petulant and meager," and "poor, weak, imbecile, helpless things," most of them as yet scarcely fit to "touch the Chariot of Liberty." Men like Douglass and Martin Delany sometimes feared that the degradation of the slave parent continued to be handed down from father even to free sons, an acquired characteristic of "submission and servitude, menialism and dependence, until it has become almost a physiological function of our system, an actual condition of our nature." They condemned black frivolity, addiction to display, and lack of concern for their own elevation. The black woman lecturer, Maria Stewart, flailed black men for their "want of laudable ambition and requisite courage" which made her "blood to boil."[25]

Liberty, then, required first of all that women and black men acknowledge that they were *not* free. They must cease to shield themselves from this insight by self-delusion and the shelter of their separate spheres. "Though we are servants; among ourselves we claim to be *ladies* and *gentlemen* . . . and as the popular expression goes, 'Just as good as anybody,'" wrote Martin Delany contemptuously, but, "we cannot at the same time, be domestic and lady; servant and gentleman. We must be the one or the other." Paulina Davis in *The Una* produced an extended comparison between the situation of women and that of both slaves and free blacks, in the hope that the analogy with "the most hated and despised race of earth, may startle some who sleep . . . and compel them to feel their own false, unnatural, and despicable position. . . . [I]f it rouse[s] one woman to feel her degradation, its suggestions will have accomplished their mission." Blacks and white women must recognize the myriad ways in which lack of freedom had contorted and vitiated the character and come to terms with the realization that they had to some extent cooperated in their own debasement. This was the crucial act of self-emancipation, and should lead, not to despair, but rather to a new vigor, self-confidence, and readiness for action.[26]

A favorite quotation, which turns up again and again in both free black and feminist discourse, is the line from Byron: "Who would be free, themselves must strike the blow." This had the implication, not merely that white men were likely to be reluctant emancipators and unreliable allies, but that the act of striking was, in a sense, in itself the liberation. Only by coming to feel their invisible chains and by taking some action, however small, to break them, could black men and women of both races begin to make themselves the free and independent individuals whose creation was the ultimate end of modern free society.

NOTES

1. Quoted in John P. Diggins, *The Lost Soul of American Politics: Virtue, Self-Interest, and the Foundations of Liberalism* (New York, 1984), 313; Jane H. Pease and William H. Pease, *They Who Would Be Free: Blacks' Search for Freedom, 1830–1861* (New York, 1974), 3–5. For the free black demands for equal rights and the black convention movement see, besides Pease and Pease, Leon F. Litwack, *North of Slavery: The Negro in the Free States, 1790–1860* (Chicago, 1961), and Leonard P. Curry, *The Free Black in Urban America, 1800–1850: The Shadow of the Dream* (Chicago, 1981), esp. chs. 12 and 13. For antebellum feminist organizations see Eleanor Flexner, *Century of Struggle: The Woman's Rights Movement in the United States* (rev. ed., Cambridge, Mass., 1975), Ellen C. DuBois, *Feminism and Suffrage: The Emergence of an Independent Women's Movement in America, 1848–1869* (Ithaca, 1978), and Elizabeth Cady Stanton et al., *History of Woman Suffrage* (6 vols., New York and Rochester, 1881–1922). The use of the term "feminist" is anachronistic for this period, yet it is the most convenient shorthand to designate demands for equality and individual self-expansion, which was one, and arguably the most important one, of the streams that fed into what later became known as the feminist movement.

2. Quoted in Stanton et al., *History of Woman Suffrage*, 1: 854. Such prominent free blacks as Charles Remond, James Forten, and Robert Purvis were all supporters of women's rights, but the most important was Frederick Douglass. See Philip S. Foner, ed., *Frederick Douglass on Women's Rights* (Westport, Conn., 1976), and Waldo E. Martin, Jr., *The Mind of Frederick Douglass* (Chapel Hill, 1984), ch. 6.

3. Stanton et al., *History of Woman Suffrage*, 1: 184; Frederick Douglass in the *North Star*, July 14, 1848, quoted in Howard Brotz, ed., *Negro Social and Political Thought, 1850–1920* (New York, 1966), 204. The feminist and temperance advocate, Clarina H. Nichols, recalled that on speaking tours she could often disarm audiences hostile to the idea of woman's rights by smuggling them into the context of woman's "wrongs." Stanton et al., *History of Woman Suffrage*, 1: 184.

4. Isaiah Berlin, "Two concepts of Liberty," in *Four Essays on Liberty* (Oxford, Eng., 1969), 155–156.

5. For the development of black organizations, see Litwack, *North of Slavery,* and Curry, *The Free Black in Urban America.* On the separation of black leaders from the mass of the black community, see Pease and Pease, *They Who Would Be Free,* 289–293. On women's culture, communities, and organizations, see Nancy F. Cott, *The Bonds of Womanhood: "Woman's Sphere" in New England, 1780–1835* (New Haven, 1977); Mary P. Ryan, "The Power of Women's Networks: A Case Study of Female Moral Reform in Antebellum America," *Feminist Studies* 5 (Spring 1979), 66–85; and Carroll Smith-Rosenberg, "The Female World of Love and Ritual: Relations between Women in Nineteenth-Century America," *Signs* 1 (Autumn 1975), 1–29.

6. Stanton et al., *History of Woman Suffrage*, 2: 266.

7. John S. Rock, 1862, in Philip S. Foner, ed., *The Voice of Black America: Major*

Speeches by Negroes in the United States, 1797–1971 (New York, 1972), 258; Charles Lenox Remond, address to a Massachusetts Legislative Committee, 1842, in ibid., 73. It was one of the principal sins of man, according to the Seneca Falls Declaration, that he had closed against woman "all the avenues to wealth and distinction which he considers most honorable to himself." Declaration of Sentiments, in Stanton et al., *History of Woman Suffrage,* 1: 71.

8. Eric Foner, "The Causes of the American Civil War: Recent Interpretations and New Directions," in *Politics and Ideology in the Age of the Civil War* (New York, 1980), 23–24. For the individualism of most feminist thinkers see James L. Cooper and Sheila M. Cooper, eds., *The Roots of American Feminist Thought* (Boston, 1973), introduction; for a critique of that individualism, see Elizabeth H. Wolgast, *Equality and the Rights of Women* (Ithaca, 1980). A recent brief essay on American individualism is J. R. Pole, *American Individualism and the Promise of Progress* (Oxford, Eng., 1980). The romantic individualism of personal growth is discussed in Yehoshua Arieli, *Individualism and Nationalism in American Ideology* (Cambridge, Mass., 1964), esp. ch. 12.

9. Stanton et al., *History of Woman Suffrage,* 1: 855; Paulina Wright Davis, *The Una* 1 (June 1853), 73. For the idea of "possessive individualism" and its more dynamic nineteenth-century developments, see C. B. Macpherson, *Democratic Theory: Essays in Retrieval* (Oxford, Eng., 1973), 199, 32.

10. Philadelphia *Public Ledger and Daily Transcript,* quoted in Stanton et al., *History of Woman Suffrage,* 1: 804. Stanton is quoted in Judith Nies, *Seven Women: Portraits from the American Radical Tradition* (New York, 1977), 67.

11. "An Indignant Factory Girl," in "Voice of Industry, August 14, 1847," in Philip S. Foner, ed., *The Factory Girls* (Urbana, 1977), 298.

12. Blackwell is quoted in Lee Virginia Chambers-Schiller, *Liberty, a Better Husband: Single Women in America: The Generation of 1780–1840* (New Haven, 1984), 66. Access to greater educational opportunities was an important goal for both feminists and free blacks since education seemed the key to achieving both individual advancement and individual development. It gave the means to develop and extend talents, to move up in the world, and to throw off the shackles of felt inferiority to well-educated white men. "Memorial to the [state] Constitutional Convention adopted by Woman's Rights Convention, Salem, Ohio" (1850), in Gerda Lerner, ed., *The Female Experience* (Indianapolis, 1977), 344. Sarah Grimké, *Letters on the Equality of the Sexes, and the Condition of Woman* (1838; rep. New York, 1970), 17. For the republican horror of dependence see, for example, Jack P. Greene, *All Men Are Created Equal: Some Reflections on the Character of the American Revolution* (Oxford, Eng., 1976), 20–21.

13. J. Elizabeth Jones at the Syracuse National Woman's Rights Convention of 1852, quoted in Stanton et al., *History of Woman Suffrage,* 1: 530; Paulina Wright Davis, *The Una* 1 (Sept. 1853), 138. Jones made her own living as a lecturer on science and insisted that it was within women's own power to apprentice themselves to skilled trades. "There is no law against this!" Lucretia Mott replied, "The Church and public opinion are stronger than law," and Lucy Stone pointed out that when some women in Massachusetts had apprenticed themselves as printers, they "were expelled because men would not set type beside them." Stanton et al., *History of Woman Suffrage* 1: 530–531.

14. For wage earning as dependency and "slavery" see, for example, Foner, *Politics*

and Ideology in the Age of the Civil War, 60; for the abolitionist attitude, see ibid., 71, and Jonathan A. Glickstein, "'Poverty is not Slavery': American Abolitionists and the Competitive Labor Market," in *Antislavery Reconsidered,* ed. Lewis Perry and Michael Fellman (Baton Rouge, 1979), 195–218. *The Una* devoted a good deal of space to the problem of women's employment and obviously struck a chord with its readers since there were several readers' letters on the subject.

15. Martin Robison Delany, *The Condition, Elevation, Emigration, and Destiny of the Colored People of the United States* (1852, rep. New York, 1969), esp. 42–43, 200 (quotation); Report of the Committee upon Agriculture, "Minutes of the National Convention of Colored Citizens: Held at Buffalo . . . 1843," 32, in *Minutes of the Proceedings of the National Negro Conventions, 1830–1864,* ed. Howard Holman Bell (New York, 1969); Frederick Douglass, "An Address to the Colored People of the United States," Sept. 29, 1848, in Brotz, ed., *Negro Social and Political Thought,* 211. See also the "Resolves of the National Colored Convention, Cleveland, 1848," 13, in Bell, ed., *Proceedings of the National Negro Conventions.* These views on "servile" occupations obviously had a constituency outside the leadership of the conventions and men like Douglass and Delany. A black in California wrote to the press making the same point. Urging every black to abandon such positions as "boot-blacks, waiters, servants and carriers," he added: "I do not wish to be understood as despising any of the callings I have mentioned above, [but] . . . so long as we follow such pursuits, so long will we be despised. The world may preach the dignity of labor. . . . But however pretty this may be in theory, everyone is aware that it does not exist in reality. The man is judged and courted, not for his inherent qualities, but for his position and wealth." San Francisco *Mirror of the Times,* in Martin E. Dann, ed., *The Black Press, 1827–1890: The Quest for National Identity* (New York, 1971), 334. For some of the acrimony over the contemptuous expressions employed by some leaders about service jobs, see "Resolves of the National Colored Convention, Cleveland," 5–6, and Howard Holman Bell, *A Survey of the Negro Convention Movement, 1830–1861* (1953, rep. New York, 1969), 102–104.

16. Catharine E. Beecher, *An Essay on Slavery and Abolitionism, with Reference to the Duty of American Females* (Philadelphia, 1837), 101–102; pastoral letter from "The General Association of Massachusetts (Orthodox) to the Churches Under Their Care" (1837), in Alice S. Rossi, *The Feminist Papers: From Adams to Beauvoir* (New York, 1973), 305; Jonathan F. Stearns, "Discourse on Female Influence" (sermon, 1837), in Aileen S. Kraditor, *Up From the Pedestal: Selected Writings in the History of American Feminism* (Chicago, 1968), 47–50. See also Litwack, *North of Slavery,* 103; and Brotz, ed., *Negro Social and Political Thought,* 283.

17. Frederick Douglass, "Advice to My Canadian Brothers and Sisters: An Address Delivered in Chatham, Canada West, on 3 August 1854," and "Self-Help: An Address Delivered in New York, on 7 May 1849," in John W. Blassingame et al., *The Frederick Douglass Papers,* Series 1: *Speeches, Debates, and Interviews,* Vol. 2: *1847–1854* (New Haven, 1982), 537, 168–169; J. R. Pole, *The Pursuit of Equality in American History* (Berkeley, Calif., 1978), xii–xiii, 150, 302.

18. Isaiah Berlin, "Two Concepts of Liberty," 131; Mary Mott to the Westchester Woman's Rights Convention, 1852, in Stanton et al., *History of Woman Suffrage,* 1: 829. On blacks' experience of travel abroad see the remarks of Charles Lenox Remond in

Foner, ed., *Voice of Black America*, 74–75, and Litwack, *North of Slavery*, 237. The English naturally liked to rub in the deficiencies of republican America: "Tell the Republicans on your side of the line," said the governor of Upper Canada to a delegation of blacks seeking to settle in Canada, "that we royalists do not know men by their color." Quoted in Litwack, *North of Slavery*, 73.

19. Pease and Pease, *They Who Would Be Free*, 173–193; Litwack, *North of Slavery*, 75–93; Charles H. Wesley, "Negro Suffrage in the Period of Constitution-Making, 1787–1865," *Journal of Negro History* 32 (Apr. 1947), 143–168; Mary P. Ryan, *Women in Public: Between Banners and Ballots, 1825–1880* (Baltimore, 1990), 136ff. Mill worker Harriet Robinson in her autobiography recalled her fellow workers as "wide-awake" and interested in the public issues of the day: "Some of us took part in a political campaign for the first time in 1840, when William H. Harrison, the first Whig president, was elected; we went to the political meetings, sat in the gallery, heard speeches against Van Buren and the Democratic Party, and helped sing the great campaign song" Glenna Matthews, *The Rise of Public Woman* (New York, 1992), 98. Lori D. Ginzberg, "'Moral Suasion is Moral Balderdash': Women, Politics, and Social Activism in the 1850s," *Journal of American History* 73, 3 (December 1986), 610.

20. Quoted in Ginzberg, "'Moral Suasion,'" 610.

21. "Indignant Factory Girl," 296.

22. John L. Stanley, "Majority Tyranny in Tocqueville's America: The Failure of Negro Suffrage in 1846," *Political Science Quarterly* 84 (Sept. 1969), 412–435. The most common argument against the enfranchisement of free blacks in the conventions for revising state constitutions in the period was that they were essentially *aliens*, "by the broad distinction of race"; since most white men were unwilling to admit any kind of equality of social intercourse with blacks, this necessarily meant that they could not be admitted to the fraternal bond of political equals. See, for example, the debate on this subject in William G. Bishop and William H. Attree, eds., *Report of the Debates and Proceedings of the Convention for the Revision of the Constitution of the State of New York, 1846* (Albany, N.Y., 1846), 1014–1036, 1045–1048. The quotation is at 1030.

23. "An Appeal to the Colored Citizens of Pennsylvania," in Philip S. Foner and George E. Walker, eds., *Proceedings of the Black State Conventions, 1840–1865* (2 vols., Philadelphia, 1979–1980), 1: 126; "Extension of the Elective Franchise to the Colored Citizens of the Free States," *The New Englander*, 5 (Oct. 1847), 523; Ohio Woman's Rights Convention, quoted in *The Una* 1 (July 1853), 86. The Seneca Falls Declaration was not the first formal claim for the suffrage for women. The constitutional convention of New York in 1846 received a petition from six women claiming complete civil and political equality with men. *Report of the Proceedings*, 646. For the fraternal and symbolic nature of antebellum politics see the brilliant article by Paula Baker, "The Domestication of Politics: Women and American Political Society, 1780–1920," *American Historical Review* 89 (June 1984), 620–647.

24. Brotz, ed., *Negro Social and Political Thought*, 279. Several black and feminist leaders would have been agreeable to accepting a qualified franchise, as long as the qualification was sex and color blind. See, for example, Robert Purvis, in Curry, *The Free Black in Urban America*, 222. For the relation of suffrage to female autonomy see DuBois, *Feminism and Suffrage*, 16–17.

25. Erik H. Erikson, "Once More the Inner Space," in Jean Strouse, ed., *Women and*

Analysis (New York, 1974), 334; Elizabeth Oakes Smith, *Woman and Her Needs* (New York, 1851), reprinted in *Liberating the Home* (New York, 1974), 106; letter from Mrs. Lydia Jane Pierson to Salem, Ohio, Equal Rights Convention, 1850, in *The Lily*, 2 (June 1850), 41; Delany, *The Condition . . . of the Colored People*, 47–48; Maria Stewart, "An Address, Delivered at the African Masonic Hall, Boston, 27 February, 1833," in Bert James Loewenberg and Ruth Bogin, eds., *Black Women in Nineteenth-Century American Life* (University Park, Pa., 1976), 196.

26. Delany, *The Condition . . . of the Colored People*, 200–201; Paulina Wright Davis, "Pecuniary Independence of Woman," *The Una* 1 (Dec. 1853), 186.

PART THREE

MODERN LIBERALISM AND THE CHALLENGE

OF GOVERNANCE

Chapter 9

THE TWO WORLD WARS AND THE IDEA OF THE STATE

A<small>LAN</small> B<small>RINKLEY</small>

THE END OF World War I brought a chorus of tributes, from many sources, to the success of the mobilization effort and to the lessons that could be learned from it. To many the war effort represented at least the partial fulfillment of a dream Walter Lippmann had expressed shortly before it began: the dream of human "mastery" over the immense forces of the modern industrial world; and end to the "drift" that Lippmann believed too often characterized human affairs.[1] Bernard Baruch, who had served as chairman of the War Industries Board, the chief agency of economic management, argued that "the experience of the War Industries Board points to the desirability of investing some government agency . . . with constructive as well as inquisitorial powers—an agency whose duty it should be to encourage, under strict Government supervision, such cooperation and coordination in industry as should tend to increase production, eliminate waste, conserve natural resources, improve the quality of products, promote efficiency in operation, and thus reduce costs to the ultimate consumer. The national Chamber of Commerce proclaimed, "War is the stern teacher that is driving home the lessons of cooperative effort." And former Secretary of War Elihu Root predicted, "There will be no withdrawal from these experiments. We shall go on; we shall expand them."[2]

Grosvenor B. Clarkson, who had directed the Council of National Defense during the war and had developed a great admiration for Baruch and his works in the process, incorporated such "lessons" into a massive semi-official history of war mobilization published in 1923:

> If we had a Government business manager with a free hand to run the business side of Government, as free as Baruch had in the War Industries Board, we should have a successful Government of business. . . . It is little wonder that the men who dealt with the industries of a nation . . . replenished and drawn on at will for the purposes of war . . . meditated with a sort of intellectual contempt on the huge hit-and-miss confusion of peace-time industry. . . . From their meditations arose dreams of an ordered economic world.[3]

The war, in other words, had shown Americans what they could do if they had the will to do it. It had proved that it was, indeed, possible to create order in the economy, to make it harmonious and efficient, to achieve mastery. And for more than a generation, the war remained an inspiration to those progressives who hoped to achieve in peacetime what they liked to think they had achieved in war: "an ordered economic world." The war helped inspire efforts throughout the 1920s to harmonize the business world through the creation of associational arrangements. It supported even larger visions of a "planned economy," in which the government would play a much more intrusive role. It served as a model in 1933 for the creation of the New Deal's National Recovery Administration. And for some, it continued throughout the 1930s, even after the failure and collapse of the NRA, to drive hopes for an economic system in which business, government, and labor would build a working partnership on behalf of the common good.[4]

The outbreak of World War II in 1939, and the American entry into the war two years later, seemed at first to encourage some of the same hopes that World War I had inspired twenty years before—including the hopes for a new political economy. "We have learned," the New Deal administrator Clifford Durr wrote in 1943, "that we cannot obtain the production we need for waging the war as an undirected by-product of what we commonly refer to as 'sound business principles.' Neither can we expect such by-product to furnish us after the war with the standard of living which we shall be warranted in expecting. . . . There must be some over-all source of direction more concerned with [these] objectives than with the profits or losses of individual business concerns."[5] Or as Herbert Emmerich, another New Deal official, wrote in 1941, "With a farewell to normalcy and an appreciation of the greater opportunities that the war crisis presents, public administrators today have an opportunity to enhance and permanently to establish the prestige of their calling in the United States."[6] The rhetoric was more muted perhaps, but the hopes seemed much the same: the war would legitimize an expanded state role in economic life and would show the way to new, more cooperative and harmonious economic arrangements; it would help produce "an ordered economic world."

But the end of the Second World War, unlike the end of the first, brought very few public tributes—from liberals or from anyone else—to the achievements of wartime economic mobilization in bringing order and harmony to the economy. There was, to be sure, substantial satisfaction with the way the economy had performed: with the "miracles" of production that had overwhelmed the Germans and the Japanese and with the new prosperity that had finally ended the Great Depression. But little of the credit for those achievements redounded to the government, to the mobilization agencies, or to the concept of a new, harmonious economic order. Bernard Baruch had emerged from World War I a national hero, a symbol of the nation's hopes for a new political economy; he remained even forty years later a celebrated sage and adviser to presidents. Donald Nelson, Baruch's World War II counterpart, emerged from that war discredited and largely forgotten. Nelson spent his last years serving as a public relations flak for a minor Hollywood trade association and pursuing obscure and unsuccessful business schemes. When he published his memoirs in 1946, many reviewers took the occasion to compare him unfavorably to Baruch.[7]

Why did these two experiences, in many ways very similar experiences, produce such different political legacies? Why did World War I come to serve as a model to many progressives and liberals of what an enlightened state could do to bring order and harmony to American economic life, while World War II produced no such model?

There were, of course, differences between the two experiments in mobilization. The most obvious difference was that the United States spent only about two years mobilizing for World War I (and only a little over a year fighting in it), while the World War II mobilization spanned more than five years (and the fighting nearly four). There was much more time during the Second World War for the problems and shortcomings of the mobilization effort to become evident, more time for things to go wrong, more time for grievances to accumulate. There were also differences in the way power was delegated among the war agencies, differences in the quality of leadership, and differences in the size and complexity of the economies the war agencies set out to manage.

But in most respects, the way the federal government mobilized and managed the economy during the two world wars was strikingly similar. Both Woodrow Wilson and Franklin Roosevelt looked beyond the existing federal bureaucracies and created special new agencies to handle the task of war mobilization. (This was not entirely a matter of choice: neither in 1917 nor in 1941—despite the New Deal—did the federal government possess anything approaching sufficient institutional capacity to manage a wartime economy from within the existing bureaucracy.)

In both wars, these new agencies staffed themselves almost entirely from the private sector, relying largely on businessmen and financiers (many of them drawn directly from the industries they were then called upon to regulate; many of them still officially in the employ of their prewar firms and paid only a token sum by the government—hence the term, common in both wars, "dollar-a-year men"). At the same time, both in 1917 and in 1942, there were efforts to balance the presence of businessmen in the war agencies with representation from other groups, especially labor: efforts to create a tripartite partnership of business, labor, and government capable of cooperating to increase production and promote the common good.

In both wars, the government stumbled through a period of unsuccessful experimentation with various decentralized or divided administrative structures before settling in the end on (to use a phrase popular in 1941, when critics were clamoring for change) "a single responsible agency with a single responsible head"—the War Industries Board, which Wilson created in 1918, headed by Baruch; the War Production Board, which Roosevelt created in 1942, headed by Nelson.

And in both wars, the war agencies, in the end, did on the whole what they were supposed to do. They oversaw impressive feats of production, which tipped the military balance decisively in favor of the United States and its allies; and they avoided major disruptions of civilian life at the same time. If anything, the War Production Board performed rather more impressively than the War Industries Board, if only because World War II was so much larger and (for the United States) so much longer than World War I and hence demanded far greater productive achievements.[8]

The two war mobilization efforts experienced similar failures as well. In neither war did labor ever achieve anything like equal standing in the supposed partnership the government was attempting to create. In neither war did business very often subordinate its own interests to a larger public good, as in theory the wartime arrangements required. Complaints about war profiteering were rampant in 1918, and for decades thereafter, just as complaints about corporate greed were rampant in World War II. Some progressives criticized the War Industries Board in 1918 for creating too many millionaires, for discriminating against small business. Twenty-five years later, liberals were criticizing the War Production Board, and the mobilization effort in general, for the same things: for failing to protect small business and for giving too much power to conservative corporate figures more interested in their own profits than in the interests of the nation.[9]

But despite the substantial similarities in both their achievements and failures, even though a strong case could be made that the mobilization experiments of World War II were considerably more successful than those of World War I, the two experiences came to have very different retrospective images. World War I became an inspiration. World War II did not. Indeed, to many liberals, it became a warning of what efforts by the government to coordinate the economy could become: a mechanism by which members of the corporate world could take over (or "capture") the regulatory process and turn it to their own advantage.

What explains that change is less the differences between the ways the United States mobilized for the two wars than the contexts in which those mobilizations occurred, the assumptions and expectations Americans brought to the two experiences. The context changed in many ways between 1918 and 1941. But three changes are particularly useful to an understanding of why Americans in 1945 thought so differently about the state, and its role in economic life, than they had a generation before.

One of those changes involved the way Americans viewed the two world wars themselves, the way they explained what the nation was fighting for—and, perhaps more importantly, against. World War I was, in the American imagination, essentially a war against German culture, which in the hysterical anti-German atmosphere of 1917 and 1918 seemed savage, and barbaric, and innately belligerent; or (as the California Board of Education noted in banning the teaching of the German language in public schools) a culture steeped in "the ideals of autocracy, brutality, and hatred." Wartime propaganda was filled with personifications of the enemy as the "Prussian cur" and "the German beast," a hostility to the German people and their society that quickly spilled over into a hostility toward German Americans as well. G. Stanley Hall, the eminent American psychologist (and the man who had first brought Freud to America), expressed a widespread assumption when he said, in 1917, "There is something fundamentally wrong with the Teutonic soul."[10]

World War II evoked a different image: less of a barbaric people than of a tyrannical regime; less of a flawed culture than of a flawed political system and a menacing state. Wartime propaganda in World War II did not personify the European enemy, at least, as an evil people (although the same cannot be said, of course, about the Japanese). It focused instead on the German and Italian states.[11]

The war, in short, pushed a fear of totalitarianism (and hence a generalized wariness about excessive state power) to the center of American political thought. In particular, it forced a reassessment of the kinds of associational and corporatist arrangements that many had found so attractive in the aftermath of World War I. Those, after all, were the kinds of arrangements Germany and Italy had claimed to be creating. "The rise of totalitarianism," Reinhold Niebuhr noted somberly in 1945, "has prompted the democratic world to view all collectivist answers to our social problems with increased apprehension." Virtually all experiments in state supervision of private institutions, he warned, contained "some peril of compounding economic and political power." Hence "a wise community will walk warily and test the effect of each new adventure before further adventures."[12]

To others, the lesson was even starker. *Any* steps in the direction of state control of economic institutions were (to use the title of Friedrich von Hayek's celebrated anti-statist book of 1944) steps along "The Road to Serfdom." One of those who had by then come to share that fear was Walter Lippmann, whose earlier dreams of an enlightened government creating "mastery" over great social forces had been replaced by a fearful opposition to the growing power of the state. Lippmann spent the war years denouncing the New Deal and corresponding with Hayek, discussing ways to mobilize what he and Hayek called the "real" liberals around the world to rescue liberalism, the liberalism of individual freedom and economic liberty, from its statist traducers.[13]

But Americans in the 1940s did not have to look to Europe for examples of state efforts to solve economic problems. They could look to their own experiences of the preceding two decades. Americans in World War I had very few previous efforts at state management of the economy against which to measure their wartime experiments. But Americans in World War II had the New Deal.

We are accustomed to thinking of the New Deal as a phenomenon that created and legitimized much of the modern American state, which in many ways it did. But the New Deal is also important for the options it foreclosed, for the way it tried to take certain paths and failed in the trying, for the ways in which it delegitimized certain concepts of the state even as it was legitimizing others. One of those concepts was the vaguely corporatist vision of economic harmony that had emerged from World War I and that culminated in the ill-fated National Recovery Administration of 1933–35.

The sorry history of the NRA is the subject of a considerable scholarly literature that needs no recapitulation here. But it is worth noting how powerfully the memory of the NRA continued to influence the way New Dealers and others thought about what the state could and should do even after the agency itself met its demise in 1935. There were, to be sure, some (including, at times, Franklin Roosevelt) who continued to defend what came to be known as the "NRA approach." But there were many more who talked instead of the "NRA disaster," the "NRA of evil memory," who saw in it a sobering lesson in what *not* to do, who considered it a disastrous mistake never to be repeated again.[14]

Chief among the complaints was that the NRA had, in the name of promoting the common good, become a license for big corporations to collude and hence to threaten the interests of small producers and consumers. The NRA, according to the *New Republic*, "gave employers the opportunity to raise prices and restrict production . . . and so encouraged monopolistic practices that interfered with the very object sought—more abundance." It had, according to the *Nation*, "hindered recovery instead of helping it." It had proved that "whenever business men are allowed to come together to 'cooperate,' the result is almost inevitably an effort to get more profits by some form of price-raising." It was "merely the trust sugar-coated," which had "pinned a policeman's badge" on monopolies.[15]

But the case against the NRA was not just a case against big business; it was also a case against certain kinds of government intervention in the economy, a case against the feasibility of imposing effective public control over the behavior of private institutions, a case against certain notions of planning, regulation, and state management. The NRA had collapsed, Thurman Arnold argued in the late 1930s, for the same reason that all economic "master plans" must collapse—because it could have succeeded only through a "vast extension of state control," an extension that Americans would not (and should not) contemplate. Henry Wallace said of it that "there is something wooden and inhuman about the government interfering in a definite, precise way with the details of our private and business lives. It suggests a time of war with generals and captains telling every individual what he must do each day and hour."[16]

The New Deal, in short, had helped teach liberals not only what the state could do, but what it could not do. And one of the things it could not do, they had come to believe, was reorder the corporate world. Such efforts would lead either to domination by private monopoly or domination by an excessively powerful state. Or it would lead, as many believed the NRA had led, to both. And thus when the United States began, for the second time in a generation, to mobilize the economy for war, liberals brought to that mobilization a much greater sensitivity than had their counterparts two decades earlier to the problems inherent in creating partnerships between the corporate world and the state, and a sensitivity to the problems inherent in giving the state responsibility for managing the affairs of private institutions. Hopes for this second wartime experiment were, as a result, much lower from the beginning; disillusionment set in much more quickly.

But there is a third, and even more fundamental, reason for the difference between the way American liberals conceived the role of their state in 1918 and the way they had come to conceive it by 1945. We cannot understand the way liberals defined the state without understanding how they defined the economic problems they were asking the state to resolve. They defined those problems very differently in 1945 from the way they had in 1918.

At the end of World War I, as for several decades before and for many years after, those who tried to prescribe a more active role for the state tended to think largely in terms of somehow changing the way private economic institutions behaved: curbing monopoly power, promoting industrial cooperation, regulating corporate activities. The problem was institutional. The function of the state was to stabilize, or regulate, or even to restructure capitalist institutions.

That belief rested not only on uneasiness about the size and power of the new corporate institutions in America. It also reflected an assumption about the way all economies worked, an assumption rooted in classical economic doctrine and in centuries of social experience. The great economic challenge, most American liberals believed in 1917, was to expand society's productive capacities and create enough goods to satisfy everyone's needs. The great economic danger was scarcity. What drove the economy, therefore, was production. The task of economic life (and, to those who believed that the state had a role to play in the economy, the task of public life) was to promote investment and production, to ensure that new factories were built, new crops were harvested, new energy sources were exploited. Economic life also required consumption, of course, but if production could be sustained and enhanced, then consumption would automatically follow.[17]

By the beginning of the 1940s, many Americans—and in particular many of those most interested in defining a role for government in the economy—had begun to embrace new assumptions. No longer did the problems of production dominate their thinking about public policy; those problems, they believed, had been largely solved. There was now no real danger of scarcity; the danger now was inadequate consumption. Consumption, not production, was now the principal force in the modern economy. Consumption drove production, not the other way around.[18] This was a significant redefinition of the nation's fundamental economic goals and, by implication, of its political goals. And the question naturally arises of why it occurred.

Anyone familiar with recent scholarship in twentieth-century American history will be aware that these new economic assumptions reflect parallel changes in popular culture—changes that have been the subject of an important literature in the last two decades exploring advertising, public education, family behavior, and other social and cultural issues. That literature has made a powerful case for the ways in which the ideas of abundance and consumption were defining the concepts of the "American dream" and the "American way of life" in the first half of the twentieth century. It is reasonable to assume, although such things are hard to demonstrate in decisive ways, that these cultural shifts were penetrating economic and political thought as well.[19]

But it was not just cultural phenomena that were changing political assumptions. It was, among other things, the economy itself, which had come to rely much more heavily on the production and sale of consumer goods than it had in the past. It was the economic boom of the 1920s, which had been driven largely by consumer spending on automobiles, appliances, and housing, and which had suggested that the traditional problems of scarcity and the traditional preoccupation with production might have become obsolete. And most of all, it was the Great Depression, which (whether or not correctly) was widely interpreted not as a problem of inadequate production but as a crisis of underconsumption and which thus reinforced the idea that the principal mission of economic life should now be to raise purchasing power and stimulate aggregate demand.[20]

The specific implications of these ideas for policy were not, at first, entirely clear through most of the 1930s. Slowly, however, one set of ideas became central to the liberal concept of the state. Government could stimulate consumption quickly and easily by using its fiscal powers. It could spend money on public works and on jobs programs. It could fund relief and welfare mechanisms. It could accumulate deliberate deficits. Public spending was the best vehicle for attacking deflation and stabilizing the economy. It need no longer be considered a necessary evil, used sparingly to achieve particular ends; it could become a positive good, to be used lavishly to promote the health of the economy as a whole.

These are ideas now associated principally with John Maynard Keynes, who by the end of World War II had developed a substantial following in the American economics profession and in broader liberal circles. But long before Keynes had found any significant audience in America, ideas that are now considered "Keynesian" were receiving independent expression from many sources: from the popular economists William Trufant Foster and Waddill Catchings, who published a series of books in the 1920s and 1930s promoting public spending as the cure for underconsumption;[21] from academic economists such as John M. Clark, Arthur Gayer, and James Harvey Rogers, who promoted the concept of "counter-cyclical" public works spending throughout the 1930s;[22] and from Marriner Eccles, the chairman of the Federal Reserve Board beginning in 1934, who had read Foster and Catchings and admired them, and who (though he was, as head of the Fed, charged with overseeing monetary policy) was principally interested in fiscal matters. Eccles, who never read Keynes, was the principal Keynesian in the New Deal's inner circle in the mid- and late 1930s—a tireless and ultimately effective advocate of using public spending to increase purchasing power.[23]

The spending argument received an important (if indirect) boost in 1937, when the administration made substantial cuts in public funding of relief and public works in order to balance the budget and almost immediately precipitated a severe recession. It received another (more positive) boost in 1938, when (partly in response to Eccles) Roosevelt reversed himself and launched a massive new spending program, justifying it for the first time not in terms of the particular, targeted problems the spending might solve but in terms of the way it would contribute to the health of the economy as a whole.[24]

But to most liberals, the clearest confirmation of the value of public spending was World War II itself. Liberals may have derived little comfort from the performance of the War Production Board and the other war agencies. But they could not fail to be impressed with the way in which massive public spending helped end almost overnight a depression that had proved resistant to institutional reforms for more than a decade. Suddenly an economy that many Americans had feared was irretrievably stagnant was expanding more rapidly and dramatically than almost anyone had believed possible. The lessons for the future seemed obvious: the government's role in supervising the behavior of institutions was less important than its role in seeing to the health of the economy as a whole. Alvin Hansen, the principal American advocate of Keynesian ideas in the 1940s and a major figure in the New Deal, expressed the new faith toward the end of the war. "Clearly fiscal policy is now and will continue to be [the principal] factor in the functioning of the modern economy." Its purpose, he said, was "to develop a high-consumption economy so that we can achieve full employment. . . . A higher propensity to consume can . . . be achieved by a progressive tax structure combined with social security, social welfare, and community consumption expenditures." If World War I's legacy to American political economy was the dream of an "ordered economic world," a more rational distribution and exercise of corporate power, World War II's legacy was the dream of full employment and economic growth.[25]

By 1945, therefore, many American liberals were rallying to a new concept of the state, substantially different from those they had embraced at the end of World War I. It was now possible, they believed, to achieve economic growth without constant involvement in the internal affairs of corporations, which was both endlessly complex and politically difficult. It was now possible for the state to manage the economy without managing the institutions of the economy. The state had already succeeded in curbing the most egregious abuses of corporate behavior, through the regulatory initiatives and labor legislation of the 1930s. The task now was to find a way for government to compensate for capitalism's remaining flaws: through aggressive fiscal policies and through expanded welfare and social insurance mechanisms. The task was to build not a corporate state nor a regulatory state, but a compensatory state.

All this is not to say that the liberals of the 1940s had consciously repudiated the dreams of their forebears a generation before. They still used much of the same language. They still spoke of planning. They still hoped for economic harmony and order. They still dreamed of what Walter Lippmann, thirty years earlier, had called "mastery." But those words meant different things in 1945 than they had meant in 1918. They referred, for example, to the principal liberal initiative of 1945: the so-called Full Employment bill, which would commit the federal government to aggressive fiscal policies to sustain purchasing power at high levels at all times. And they referred to the raft of legislative initiatives that Harry Truman promoted throughout his eight years as president: the expansion of social security, the creation of national health insurance, the construction of public housing, the protection of the consumer. The older, more institutional dreams—of partnerships between government and business, of planning production and investment (or what we now call "industrial policy"), of extensive state regulation of corporate behavior—had come, in the view of many Americans, to seem politically unrealistic, bureaucratically impossible, and socially dangerous. But most of all, to many liberals, at least, they had come to seem irrelevant.

And yet when one looks back from the perspective of a later era at the bright liberal hopes of 1945, it is hard not to sense that the confidence of that time was to some degree misplaced. Liberals in the postwar decades did follow, and to some degree still follow, the path they devised for themselves in the 1940s. But the weak and embattled liberal state that has emerged from their efforts has fallen far short of their hopes—its cumbersome and inadequate welfare mechanisms battling constantly for legitimacy, with uncertain results; its primitive fiscal mechanisms never coming close to fulfilling the liberal dreams of the 1940s and ultimately, in the 1980s, becoming a grotesque inversion of the Keynesian model; its claim on popular loyalties consistently frail.

Nor is it at all clear that the model of state development liberals rejected in the 1940s—the model of war mobilization, of the War Industries Board and the War Production Board—was as irrelevant to the nation's future as they believed it to be. For in the postwar era there emerged—alongside this frail and struggling liberal state—what became, in a sense, a second government: a national security state, powerful, entrenched, constantly expanding, and largely invulnerable to political attacks; a state that forged intimate partnerships with the corporate world, constantly blurring the distinctions between public and private; and a state that produced some of the very things— strengthened private monopolies and expanded state power to sustain them— that the liberal vision was supposed to prevent.[26]

Sometime in the early 1930s (it is not clear exactly when), Franklin Roosevelt read a book by William T. Foster and Waddill Catchings, the proto-Keynesian popular economists who helped draw public attention to the idea of dealing with economic problems through public spending. The book was called *The Road to Plenty,* and its distinctly Utopian overtones made it reminiscent of William Harvey's free silver tract of thirty years earlier, *Coin's Financial School. The Road to Plenty* outlined what Foster and Catchings considered a safe, painless, and certain route to prosperity and social justice: a redirection of government's efforts away from the profitless (and, in their view, dangerous) effort to manage economic institutions and toward the safer and more promising effort to manage the aggregate economy through taxation and public spending, through attention to consumption instead of to investment. Roosevelt's copy of the book is in the Franklin D. Roosevelt Library in Hyde Park. It contains his marginal commentary, of the sort one sometimes finds scrawled in books in undergraduate libraries. Toward the end, he recorded a general reaction: "Too good to be true—You can't get something for nothing."[27]

Later, of course, Roosevelt seemed to change his mind, if not about Foster and Catchings themselves then about the general constellation of ideas they expressed. But there is, I think, room to wonder whether, had Roosevelt lived to see where this new concept of the liberal state would eventually lead, he might have concluded that he had it right the first time.

NOTES

1. Walter Lippmann, *Drift and Mastery: An Attempt to Diagnose the Current Unrest* (New York: Mitchell Kennerley, 1914), pp. 147–148; Lippmann expressed similar hopes for the war itself in the spring of 1917 in "The World Conflict in its Relation to American Democracy," *The Annals* 72 (July 1917), 7–8.

2. Bernard M. Baruch, *American Industry in the War* (New York: Prentice-Hall,

1941), pp. 105–106; Paul A. C. Koistinen, "The 'Industrial-Military Complex' in Historical Perspective: World War I," *Business History Review* 41 (1967), 393.

3. Grosvenor B. Clarkson, *Industrial America in the World War: The Strategy Behind the Line, 1917–1918* (Boston: Houghton Mifflin, 1923), pp. 312, 475–488.

4. Ellis W. Hawley, "Herbert Hoover and Economic Stabilization, 1921–22," in Hawley, ed., *Herbert Hoover as Secretary of Commerce* (Iowa City: University of Iowa Press, 1981), pp. 43–77; Robert F. Himmelberg, *The Origins of the National Recovery Administration: Business, Government, and the Trade Association Issue, 1921–1933* (New York: Fordham University Press, 1976), pp. 43–74; Louis Galambos, *Competition and Cooperation: The Emergence of a National Trade Association* (Baltimore: Johns Hopkins University Press, 1966), pp. 89–138; Rexford G. Tugwell, *The Industrial Discipline and the Governmental Arts* (New York: Columbia University Press, 1933), pp. 4–6, 189–219; Tugwell, *The Democratic Roosevelt* (Garden City: Doubleday, 1957), pp. 229–230, 284–286, 308–311; Adolf A. Berle, Jr., and Gardiner C. Means, *The Modern Corporation and Private Property* (New York: Macmillan, 1932), pp. v., 124–125, 352, and 356; Charles R. Van Hise, *Concentration and Control: A Solution of the Trust Problem in the United States* (New York: Macmillan, 1912), esp. pp. 8–20, 277–278. For a discussion of the roots of New Deal corporatism in the decades preceding the Depression, see (in addition to the works cited above) Donald Brand, *Corporatism and the Rule of Law: A Study of the National Recovery Administration* (Ithaca: Cornell University Press, 1988), Part I.

5. Clifford Durr, "The Postwar Relationship Between Government and Business," *American Economic Review* 33 (1943), 47. See also George Soule, "The War in Washington," *The New Republic* 101 (September 27, 1939), 205–206; "New Deal Plans Industry Council," *Business Week,* March 20, 1943, p. 15.

6. Robert D. Cuff, "American Mobilization for War 1917–1945: Political Culture vs Bureaucratic Administration," in N. F. Dreisiger, ed., *Mobilization for Total War: The Canadian, American, and British Experience, 1914–1918, 1937–1945* (Waterloo, Ont.: Wilfred Laurier University Press, 1981), p. 80.

7. *New York Times,* September 21, 1948; *New York World Telegram and Sun,* March 10, 1950; W. M. Jeffers to Eberstadt, March 20, 1950, Eberstadt Papers, Box 116, Princeton University Library; Eliot Janeway, "Where was Mr. Nelson?" *Saturday Review,* September 7, 1946, p. 11; Eberstadt letter to multiple correspondents, August 23, 1946, Eberstadt Papers, Box 116.

8. The best account of economic mobilization during World War I is Robert D. Cuff, *The War Industries Board: Business-Government Relations during World War I* (Baltimore: The Johns Hopkins University Press, 1973). For World War II, see Richard Polenberg, *War and Society: The United States, 1941–1945* (Philadelphia: J. B. Lippincott, 1972), chapters 1, 6; and Alan Brinkley, *The End of Reform: New Deal Liberalism in Recession and War* (New York: Alfred A. Knopf, 1995), chapter 8.

9. I. F. Stone wrote caustically of the WPB in 1942, in a statement typical of liberal complaints: "The arsenal of democracy . . . is still being operated with one eye on the war and the other on the convenience of big business. . . . [T]he men running the program are not willing to fight business interests on behalf of good will and good intentions." Stone, "Donald Nelson Has Chosen," *Nation,* March 21, 1942, p. 332. See also Stone, "Nelson and Guthrie," ibid., June 27, 1942, p. 731; Michael Straight,

"Dollar-a-Year Sabotage," *New Republic,* March 30, 1942, p. 418; "Don Nelson's Men," *Business Week,* July 4, 1942, pp. 50–52; "The Pain and the Necessity," *Time,* June 29, 1942, p. 18; *Kiplinger Washington Letter,* August 15, 1942, Nelson Papers, Box 2, Huntington Library, San Marino, Calif.; Bruce Bliven to Max Lerner, August 24, 1942, Lerner Papers, Box 1, Yale University Library.

10. David M. Kennedy, *Over Here: The First World War and American Society* (New York: Oxford University Press, 1980), pp. 55–56, 62–69; John Higham, *Strangers in the Land* (New Brunswick: Rutgers University Press, 1963), pp. 201–202; Paul L. Murphy, *World War I and the Origin of Civil Liberties in the United States* (New York: W. W. Norton, 1979), chapters 4–5.

11. See Allan M. Winkler, *The Politics of Propaganda: The Office of War Information, 1942–1945* (New Haven: Yale University Press, 1978), pp. 38–72; John Morton Blum, *V Was for Victory: Politics and American Culture during World War II* (New York: Harcourt Brace Jovanovich, 1976), pp. 45–52; Clayton R. Koppes and Gregory D. Black, *Hollywood Goes to War: How Politics, Profits and Propaganda Shaped World War II Movies* (Berkeley: University of California Press, 1987), pp. 82–112, 278–316.

12. Reinhold Niebuhr, *The Children of Light and the Children of Darkness* (New York: Charles Scribner's Sons, 1945), p. 117. See also Niebuhr, "The Collectivist Bogy," *Nation,* October 21, 1944, pp. 478–480.

13. Friedrich A. Hayek, *The Road to Serfdom* (Chicago: University of Chicago Press, 1944); Hayek to Walter Lippmann, April 6, 1937, Walter Lippmann Papers, Series III, Box 77, Yale University Library. See also Theodore Rosenof, *Patterns of Political Economy: The Failure to Develop a Democratic Left Synthesis in America, 1933–1950* (New York: Garland, 1983), pp. 228–232; Rosenof, "Freedom, Planning, and Totalitarianism: The Reception of F. A. Hayek's *Road to Serfdom,*" *Canadian Review of American Studies* 5 (Fall 1974), 150–160.

14. James T. Flynn, "Other People's Money," *New Republic,* January 26, 1938, p. 337; Walter Millis, "Cross Purposes in the New Deal," *Virginia Quarterly Review* 14 (Summer 1938), 357–367. The best account of the NRA is Ellis W. Hawley, *The New Deal and the Problem of Monopoly* (Princeton: Princeton University Press, 1966), chapters 1–7. See also Brand, *Corporatism and the Rule of Law.*

15. "National Minima for Labor," *New Republic,* December 1, 1937, p. 88; "Again— The Trust Problem," *New Republic,* January 19, 1938, p. 295; "A New NRA," *Nation,* March 25, 1939, p. 337; "Liberals Never Learn," *Nation,* March 18, 1939, p. 309; George Soule, "This Recovery: What Brought It? Will It Last?" *Harper's,* March 1937, p. 342; Robert Jackson, speech entitled "Business Confidence and Government Policy," December 26, 1937, Raymond Clapper Papers, Box 200, Manuscripts Division, Library of Congress.

16. Thurman Arnold, *The Folklore of Capitalism* (New Haven: Yale University Press, 1937), pp. 221, 268; Arnold, "Feathers and Prices," *Common Sense,* July, 1939, p. 6; William E. Leuchtenburg, "The New Deal and the Analogue of War," in John Braeman et al., eds., *Change and Continuity in Twentieth-Century America* (Columbus: Ohio State University Press, 1964), p. 135.

17. Alan Brinkley, "Origins of the 'Fiscal Revolution,'" *Storia NordAmericana* 6 (1989), 37–39.

18. Ibid., pp. 37–42.

19. On the role of the advertising industry in encouraging and legitimizing consumption, see Roland Marchand, *Advertising the American Dream, 1920–1940* (Berkeley: University Of California Press, 1985), 25–43, 120–163; Stuart Ewen, *Captains of Consciousness: Advertising and the Social Roots of the Consumer Culture* (New York: McGraw-Hill, 1976), pp. 81–109; T. J. Jackson Lears, "From Salvation to Self-Realization: Advertising and the Therapeutic Roots of the Consumer Culture, 1880–1930," in Lears and Richard Wightman Fox, eds., *The Culture of Consumption: Critical Essays in American History, 1880–1890* (New York: Pantheon, 1983), pp. 1–38.

20. Michael Bernstein, *The Great Depression: Delayed Recovery and Economic Change in America, 1929–1939* (New York: Cambridge University Press, 1987), pp. 21–40; Stanley Lebergott, *Pursuing Happiness: American Consumers in the Twentieth Century* (Princeton: Princeton University Press, 1993), pp. 69–72, 148.

21. William Trufant Foster and Waddill Catchings, *Money* (Boston: Houghton Mifflin, 1923), pp. 351–356; Foster and Catchings, *Profits* (Boston: Houghton Mifflin, 1925), pp. v–vi, 223–246, 398–418; Foster and Catchings, *Business Without a Buyer* (Boston: Houghton Mifflin, 1927), pp. v–vii; Foster and Catchings, *The Road to Plenty* (Boston: Houghton Mifflin, 1928), pp. 3–10.

22. Arthur D. Gayer, *Public Works in Prosperity and Depression* (New York: National Bureau of Economic Research, 1935), pp. 366–401; John M. Clark, *Economics of Planning Public Works* (Washington: The National Planning Board, 1935), pp. 155–159; Alan Sweezy, "The Keynesians and Government Policy, 1933–1939," *American Economic Review* 62 (May 1972), 118–119; James Harvey Rogers to Marvin McIntyre, October 28, 1937, James Roosevelt to Rogers, November 8, 1937, Rogers to Robert S. Shriver, December 9, 1937, all in Rogers Papers, Box 21, Yale University Library; Byrd L. Jones, "James Harvey Rogers: An Intellectual Biography," Ph.D. diss., Yale University, 1966, pp. 146, 175, 210–211, 297, and 506–507.

23. Brinkley, "Origins of the 'Fiscal Revolution,'" pp. 48–56.

24. Herbert Stein, *The Fiscal Revolution in America* (Chicago: University of Chicago Press, 1969), chapters 6–7; Dean L. May, *From New Deal to New Economics: The American Liberal Response to the Recession of 1937* (New York: Garland, 1981).

25. Alvin Hansen, "Planning Full Employment," *Nation* 159 (October 21, 1941), 492; Hansen to Marriner Eccles, August 18, 1944, enclosing a copy of "Postwar Employment Program," August 17, 1944, Eccles Papers, Box 7, Folder 12, University of Utah Library; "Is There a New Frontier?" *New Republic,* November 27, 1944, pp. 708–710; "A New Bill of Rights," *Nation,* March 20, 1943, 402; Stein, *Fiscal Revolution,* pp. 175–77.

26. The literature describing the origins and character of what has come to be known as the military-industrial complex is vast. C. Wright Mills was among the first scholars to describe its characteristics in *The Power Elite* (New York: Oxford University Press, 1956), pp. 171–224. William Appleman Williams, similarly, cited the "military-industrial complex" as part of "an imperial complex" that dominated American foreign policy and political economy; see *Americans in a Changing World: A History of the United States in the Twentieth Century* (New York: Harper & Row, 1978), p. 375. Daniel Yergin describes the complex as a central element of the "national-security state" in *Shattered Peace: The Origins of The Cold War and the National Security State* (Boston: Houghton Mifflin, 1977). See also Paul A. C. Koistinen, *The Military-Industrial Complex: A Histori-*

cal Perspective (New York: Praeger, 1980), and "Mobilizing the World War II Economy"; Bruce G. Brunton, "The Origins and Early Development of the American Military-Industrial Complex," Ph.D. diss., University of Utah, 1989, and "An Historical Perspective on the Future of the Military-Industrial Complex," *Social Science Journal* 28 (1991), 45–62; Charles A. Cannon, "The Military-Industrial Complex in American Politics, 1953–1970," Ph.D. diss., Stanford University, 1975; Gregory Hooks, *Forging the Military-Industrial Complex: World War II's Battle of the Potomac* (Urbana: University of Illinois Press, 1991); Steve Fraser, *Labor Will Rule: Sidney Hillman and the Rise of American Labor* (New York: The Free Press, 1991), pp. 481–483; Gerald D. Nash, "The West and the Military-Industrial Complex," *Montana* 40 (1990), 72–75; Ben Baack and Edward Ray, "The Political Economy of the Origins of the Military-Industrial Complex in the United States," *Journal of Economic History* 45 (1985), pp. 369–375; Roger W. Lotchin, "The Political Culture of the Metropolitan-Military Complex," *Social Science History* 16 (1992), 275–299; Huntington, *The Soldier and the State,* chapters 12–13; Gautam Sen, "The Economics of US Defense: The Military Industrial Complex and Neo-Marxist Economic Theories Reconsidered," *Millennium: Journal of International Studies* 15 (1986), 179–195.

27. Foster and Catchings, *Road to Plenty,* pp. 3–10; Arthur M. Schlesinger, Jr., *The Crisis of the Old Order* (Boston: Houghton Mifflin, 1957) pp. 134–136.

Chapter 10

WOMEN, POLITICS, PHILANTHROPY: SOME HISTORICAL ORIGINS OF THE WELFARE STATE

Kathleen D. McCarthy

ONE OF THE most provocative questions to emerge from the field of women's studies asks why women in the United States exercised considerable political influence before winning the right to vote. Denied access to direct political participation at the federal level for almost a century and a half after Independence, middle-class women nonetheless left their distinctive imprint on the country's laws, its public services, and its "maternalist" social agendas for women and children. This in turn raises a number of related questions concerning the boundaries between "public" and "private" activities, politics and the voluntary sphere. Are these realms genuinely separate, or do we need to devise new ways of thinking about government that embrace ostensibly "private" philanthropic and nonprofit initiatives more fully? Women's activities provide an ideal laboratory for tracing the role of philanthropy— "gifts of time, money or material goods for public purposes"—in enabling even politically disadvantaged groups to shape the course of American government and the rise of the welfare state.[1]

Unlike the United States, most industrialized nations developed their welfare states around the needs of male breadwinners rather than women and children. Aside from Civil War veterans' pensions, which were categorized as a military expense, the first widespread public welfare initiatives in the United States were the forty-one state programs to provide mothers' pensions, and the federal grants-in-aid for child health activities mandated by the Sheppard-Towner Act in the 1920s. The United States Children's Bureau (USCB), which administered the Sheppard-Towner funds, was the first national bureaucracy in any country to be created and managed almost entirely by women. Theda Skocpol describes the organization as "an internationally distinctive maternalist welfare state" headed and administered by female professionals.[2]

Skocpol and others have traced these patterns to the power of women's networks. What began as isolated charitable endeavors at the threshold of the nineteenth century matured into a dense array of local, state, and national women's organizations after the Civil War. By 1900, they were "knit together in huge, nation-spanning federations, networks that paralleled the local/

state/national structures of U.S. parties and government." This organizational infrastructure enabled groups like the Women's Trade Union League, women's clubs, the National Consumer's Leagues and the National Congress of Mothers to spread ideas and marshall volunteers for lobbying efforts with impressive speed. Their numbers were impressive as well. For example, the National Congress (which later became the PTA) counted over 190,000 members in 37 states as of 1920.[3]

But just underscoring the existence of these groups falls short of explaining how they actually functioned as networks, and why they were so effective as a policymaking bloc. Some scholars, such as Kathryn Kish Sklar, and Seth Koven and Sonya Michel, have concluded that the efficacy of "women's activism is inversely related to the power of the state," and that the weakest governments will produce the strongest civil societies, opening wider opportunities for public influence for women. However, this interpretation still leaves a host of unanswered questions. For example, why were voteless women able to assume such an important policymaking role?[4]

Three factors are particularly important for understanding women's roles within the United States before 1920: (1) the extent to which service provision was historically rooted in public/private partnerships; (2) the fact that middle-class women used philanthropy—particularly their ability to build organizations through an economy of time rather than money—to carve out a significant role for themselves within this context; and (3) the ways in which they used these activities to forge their own "parallel power structures" that resembled, but rarely precisely replicated, the commercial and political arenas of men.[5]

Public/private partnerships were deeply rooted in the American past, tracing their origins to the colonial era. A few examples suffice to illustrate this point: Benjamin Franklin helped to launch the Pennsylvania Hospital for Sick Poor in 1751 by raising funds through his newspaper to match a £2000 challenge grant offered by the colonial assembly. Harvard began to blend endowment income and private gifts with legislative grants and tuition fees in the seventeenth century. Colonial New Yorkers conducted private subscription campaigns to augment the city's outlays for poor relief, while Virginia funneled its welfare funds through the vestrymen of the Anglican Church. In each instance, public and private resources and revenues were blended in the provision of public services.[6]

These trends were strengthened by the Revolution. Unlike its European counterparts, the American government was cast in the crucible of skeptical Enlightenment thought, and tinged with a strong distrust of the corrupting influence of political power. As such, the federal government was initially designed with only limited authority, including a circumscribed capacity to tax that was reflected at the state and local levels as well.

While popular misgivings and scanty tax revenues limited governmental capacities to deliver public services, constitutional guarantees of the right of citizens "peaceably to assemble and to petition the Government for a redress of grievances" encouraged the growth of citizen initiatives. Although not initially conceived as a manifesto for voluntary associations, First Amendment assurances of the right to assemble and petition for legislative change opened opportunities for even disfranchised groups to participate in public policy-making.

Geographical expansion played a role as well. In 1790, the United States consisted essentially of a strip settlement along the Atlantic seacoast. Seventy years later it stretched three thousand miles across the continent to the Pacific Ocean. This rapid growth engendered a voracious appetite for educational and welfare services in newly minted towns across the moving frontier. Since government funding for these services was limited, the need for continuing public/private partnerships added a value to women's volunteer activities that they might not have attained in a more centralized political milieu, or a less volatile geographical setting.

In the process, middle- and upper-class women were involved in extra-political activities that enhanced their political and economic roles. Prior to the introduction of Married Women's Property Acts in the mid-nineteenth-century, the common-law doctrine of *femme couverte* prohibited wives from owning and alienating property in their own right. Nor did they legally control their dowries or wages. Indeed, women's legal dependency on their husbands was one of the arguments used to deny them the vote, since wives were deemed incapable of acting independently from their spouses.[7]

But once they gathered together to form a legally chartered charitable corporation, even married women assumed a part of a collective identity that imbued them with legal prerogatives that they lacked as individuals, including the right to buy, sell, and invest property and to sign binding contracts. They gained a voice in public policymaking as well. Despite their political invisibility, the women who ran urban charities were often quite adept at lobbying for municipal appropriations for their organizations.[8]

They also exercised significant economic roles under the mantle of what would now be termed "nonprofit entrepreneurship." As the combined forces of industrialization and marketization gathered momentum, many middle-class white women were eased out of the paid workforce. Although opinions vary about the degree of leisure this created for them, by 1830 some of these women began to have more surplus time to contribute to voluntary activities than either their spouses or working-class women or men. In an economy of scarcity where only limited funds were available for charitable activities, volunteer labor often provided the margin that guaranteed institutional survival.[9]

Men, rather than women, were more likely to build their nonprofit organizations on a solid framework of private donations, occasionally resorting to joint-stock companies to ensure long-term sustainability. Women, on the other hand, built institutions such as orphanages through contributions of time and domestic skills, often cooking, sewing, and caring for the inmates themselves. They also became highly adept at income generation, turning handmade household goods into cash through charity fairs, benefits and bazaars, activities that culminated in the million-dollar profits generated for the Union troops through Civil War Sanitary Commission fairs.[10]

With the rise of America's first generation of millionaires in the wake of the Civil War, men's and women's philanthropic styles began to move in different directions. While wealthy businessmen such as John D. Rockefeller and Andrew Carnegie lavished massive donations on growing crops of foundations, universities, museums, and think tanks created in the corporate image of their business ventures, women—even very wealthy women—continued to build their own organizations through an economy of time, rather than cash. Middle- and upper-class women were the only group in America's industrializing economy with sufficient leisure and financial security to embrace voluntarism as a full-time career. This vocational advantage reinforced their ability to donate large amounts of time, thereby enhancing the importance of these donations within the arena of American governance.[11]

Philanthropic organizations also enjoyed a special status. That they operated outside the spheres of both the profit economy and of patronage politics reinforced their moral authority, enabling them to lobby for and to implement public programs. Underscoring "the political uses of moral rhetoric," Skocpol notes that "the party-based 'corruption' that many U.S. reformers associated with the implementation of Civil War pensions prompted them to argue that the United States could not administer any new social spending programs efficiently or honestly." Because of public fears about political corruption, "adult males could not become legitimate beneficiaries of public social spending for workers." Conversely, "women's rhetoric appeared to rise above narrowly partisan considerations" by invoking symbols of motherhood and "notions of selfless morality."[12]

Recent research suggests that women rather than men were the primary architects of the American welfare state, successfully promoting the introduction of "maternalist" legislation for mothers and children in the 1910s and 1920s, well before the New Deal programs that have traditionally been thought to mark the advent of modern American welfarism. Yet the point that should be stressed is that women's groups were able to do so because they relied so heavily on voluntarism, and could therefore develop even national public programs at minimal cost through what economists would term a "commodity of time" rather than money. Women's voluntary networks played an indispensable role in helping to implement the work of the Children's Bureau by distributing information and literature, coordinating local meetings, and conducting research. In the process, they also obviated the need for salaried, male-controlled administrative bureaucracies.

In effect, voluntary associations were unusually influential in weak governmental systems, such as that of the United States in this era, precisely because these countries lacked the funds to create large, permanent, public bureaucracies to administer welfare programs. Quite simply, strong governments and the elaborate bureaucratic infrastructures that support them cost money. And the American government did not have a great deal of surplus cash at its disposal before the 1930s. Moreover, public sentiment militated against the expansion of government spending, particularly after the veterans' pension programs became embroiled in pork barrel politics.[13]

In 1915, the tab for the pension program tallied over $6 million in Massachusetts alone. By comparison, the Children's Bureau initiated its national programs with an annual budget of $26,000 in 1912. By 1915, that figure had risen to $165,000. When the Bureau was charged with the administration of the national grants-in-aid program for the Sheppard Towner program in 1921, its annual appropriations finally topped the million dollar mark. With that amount of money it distributed 22 million pieces of literature, coordinated 183,000 health conferences, and established almost 3,000 clinics for prenatal care. It simply would not have been possible to achieve a record like this without the aid of a virtual army of unpaid workers.[14]

Ironically, when women won the vote in 1920, much of their former moral authority was lost, because the voting returns revealed the extent to which the "female dominion" created by alliances of women reformers, professionals, and volunteers was a middle-class construct that never truly represented American womanhood as a whole. To quote historian Paula Baker, "Women gained little real public power upon winning the vote." Once the suffrage amendment was ratified, all of the centrifugal forces of class and kin, ethnicity, religion, and race surfaced, dissipating the political clout inherent in the power of numbers, which had traditionally undergirded women's organizations as the basis of their political authority.[15]

There were professional implications as well. Robyn Muncy's book *Creating a Female Dominion for Reform* highlights the dichotomies surrounding men's and women's professional cultures during the period from 1900 to 1930. Social settlements played a particularly important role in the promotion of "maternalist" legislation. They also provided the primary base for female researchers in medicine, social work, and social policy, since discriminatory hiring practices generally barred women from the faculties of the nation's leading research universities. Like the majority of nonprofit organizations run by women, Chicago's renowned Hull House operated on a shoestring budget for much of its history, backed primarily by its founder, Jane Addams, and two close female friends. Nonetheless, it served as a major institutional resource for training, research, and career development by and for a spate of prominent female experts and policymakers, including the head of the Children's Bureau, Julia Lathrop.[16]

While male social scientists ascended through the ranks of academe, even the most gifted women professionals remained mired in charity before they began to acquire government jobs. Addams initially tried to support researchers at Hull House by conscripting women donors to provide monthly $50 fellowships to cover the residents' salaries.[17]

Those who found these charitable relationships too constraining (or demeaning) eventually turned their attention to the pursuit of government jobs. As a result, women, rather than men, took the lead in calling for the creation of public welfare services. As Skocpol explains, they were far more likely "to favor the expansion of the public sector through reform, rather than its contraction in deference to business preferences for low taxes and business-oriented government." Their crowning achievement was the creation of the Children's Bureau. Ignored by the universities, foundations, and think tanks supported by and for men, women embraced the state. And in view of the Jeffersonian bias against the state that Arthur Schlesinger emphasizes, it is interesting that women endorsed the expansion of government-funded social welfare programs as a positive idea.[18]

It proved to be a precarious strategy. As it became increasingly apparent that female voters would not cast their ballots as a cohesive gender bloc after they won the vote in 1920, the political influence of women reformers waned. Federal appropriations for the Sheppard Towner program, which was the main source of revenue for the Children's Bureau, began to be phased out in 1927. To quote Muncy, as child welfare services "slid into the mainstream of public policy, women lost their exclusive hold" on these programs, and the public dominion created by settlement-trained researchers and social workers "dissolved."[19]

How does this analysis alter our understanding of the political roles of women's voluntary associations in the United States? Since the mid-1980s, a small but growing number of scholars have underscored the political nature of female voluntarism. One defined its primary role as gap-filling: providing services for causes and constituencies overlooked by political policymakers. Another lauded its contributions as "an early warning system" that continually identified and acted upon emerging needs. The analysis has been carried further by underscoring women's capacity to lobby effectively for public legislation and funds in the antebellum era. But it has also been suggested that these activities diminished before the Civil War, an interpretation that provides little continuity with the scenario that Skocpol describes.[20]

Contrary to some findings, women's voluntary associations continued to function as an inherent part of the American system of governance. Rather than simply filling gaps or identifying needs, they worked in tandem with government, blending their contributions as volunteers with public and private donations, income generation activities, and fees-for-service to provide crucial social welfare services. The special advantage that middle-class women brought to their charities and their legislative campaigns was their ability to run these organizations primarily through an economy of time, rather than relying on large-scale public or private expenditures. This ostensibly placed them above the marketplace, above the political arena, and above the scramble for extensive federal funding.

In the process, their organizations became powerful political tools in the decentralized and relatively impoverished governmental milieu of the United States. The federal government was often hamstrung in the expansion of its powers to implement national welfare programs in the decades before the New Deal, which led it to forge alliances with private philanthropies. Barry Karl and Stanley N. Katz have illustrated the extent to which large foundations created three-tier tracks of managerial elites that linked foundations, government, and academe, helping to develop and test public policies on a national scale in the early decades of the twentieth century. Similarly, women's groups that could volunteer the use of their existing local, state, and national infrastructures were ideally positioned to administer welfare initiatives on a national scale while applying minimal pressure on the public till.[21]

Toward the end of his treatise on democracy in the United States, Alexis de Tocqueville mused that if he were asked "to what the singular prosperity and growing strength of [the American] people ought mainly to be attributed," he would reply, "to the superiority of their women." For Tocqueville, the quintessential American woman was white, middle class, and politically invisible. Despite his keen perception of the importance of voluntary associations in fostering American governance and American democracy, he ultimately concluded that women in this country "irrecoverably" lost their independence "in the bonds of matrimony," and therefore they never "take part in political life."[22]

It was an odd omission, one that suggests that the normally canny French aristocrat fundamentally misinterpreted the extent and nature of the civil society that he sought to portray. Far from being apolitical, many middle-class housewives were deeply enmeshed in the practice of governance well before they won the right to vote. Over the past two centuries, American women effectively invested their time in building an array of public services. These activities enabled them to win political, economic, and legal prerogatives for themselves, and to accord women's and children's issues a prominent place on the public agenda.

Through a vast network of voluntary associations, middle-class and upper-class women (who became the country's primary leisure class in the wake of the industrial revolution) created parallel power structures at the local, state, and national levels that enabled them to expand their own prerogatives while promoting social change to a degree unmatched in other industrialized nations. In the process, they managed to shape American government and the American welfare state from the periphery of the political arena. Ironically, philanthropy, rather than the franchise, was the key to their success.

Notes

1. Definitions of nonprofits and philanthropy are discussed in Lester M. Salamon, *America's Nonprofit Sector: A Primer* (New York: The Foundation Center, 1992), 5–7.

2. Theda Skocpol, *Protecting Soldiers and Mothers: The Political Origins of Social Policy in the United States* (Cambridge: Harvard University Press, 1992), 526.

3. Ibid., 529, 336.

4. Kathryn Kish Sklar, "A Call for Comparisons," *American Historical Review* 95:4 (October 1990): 1112; Sonya Michel and Seth Koven, "Womanly Duties: Maternalist Politics and the Origins of Welfare States in France, Germany, Great Britain, and the United States, 1880–1920," *American Historical Review* 95:4 (October 1990), 1079.

5. Political scientists have recently begun to examine the role of "third-party government." This is the idea that beginning in the 1930s, the American welfare state was built on webs of public/private partnerships between government and nonprofit organizations, rather than the expansion of permanent federal bureaucracies for the delivery of many public services. Funded by varying combinations of individual, corporate, and foundation donations; state, local, and federal contracts and grants; endowment income; and in-kind donations, volunteer time, and fees for service, nonprofits constitute one of the cornerstones of American governance by virtue of their roles in the provision of public health, educational, and welfare services. See, for example, Salamon, *America's Nonprofit Sector,* chapter 4. The concept of "parallel power structures" is discussed in Kathleen D. McCarthy, "Parallel Power Structures: Women and the Voluntary Sphere," in McCarthy, ed., *Lady Bountiful Revisited: Women, Philanthropy and Power* (New Brunswick: Rutgers University Press, 1990), 1–54.

6. Gary B. Nash, *The Urban Crucible: Social Change, Political Consciousness, and the Origins of the American Revolution* (Cambridge: Harvard University Press, 1979), 254, 188; Peter Dobkin Hall, *Inventing the Nonprofit Sector* (Baltimore: Johns Hopkins University Press, 1992), 17; Raymond A. Mohl, *Poverty in New York, 1783–1825* (New York: Oxford University Press, 1971), 45; Rhys Isaac, *The Transformation of Virginia, 1740–1790* (New York: W. W. Norton, 1982), 65.

7. Linda K. Kerber, *Women of the Republic: Intellect and Ideology in Revolutionary America* (Chapel Hill: University of North Carolina Press, 1980), 9, 120.

8. For a fuller discussion of these issues, see McCarthy, "Parallel Power Structures," and Lori D. Ginzberg, *Women and the Work of Benevolence: Morality, Politics and Class in the Nineteenth-Century United States* (New Haven: Yale University Press, 1990).

9. On the issue of middle-class women and leisure, see Jeanne Boydston, *Home and Work: Housework, Wages, and the Ideology of Labor in the Early Republic* (New York: Oxford University Press, 1990).

10. The Sanitary Fairs are discussed in Ginzberg, *Women and the Work of Benevolence,* chapter 5.

11. These differences are discussed more fully in Kathleen D. McCarthy, *Women's Culture: American Philanthropy and Art, 1830–1930* (Chicago: University of Chicago Press, 1991); Kathleen D. McCarthy, "Women and Philanthropy: Three Strategies in Historical Perspective," Working Paper (New York: Center for the Study of Philanthropy, CUNY, 1994).

12. Skocpol, *Protecting Soldiers and Mothers,* 367, 59–60, 465, 368.

13. For example, in 1913, when the nation's first permanent income tax legislation was written into law, the entire federal budget for education was less than the annual budget of the Carnegie Corporation, a single private foundation.

14. Skocpol, *Protecting Soldiers and Mothers,* 142, 481.

15. Paula Baker, "The Domestication of Politics: Women and American Political Society, 1780–1920," *American Historical Review* 89:3 (June 1984): 645.

16. Robyn Muncy, *Creating a Female Dominion for Reform, 1890–1935* (New York: Oxford University Press, 1991). For the settlement's financial history, see Kathryn Kish Sklar, "Who Funded Hull House?" in McCarthy, ed., *Lady Bountiful Revisited,* 94–118.

17. Muncy, *Creating a Female Dominion,* 17.

18. Skocpol, *Protecting Soldiers and Mothers,* 355. However, the political power of women's networks reemerged in the New Deal. See, for example, Susan Ware, *Beyond Suffrage: Women in the New Deal* (Cambridge: Harvard University Press, 1981).

19. Muncy, *Creating a Female Dominion,* xvii.

20. Baker, "The Domestication of Politics"; Scott, *Natural Allies;* Ginzberg, *Women and the Work of Benevolence.*

21. Barry D. Karl and Stanley N. Katz, "The American Private Philanthropic Foundation and the Public Sphere, 1890–1930," *Minerva* 19:2 (Summer 1981), 236–270.

22. Alexis de Tocqueville, *Democracy in America* (1835, 1840; reprint, New York: Modern Library, 1981), 501, 488, 498.

Chapter 11

THE NEW LEFT, THE NEW RIGHT, AND THE NEW DEAL

FRED SIEGEL

"LISTEN TO these guys," my father shouted with a mixture of annoyance and admiration. It was 1986 and my parents and I were watching President Reagan introduce Frank Sinatra during the televised extravaganza honoring the Statue of Liberty's centennial. Frank Sinatra, like Reagan a former liberal Democrat, was singing "The House I Live In," a Popular Front standard celebrating an inclusive Americanism. "How did they pull this off?" my mother asked, not quite rhetorically. "How the hell can they enlist a Communist song in the cause of right-wing Republicanism?" And then my father, a copy of Arthur Schlesinger's *Crisis of the Old Order* visible on the shelf behind him, turned to me and growled, "You're the professor: how did Reagan steal the New Deal out from under the Democrats' noses?" "Reagan didn't exactly steal it," I replied. "He picked up what many Democrats had discarded in the disarray of the late 1960s."

Returning home, I rose to the bait and sent my parents a note. The short answer, I told them, came in two parts. First off, historians writing against the backdrop of the "revolutionary" 1960s downplayed Roosevelt's achievements by mistakenly assuming that the New Deal either missed a chance for radical change or was actively designed to squelch it. But the great mass movement of the early 1930s, I pointed out, was not proletarians on the march, but states' rights supporters of the repeal of prohibition triumphing over the power of the federal government.

Second, I wrote, "it's hard to remember that the first politically effective intellectual assault on the New Deal's attempt to reconcile liberty and equality came not from the Goldwaterites of the New Right but from the New Left of the 1960s." While an older generation had been impressed by the way the institutionalized conflicts that were built into the New Deal prevented all but the most distant resemblance to the overpowerful regimes of Europe, the New Left echoed both left- and right-wing isolationists in denouncing Roosevelt's "fascist" tendencies. Roosevelt's reputation, I argued, had been ground down by the ascendancy of New Left academics and New Right politicians. What follows is an extension of that brief answer I dashed off to my parents.

The standard bearers among the New Left historians of the New Deal, Barton Bernstein and Howard Zinn, paid scant attention to the political history of the early 1930s. Instead they assumed that forces unleashed by the Great Depression lead inexorably leftward, so that the only measure of Roosevelt's achievement was how far he was willing to be carried by those currents. The New Left, like the old, argued that the sheer scope of the economic collapse compelled radical changes commensurate with the catastrophe.[1]

But in Britain, France, Canada, and Australia, the Great Depression produced not radical change but conservative governments appealing to the public demand for stability and order. In Canada, for instance, former prime minister W. L. Mackenzie King, whose slogan was "It's King or Chaos," was returned to power in 1935 in opposition to the New Deal style programs of his predecessor. Similarly, the 1931 British elections produced a largely Tory National government, the only British government of the twentieth century elected by a majority of the voters in Britain's three-party system.

Hoover's relative inaction was typical of the period. In Britain, Labor, led by Ramsay MacDonald, was paralyzed by the almost theological belief that there was no part-way point between a total transformation to socialism or a return to full-blooded laissez-faire. A practicing platonist of sorts, MacDonald, and for that matter almost all the leaders of the European left, saw practice as legitimate only when it was the shadow cast by theory. French socialists, Blum excepted, similarly refused to cooperate in any schemes to fight the depression. "Before any plan," they insisted on "the total conquest of power by socialism."[2]

If any of the candidates other than Roosevelt had won the 1932 Democratic nomination, it is likely that the United States would have remained as immobilized as the other industrial democracies. FDR's New Deal policies were opposed by all the living presidential nominees of both parties with the partial exception of his 1920 ticket-mate, James Cox, who gave lukewarm support. The 1924 Democratic nominee, John W. Davis, capturing the mood of what was still a Jeffersonian party doing battle with Republican Hamiltonians, condemned Hoover's tentative 1931 anti-depression measures for "following the road to socialism at a rate never before equaled in time of peace."[3]

Two of Roosevelt's rivals for the 1932 nomination, New York governor Al Smith and Maryland governor Albert Ritchie, both fervent supporters of states' rights, would join the Liberty League, and a third, Newton Baker, Woodrow Wilson's secretary of war and heir apparent, was so similar to Hoover on economic issues that a Baker race against Hoover would have centered on the tariff. A fourth rival, "Cactus" Jack Garner, who had served Texas in Congress since 1903 and was then Speaker of the House, proposed to end the Depression with a regressive national sales tax to balance the budget.[4]

"The great puzzle," wrote Walter Lippmann covering the 1932 Republican convention, "is the total absence of economic insurgency." The Western Progressives who might have been expected to raise hell had largely been beaten into a stunned quiescence by the collapse. Hoover was renominated without opposition. Lippmann pointed to a similar absence of action on the part of the Democratic-controlled House. Led by Garner, the bourbon-and-branch water Speaker, the House pursued a "don't disturb business" strategy, Lippmann noted. "The great majority of the people," he concluded, "is more concerned with defending and preserving what it has left than it is hopeful of much better things from experiments." The Democratic Party of the early 1930s was still the culturally divided party (united only by its opposition to the tariff) that had met in Madison Square Garden in 1924 and had been unable to condemn the KKK.[5]

With the exception of the Democrats' call for the repeal of Prohibition, neither party's 1932 platforms showed the slightest hint of innovation, though the Republican Party was somewhat more forward-looking on civil rights and economic policy. The keynote speaker at the Democrat's nominating convention, Senator Alben Barkley of Kentucky, captured the prevailing mood of a party dominated by saloonkeeps and segregationists. Depicting the Depression as retribution for a failure of faith, he called for a return to the old ways, back to Jeffersonian states' rights. The Democratic platform, which was "not conservative, but in the exact sense of the word reactionary," called for a balanced budget and drastic spending cuts as ways of reducing the size of government. The portions of the platform written by Wilsonians, who excised any attempt by the Bryanite wing of the party to call for a more activist economic policy, put forward free trade as the answer to all economic questions.[6]

The few times during the 1932 presidential election that Roosevelt enunciated thoughts that even approached the foothills of radicalism, as in his radio speech about the "forgotten men," the largely silent victims of Hoover's principled intransigence, he paid an unmistakable price. Al Smith, the party's 1928 nominee and the political hero of Catholic and big-city America, warned that he would "take off my coat" and "fight to the end against any candidate who persisted in a demagogic appeal . . . by setting class against class."[7]

For Smith, much beloved by the "what's-it-to-you," Irish, upwardly mobile wing of the New Deal coalition, talk of class conflict, however muted, was a threat to the promise of personal mobility that defined America. An attack on the promise, even in the midst of the Depression, was politically dangerous. In the period following the "forgotten man" speech, FDR's fortunes sunk to their lowest level; he was beaten badly (73–27 percent) by Smith in the Massachusetts primary, and finished behind Garner in a three-way race in California.

Smith's furious talk of Roosevelt's bolshevism was matched by Hoover's reaction to FDR's Commonwealth Club speech, in which Roosevelt unveiled the concept of a New Deal with mild proposals for a stronger administrative government. The "fighting Quaker" warned that the New Deal would regiment and bureaucratize. It was, he said, "sliding from abstraction into melodrama," "an un-American scheme," "a proposal to alter the whole foundation of our national life." Again FDR backed off, "reverting to the standard attacks on Republicans as the party of budget-busting centralizers."[8]

Roosevelt assumed office shadowed by two nearly simultaneous developments. On the one hand the great centralizer Hitler had taken power in Germany two months earlier; on the other, the 1932 elections were a great victory for the states'-rights supporters of prohibition repeal.

In the first year of the New Deal, repeal conventions around the country voted decisively for restoring the power of local government and protecting individual rights by ending prohibition. Acutely aware of the divisions within his own party, Roosevelt was faced with the dauntingly difficult task of reconciling the wet, urban, anti-federal, eastern Catholic wing of the party with its bitter, southern and western, dry, populist, and economically interventionist rivals.[9]

The rural, Protestant, Bryanite wing of the Democratic Party supported both economic and social intervention by the federal government to reduce economic inequality and impose prohibition. The urban Catholic half of the party, while culturally more tolerant, was also deeply hostile to a federal government powerful enough to impose either moral or economic regulation. FDR's achievement was to bring the two wings together. First in the campaign and then as president, Roosevelt mastered the art of what one commentator described derisively as the unprincipled "art of carrying water on both shoulders."[10]

Historians like to quote Raymond Moley's anecdote about how, when presented with two conflicting viewpoints, FDR told Moley to "weave them together" in order to note Roosevelt's indifference to substance. But in a party riven, wrote Lippmann, "Governor Roosevelt could only divide his own friends if he had a policy." It was Roosevelt's lack of dogmatism that allowed him to both win and govern, a talent lost to most Democrats since that era. Roosevelt, for instance, enraged friends and foes with his ability to both draw on and distance himself from Tammany Hall. "In the case of Mr. Roosevelt," wrote Lippmann, anticipating the confusions of critics to come, "it is not easy to say with certainty whether his left-wing or his right-wing supporters are more deceived."[11]

FDR, the driest of the Democratic candidates, managed to both draw on and distance himself from his Prohibitionist supporters, as embodied in his brilliant and double-edged 1930 slogan, "Bread, not booze." One reading suggested that it was time to focus on the Depression and not on cultural clashes. Another suggested to Prohibitionists that people ought to be spending their scant income on what was really important, sustenance instead of stupefaction. FDR, "the chameleon on plain," as Hoover derided him, chose as his chief political operative James Farley, a small-town dry Catholic who in his very person bridged the divisions within the party.

Roosevelt managed to forge the liberal New Deal out of a country at once insecure and conservative. His achievement in containing the cultural conflicts in his party could have been an instructive achievement for the liberal and left-wing historians of the 1960s and 1970s, another period of intense cultural conflict. But it wasn't. Instead an appreciation of Roosevelt's rare abilities were overshadowed by Reagan-like accusations about the "fascist" tendencies of the New Deal.

The impression that America was on the road to fascism took root on the pacifist left and the isolationist right in the mid-1930s when both predicted that war abroad entailed fascism at home. Haunted by the memories of post–World War I repression, Oswald Garrison Villard, the heir of the abolitionist tradition in American reform, charged that Roosevelt's "stupendous national debt, unbalanced budget, and vast public expenditures inevitably meant Fascism in one form or another." Norman Thomas, heir to the tradition of Debsian socialism, concurred with conservative isolationist Robert Taft. He agreed that war meant a "dictatorship" that would "live on even when exhaustion temporarily stills the guns."[12]

The increasingly centralized character of modern industrial societies fueled the critics' enduring assumptions about America's fascist fate. For Villard, the industrial concentrations described by Berle and Means, in their seminal 1933 study *The Modern Corporation and Private Property*, posed a mortal danger to the nineteenth-century traditions of limited government he assumed essential if America was to remain a free society. Both Villard and Thomas assumed, wrote George Orwell, that "industrialism must end in monopoly, and that monopoly must imply tyranny."[13]

The specter of an American fascism was carried into the postwar left-liberal world and eventually into the 1960s by a variety of writers, including Dwight Macdonald, who quipped that "Europe has its Hitlers but we have our Rotarians." But Macdonald's Menckenesqe hostility to the American middle class was less influential than writings of two remarkable figures, the radical sociologist C. Wright Mills and the neo-isolationist historian William Appleman Williams. They were to become godfathers to the New Left, not only by challenging the anti-Communism of the Cold War consensus but by arguing that anti-Communism itself was a manifestation of the disguised fascism the anti-New Dealers and isolationists had warned against.

"There are," wrote Mills in 1942, "structural trends in the political economy of the U.S. which parallel those of Germany." By 1956, writing at the moment when American industry reached an unprecedented level of concentration, Mills argued in *The Power Elite* (1956) that the corporate structure had put the United States in the grip of a controlling cabal almost as all powerful as those that had recently gone down to defeat.[14]

A parallel indictment came from University of Wisconsin historian William Appleman Williams. Williams had been convinced, even before his persecution by HUAC in the early 1960s, of the isolationist claim that Roosevelt's war for democracy abroad had produced something like dictatorship at home. Strongly influenced by Charles Beard, Williams helped define what would become the New Left with his influential *Contours of American History*. An antipolitical mytho-history in which elections go virtually unmentioned, *Contours* argues that America's commitments to private property and free markets lead inexorably to a future of either "literal isolation," as the United States is surpassed by the nations inspired by the Bolshevik Revolution, or "nuclear destruction."

Williams was supremely indifferent to totalitarianism abroad—the names of Stalin and Hitler are absent from the index to *Contours*—even as he could sniff it out in the most unlikely places in the United States. While Williams the isolationist minimized the impact of Nazism, Williams the life-long apologist for the Bolshevik coup as an expression of popular desires saw in the Soviet Union "a fundamental critique of capitalist society" that necessitated a militarized American response.[15] Williams became both a leading critic of American involvement in Vietnam and a convert of sorts to the counterculture. Tracing the war in Vietnam back in part to FDR's "corporate liberal" response to the Depression, Williams tried to redeem Herbert Hoover from the political hell into which he had been cast by the New Deal. He depicted Herbert Hoover as a Christ figure who had sacrificed himself to redeem America from a fascist "Hell-on-earth" imposed by treacherous cosmopolitans and internationalists. In a burst of 1960s pathos Williams urged the readers of the *New York Review of Books* to understand Hoover as a man who had been failed by the people. If you want to see why the martyred Hoover was forced to sic General MacArthur on the Bonus Army marchers, you must, Williams tells us, "listen to the Doors doing the first verse of 'the Soft Parade.'"[16]

Hoover, in fact, was not much of an anti-fascist. He had, through his close ties to the House of Morgan, been willing to supply financial credits to Mussolini. But if Williams, who was to become president of the Organization of American Historians, had written bad history, that was beside the point. His prose poems about "corporate liberalism" provided some of the most important lyrics for the 1960s music of political alienation.[17]

In the early 1960s a group of talented young academics influenced by Williams mounted a concerted attack on both the Cold War consensus and the New Deal tradition in the pages of the formative New Left journal *Studies on the Left*. Bringing together the losers in the debates of the 1940s, the Communists and the isolationists, the *Studies* iconoclasts at the University of Wisconsin redefined the New Deal as a "late capitalist" strategy for maintaining ruling class control.

Earlier leftists, anticipating the full scale transformation of the United States, had seen the struggles of farmers and workers as the engine of reform. But New Leftists, dismayed by the failure of capitalism to collapse after World War

II, relegated such struggles to mere shadow play. Drawing on the concept of what Gabriel Kolko had described as "political capitalism," they argued that New Deal reform was really the use by capitalists of "a centralized state power to meet problems they could not solve themselves." As with Mills writing on a "power elite," the particulars of how the executive committee of the bourgeoisie pulled the strings was left largely unspecified. What was clear, however, was the upshot—"co-optation." As noted by Howard Zinn, "In the United States every little rebellion, every crisis has been met with enough concessions to keep general resentment below the combustible level."

In a series of spirited debates with the New Deal's defenders, some *Studies* writers insisted that America had become as "complete a dictatorship as ever existed in history." This dictatorship was all the more insidious, it was argued, for being masked in the guise of formal democracy. "Hitler," it was asserted, "had no more power than John F. Kennedy—in fact he had less." The escalation of the war in Vietnam only confirmed the belief in American fascism—friendly at home and ferocious abroad.

The idea that liberalism was a disguised form of fascism became an article of faith for many in the New Left. Paul Potter of Students for a Democratic Society spoke to that faith in his influential 1964 "We Must Name the System" speech, which attributed the war in Vietnam, southern lynching, and "all the incalculable, innumerable more subtle atrocities that are worked on people all over—all the time," to what *Studies on the Left* called "corporate liberalism."

In the 1960s the "paranoid style" long associated with the anti-Roosevelt right took hold of the New Left and even many liberals. Fears of an incipient American totalitarianism were stoked by the writings of the Frankfurt school, a group of German intellectual exiles who had failed to see the rise of fascism in Germany but were convinced it was imminent in America. In Herbert Marcuse's *Eros and Civilization* and *One-Dimensional Man,* campus radicals found an erudite explanation for how American society could maintain the trapping of freedom even as it was organized to suppress both dissent and joy.

In the turmoil of the late 1960s, fears of "friendly fascism" were broadly popularized and widely disseminated far beyond narrow left-wing circles to what was broadly defined as the movement for a New Politics. The widely read journalist Peter Schrag captured the sentiments of New Politics activists, the activists who transformed the Democratic Party in the 1970s, when he wrote that the "tyranny of experts and planners isn't much of an improvement over a tyranny of gauleiters and commissars." In his book *The Decline of the WASP,* he laid the blame for cultural conformity at the New Deal's doorstep. Once praised for bringing forty million ethnic Americans into full citizenship by breaking the Protestant stranglehold on public life, the New Deal was now disdained as a dispenser of Protestant privilege. For Schrag the New Deal and the New Right were just different sides of the debased coin of middle-class sterility.[18]

Lost in Schrag's account were the real fascists and commissars confronted abroad, as well as American party politics. But he was hardly alone. Barton Bernstein's much-discussed and oft-praised "Conservative Achievements of Liberal Reform," probably the single most influential article written on the New Deal during the 1960s, was similarly lacking. Bernstein added little to criticisms of the New Deal that hadn't already been noted at length by historians more kindly disposed to Roosevelt. What was new was more a matter of attitude than evidence.

Written as part of a collection of New Left essays entitled *Toward a New Past,* Bernstein's article was indifferent to the distinctions between the early or the late New Deal, indifferent to party politics. In fact Bernstein was largely indifferent to all but one point—why the New Deal failed to measure up to his Aquarian expectations.

Bernstein faulted the New Deal for failing to create more social and racial equality, while at the same time he condemned as bureaucratic the institutions which furthered that end. Bernstein had, without realizing it, replicated the arguments of one of Roosevelt's most prominent left-liberal critics of the 1930s, Oswald Garrison Villard. The longtime editor of the *Nation,* Villard was unwilling to accept the need for trade-offs. He wanted a social welfare society without a welfare state. Like the New Leftists, Villard saw society as a kind of giant jigsaw puzzle. If you could only arrange all the pieces correctly it would be possible to fully and for all time reconcile liberty and equality. Villard began the 1930s as a left-wing critic of the New Deal, but, confronted with the permanence of a more powerful yet less idealistic government, he ended up prophetically for the New Left in a de facto alliance with Roosevelt's right-wing critics.[19]

Bernstein's article influenced historians, but the 1960s critique of New Deal liberalism reached its widest audience in Charles Reich's celebrated *Greening of America.* The book's mix of "apocalyptic anticipation and utopian aspiration" both captured and catalyzed the mood of the moment, turning the book into a publishing sensation when it first appeared in the pages of the *New Yorker.* *Greening* carried blurbs of praise from Justice William O. Douglas and Senator George McGovern, the latter of whom pronounced it "one of the most gripping, penetrating and revealing analyses of American Society I have yet seen."[20]

Many of Reich's claims about the sheer horror of machines and mass production had already been introduced into twentieth-century American culture by Lewis Mumford, who in the 1920s and 1930s had in turn been heavily influenced by Oswald Spengler's prophecies of Western decline. An elitist who endorsed egalitarianism, Reich mastered the technique of literary radicalism by both denouncing as drones the great mass of Americans, while flattering his readers who, by the very act of reading him, were among the elect who had heroically escaped the temptations of technology.[21]

The New Deal, said Reich, furthered the creation of a hierarchical, elitist society. Its bureaucracies betrayed the Whitmanesque dream of untrammeled individuality. It had failed utterly to solve any of "the great modern problems, such as a loss of meaning, loss of community and self." In fact, it had "encourage[d] the trends toward making them worse." Reich's accusation echoed those of the progressive Newton Baker, who decried the New Deal for shutting off America's "wide spiritual spaces" for the individual. He bemoaned the New Deal "departure from our old beliefs" about government, and he compared America under the New Deal to a Marxist ant colony.[22]

Baker, like Reich a constitutional lawyer, was particularly offended by the New Deal's hostility to the preeminent role of lawyers and legal formalism in politics. The New Deal emphasis on a government that got results clashed with the legal priesthood's insistence that all government activity be mediated through the courts. In 1969 the political scientist Theodore Lowi took up Baker's themes in his influential work *The End of Liberalism*. Lowi attacked the New Deal's experiments with planning as an attack on the rule of law and a mere masquerade for big business domination of the reform process.[23]

A decade later, the concept of "corporate liberalism" began to crumble with the collapse of the Carter administration. Politically, at least, Reagan's election in 1980 called into question the blinding revelation of first the New Left and then the New Politics Democrats. New Deal liberals, it turned out, were not "the real enemy," at least not anymore.

In 1982, four years before the Statue of Liberty festivities, there was another centenary, one that went largely unnoticed. The hundredth anniversary of Franklin Roosevelt's birth was virtually ignored by his own party. In 1974 the Democratic-controlled Congress appropriated seven million dollars for the upcoming Herbert Hoover centenary. But in the late seventies, when planning would have to get under way for the Roosevelt festivities, the Democratic-controlled Congress refused to do the same for FDR. At the same time President Carter, a Democrat whose history and presidential career were conspicuous by their distance from the New Deal tradition, "refused to lift a finger." It was left to a young unknown citizen, Peter Kovler, to organize the commemoration on his own. Congress, at Kovler's urgings, went along with a joint session in FDR's honor but insisted that the costs could not exceed $25,000.[24]

Ronald Reagan supported the idea of an FDR memorial enthusiastically, but in characteristic fashion never funded it. Reagan speech-writer Peggy Noonan claims to have "invented" "RR" by working FDR's speeches into Reagan's own. But long before Ms. Noonan, Reagan had immersed himself in Rooseveltian rhetoric. Reagan, who, in 1932 at the age of twenty-one cast his first ballot for FDR, not only voted for Roosevelt in each of the Democrat's subsequent campaigns, he was a devoted listener to FDR's speeches and fireside chats. He learned part of Roosevelt's first inaugural by heart and even as president was still in awe of the way Roosevelt's rhetoric "gave confidence to the people." "I still believe," he told a reporter in 1976, that when FDR "was first inaugurated, yes, if he didn't do anything else, he gave back to the people of this country their courage."[25]

Reagan, who admitted to having been "a near-hopeless hemophiliac liberal," didn't change his voter registration to Republican until 1962. But culturally he continued to be a New Deal Democrat. Long after he had left the Democratic Party, notes Lou Cannon, "he continued to draw his metaphors and inspirations from the New Deal." The language of Reagan's 1981 inaugural speech was so Rooseveltian that the *New York Times* wrote of "Franklin Delano Reagan." Ronald Reagan, says Cannon, "undermined the New Deal in its own vernacular." For his part Reagan, who argues that the Democrats deserted him, insists that he remained loyal to the New Deal, or at least one version of it.

Like many Americans who loved FDR but hated many of his policies, Reagan was confused about just what the New Deal was, a confusion that he shares with a great many New Deal critics then and since. "The Roosevelt that I voted for," Reagan told interviewer Ben Wattenberg, "had promised to cut federal spending by 25 percent, had promised to return to the states and local communities authority and autonomy that had been unjustly seized by the federal government." True enough, those were some of FDR's 1932 campaign pledges. But the New Deal went on, Reagan argued, to introduce fascist and communist tendencies—a more powerful state—into American life. Reagan was pilloried for his comments about fascism and Roosevelt's policies, but his assertions reflected confusion about the nature of the New Deal as deep and as widespread on the left as on the right.[26]

NOTES

1. Barton Bernstein, "The Conservative Achievements of Liberal Reform" in Bernstein, ed., *Towards A New Past: Dissenting Essays in American History* (New York: Pantheon, 1968), and Howard Zinn, ed., *New Deal Thought* (Indianapolis: Bobbs-Merrill, 1966); Carl Degler, in "What Was the New Deal," *The New Deal* (Chicago: Quadrangle, 1971), pp. 3, 4, notes that "no other depression gave birth to a major reform movement, and no other reform movement of national proportions achieved success during a depression."

2. On the European paralysis see John A. Garraty, *The Great Depression* (New York: Harcourt Brace, 1986) and William Leuchtenburg, "The Great Depression," in C. Vann Woodward, ed., *The Comparative Approach to American History* (New York: Basic, 1968).

3. David Burner, *The Politics of Provincialism: The Democratic Party in Transition, 1918–1932* (reprint, Greenwood, Conn.: Greenwood, 1981).

4. Governor Ritchie, notes Arthur Schlesinger, thought that, with the exception of

fascist Italy and Communist Russia, Americans were already among the most regimented people in the world. "Inspectors and spies and official regulators," said Ritchie, "follow the one-hundred-percent American from the day he draws his first nourishment from his inspected mother's breast" (Schlesinger, *The Crisis of the Old Order* [Boston: Houghton Mifflin, 1957]).

5. Walter Lippmann, *Interpretations: 1931, 1932* (New York: Macmillan, 1932), pp. 286, 302, 309–10.

6. Ibid. Wilsonians agreed the state had social welfare obligations but at the same time argued that any attempt to control the domestic economy led to imperialism, trade wars, and obstructed interdependence. The term "New Deal" was first used by Raymond Moley in a memorandum to FDR that read, "Unlike most depressions this one has as yet produced only a few of the disorderly manifestations usually attendant upon such times" (Moley, *After Seven Years* [New York: Harper and Brothers, 1939] p. 23).

7. Michael Barone, *Our Country: The Shaping of America from Roosevelt to Reagan* (New York: Free Press, 1990), p. 52.

8. Ibid., pp. 50–57.

9. David Kyvig, *Repealing National Prohibition* (Chicago: University of Chicago Press, 1979), pp. 2, 168, 181.

10. Lippmann, *Interpretations,* p. 256; Lippmann wrote of the Democrats, "They are a party which is much stronger in its parts than as a whole, whereas the Republicans are almost always stronger nationally than they are locally."

11. Ibid., pp. 262, 277.

12. Stephen Thernstrom, "Oswald Garrison Villard and the Politics of Pacifism," *Harvard Library Bulletin* (Winter 1960), p. 148. Villard, the grandson of the great abolitionist William Lloyd Garrison, compared FDR unfavorably with Grover Cleveland: "The best, the bravest, the most honest, the truest, of all presidents for his willingness to go down to a principled defeat."

13. George Orwell, *In Front of Your Nose: 1945–50* (New York: Harcourt Brace, 1968), p. 163.

14. Howard Brick, *Daniel Bell and the Decline of Intellectual Radicalism* (Madison: University of Wisconsin Press, 1986), chapter 2, "The Politics of War." See also Daniel Bell's review of *The Power Elite,* reprinted as chapter 3 of his *End of Ideology* and Irving Louis Horowitz's *C. Wright Mills: An American Utopian* (New York: Macmillan, 1983).

15. William Appleman Williams, *The Contours of American History* (Cleveland: World Publishing, 1971).

16. William Appleman Williams, "What This Country Needs. . . ," *New York Review of Books,* November 5, 1970; in *Contours,* Williams argues that Hoover represented what was in effect the second political coming of the self-conscious gentry personified by John Adams in the nineteenth-century. Williams's story of America's fall from grace makes for riveting reading. But the book is often as incoherent as it is fascinating. Williams argued at different times for three largely mutually exclusive paths to redemption: (1) rule by the self-conscious gentry; (2) Debsian socialism; and (3) regional decentralization.

17. At its core, the concept of "corporate liberalism" was an updated version of the old question of "Why is there no socialism in America?" The implicit assumption was that socialism was the natural state of affairs for industrial societies; hence what has to

be explained is its absence. On this see Gabriel Kolko, *The Triumph of Conservatism* (New York: Free Press, 1963), pp. 302–4, on the theory of "political capitalism"; a special issue of *Radical America* on historiography defined "corporate liberalism" as a way for the "social system to contain the contradictions of capitalism" (November 1970 [4], 100). Martin Sklar, whose seminal *Studies on the Left* essay on Woodrow Wilson paved the way for Kolko and others, later rejected the "corporate liberalism" thesis as too rigid and limited. See his recent *Corporate Reconstruction of American Capitalism, 1896–1916: The Market, the Law, and Politics* (New York: Cambridge University Press, 1988) for a more nuanced account of the relationship between government and business.

18. Peter Schrag, *The Decline of the WASP* (New York: Simon and Schuster, 1971), pp. 229, 241, 252; Theodore Draper, the historian of American Communism, discussed an antecedent cousin of the "corporate liberalism" thesis in "The Specter of Weimar," *Commentary,* December 1971.

19. The New Left revisionists had a profound impact on the writing of American history. While the revisionists served as a useful corrective to some of the more hagiographic treatments of Roosevelt, their impact, according to Donald McCoy's 1979 article "Trends in Viewing Herbert Hoover, Franklin D. Roosevelt, Harry S. Truman, and Dwight D. Eisenhower" (*Midwest Quarterly* 26, Jan. 1979, p. 124) went far beyond that. McCoy concluded, referring to the revisionists, "Thanks to their work as well as to the recent probings of more traditional researchers, there are few historians today who are unaware that Franklin D. Roosevelt claimed far more than he achieved, that a good deal of what he did was either insignificant, mischievous, or contradictory; and that he missed numerous opportunities for constructive action. He was in many ways Dr. Wrong Too Often." The new revised conventional wisdom was popularized in a 1973 *American History Illustrated* article asserting that FDR "was not a deep thinker. . . . His intentions were as sincere as his ideas were shallow." The New Deal failed, argues author Murray Klein, because it failed to lead us down the revolutionary road.

20. Charles Reich, *The Greening of America* (New York: Random House, 1970).

21. Lewis Mumford, *Technics and Civilization* (New York: Harcourt Brace, 1934).

22. Reich, *Greening;* see Jerold Auerbach, "New Deal, Old Deal, or Raw Deal: Some Thoughts on New Left Historiography," *Journal of Southern History* 35 (February 1969). Writing in *The Atlantic Monthly* (December 1934), Newton Baker complained that FDR was unprincipled and had nothing more in mind than greater abundance. "This object I am sure is the central thought of highwaymen as well as of philanthropists." FDR, he charged, encouraged "truculent, assertive, and selfish interests" which were "incompatible with any rational theory of permanently organized society."

23. The New Deal critics of the sixties had, without realizing it, rhetorically rewrapped the criticism of the thirties. Roosevelt's critics of both the 1930s and the 1960s never tired of complaining about his lack of intellectual curiosity and sophistication. "People who were merely 'intellectual,'" wrote Columbia professor and FDR advisor Raymond Moley in 1932, "were almost unanimous on the subject of Roosevelt's inadequacy." Similarly, Paul Conkin, one of FDR's 1960s critics, was appalled by Roosevelt's unprincipled "lack of philosophical concern" and failure to understand "subtle philosophical differences." Conkin echoed Progressives like Amos Pinchot, who called FDR "the Great Uncertainty" for failing to provide a clear philosophical orientation. Sim-

ilarly, Newton Baker, speaking for the bar, criticized the New Deal's incoherence. Baker anticipated Theodore Lowi, the proponent of juridical democracy, who in the 1960s complained that "the [Roosevelt] Administration seems to me to have no philosophy or principles."

24. William Leuchtenburg, *In the Shadow of FDR: From Harry Truman to Ronald Reagan* (Ithaca: Cornell University Press, 1983), p. 233; Benjamin Forgey, "FDR Memorial on Hold Again," *Washington Post,* April 20, 1990; Brendan Cooney, "Lobbying for Money to Honor Roosevelt," *National Journal* (September 8, 1990, p. 2140.

25. Leuchtenburg, *In the Shadow of FDR,* pp. 213, 1.

26. Ibid., p. 225, *New Republic* January 27, 1982, p. 8. Frank Freidel's *Franklin D. Roosevelt: His Rendezvous with Destiny* (Boston: Little, Brown, 1991) discusses the FDR/Reagan continuities, particularly on the question of traditional values. FDR's rhetoric, he notes, repeatedly affirmed God, work, family, the flag, and American nationalism.

Chapter 12

"MALAISE" REVISITED: JIMMY CARTER AND THE CRISIS OF CONFIDENCE

LEO P. RIBUFFO

ON JULY 15, 1979, Jimmy Carter delivered what remains one of the most famous speeches by a modern American president. Yet, unlike Franklin D. Roosevelt's exorcism of "fear itself," John F. Kennedy's appeal to "do for your country," and Dwight D. Eisenhower's warning against the "military-industrial complex," Carter's speech is recalled not as a source of inspiration and prophecy, but as a fount of peculiarity and sanctimony. Hardly anyone remembers the formal title, "Energy and the Crisis of Confidence." Instead pundits and opponents alike remember the "malaise" speech, a phrase popularized by Carter's rival, Senator Edward M. Kennedy, even though the word appeared nowhere in the text. In the last days of the 1992 campaign, President George Bush warned that Bill Clinton would return the country to the "malaise days" of the late 1970s. Subsequently numerous commentators urged President Clinton to avoid the mistakes of Carter's allegedly failed presidency, failure supposedly rooted in his preference for brooding over back-slapping.[1]

Since Carter and malaise seem inextricably linked for the foreseeable future, this article uses the July 15 speech as the focal point for interpreting the man and his presidency. In addition, I offer (progressively more speculative) thoughts on Carter's presidential record, on the ways in which scholars, pundits, and citizens evaluate all recent presidents, on the role of "malaise" in American (and some other) histories, and on the vices and virtues (or at least the inevitability) of symbolic politics orchestrated from the White House.

In 1979, "Energy and the Crisis of Confidence" was largely interpreted according to two frames of reference that commentators had used since 1976 in a vain effort to understand Carter. From one perspective, called the "weirdo factor" by campaign manager Hamilton Jordan in 1976, Carter was thought too peculiar to lead the country. The original source of peculiarity was said to be Carter's "born again" Protestantism, something that remained mysterious to virtually everyone except the eighty million Americans who shared it. Once weirdness was established as an interpretive convention, new evidence was quickly found or manufactured to support the point. Not only did Carter try to explain the sin of pride in *Playboy*, but he corrected typing and spelling errors in memoranda.[2]

The second frame of reference, which highlighted Carter's use of symbolic politics to win the presidency and subsequently to rally support for his legislative agenda, was dubbed "Rafshoonery" by cartoonist Garry Trudeau. Yet even in the absence of media advisor Gerald Rafshoon, Carter had an intuitive feel for the techniques of symbolic politics. Following the Vietnam War and Watergate scandal, Carter said in 1975, he would be elected if he could "personify in my personal life the aspirations of the American people." Accordingly, while assailing President Gerald R. Ford for lack of leadership, Carter symbolized his rejection of the "imperial presidency" by occasionally carrying his own luggage and emphasized his trustworthiness by promising in various locutions never to lie to the American people.[3]

Yet the American people in general and the Democratic Party in particular were divided about economic policy, race relations, and foreign policy. Thus Carter shrewdly advertised different sides of himself to different constituencies. He was variously a peanut farmer and nuclear engineer, a devotee of Bob Dylan and Dylan Thomas, an integrationist and defender of ethnically homogeneous neighborhoods, a critic of detente and a champion of human rights in the Third World. To Rafshoon and pollster Patrick Caddell, such variations merely reflected the "fine tuning" necessary to project Carter's image. To journalist Stephen Brill, they were examples of Carter's "pathetic lies." The Ford campaign almost convinced the electorate that Carter was totally untrustworthy, at best indecisive and opportunistic, and perhaps downright mean. From 1976 onward, Rafshoonery and the weirdo factor were two sides of the same political coin. Because Carter weirdly stressed his own good character, he would be held to higher standards than other recent presidents whose advertising puffery, smooth deception, and outright lies were often viewed, by pundits, scholars, and citizens alike, as standard operating procedure or even marks of higher statesmanship.[4]

Although Carter was arguably much less weird than John Kennedy, Lyndon Johnson, and Richard Nixon, he may have been the most psychologically complex president in this century. He absorbed information easily and viewed complicated issues from several angles, yet he not only became bogged down in detail, but also had trouble synthesizing information and deciding what perspective was most pertinent. A trained engineer who prided himself on making technical decisions unburdened by ideology, Carter was nonetheless stubborn, often letting his determination to succeed blind him to unpleasant facts. Uncomfortable with loose ends, he proposed—to use his own favorite adjective—"comprehensive" solutions to problems where even slight amelioration would have been difficult to achieve. In addressing these problems, he spoke with a mixture of precision and hyperbole. He demanded excellence and loyalty from subordinates, but was stingy with praise, oblivious to fair complaints, and prone to sarcasm. Carter took pride in his achievements and abilities, sometimes to the point of self-righteousness, but nevertheless considered pride the "number one sin."

Carter held mixed feelings about politics itself. He enjoyed the applause and the competition to which, he said often, he "didn't intend to lose." To avoid losing, he hedged on issues, denigrated opponents, and made unsavory alliances. But by politics he meant primarily wheeling and dealing with legislators and so-called special interests, a practice he disdained. Symbolic politics conducted on a grand scale seemed less corrupt than wheeling and dealing because it involved open contact with ordinary citizens and perhaps also because Carter was more adept at it. Even here, however, the inevitable manipulation and blarney bothered Carter, and he tried hard to minimize or deny them, refusing, for example, to improve his choppy speaking style.[5]

Probably the weirdest thing about Carter was that he was elected president as a Democrat in 1976. Unlike all Democratic presidents since Franklin D. Roosevelt, Carter neither reconciled himself to the constraints of interest group politics nor considered expansion of the welfare state a domestic priority. Rather, he advocated an updated version of the kind of liberalism dominant before the New Deal, what we still (warily) call progressivism. Like Theodore Roosevelt, Woodrow Wilson, and their primarily middle-class allies, Carter promoted efficiency instead of economic equality, tried to raise the nation's moral tone, and assailed ill-defined "special interests" in the name of an ill-defined common good. Thus, unlike most Democrats on Capitol Hill, including Speaker Thomas P. O'Neill and Senator Edward Kennedy, Carter was personally more concerned with deregulating major industries, reorganizing the executive branch, and reducing alleged government waste than with increasing unemployment benefits, stimulating the economy, and establishing national health insurance.[6]

Nor was this split between the latter-day progressive in the White House and welfare state liberals on Capitol Hill the only serious division among Democrats. In addition, supporters of detente with the Soviet Union were arrayed against unreconstructed cold warriors, advocates of affirmative action confronted Democrats barely acquiescent in integration, and feminist supporters of *Roe v. Wade* coexisted with Roman Catholic opponents of abortion. Whatever Carter's personal feelings, and they were characteristically mixed on the Cold War and abortion, he tried to solve the problem of intraparty and national divisiveness the old-fashioned way, by appointing diverse subordinates and trying to bury differences under amorphous rhetorical solidarity, in this case about creating a government as good as the people. Even in retrospect, an alternate strategy is hard to imagine. Certainly no Democratic president has found one in the past six decades. Nonetheless, the perils soon became apparent. By early 1978, as congressional Democrats battled over dams and deregulation, and as Carter's appointees proclaimed or leaked incompatible opinions on Soviet emigration and affirmative action, pundits in a pack viewed him as an inept leader devoid of vision. Many of the same pundits had proclaimed him a shrewd but moral leader only a year earlier.[7]

Contrary to the conventional wisdom, these divisions within the Democratic Party and the country at large, not Carter's alleged peculiarity, were the primary domestic cause of his chronic embattlement. Yet the conventional wisdom is not entirely wrong. Carter's insularity and inflexibility compounded his political problems. From the outset, he received excellent advice from a (still underrated) White House staff to court important members of Congress, control his hyperbole, beware of self-righteousness, avoid arbitrary deadlines, recognize the power of organized labor and other unfamiliar allies, and settle for partial rather than "comprehensive" solutions to complex problems. Carter tried with customary earnestness to modify his demeanor and modus operandi but his heart just wasn't in it.[8]

No issue was more complex than energy; none better illustrates Carter's tenacious commitment to "comprehensive" solutions as well as the limits of both symbolic politics and wheeling and dealing. By 1977, the United States imported 36 percent of its petroleum from Arab countries in the Organization of Petroleum Exporting Countries (OPEC). In Carter's view, this left the United States vulnerable to the threat of "political blackmail" and might even provoke enthusiasm for military intervention, something he abhorred even more than being "jerked around by a few desert states." On February 2, 1977, dressed in an energy-saving, populist cardigan sweater, he gave a fireside chat in which he promised a comprehensive energy plan within ninety days. Despite much internal administration grumbling about this arbitrary deadline, a basic plan was available for presentation, this time by a more formally attired president, on the night of April 18. Borrowing a phrase from William James via Admiral Hyman Rickover, Carter called the energy crisis the "moral equivalent of war" and a "test [of] the character of the American people."[9]

Carter was not the first president to postulate an "energy crisis" and to conceive it as both a threat to national security and a challenge to American character. On the contrary, he was the third. In the midst of the OPEC embargo of 1973–74, Richard Nixon had compared the quest for "energy independence" to the Apollo space program. The next year Gerald Ford had used comparable inspirational language to urge energy independence by 1985. Moreover, many of the means Carter endorsed to increase domestic production of energy while curtailing imports and consumption had been proposed by his predecessors. These included complicated procedures for deregulating the price of natural gas and petroleum in order to expand supply and promote conservation, a wellhead "equalization tax" to finance energy research and subsidies for the poor while preventing oil companies from reaping unjustified profits, a tax on "gas guzzling" automobiles, a standby five-cent-per-gallon increase in the gasoline tax, tax credits to encourage conservation, regulations to encourage industrial use of coal, nuclear power, and solar energy, and a federal agency to explore alternate sources of energy. Carter differed from his predecessors mainly in two respects: a greater commitment to environmental protection, long a personal interest, and greater concern for equitable distribution of the economic burden, a product of Carter's visceral distrust of big business and his position as a Democratic president.[10]

Carter understood that there was no popular demand for a comprehensive energy policy. Indeed, cardigan Rafshoonery and William James were enlisted to create a demand. Carter also understood in principle that the minority of Americans deeply concerned with the issue was itself bitterly divided in cross-cutting ways among oil companies, gas companies, coal companies, consumer groups, environmentalists, and residents of different regions. With customary positive thinking Carter believed that he could transcend these "special interests" where Nixon and Ford had failed. After passing the House relatively unscathed, Carter's comprehensive plan bogged down in the Senate in late 1977. Although faulty White House liaison and outsize congressional egos played their part, the problem centered on the allocation of gain and pain to energy producers and users. On the one hand, Edward Kennedy and other Senate liberals fought natural gas deregulation with denunciations and a filibuster; on the other hand, conservative Senator Russell Long, the powerful chairman of the Finance Committee, maneuvered to undermine the equalization tax. A stripped-down version of Carter's program finally passed the Senate in late October 1977. Unfortunately, despite Carter's persistent attempts to mobilize American opinion, including a third major energy speech on November 8, most citizens remained apathetic and the legislation floundered in a House-Senate conference committee. Yet Carter's reputation suffered more than that of "characteristically uncompromising" liberals whom he blamed for the impasse. By March 1978, only 34 percent of Americans in an ABC–Associated Press poll rated his presidential performance as good or excellent.[11]

Carter and his closest advisors took concerted action in the first six months of 1978 to improve his standing in the press and the polls. Hamilton Jordan became *de facto* chief of staff, Gerald Rafshoon was appointed to the White House staff, and Patrick Caddell stepped up the pace of his memoranda and polls on the grouchy American mood. At Rafshoon's urging, Carter granted interviews to major magazines and grudgingly hosted White House dinners for members of the media elite and the usual overrated Washington "wise men." Throughout, Rafshoon urged repeatedly, the president must deliver the message of "Carter in control"—in control of the government, the economy, and the energy crisis.[12]

Although such claims of control combined equal parts puffery (from Rafshoon) and positive thinking (from Carter), the administration did win a series of victories between spring 1978 and spring 1979. These included ratification of the Panama Canal treaties, a strategic arms limitation treaty with the Soviet Union, and mediation of an Egyptian-Israeli peace. Furthermore, following capable administration lobbying, Congress passed the National Energy Act of 1978. Neither the standby increase in the gasoline tax nor the wellhead equalization tax had survived the legislative odyssey. But the final bills did include appropriations and modest tax levies to encourage conservation, prod utilities to use coal instead of gas or oil, and develop solar power and other renewable energy sources. Most important, the act set procedures to speed the deregulation of natural gas. Putting the best face on the situation and evidently speaking with a sense of relief, Carter proclaimed the creation of the first "conscious national [energy] policy" and said that "we've acquitted ourselves well as a nation."[13]

Unfortunately, Carter had won only pyrrhic victories because, from Camp David to the Energy Act, his actions energized Republican conservatives or alienated major Democratic constituencies. Nevertheless, the president and most of his advisors entered 1979 with chastened optimism. The consumer price index had risen by 7.8 percent in 1978 and voters were suspicious and "bitter," according to Caddell's polls, but the administration might ride the tide by stressing its competence and integrity during unavoidably tough times.[14]

Even cautious optimism proved unwarranted. Carter's fragile and unenthusiastic coalition began to shake apart during the first six months of 1979. When chronic economic problems turned acute in another round of "stagflation," Carter's commitment to fight inflation rather than unemployment further alienated welfare state liberals. The Iranian revolution caused a shortfall in petroleum imports, which led in turn to higher inflation, regional gasoline shortages, and lines of angry motorists.

In April, Caddell surmised from his polls and from such social criticism as Christopher Lasch's *Culture of Narcissism* and James MacGregor Burn's *Leadership* that Americans were even angrier and more pessimistic about the future than they had been during the Watergate scandal. His positive thinking faltering for a moment, Carter groused that the country was "going to hell." Increasingly sympathetic to Caddell's argument that the basic problem was, broadly speaking, psychological, Carter on May 30 met with a group of intellectuals (including Lasch and Daniel Bell) and demi-intellectuals (including John Gardner and Charles Peters). The confused session apparently reinforced Carter's feeling that the country was facing, in Lasch's phrase from *The Culture of Narcissism*, a "crisis of confidence," but offered no solace or solutions.[15]

In addition to reflecting on the national mood, Carter reluctantly reentered the quagmire of energy politics. Addressing the nation on April 5, he focused on a "painful" but necessary step that would force Americans to "use less oil and pay more": the phased decontrol of oil prices that he ordered to begin on June 1. But to prevent oil companies from reaping unjustified gains, he proposed a windfall profits tax with proceeds going to mass transit, energy research, and poor families burdened by the price rise. No more than its three predecessors did this speech stir popular enthusiasm or dissolve disagreements between congressional liberals and conservatives.[16]

In June, Carter joined the leaders of other major industrialized nations at an economic summit meeting in Tokyo and, recognizing that the windfall profits tax was stalled on Capitol Hill, asked his aides to prepare yet another major speech on energy. OPEC, taking advantage of the Iranian revolution, announced the fourth—and largest—oil price rise in five months. By the time Carter returned to Washington from the Far East on Sunday, July 1, long lines at gasoline stations had come to symbolize his presidency as vividly as soup kitchens had symbolized Herbert Hoover's.[17]

On July 4, encouraged by his wife Rosalynn, Carter decided with a feeling of relief to cancel the energy speech scheduled for the next day. Settling in at Camp David, he began a systematic evaluation of his administration and the American mood. The basic motifs for the next week and a half were established on Thursday, July 5, when he met with his closest advisors. Vice President Walter Mondale and Stuart Eizenstat, head of the domestic policy staff, argued that the country's problems were primarily economic and centered on the end of cheap energy. The vice president, who had often been skeptical of Caddell's sweeping formulations, worried that "you can't castigate the American people or they will turn you off once and for all." Eizenstat bluntly called Caddell's reiteration of his psychological argument "bullshit," but Carter thought it a "masterpiece." That question settled, the group discussed the removal of cabinet secretaries who seemed less than fully loyal. Between sessions, they chuckled at television reporters trying to make sense of Carter's sudden cancellation of his energy speech. Soon the chuckling would be reciprocated.[18]

During the next week, 130 men and women were brought to Camp David to consult with Carter in more-or-less functional groups. Some of the invitees were utterly predictable: leading Democratic governors, mayors, and members of Congress, corporate leaders with reputations for business statesmanship, officers of major unions, and such Washington insiders as Clark Clifford and Robert Strauss. Nonetheless, the choice of advisors was notable in two respects. First, in terms of race and gender, this was the most diverse group ever chosen to help out during a presidential crisis. The African-Americans included four mayors, such organizational leaders as Jesse Jackson and Vernon Jordan, and Eleanor Holmes Norton and Mary Frances Berry from within the administration. Second, this was probably the first presidential crisis in which advice was seriously solicited from clergy and scholars of religion, including Cardinal Terence Cooke, Rabbi Marc Tanenbaum, Rev. Jimmy Allen of the Southern Baptist Convention, and sociologist Robert Bellah.[19]

Carter, who listened intently and took copious notes, was chided for bogging down in detail and failing to provide something called "leadership." Other advice was more congenial, especially that disloyal cabinet secretaries must not be tolerated, that the country indeed suffered from a "crisis of confidence," and that grassroots America would accept sacrifice if he offered "bold" leadership. Carter was especially moved by the religious leaders and least impressed by the economists, whom he later criticized for holding tenaciously to impractical and "conflicting theories."[20]

From the outset, members of Carter's inner circle were concerned about how the Camp David retreat would be perceived. The president needed to exude confidence when he met a group of governors on July 6, the first representatives from what cabinet secretary Jack Watson called the "outside world." In part, the Camp David sessions lasted more than a week so that Carter could deliver his speech on July 15, the third anniversary of his nomination. In the meantime Rafshoon and Caddell strived to build a national sense of anticipation while Rosalynn Carter, Vice President Mondale, and Press Secretary Jody Powell served as upbeat emissaries to the outside world.[21]

The news media cooperated fitfully. If Carter was going to mull over the national mood and the state of his administration, then they were going to offer advice on those subjects. Above all, metropolitan newspapers and network commentators urged this "leader racked by indecision" (*Wall Street Journal*) to demonstrate "resolution and leadership" (*St. Louis Post-Dispatch*) in order to end "Washington's drift" (*New York Newsday*). The *Charlotte Observer* cartoonist portrayed Carter as Rodin's thinker seated on an oil can. *NBC Nightly News* observed that CBS was canceling a movie on Moses to broadcast Carter's speech, and CBS commentator Bruce Morton wondered if Carter would come down from the Catoctin Mountains "with a few stone tablets of his own."[22]

Yet most commentators were willing to give some benefit of the doubt to a president, even one afflicted by the weirdo factor. They overwhelmingly agreed that there was an energy "crisis," a failure of leadership, and a national "malaise" (a term used by the *Wall Street Journal* as early as August 1978). Occasionally a regional newspaper broke from the pack. The *Bergen Evening Record* (New Jersey) pointed to the "unpleasant truth . . . that 'leadership' isn't what's lacking here. What is lacking, instead, is an easy, painless way out of the fix."[23]

As the speech title, "Energy and the Crisis of Confidence," suggests, Carter and his advisors attempted to yoke together an inspirational discussion of the national mood and specific proposals for mitigating the energy crisis. This was no easy task. After Carter canceled the July 5 address, everyone was "grasping at straws," as Rafshoon put it. Rafshoon himself favored some treatment of the "malaise in the country" but wanted to avoid Caddell's "apocalyptic" version and warned that a weak, confessional speech "could even be a disaster." Mondale and Eizenstat continued to urge an emphasis on energy legislation. Alfred Kahn, head of the Council of Wage and Price Stability, gently reminded the president that his fellow economists gathered at Camp David differed primarily because there was no way immediately to lower energy prices and expand supply; both decontrol of gasoline prices (recommended by Lawrence Klein) and rationing (suggested by John Kenneth Galbraith) had liabilities and should be avoided if possible.[24]

The president was much less concerned with the reiteration of familiar energy proposals than with the inspirational portion of the speech, which he essentially wrote himself. Journalists reported that Carter and his advisors were digging deeply into the ideas of Daniel Bell, Christopher Lasch, and Alexis de Tocqueville, but these reports were unwarranted. Caddell summarized Lasch's *Culture of Narcissism* in two sentences: "People who lose sense of future turn inward for fulfillment which leads to vacuum and greater unhappiness. Explores this phenomenon through damage of advertising, consumption, personal relationships, education, child rearing, and public interest— building of dependency—loss of sense meaning of life for future." After the gathering of intellectuals on May 30, Lasch himself had sent the White House a long letter expanding his views. This Marxist-Freudian critique of the idea of progress did reach the president but had little impact. Carter underlined three phrases—"decline of the work ethic . . . lack of faith in the future, a desire to enjoy life in the present"—and continued searching for ways to restore the electorate's faith in progress.[25]

Not abstract ideas but "personal advice" from the ad hoc advisors summoned to Camp David, channeled through Carter's visceral determination, distrust of insiders, and latter-day progressive belief that "we simply must have faith in each other," set the tone for his speech. Crafting a deliberately inspirational but not overtly religious address, he considered but ultimately dropped Robert Bellah's line, "Let us covenant together."[26]

Twice Carter left Camp David for brief visits to middle-class families in West Virginia and Pennsylvania, several of whom vouched for his sincerity when the news media descended. On Sunday, July 15, he returned to Washington, attended church, and practiced his speech. At 10:00 P.M. that night Carter addressed 65 million television viewers.[27]

In the years since his election, the president said, he had become "isolated" from the people and, concentrating on day-to-day government affairs, had spoken "less and less about the nation's hopes." Now the United States faced problems "much deeper" than the energy crisis—problems that constituted a "crisis of confidence." Carter quoted complaints by fifteen of the visitors to Camp David in order to underscore pertinent aspects of the crisis. According to these citizens, whom he identified by race, gender, class, or other politically useful traits, "big shots" exercised too much power, material things counted for more than eternal truths, and the president himself "had ceased to be a spiritual leader." An unspecified southern governor had warned that Carter was not leading the nation at all, "just managing the Government."[28]

Following Caddell and Rafshoon's analysis, Carter found some causes of the crisis in recent history. "We were sure that ours was a nation of the ballot, not the bullet, until the murders of John Kennedy and Robert Kennedy and Martin Luther King, Jr. We were taught our armies were always invincible and our causes were always just, only to suffer the agony of Vietnam. We respected the Presidency as a place of honor until the shock of Watergate." Then, too, Carter indicted familiar scapegoats—government insiders who practiced "politics as usual," rejecting even the small sacrifices necessary for "balanced and fair" solutions.

Yet the problem went deeper than recent tragedies and flawed officials. Carter implied that the crisis of confidence was actually a crisis of national character, and that contemporary Americans were inferior to ancestors who had overcome truly "awesome" threats. There was "growing disrespect" for churches, schools, and other institutions. Even worse for a country formerly "proud of hard work, strong families, close-knit communities, and our faith in God, too many of us now tend to worship self-indulgence and consumption. Human identity is no longer defined by what one does, but by what one owns." Unintentionally and ironically, Carter implied that his government was—unfortunately—just about as good as the people.

Still he remained hopeful. Americans were discovering that "owning things and consuming things does not satisfy our longing for meaning." From this perspective, the energy crisis was not only a "clear and present danger," but also an opportunity for Americans to redeem themselves. Echoing Nixon, Carter recalled the successful moon landing, and echoing himself in April 1977, Carter called the energy crisis a test of character. Roughly one-third of the speech sketched Carter's energy proposals. His major new initiative was an Energy Mobilization Board analogous to the War Production Board during World War II, which would cut through the "endless roadblocks to completing key energy projects."

Most commentators gave the president the benefit of the doubt. The *Los Angeles Times* questioned Carter's "scolding" of the country in the manner of a "pastor with a profligate flock," but nonetheless called the speech a "good first step." A cartoonist who portrayed Carter blowing the trumpet of "energy war" from the White House balcony was similarly ambivalent. Other observers overlooked weirdness entirely and suddenly discovered qualities of "leadership" in Carter that they had missed only a week earlier; to *New York Newsday* he even qualified as "forceful, realistic, and politically savvy." Many also anticipated what the *Hartford Courant* called "another beginning" for his administration. Several editorials credited Carter with eloquence, and Robert Pierpoint of CBS News, who had previously ruminated on Carter's peculiarity, now praised the "best speech of Carter's presidency."[29] Only Carter's most implacable conservative critics were entirely unmoved. Beneath the "sermonic and confusing rhetoric" lay an "almost unbelievable government intrusion" into the energy business, the *Wall Street Journal* complained.[30]

Asked point-blank by ABC–Associated Press pollsters whether or not there was a national "crisis of confidence," 79 percent of the sample answered in the affirmative. Yet these figures meant primarily that most citizens would not contradict their president immediately after such an earnest speech. The same poll revealed that only 56 percent of Americans believed that there was an energy crisis and only 48 percent thought that Carter was doing an adequate job. According to the *New York Times*–CBS survey, 42 percent of those polled now felt more optimistic about the future and Carter's approval rating had moved upward by 11 percent—to a mere 37 percent.[31]

Carter himself did not doubt the speech's success. Examining the first favorable letters to the White House, he predicted to Hamilton Jordan that there would be "25,000 Americans eager to help us." With his customary attention to detail, he instructed subordinates to turn off White House lights at day break and check thermostats weekly, transfer to the National Gallery of Art any paintings that might be damaged by reductions in air conditioning, and examine Georgia Tech studies of the minimum lighting required for health and safety. Reiterating the basic themes of "Energy and the Crisis of Confidence," Carter spoke twice in the midwest on July 16 to lead off the administration's concerted effort to use the "crisis" mood to pass his energy program and enhance his reputation.[32]

But Carter's most important action, reorganization of the cabinet and White House staff, undercut whatever political and inspirational benefits that followed from the speech. By Friday, July 20, five cabinet secretaries had been replaced. Although this action constituted the largest cabinet reorganization in history, it meant less than met the eye and would have caused minimal damage to Carter if it had not followed his Sunday night self-presentation as an inspirational leader. Attorney General Griffin Bell was already scheduled to leave. Secretary of Energy James Schlesinger had offered to resign at least twice. Secretary of the Treasury Michael Blumenthal was willing to go amicably. Secretary of Transportation Brock Adams might have stayed if Carter had not required him to fire subordinates. Only the departure of Secretary of Health, Education and Welfare Joseph A. Califano, whose relations with the White House staff had steadily deteriorated, would have caused a stir. For welfare state liberals, the removal of Califano, the administration's living link to Lyndon Johnson and the Great Society, represented the latest step in a conservative direction.[33]

In retrospect, even Carter admitted that he had mismanaged the reorganization. On Tuesday, July 17, he told the cabinet that Jordan would now be *de jure* chief of staff, raised questions about their loyalty, and asked for their written resignations as well as systematic evaluations of potentially disloyal subordinates. The assembled secretaries were variously amazed, annoyed, and reminded of Richard Nixon. Ultimately there was reluctant agreement on the fiction that they had orally submitted their resignations. These developments quickly leaked to the news media, prompting renewed editorial speculation about Carter's weirdness and failure to lead.[34]

What the *New York Daily News* called a "purge" was welcomed almost nowhere outside Carter's inner circle. The erstwhile moral leader now looked like a "petulant President," in the *Philadelphia Inquirer*'s opinion. Furthermore, the reorganization increased the power of those whom the *Wall Street Journal* called Carter's "shallow and callow" campaign advisors. Finally, perhaps everything since July 4 had been an exercise in Rafshoonery. Carter was guilty of a "showy stunt" (*Boston Globe*), a "grandstand play" (*Dallas Times-Herald*), a "contrived high school drama" (*Atlanta Journal-Constitution*), or a "possibly dangerous media ploy" (*New York Newsday*). Academic observers were no kinder. Political scientist Fred Greenstein of Princeton University discerned a "certain spookiness about Camp David," and Stephen Hess of the Brookings Institution thought the recent turn of events "bizarre, absolutely bizarre."[35]

Further left, the *Nation* declared: "Had a purge like the President's taken place in the Soviet Union, Kremlinologists would have been pontificating about the problems of transition in a totalitarian state." After an unrepentant Joseph Califano gave his version of events on three morning network news shows, Jody Powell denied that Carter had called him the "best" HEW secretary in history. Such petulance also marked Carter's off-the-record press briefing. The president's demeanor aside, it was "probably no disgrace to be fired from his cabinet," the now critical *Hartford Courant* observed. Similarly, a cartoonist portrayed Carter as a failed magician who fires his rabbit. Vice President Mondale, leaving on a mission abroad, never felt "happier to get out of the country. It went from sugar to shit right there."[36]

In 1979–80, the president's latest energy initiatives enjoyed mixed success. Congress rejected the Energy Mobilization Board but enacted a mild windfall profits tax, established an Energy Security Corporation to finance development of synthetic fuel, and authorized a Solar Energy and Conservation Bank to subsidize adoption of that energy alternative by business and home owners. By early 1980, the "energy crisis" per se was dwarfed by worsening stagflation, Kennedy's challenge to Carter's renomination, the Soviet invasion of Afghanistan, and the Iran hostage crisis. In this context, Republican nominee Ronald Reagan convinced a plurality of voters that Carter's government was not as good as they were. Some said "that a great national malaise is upon us," Reagan noted in his election eve television address, but he knew that there was "nothing wrong with the American people."[37]

In the years since Carter's defeat, his reputation has followed the familiar trajectory characterizing that of other modern presidents who left office widely regarded as failures. That is, after lingering in the doldrums for several years, his reputation began to rise. This pattern is hardly surprising. Not only do most Americans, including the few historians still interested in presidents, want to think well of them (as the initial response to "Energy and the Crisis of Confidence" showed), but also no consequential public figure could be so one-dimensional as the caricatures of vanquished presidents painted by jubilant victors and gloating journalists in the aftermath of defeat.

Although the general trajectory is familiar, each upward revision in reputation bears distinctive features. Two aspects of the Carter revival stand out. First, unlike Herbert Hoover and Dwight D. Eisenhower, for example, Carter has enjoyed a renaissance among pundits and Americans at large before scholars have made substantial use of his presidential papers (which began to open in 1987). Second—and this point is surely connected to the first—academic and lay participants in the Carter renaissance view him as he would like to see himself. Certainly Hoover would have qualms about his revisionist reputation as a precursor of the New Deal, and Eisenhower would rather be known for disinterested public service than as a shrewd behind-the-scenes operator. Conversely, Carter basks in his growing reputation as a good man who tried to "do what is right," as political scientist Charles O. Jones puts it. This motif not only characterizes folklore and encomiums on "Larry King Live," but also undergirds standard accounts of the Carter administration by Jones and his fellow political scientist Erwin C. Hargrove. While King pronounced Carter "beloved," Hargrove and Jones chide congressional Democrats and "special interests" for failing to accommodate Carter's latter-day progressivism.[38]

There is no reason to dispute Professor Jones's judgment that Carter tried to do the right thing. On the contrary, as the Camp David retreat shows, he reflected on right and wrong more than the typical modern president. Still, any serious evaluation of Carter's record requires an appreciation of the tensions within his complex personality and worldview: between generosity and pettiness, provincialism and tolerance, efficiency and uplift, reflectiveness and stubbornness. Only in comparison to Richard Nixon and Lyndon Johnson does this president look like an easy man to work for or work with. A less stubborn Carter could have prevented the split between latter-day progressives and welfare state liberals from turning into a chasm. As late as 1979, Edward Kennedy and the White House staff worked together on issues ranging from trucking deregulation to international human rights, and Kennedy's challenge might well have been avoided if Carter had been less determined to "whip his ass."[39]

"Energy and the Crisis of Confidence" reveals both the special problems Carter faced, problems that probably would have cost any president reelection, and the distinctive ways he handled them. The basic economic difficulty, which had also afflicted Nixon and Ford, was the rising price and precarious supply of petroleum. In this context, it made some strategic sense to limit the country's dependence on imported oil. Given Carter's temperament, it is no surprise that he expected to succeed where Nixon and Ford had failed, and given his relative conservatism, it is no surprise that he ultimately emphasized decontrol of gas and oil prices instead of subsidies or regulations to promote conservation. Although plausible, these choices were not (as Carter himself often failed to see) self-evidently "what was right." Rather than a test of American character, energy policy was better understood as a contentious political and economic issue that needed to be considered along with other important issues.

A more flexible president might have concluded that the slight decrease in petroleum imports made possible by accelerated price decontrol was not worth the congressional gridlock and intraparty divisions entailed. Along with many others in political or moral authority, Carter chastised Americans for failing to rally against the energy *crisis* when they might have responded better to modulated advice for muddling through an energy *problem*. Not only did the problem turn out to be less severe during the next two decades then Carter had anticipated, but also apathetic citizens were no further from the mark in their optimism than the energy experts and oil company executives who expected petroleum to cost $100 per barrel by 1990.

Although motorists in long lines at gasoline stations were no happier in 1973 than in 1979, Carter made himself especially vulnerable because— unlike Nixon and Ford—he repeatedly highlighted energy as the signal "crisis" of the 1970s and made achievement of a "comprehensive" solution the preeminent symbol of his administration's domestic success or failure. Essentially he talked himself into an unwinnable position. No comprehensive "solution" to the problem of precarious oil supply was possible before the end of the Cold War and the reassertion of American military power in the Middle East. If, as critics joked, the energy crisis became the moral equivalent of the *Vietnam* War, then perhaps Carter should have stuck to his decision after the legislative victories of 1978 to declare victory and let the issue subside.

Once trapped in the unwinnable position, however, Carter's decision to recast the energy issue as a crisis of confidence not only fit his own ascetic temperament and earlier successful use of symbolic politics, but it also was as plausible as Mondale and Eizenstat's supposedly realistic focus on the pending energy bills. As everyone understood, their passage would bring no quick relief from rising prices. Nor was all of the legislation worthy of support on the merits. For example, the synthetic fuels program opened the kind of pork barrel that Carter loathed in other circumstances.

Under these difficult circumstances in mid-1979, Carter had little to lose by trying once again to raise the nation's moral tone. Nor was the effort without precedent from presidents widely regarded as "pragmatists." In his own idiom, Carter was telling Americans that the only thing they had to fear was fear itself, and urging them to ask not what their country could do for them, but what they could do for their country.

Was the United States enduring a crisis of confidence in the late 1970s? Probably so, since American history can be interpreted as one long crisis of confidence broken occasionally by extraordinary disasters—such as the Civil War or Great Depression—in which public spirits are incongruously high. A long line of malcontents, as Christopher Lasch described himself in 1979, stretches back through Henry Adams to Cotton Mather, who complained at the turn of the eighteenth century that great men had formerly done Christ's work in America. In the absence of polls by Pat Caddell and Robert Bellah we cannot be certain, but malaise does not seem to have been confined to the elite during, for example, the antebellum mourning of the last of the Founders or the romanticization of Civil War heroes at the turn of this century. Fears that one's country is less than it ought to be are not uniquely American, and we might usefully compare our crises of confidence with those abroad. For instance, in late-nineteenth-century Britain, muscular Christians exhorted school boys to revive their sagging nation, and sub-Saharan Africans in the 1980s wondered why the bright prospects for independence seemed so far from fulfillment. Students of comparative malaise might nonetheless conclude that centuries of Protestant perfectionism have rendered the United States peculiarly vulnerable to this malady.

At least since the Great Depression, and probably since the Progressive era, Americans have held presidents responsible for the national mood as well as the national defense and the national economy. The famous Clinton campaign slogan to the contrary, it wasn't just "the economy, stupid," that elected Bill Clinton or Ronald Reagan or Jimmy Carter or John Kennedy. When commentators assailed Carter for lack of "leadership," they were trying incoherently to make sense of this question. Few historians have addressed it systematically, and the best of them—Richard Hofstadter and Bruce Kuklick—tend to contrast mere "symbolic politics" with solid "interest politics." The subject of presidential symbolism deserves more attention and less condescension. Franklin D. Roosevelt and Dwight D. Eisenhower would not have been able to establish themselves as national father figures if the former had not begun direct relief for the unemployed and the latter had not ended the Korean War. Nonetheless, the psychological success of their administrations is significant in itself. Ultimately, a president's manipulation of powerful symbols should be viewed less as a matter of technique—politics as exemplified by Pat Caddell and Jerry Rafshoon—than as a matter of ethics—politics as exemplified by Mahatma Gandhi and Martin Luther King, Jr. Or, as Reinhold Niebuhr, Jimmy Carter's favorite theologian, pondered for forty years, how do we move apathetic men and women to make the world slightly more moral?

These questions are particularly pertinent during the Clinton administration. Carter and Bill Clinton have known each other since the late 1970s. In

1976, while running for attorney general of Arkansas, Clinton also served as state coordinator of the Carter campaign. After their respective victories, he flooded the transition team and then the White House staff with the resumes of friends, invited the president to visit, and offered advice on executive reorganization. The correspondence escalated after Clinton's election as governor in 1978; he also attended briefings at the White House and welcomed Rosalynn Carter to Arkansas.[40]

Carter was sufficiently impressed to include Clinton in the Camp David ruminations. Sitting next to Carter during a three-hour group meeting on July 11, Clinton told him that he was "too withdrawn," warned that the country lacked a sense of his intelligence and dedication, and urged him to emphasize the opportunities rather than the sacrifices latent in the energy crisis. According to Clinton, Carter responded "very well" to this frank and "emotional exchange." On July 15, Clinton hailed Carter's "terrific speech . . . exactly what I thought he should say." Perhaps, Clinton speculated, he was the unspecified southern governor mentioned at the outset. Covering a different base, Clinton telephoned his sympathy to Joseph Califano after the cabinet reorganization.[41]

In 1992, Carter voted for Clinton in the Georgia Democratic primary and regarded his election as a kind of personal vindication. Not only was Clinton a fellow southerner victimized by Yankee stereotypes, but he also "very courageously" stressed that Americans were "all in this together." Although Carter urged a "comprehensive" plan of health care reform in which all Americans sacrificed "a little," he initially declined to burden Clinton with detailed advice drawn from his own years in office. Their relationship soon cooled because the Clinton White House was less cooperative with Carter's independent postpresidential diplomacy than the Bush administration had been. In 1994, despite misgivings, Clinton sanctioned both Carter's meeting with Kim Il Sung to defuse the crisis over North Korea's evident attempt to build nuclear weapons and his negotiations with Haiti's junta to prevent an American invasion. Carter subsequently complained that his efforts were insufficiently appreciated by the administration. To post–Cold War cold warriors like William Safire, however, the White House's reluctant endorsement of Carter's missions to Pyongyang and Port-au-Prince constituted appeasement and evidence that "Jimmy Clinton" now occupied the Oval Office.[42]

On the domestic front, pundits in a pack during early 1993 discerned alarming similarities between Clinton's routine transition troubles and Carter's "failed" presidency. In the most ominous comparisons, they pointed to the new president's advocacy of too much complex legislation and apparent lack of "leadership." Members of the Clinton administration extracted similar lessons from the now-stylized portrayal of the malaise-laden late seventies. "The shadow of Carter haunts everyone," said Leon Panetta, Clinton's first director of the Office of Management and Budget. These comparisons subsided after

Clinton won a series of victories on Capitol Hill, yet they were readily retrieved in 1994 after his legislative program bogged down and his poll ratings slipped.[43]

Most journalistic comparisons of Carter and Clinton missed the important point waiting to be made. Although Clinton represented a later generation of white southerners, came from a lower social stratum, and thrived on political maneuvering, his self-consciously centrist worldview was nonetheless closer to Carter's updated progressivism than to welfare state liberalism. During the 1992 campaign, he assailed "Washington insiders," promised to cut a bloated "federal bureaucracy," and emphasized that Americans shared a common destiny regardless of their race, gender, or class. Clinton, too, used broadly psychological appeals to win votes and convince Americans of their common destiny. He even diagnosed a "crisis of the American spirit" that, fortunately, could be blamed on a Republican president this time around. During his first year in office, Clinton made deficit control and the North American Free Trade Agreement rather than unemployment relief his legislative priorities. Criticism of these choices elicited Clinton's condemnation of the "knee-jerk liberal press."[44]

Those pundits and politicians who expect Clinton to avoid Carter's presidential "failure" point to his greater charisma and preference for back slapping over brooding. His major advantages, however, are two things Carter had and he does not: a Cold War and a strong left-liberal wing of the Democratic Party. Even so, it remains uncertain whether charisma combined with the rhetoric of social solidarity can sustain Clinton's coalition under the banner of latter-day progressivism. It is even less clear that this latest version of progressivism can meet the country's needs.

NOTES

An earlier version of this article was presented at the American Historical Association convention, December 28, 1992. I want to thank William Becker, Lee Fleming, and Diana S. Rodriguez for their suggestions for revisions.

1. WTOP Radio, October 28, 1992; "Monumental Mandate. But Fragile," *New York Times,* November 4, 1992; Adam Clymer, "Clinton Tries to Learn from Carter and History," *New York Times,* December 6, 1992.

2. For a good treatment of the 1976 campaign, see Kathleen Hall Jamieson, *Packaging the Presidency: A History and Criticism of Presidential Campaign Advertising* (New York: Oxford University Press, 1984), chap. 8.

3. Carter is quoted in my article, "Jimmy Carter: Beyond the Current Myths," *Magazine of History* 3 (Summer-Fall 1988), 19. For a more detailed discussion of Carter's use of symbolic politics, see Leo P. Ribuffo, "Jimmy Carter and the Selling of the President, 1976–1980," in Herbert Rosenbaum and Alexej Ugrinsky, ed., *Keeping Faith: The Presi-*

dency and Domestic Policies of Jimmy Carter (Westport, Conn.: Greenwood Press, 1993), 143–162.

4. James Wooten, *Dasher: The Roots and the Rising of Jimmy Carter* (New York: Summit Books, 1978), 347; Stephen Brill, "Jimmy Carter's Pathetic Lies," *Harper's* 252 (March 1976), 77–80, 82, 84, 88.

5. For further explorations of Carter's personality and worldview, see my "God and Jimmy Carter," in Ribuffo, *Right Center Left: Essays in American History* (New Brunswick: Rutgers University Press, 1992), 214–248, and Betty Glad, *Jimmy Carter: In Search of the Great White House* (New York: Norton, 1980).

6. For further discussion of Carter as a latter-day progressive and the problems this position caused within the Democratic coalition, see Leo P. Ribuffo, "Jimmy Carter and the Ironies of American Liberalism," *Gettysburg Review* 1 (Autumn 1989), 738–749; Burton I. Kaufman, *The Presidency of James Earl Carter, Jr.* (Lawrence: University Press of Kansas, 1993); and Erwin C. Hargrove, *Jimmy Carter as President: Leadership and the Politics of the Public Good* (Baton Rouge: Louisiana State University Press, 1988).

7. For the shifting treatment of Carter as a leader in this period, see Mark Rozell, *The Press and the Carter Presidency* (Boulder: Westview Press, 1989), 35–40, 74–75, 82–88.

8. Ribuffo, "Selling of the President," 149–150.

9. Carter, *Keeping Faith: Memoirs of a President* (New York: Bantam, 1982), 92; *Public Papers of the Presidents of the United States: Jimmy Carter 1977* (Washington: Government Printing Office, 1977), 69–77, 656–662.

10. Neil de Marchi, "Energy Policy Under Nixon: Mainly Putting Out Fires" and "The Ford Administration: Energy as a Political Good," and James L. Cochrane, "Carter Energy Policy and the Ninety-fifth Congress," in Crauford D. Goodwin, ed., *Energy Policy in Perspective: Today's Problems, Yesterday's Solutions* (Washington: Brookings Institution, 1981), 395–473, 475–545, 553, 564–577; Franklin Tugwell, *The Energy Crisis and the American Political Economy: Politics and Markets in the Management of Natural Resources* (Stanford: Stanford University Press, 1988), 97–113.

11. Kaufman, *James Earl Carter,* 66–68; Tugwell, *Energy Crisis,* 114–118; Barbara Kellerman, *The Political Presidency: Practice of Leadership* (New York: Oxford University Press, 1984), 192–206; Robert Mann, *Legacy to Power: Senator Russell Long of Louisiana* (New York: Paragon, 1992), 342–346; Russell D. Motter: "Seeking Limits: The Passage of the National Energy Act as a Microcosm of the Carter Presidency," in Rosenbaum and Ugrinsky, *Domestic Policies of Jimmy Carter,* 581–586; Carter, *Keeping Faith,* 92.

12. Ribuffo, "Selling of the President," and John Anthony Maltese, "'Rafshoonery': The Effort to Control the Communications Agenda of the Carter Administration," in Rosenbaum and Ugrinsky, *Domestic Policies,* 150–151 and 437–447; Rafshoon to Carter, July 20, August 8, 1978, Box 9; Rafshoon to Carter, August 17, 1978, Box 10; Rafshoon to Carter, November 11, 1978, Box 13, Rafshoon Collection, all from the Jimmy Carter Library, Atlanta.

13. Kellerman, *Political Presidency,* 206–209; Cochrane, "Carter Energy Policy," 584–587; Pietro S. Nivola, *The Politics of Energy Conservation* (Washington: Brookings Institution, 1986), 118–120, 229–233; *Public Papers 1978,* 1978–1985.

14. Ribuffo, "Ironies of Liberalism," 743–744. Rafshoon to Carter, September 27,

1978, and [Rafshoon], "Public Strategy, January 1–March 31 (1979)," Box 29; Pat Caddell to Carter, December 17, 1978, Box 32; Rafshoon Collection.

15. Theodore H. White, *America in Search of Itself: The Making of the President, 1956–1980* (New York: Harper and Row, 1982), 259–260; James MacGregor Burns, *Leadership* (New York: Harper and Row, 1978); Christopher Lasch, *The Culture of Narcissism: American Life in an Age of Diminishing Expectations* (1979,: reprint, New York: Norton, 1991), xiii; Robert A. Strong, "Recapturing Leadership: The Carter Administration and the Crisis of Confidence," *Presidential Studies Quarterly* 16 (February 1986), 640.

16. *Public Papers 1979,* 609–614; Joseph A. Yager, "The Energy Battles of 1979," in Goodwin, *Energy Policy,* 610–616; Mann, *Legacy of Power,* 362–365; Kaufman, *James Earl Carter,* 137–139.

17. Yager, "Energy Battles," 618–623; Kaufman, *James Earl Carter,* 143.

18. *New York Times,* July 1, 1979; White, *America in Search,* 266; Carter, *Keeping Faith,* 114; Rosalynn Carter, *First Lady from Plains* (New York: Fawcett, 1984), 286; Strong, "Recapturing Leadership," 664–665; J. William Holland, "The Great Gamble: Jimmy Carter and the 1979 Energy Crisis," *Prologue* 22 (Spring 1990): 66–70; Steven M. Gillon, *The Democrats' Dilemma: Walter F. Mondale and the Liberal Legacy* (New York: Columbia University Press, 1992), 261–262; Carter to Caddell, July 16, Box 139, President's Handwriting File.

19. "Camp David Advisers: Who Carter Met," from *Congressional Digest,* in Box 139, President's Handwriting File.

20. Holland, "Great Gamble," 70–71; Carter, *Keeping Faith,* 116–118. For some of Carter's notes, in the form of brief quotations from his visitors, see "Mr. President" and "Draft # 3," Box 139, President's Handwriting File.

21. Carter memorandum of his telephone conversation with Robert Strauss, July 6, 1979, Jack Watson to Carter, July 6, 1979, Zbigniew Brzezinski to Carter, July 6, 1979, Box 137, Caddell to Carter, July 12, 1979, Box 138, President's Handwriting File; "White House News Summary," July 9, 10, 11, 1979.

22. *Wall Street Journal,* July 10, 1979; *St. Louis Post-Dispatch,* July 8, 1979; *New York Newsday,* July 11, 1979; "White House News Summary," July 11, 13, 1979.

23. Rozell, *Press and Carter Presidency,* 87; *Christian Science Monitor,* July 9, 1979; *Sarasota Herald Tribune,* July 6, 1979; *Milwaukee Journal,* July 6, 1979; *Atlanta Constitution,* July 8, 1979; *New York Newsday,* July 7, 1979; *Bergen (New Jersey) Evening Record,* July 11, 1979; *Los Angeles Times,* July 8, 1979; *Baltimore Sun,* July 9, 1979; *Chicago Tribune,* July 7, 1979; "White House News Summary," July 6, 1979.

24. Rafshoon to Carter, July 10, 1979, Box 50, Speechwriters' File; Alfred Kahn to Carter, July 12, 1979, Box 139, President's Handwriting File.

25. White, *America in Search,* 268; Rafshoon, "Exit Interview"; Caddell to Carter, July 12, 1979, Box 138, Lasch to Jody Powell, June 10, 1979, Box 140, President's Handwriting File.

26. "Draft # 3," 3, 8, 14.

27. "White House Press Summary," July 14, 1979; White, *America in Search,* 268.

28. "Energy and the Crisis of Confidence," *Public Papers 1979,* 1235–1241.

29. *Los Angeles Times, New York Newsday,* and *Hartford Courant,* July 17, 1979;

"White House News Summary," July 17, 1979. See also *Boston Globe, Milwaukee Journal, Minneapolis Tribune,* and *Baltimore Sun,* July 17, 1979; *Charlotte Observer,* and *Shreveport Journal,* July 16; *Bangor Daily News,* July 18.

30. *Wall Street Journal,* July 17, 1979. See also *Chicago Tribune* and *Richmond Times-Dispatch,* July 17, 1979.

31. "White House News Summary," July 17, 18, 1979.

32. *Presidential Papers of Jimmy Carter 1979,* 1241–1258; Janet R. Albrecht to Carter, July 15, 1979, Box 139, Carter to Rex Scouten, July 24, 1979, to Administrator Freemason, July 27, 1979, to Clement Conger, July 26, 1979, Box 140, President's Handwriting File; "White House News Summary," July 16, 1979.

33. Joseph A. Califano, *Governing America: An Insider's Report from the White House and the Cabinet* (New York: Simon and Schuster, 1981), 428–445; Michael Blumenthal to Carter, July 19, 1979, Box 139, President's Handwriting File.

34. Carter, *Keeping Faith,* 121; Califano, *Governing America,* 430; "White House News Summaries," July 18, 19, 1979.

35. *New York Daily News,* July 22, 1979, *Philadelphia Inquirer, Chicago Tribune,* July 20, 1979, *Wall Street Journal, Boston Globe, Dallas Times-Herald, New York Newsday,* July 19, 1979, *Atlanta Journal-Constitution,* July 21, 1979; Dom Bonafede, "Carter Turns on the Drama—But Can He Lead?" *National Journal* 11 (July 28, 1979), 1236–1240.

36. Rosalynn Carter, *First Lady,* 287; "Energy and Imagery," *Nation* (July 28–August 4, 1979), 65; "White House News Summary," July 20, 21, 1979; *Hartford Courant,* July 20, 1979; Gillon, *Democrats' Dilemma,* 264–265.

37. Tugwell, *Energy Crisis,* 125–126; Nivola, *Politics of Energy,* 233–235; G. John Ikenberry, *Reasons of State: Oil Politics and the Capacities of American Government* (Ithaca: Cornell University Press, 1988), 132–135; Jamieson, *Packaging the Presidency,* 444.

38. "Larry King Live," CNN, December 10, 1992; Hargrove, *Carter as President;* Charles O. Jones, *The Trusteeship Presidency: Jimmy Carter and the United States Congress* (Baton Rouge: Louisiana State University Press, 1988), 217; Kai Bird, "The Very Model of an Ex-President," *Nation* (November 12, 1990), 558, 560–564.

39. Kaufman, *James Earl Carter,* 140; Frank Moore, Dan Tate, and Robert Thomson to Carter, June 20, 1979, President's Handwriting File; Carter to Edward Kennedy, March 1, 1979, July 25, 1979, Edward Kennedy to Jimmy Carter, April 27, 1979, June 21, 1979, July 9, 1979, Edward M. Kennedy Name File (White House Central Files). I deal with the Carter-Kennedy relationship in "'I'll Whip His Ass': Jimmy Carter, Edward Kennedy, and the Latest Crisis of American Liberalism," paper delivered at the Organization of American Historians convention, April 1994.

40. Frank Moore to Bill Clinton, March 18, 1977, Hamilton Jordan to Bill Clinton, November 15, 1977, Jack Watson to Bill Clinton, July 18, 1979, Rosalynn Carter to Hillary Rodham and Bill Clinton, July 25, 1979, Stuart Eizenstat to Bill Clinton, December 19, 1979, Bill Clinton Name File (White House Central File).

41. *Arkansas Gazette,* July 11, 12, 16, 1979; Califano, *Governing America,* 443.

42. "A Town Meeting with President Jimmy Carter," Southern Historical Association, November 5, 1992; "Nightline," ABC, February 8, 1993; *New York Times,* January 14, 1993, April 3, 25, 1993; Steven H. Hochman, "The Post-Presidential Foreign

Policy Initiatives of Jimmy Carter," paper presented at the meeting of the Society for Historians of American Foreign Relations, June 25, 1994; William Safire, "Jimmy Clinton," *New York Times,* June 27, 1994; George F. Will, "Communing in Korea," *Washington Post,* June 23, 1994; "The Empty Suit, Cont'd," *New Republic* 211 (July 22, 1994), 7; Maureen Dowd, "Despite Role as Negotiator, Carter Feels Unappreciated," *New York Times,* September 21, 1994; William Safire, "Jimmy Clinton, II," *New York Times,* September 22, 1994.

43. *New York Times,* April 3, 25, 1993; *Washington Post,* May 27, 1993, November 9, 1993; Andrew Ferguson, "The New New Democrats," *National Review* (February 15, 1993).

44. "A Town Meeting with President Jimmy Carter," Southern Historical Association, November 5, 1992; *A Plan for America's Future* (n.p.: Clinton for President Committee, 1992), 8, 11; "Listening to America with Bill Moyers: A Conversation with Governor Bill Clinton," PBS, July 7, 1992, 14, 19; *New York Times,* November 22, 1993.

Chapter 13

HISTORICAL ANALOGIES AND PUBLIC POLICY:

THE BLACK AND IMMIGRANT EXPERIENCE

IN URBAN AMERICA

RICHARD C. WADE

H ISTORICAL ANALOGIES are one of the games historians play. In its most serious exercise, it is the way scholars deepen insights into major historical problems. Arthur Schlesinger, for example, illustrated the moral dimension of the coming of the Civil War by comparing the sectional conflict of the 1850s with the dilemma of democratic nations in the face of totalitarian aggression in the 1930s. Herbert Gans discovered an interesting parallel in Italian neighborhood life and its village antecedents in the old world. Not all analogies have been equally convincing, but at their best they provided an arresting perspective on persistent historical problems.

Analogies not only are a convenient construct of historians, but also provide a basis for making public policy. Leaders examine past experience while developing their own programs, using what they consider to be the "lessons of history" as a broad framework for contemporary action. Woodrow Wilson, for instance, approached World War I from his historical understanding of the War of 1812. He had concluded from his own work that President Madison had made a mistake in that conflict by bringing the United States into the war in effect on the side of Napoleon and his imperial ambitions. Wilson always felt that Madison had viewed the war too narrowly, seeing it as an issue of freedom of the seas when he felt the deeper question was the prospect of democracy and liberty in Europe. If the young Republic could not avoid involvement, at least it ought to have gone to war on the right side. When confronted with another war a century later, Wilson faced the question of freedom of the seas for both sides. His reluctant neutrality always tilted toward the Allies, and when Wilson did take the country to war he raised it above the legal argument concerning international law and placed it on the high ideological ground of the defense of democracy.

A better-known analogy involves the famous Maginot line in which the French believed that the lesson of its many wars with Germany dictated a comprehensive defensive strategy. Expecting an analogous problem in the future, they created a complex system of fortifications admirably designed to defend France in 1870 or 1914, but which had become hopelessly dated by 1939. And, of course, in diplomacy no word is more often used than Munich. Referring to the Western betrayal of Czechoslovakia during the European crisis in the thirties, it became a popular code word for the consequences of cowardice in international affairs. This analogy was not simply invoked in the same geographic area but was widely used by American spokesmen in East Asia, Africa, and Latin America as well.

Historical analogies obviously are not always correct; indeed, they can be misleading. But we do not know how to think about big problems without them. They broaden our perspective, allow us to put new problems into a more comfortable and intelligible context, and remind us of the shared experience of others under similar circumstances either earlier or elsewhere. Sometimes these analogies are explicit, clearly stated by policy makers, and more or less precise in application. At other times, the analogy is assumed, perhaps being so apparent or so widely understood that it needs no elaboration.

I want to examine a case that falls into both these categories—a historical analogy that earlier lay unarticulated but assumed and later became the acting hypothesis of policy makers. Moreover, the problem involved is the most important facing the nation: the elemental question of race. The outlines of the issue need only restatement, not elaboration.

Beginning at about the turn of the century, southern blacks began to move into northern cities. In one of the most massive migrations in history, Dixie's black population moved off the countryside into the nation's booming urban centers. For the past century, the accommodation of these newcomers has been a central problem for city officials.

It was assumed by everyone that the blacks were simply the last of a whole series of migrants, and that what happened to the Irish, Germans, Italians, Poles, and Jews would also happen to southern blacks. The same natural forces that had facilitated the acceptance of white newcomers would also ease the entrance of those from the South. And the public policies appropriate for the earlier groups would be applicable for the most recent arrivals regardless of race. The analogy was widely accepted and provided the framework for official thinking and action for the five decades when the blacks swarmed into northern cities. The analogy, however, proved mistaken; the experiences of the white and black immigrants turned out to be fundamentally different.

The process by which the American city incorporated its European newcomers into municipal life is well known. The immigrants came from all over the old world. Most were poor and without marketable skills. As they piled into the crowded downtowns, they found housing where they could. Some owners carved small apartments out of old mansions, others converted rooms in warehouses, and still others constructed tenements for immigrant lodging. No space was too small for use. Whole families were stuffed into single rooms;

unattached men made barracks out of basements. The population densities exceeded anything known before. New York's Lower East Side had heavier concentration than London, Paris, Naples, or even Bombay.

The crowding brought with it predictable consequences. Sanitation facilities, primitive at best, quickly became overburdened, and immigrant sections of town stood out on every health map drawn by city officials. Conditions coaxed disease; congestion permitted its rapid spread throughout the neighborhood. Quarantine required precisely the distance and space that were missing in the area. Hospital capacities were hopelessly small. No age or group was spared. In Chicago, one out of every three children in downtown precincts died by the age of one. Life, indeed, was mean, brutish, and short. By the nineties, public bodies and private agencies continuously published depressing accounts of slum conditions in every American city.

Moreover, jobs were scarce and unpredictable. Few newcomers could command much better than the least skilled work; most depended on seasonal employment. Ironically, the fact that so many people poured into cities forced municipal authorities into ambitious construction programs. New streets had to be paved, schools constructed, sewers put underground, bridges built, trolley lines laid, new city halls and court houses erected, and parks planned and developed. In short, the modern physical infrastructure of most American cities was built during the height of immigration. Since all this activity required unskilled labor on a grand scale, there were jobs enough to take the edge off want and desperation. Nonetheless, there were always too few jobs and too many mouths to feed.

The neighborhood had little to compensate for the congestion, inadequate housing, poor health, and low income of its residents. Schools were overcrowded, underfinanced, and usually poorly staffed. Religious organizations struggled vainly to provide enough buildings and schools for their growing numbers. Saloons alone kept pace with the population, dotting every street and forming a social focus for male activity outside the home. On the lower level, rampant crime and vice added danger and uncertainty to street life.

In short, conditions in immigrant ghettos in the late nineteenth and early twentieth centuries were never very pleasant. For the city, they were centers of continuous trouble, afflicted with wretched housing, erratic and low-paying jobs, inadequate schools, dirt and filth, high crime, and endemic disorder. Later these neighborhoods would be invested in retrospect with qualities their residents seldom knew. Writers and planners would find a benignancy in their clutter and crowding, in their intense ethnicity and religious diversity, and in their uncertain and fragile institutions. A whole nostalgic literature grew up to contrast urban life of the present with what authors took to be true in 1900. But most of the "good old neighborhood" nostalgia would be written thirty years and sometimes thirty miles from childhood ghetto streets.

The fact is that most of the residents who could moved out into better areas in the city. Indeed, they found life tolerable in the old ghetto only because it was perceived to be temporary, a kind of staging ground for movement into an improved life elsewhere. And experience bore out this expectation. Every family knew of people who had once lived on the block and later found better quarters in another part of town. Sometimes it would be a member of the family, or perhaps someone in the parish, or a neighbor down the street, but the outward mobility was a continuing process. This fact was central to ghetto life because it made difficult conditions tolerable. If one could survive now, things might get better—at least for the younger ones. To be sure, the number "making it" comprised only a modest percentage, but the hope was more pervasive.

Constant movement, then, was a critical component of the immigrant ghetto. Scholars later discovered what residents knew so well; they also gauged its extent. Howard Chudacoff's study of Omaha is, perhaps, the clearest account of this internal urban migration. Tracing immigrant mobility in the Nebraska boom town at the turn of the century, he concluded that "the overwhelming majority" of men living for twenty years in Omaha "occupied three or more homes" and only about 3 percent remained in the same dwelling for that period. Peter Knights and Stephen Thernstrom found the same movement among Boston's Irish in the nineteenth century, while Thomas Philpott's volume on Chicago brilliantly demonstrated the universality of white immigrant residential instability in that polyglot metropolis.

Much of this residential movement was mere transience within the same neighborhood; some of it was forced by the tenant's inability to pay even small rents; and family additions required a constant search for larger quarters. Yet a significant amount represented genuine, if modest, social mobility. A better job and the accumulation of savings permitted purchase of a home in a better neighborhood farther away from the noise, congestion, and pollution of downtown. A single-family home or a two-flat replaced rooms in a crowded tenement or a converted mansion. Occasionally, the move was dramatic, involving a leap into a middle-class community well outside the original block. But usually the movement was gradual, involving several moves and many years. Nonetheless, the centrifugal action was unmistakable. Indeed, it was the genius of America's metropolitan system, allowing millions of people from different countries, with different languages and religions, to be incorporated into the nation's urban mainstream.

When blacks began to move into northern cities on a large scale at the turn of the century, it was widely believed that they would repeat the process that had so successfully served millions of European immigrants. Policy makers assumed that the newcomers would, like their predecessors, concentrate in the center of cities, find some jobs, get an economic footing, discover their numbers, and slowly move outward toward the more pleasant residential areas of town. And, at first, it appeared that this calculation was correct. Blacks indeed did huddle in the congested center; jobs, while not plentiful or well paid, were available to some; and a group consciousness gradually emerged. Yet there was little outward movement; residential segregation increased with each decade and with each new wave of black migrants. Far from breaking, the ghetto held and expanded, oozing out into white neighborhoods on its borders. In the North this rigidity was new; in the South it was traditional.

In fact, the proper analogy for northern cities was not the immigrant experience, but rather the black experience in southern cities in the decades following the Civil War. For, in urban Dixie, blacks had been a substantial part of the population for at least four generations. In some cities the proportion reached almost half, seldom dropped below a quarter, and usually hovered around a third. Out of the tangled race relations bequeathed by the institution of slavery emerged a pattern that would later be re-created in northern cities. An examination of that process suggests something of the dimension of the race problem that so afflicts metropolitan America.

Even before slavery had been abolished, a system of segregation had grown up in southern cities. The whites thought some such arrangement was necessary if they were to sustain their traditional supremacy over the blacks in an urban setting. The countryside provided enough room to give meaning to racial separation. The master could be physically quite removed from his blacks, though sharing the same plantation or farm. And together both were isolated from others. In cities these spatial relationships were quite different. Both races were thrown together; they encountered each other at every corner; they rubbed elbows at every turn; they divided up, however inequitably, the limited space of the town site. Segregation sorted people out by race, established a public etiquette for their conduct, and created social distance where there was a physical proximity. Urban circumstances produced this system long before the destruction of slavery itself.

Of course, the complete separation of races was impossible in the city, and practices differed from place to place. In some towns, public conveyances remained mixed; in others Negroes were not excluded from all public grounds; in still others housing continued to be scrambled. Yet every city developed its own arrangement expressed in the contrived separation of black and white in countless ways. Though never total, the segregation was so extensive that blacks were never permitted to forget their inferior position.

The rising incidence of segregation characterized race relations even before emancipation. Rooted in the white's need for discipline and deference, it developed to take up the slack in the loosening system of slavery. It provided public control to replace the dwindling private supervision of master over slave. To do this, the difference between free and enslaved blacks had to be narrowed, depriving the free of part of their freedom even while permitting a wider latitude to bondsmen. To most whites, however, there seemed no alternative. The old system no longer really controlled; the walls no longer really confined; the chains no longer really held.

After the Civil War, the South had to produce a new system of race relations. Slavery was dead, and, except for the nascent segregation in the cities, there were no guidelines to inform public policy. In the countryside the problem was not as acute; space provided racial separation. Local governments had very limited jurisdiction—schools, roads, almshouses—which required no immediate racial decisions. The schools would, of course, be segregated but the broader question of a new racial system was not so urgent. But in the cities the question could not be postponed. Blacks in large numbers, landless and unskilled, drifted from the countryside into the cities. Local authorities were overwhelmed by this migration. They had neither the facilities nor a program to deal with the new situation. Yet they had to act, and in the racial assumptions underlying their response lay the seeds of modern urban segregation.

A close look at the development of race relations in Atlanta perhaps best illustrates the case. As the capital of Georgia, it lay in the heart of Dixie; as a city leveled by the war, it had to start from scratch in both its physical and its social rebuilding. To be sure, as a small town in the fifties, it had been governed by the institution of slavery, and its race relations looked very much like those in other southern cities. Yet emancipation and destruction offered a new opportunity to find a racial system appropriate for a new South.

By 1870 Atlanta's population was about 40 percent black, a proportion that has remained stable until recent times. The crisis in the young city was immediate. Former slaves came into the city as soon as the war ended. Most had no skills, and jobs were scarce. As a result the number of poor mounted rapidly, forcing the city to produce facilities for their care. From the beginning, local authorities established separated almshouses, initially by leasing and then with new construction. Vagrancy was inevitably the handmaid of poverty, and blacks picked up for loitering were placed in custody. They were then taken before a separate court, and, if guilty, placed in segregated quarters in the jail. Later a black facility replaced the single institution.

Public health also had to be faced. The city needed hospital care for both races but lacked the money to construct two buildings. Hence, they erected only one; yet the new facilities included separate rooms and separate entrances. Whites entered from the main street and blacks by the side door. Inside, segregated quarters served whites and blacks in different parts of the hospital. Inevitably, the newcomers would die, and, just as separate as in life, blacks would be interred in separate plots. In the years before the war the city's central cemetery had a quadrant reserved for the black dead. But in 1871 a new area was set aside on the west end, and, in the cool notation of the city council minutes, the bones of blacks were dug up and moved to the new area. Moreover, for the nameless or poor separate pauper fields were available.

In short, when public policy had to be made clear exigencies, the racial assumptions of local officials were abundantly clear. They believed in the separation of the races and they devised elaborate means to keep black and white apart. Moreover, all this happened in the Reconstruction South under federal supervision when official statements gave presumption to equality. Yet when confronted with very practical problems and the need to act, white officialdom opted for segregation.

Educational development revealed the same tendencies. From the outset white and black students attended different schools. Black teachers taught only in their own system, though whites occupied both the school board and, until the 1890s, all the principals' chairs. Moreover, public library facilities excluded blacks from the beginning. In Atlanta this handicap was not as fatal as elsewhere, because what would later become Atlanta University offered a whole range of education not available to blacks elsewhere in the South. Yet any learning in the Georgia capital took place in segregated units.

The development of parks displayed the same racial policy. Small parks created no problem since they were easily segregated, but larger ones needed interior separation. When a zoo was established, authorities met the delicate problem by keeping visitors separated by the central cages where, as the *Atlanta Constitution* observed with satisfaction, "an aisle 7 feet wide was railed off on each side of the cases—one for whites, and the other for blacks," and "there is no communication between them." Thus the occupation of open space as well as the more congested places demonstrated the same racial assumption.

Quasi-public facilities also fell into separated categories. In the theaters, blacks entered by different doors, occupied designated areas, and fended for themselves for refreshments. Hotels and restaurants excluded them, and except for a few downtown bars the color line also prevailed. Occasionally a traveler, especially if politically connected, would be accommodated for a short time, but in 1872 the Calhoun opened to meet "a necessity long felt by colored citizens" because the "better class" of blacks would not travel due to the "ill and unjust treatment" they suffered at the hands of "public carriers and innkeepers . . . who claim the right to discriminate." When the horse-drawn street car was introduced in the same year, it adopted the same restrictions.

Employment and housing involved less overt public policy. Moreover, the legacy of slavery in these areas was more ambivalent. Yet the trend in both was the same—toward more separation. Under the peculiar institution, workers mingled on many jobs and, though blacks usually did the most menial tasks, 6 percent were classified as skilled in 1870. Georgia law had reserved most of the high-paying skills for whites in antebellum years, but the postwar practice began with some mixing. As the decades wore on, however, exclusion became more frequent and even the small percentage of black skilled labor almost disappeared.

Residential segregation was similarly a result of white practice with some public encouragement. Before abolition, blacks and whites had shared the same urban plot, and though the slave lived in back quarters, racial proximity was a central fact. Over the three decades after emancipation another residential pattern emerged. A racial map of 1870 showed blacks living in all parts of Atlanta. To be sure, there were heavier concentrations on the east and south sides. But only a few blocks were wholly black. By 1880 the new system became visible. Black residents in the northern part of the city diminished, and the areas of full black occupancy expanded. It was possible to identify the "colored sections" of town. After ten more years the present areas of concentration appeared clearly. Eastern downtown areas—"buttermilk bottom" and "sweet Auburn"—were wholly black. The area around Atlanta University on the west side had developed a homogeneous community. Elsewhere in the city, some residual black residents could be found scattered throughout white neighborhoods. Yet the tendency was clear: the index of racial segregation in housing rose with each census. By 1890 the shape of the modern ghettos had been fixed.

Just as revealing was the racial composition of new housing. Atlanta was one of the great boom towns of the new South with a population that jumped from 9,500 in 1860 to 37,500 in 1880 to 65,000 in 1890. This expansion required new residential building, most of which took place on the outer edges of town where land was vacant and cheap. In these new areas all the construction was for whites. Areas later annexed by the city had no black residents at all. The meaning was clear enough: when whites had a choice they moved into racially exclusive areas. Blacks were more and more confined to the old areas of town with hand-me-down buildings or jerry-built wooden dwellings. The historic urban forces that have produced the white ring around the black center had begun; the modern ghetto appeared even before the present century.

By 1885 race relations in Atlanta had been set. Over two decades a series of public decisions and private practices created a pervasive pattern of segregation. Though there were a few crevices, the system left little room for leakage. At any moment blacks were confronted with discrimination. Whether it was in a public facility, school, or church, or on the job, their "place" was clear. Moreover, whites believed that blacks liked it that way. Revealing both local customs and the official view, the *Atlanta Constitution* asserted: "We believe that negroes themselves do not, and would not if they had the power, insist on miscellaneous assemblages. Here in Atlanta they have their own churches, are ministered by their own pastors and conduct their own affairs. . . . In this city they have their own schools, equal in all respects to white schools. . . . They have their own secret societies of Odd Fellows, Masons, military companies and societies. . . . They have their own restaurants, hotels and largely their own doctors, lawyers and merchants. This is the proper adjustment of this matter in our opinion."

What happened in Atlanta developed in other southern cities, though of course with variation. Not all places segregated the same categories. Some permitted mixing in a few public places or on street cars; others never separated the races in the theaters or parks; and in the more stagnant postwar towns, such as Charleston, it took longer to untangle housing and employment patterns. Yet by 1880 the urban South was effectively segregated. No matter where the black might turn, on the street, in the school or church, in recreational or health facilities, on his job or in his neighborhood, he was reminded of the general white judgment that the races ought to be separate. This public etiquette governed behavior everywhere and was embodied in numberless ordinances and governmental regulations. Later Jim Crow laws formalized this segregation on a statewide level.

This development was fixed by the time the great black migration began to northern cities. And it would be repeated there. When the vanguard reached Chicago, for example, it found blacks living in many parts of the city. To be sure, most lived in minighettos in out-of-the-way locations and suffered racial discrimination in many ways. But the numbers were small and whites felt no general threat. As the migration mounted, however, so did the separation. The newcomers flocked into the south and west sides. Low incomes and real estate practices confined black residents to certain areas. In 1917, the real estate board formally embodied the segregation by declaring it a violation of its rules to sell to blacks outside the concentrated areas. School board policy, using district line changes and branch schools, separated youngsters in public education. Whites living near black neighborhoods resisted the spread of the ghetto, often with violence. In 1919 a race riot revealed the grim dimensions of Chicago's ghetto as it fractured the town's racial peace.

A similar pattern developed in other northern cities. As the proportion of blacks rose, so did the size of the ghetto. Unlike in the South, public policy seldom consciously underwrote the process; indeed, even as the separation proceeded, public officials condemned segregation and city councils legislated against discrimination. No one denied the problem; in fact, government reports laid it out in agonizing details and sponsored programs to foster equality. Political rhetoric warned against creating southern relations in northern metropolises. Yet, inevitably, the ghetto grew, absorbing white neighborhoods as it spread. Through the century, the index of residential segregation rose and the distinction between North and South narrowed. By 1950 every city of considerable size had its black sector.

This new black ghetto was fundamentally different from the old immigrant ghetto. Unlike its earlier white counterpart, the new ghetto did not disperse part of its population into other parts of the city. The escape valve of the immigrant concentrations was missing; the black areas simply filled up and spread out. The earlier ghetto had been tolerable because its residents thought it temporary; the new ghetto became intolerable because its inhabitants increasingly considered it permanent. Initially, blacks thought escape was always possible and that hard work, education, and some luck would spring at least their most successful into the middle-class-white world beyond. The last generation has seen this hope fade and the ghetto triumph.

This confinement produced two consequences that were new. The first was the increasing embitterment of the rising black middle class, which became increasingly frustrated by the intractability of residential restrictions. After all, they had met every traditional criteria for acceptance. They had education, good employment, and considerable income. Yet they were denied the most important symbol of American success—the right to live where they wanted, in neighborhoods of their own choosing with schools appropriate to their children's abilities or their own ambitions. They now learned that the only basis of their exclusion was the color of their skin. A college degree and a substantial income could carry the black family into better housing but, with a few exceptions, not into genuinely integrated communities. When the white middle class abandoned the city, the suburbs offered competitive possibilities. For the emergent blacks that option only occasionally appeared.

Ironically, the excluded comprised one of the most successful classes in American history. No other group had produced such a large middle class in such a short period of time as did the North's urban blacks. In 1950 the federal census classified their proportion as about 8 percent; by 1960 that figure more than doubled; in 1970 the black middle class in the cities comprised one-third of their total. In 1980 it reached 40 percent and in 1990 about half. There are, of course, problems with the census definition, especially because black middle-class families frequently involved two breadwinners. But this fact simply underlined the ambition of the new group at the same time it added some ambiguity to the figures.

The civil rights revolution of the fifties and early sixties was led by this energetic, intelligent, and embittered middle class. After more conventional strategies failed, this group, despairing of breaking the ghetto, turned inward to organize it. This had not happened with immigrant graduates of the ghetto, who quickly identified themselves with their new communities and gradually loosened their ties with the old neighborhoods. As the Irish, for example, fled the ghetto they might send some money back to the church, keep a few memberships in old associations, and drop in on St. Patrick's Day. But the focus of family life was in the new area and what lay ahead there for the family.

The black middle class was never offered that opportunity. Denied a new community, they turned back into the old. Here they discovered the second major difference between the new and old ghettos. The young, often now a majority in black neighborhoods, had already given up on the system. A young boy of fourteen could look around and say to himself: "What difference does it make for me to do what they tell me to? All around are people who did that. They stayed in school and out of trouble; they got their jobs and money.

But they are still just like we are—living in bad neighborhoods, with crime, rip-offs, bad schools, high prices, and impossible rent. What difference does it make what I do?" Nearly every poverty program has floundered on the question of motivation. "Why don't they act like the Italians, Irish, Poles, and Jews did?" is the familiar bureaucratic lament. But the answer is clear: they were never treated like the Italians, Irish, Poles, and Jews. In this fact lie the hopelessness, frustration, and feckless violence of the American city.

The ghettos first erupted in the sixties when the frustrated young people struck out at what appeared to them to be the oppressor. Though most of the deaths, injuries, and damages were suffered by blacks in black neighborhoods, the mutiny shook white America and damaged, at least temporarily, the fragile racial bonds of the country. What was significant through those grim years was the retrospective sampling of black middle-class opinion. In large numbers, they deplored violence, noting that the casualties were almost always black. At the same time, however, they refused publicly to denounce the rioters, because they said they understood the cause that lay behind the explosions. The Italian American middle class, on the other hand, has always been anxious to separate themselves from illegal action, especially the Mafia, when it tends to reflect adversely on the whole group within the wider community. The new ghetto has denied its successful middle class the luxury of those internal distinctions.

Moreover, the shape of the black ghetto frustrated political attempts to lessen tensions and provide an orderly dissolution of the infected spots. For the black neighborhoods almost invariably abutted on low-income white residential areas. The people living there had already moved several times before and now lacked the resources for the final leap into the suburbs. Resistance was everywhere strong; in places it was marked by violence. The racial guerrilla warfare in these urban communities shattered the Democratic Party and encouraged a new demagoguery on both sides. The disintegration of central policy making resulted in endless vetoes applied by one local group or another on city, state, and national programs.

In the larger context, the situation was almost bizarre. Race was, and is, the country's most persistent and dangerous problem. Yet its future was being determined by the group least able to handle it. The white residents at the edge of the ghetto are among the least educated, have the lowest incomes, and are the most insecure people in American society. Yet the nation places on their backs its most difficult question. Meanwhile, those with the highest education, greatest resources, and most security are far removed from the battle. And from the safety of the suburbs they judge the merits of the contesting forces, chiding the blacks with being too militant and labeling blue-collar whites as "backlashers." Hence, decisions on race, surely the most delicate and explosive of this century, repose in the hands of people whose margins of maneuver are very thin.

The new ghetto thus upsets expectation. Its intractability is new and obviously dangerous. What is now important is to devise a new national housing program that takes into account the difference between the black and immigrant experiences in American cities. The most recent newcomers will need a new policy designed to break the walls of the ghetto and permit their residents to disperse throughout the metropolis. The beginning of wisdom in developing a new approach is to understand the immigrant analogy has not worked and if the present historical forces continue to govern residential patterns, the indices of segregation will continue to fester.

The present condition contrasts sharply with the historic situation. Was there a coherent public policy? The older ways that incorporated immigrant millions into metropolitan America have proved inappropriate for blacks. It is now time for urban historians and public policy makers to think of new ways to tackle this urgent problem.

PART FOUR

AMERICA AND THE WORLD

Chapter 14

WOODROW WILSON AND THE COLD WAR

Betty Miller Unterberger

ALTHOUGH THE COLD WAR has ended, debate over its origins and development continues. As late as the Gorbachev regime, the Soviet Union was still seeking damages for America's role in the Allied interventions of 1918–1920, which they regard as the catalyst for the Cold War. More recently, American and Soviet analysts and interpreters have seen in American interventions abroad during the Cold War a continuation of Woodrow Wilson's policy of intervention in Bolshevik Russia. In the forty years between Harry Truman and Ronald Reagan, American combat forces intervened in Korea, Lebanon, Vietnam, the Dominican Republic, and Grenada to support governments threatened by perceived Communist takeovers. Although these latter interventions were clear in their stated anti-Communist motivations and objectives, there is no hint in *The Papers of Woodrow Wilson* that Wilson's purposes were in any way similar. Actually, Franklin D. Roosevelt faced similar charges at the conclusion of World War II for his decisions at Yalta. While many have exonerated Roosevelt as a major culprit in the origins of the Cold War, Wilson continues to be regarded as the villain. Now that the Cold War is over, it is time to reexamine these charges.

The record is clear that in the summer of 1918, in the midst of the carnage of World War I, and nine months after the Bolshevik revolution, thousands of American soldiers landed in Russia to engage in one of the strangest adventures in American diplomatic and military history. While contemporary critics described the enterprise as "Mr. Wilson's little war with Russia," most Americans today have long since forgotten it. Not so the Russians! Soviet leaders from Lenin to Gorbachev have repeatedly spoken with bitter reproach of the role of the United States as hostile promoter and participant in a military intervention designed to overthrow the Soviet government. But was this the reason for American intervention in Russia? Woodrow Wilson would have rejected the charge vociferously and he would also have rejected the charge that the American expeditions to Russia in 1918 provided the pattern for interventions against Communism throughout the Cold War.[1] As president, he consistently sought a policy of self-determination for the Russian people. But the story is a complicated one and cannot be understood outside of its setting in world conflict and coalition diplomacy.

Wilson would have been particularly distressed about Soviet allegations that the United States attempted to destroy the Soviet state at birth. On the contrary, Wilson attempted to encourage the Russian people to play their own role in their destiny, whatever the results. As he later explained to Sir William Wiseman, chief British intelligence officer in the United States: "My policy regarding Russia is very similar to my Mexican policy. I believe in letting them work out their own salvation, even though they wallow in anarchy for a while."[2]

Americans greeted the Russian Revolution of March 1917 with genuine enthusiasm. After the abdication of Nicholas II, a provisional government had been established and steps had been taken toward long awaited political and social reforms. It appeared as though democracy had finally broken through the hard crust of despotism. Within a few days the United States hurriedly recognized the new government—the first among the great powers to do so. Wilson had been reluctant to enter the war on the same side as the blackest autocracy in the world. Now Wilson could call Russia "a fit partner for a League of Honor," an ally dedicated to a common cause.[3] Americans also were inspired by the naive assumption that a democratic Russia would continue the war with renewed zeal.

By the fall of 1917, American hopes for a strong ally were diminished as a second revolution rocked Russia. The Bolsheviks, led by Nikolai Lenin, Leon Trotsky, and a virtually unknown Stalin, seized power. They instituted sweeping changes, some more rapidly than others. Not only did the revolution appear to be a menace to capitalistic society but, more immediately, Bolshevik peace negotiations with the Germans threatened the possible withdrawal of some forty divisions, or several hundred thousand German veterans from Russia and their deployment on the Western Front. A peace would make available to Germany the vast resources of Russia, thereby prolonging the struggle by billions of dollars and millions of lives. If this happened the democracies might be overwhelmed.

In these circumstances, the Allied statesmen and military leaders sought Allied military action in Russia for the purpose of restoring an Eastern Front against Germany. They turned to America and to Japan for possible sources of manpower and supply for such a military effort. The American response was consistently negative, while, in the case of Japan, the request raised geopolitical issues of major importance.

Wilson had stated his position toward Russia clearly in his memorable Fourteen Points address on January 8, 1918.[4] His sixth point was of special interest as it represented the official attitude of the American government toward Russia. He called for

the evacuation of all Russian territory and such settlement of all questions affecting Russia as will secure the best and freest cooperation of the other nations of the world in obtaining for her an unhampered and unembarrassed opportunity for the independent determination of her own political development and national policy and assure her of a sincere welcome into the society of free nations under institutions of her own choosing; and, more than a welcome, assistance also of every kind that she may need and may herself desire. The treatment accorded to Russia by her sister nations in the months to come will be the acid test of their good will, of their comprehension of her needs as distinguished from their own interest, and of their intelligent and unselfish sympathy.[5]

Wilson's policy toward Russia thus advocated nonintervention, self-determination, and friendly assistance. His position was reflected in a number of official statements of the United States government in the winter and spring of 1918, all of which had his approval and some of which he drafted personally. For example, in a communication to the Japanese government on January 20, 1918, he stated, "The common interests of all the powers at war with Germany demand from them an attitude of sympathy with the Russian people. . . . Any movement looking toward the occupation of Russian territory would at once be construed as one hostile to Russia and would be likely to unite all factions in Russia against us."[6]

Events of February and March 1918—the Germans' reopening hostilities against Russia as a means of bringing pressure in the peace negotiations, the final signing of the Russian-German peace treaty on March 3, and its ratification on March 16, and the opening of the great German offensive on the Western Front five days later—caused the Allies to exert even heavier pressure on Wilson to change his stand and to sanction an intervention in Siberia by the Japanese. The Japanese themselves were not yet ready to take action independently, and they refused to act as mandatory for the Allies unless the United States joined in making the request. Everything appeared to hang on Wilson's decision. Yet despite these pressures, the president remained unmoved. Throughout the winter and spring of the year, he questioned the wisdom of intervention. If any action were to be taken by the Japanese, he assumed it would be accompanied by a declaration to the effect that they were acting "as an ally of Russia, in Russia's interests, and with the sole view of holding it safe against Germany." But even with such a declaration, he thought the action would be misinterpreted, that "a hot resentment would be generated in Russia itself, and that the whole action might play into the hands of the enemies of Russia, and particularly of the enemies of the Russian Revolution, for which the Government of the United States entertains the greatest sympathy, in spite of all the unhappiness and misfortune which has for the time being sprung out of it."[7] In the absence of Wilson's approval, the Japanese for the moment abstained from action, but chaotic conditions in Manchuria and along the line of the Trans-Siberian Railway encouraged rumors of lone Japanese intervention.

In April-May 1918, confronted with a new German offensive in the west, the French and British military planners conceived a somewhat more elaborate scheme for intervention in Russia with or without the consent of the Bolsheviks. They proposed Allied landings both at Vladivostok and at the northern ports of European Russia. The Japanese were to bear the main burden at Vladivostok; a mixed Allied force, in which it was hoped the Americans would play a prominent part, was to bear the responsibility at Murmansk and Archangel. The expeditions at these widely separated points would combine with local anti-Bolshevik forces loyal to the Allied cause, advance toward each other, and eventually link up, thus creating a solid Allied front from Siberia to the Upper Volga region, forcing the Germans to reconstitute their military position in the east.[8]

It was obvious at the time that Wilson never would have given his approval to such a plan, and when he did learn of it, he was outraged. Nevertheless, the French and British military planners did not wait for American approval before beginning to implement the project to the extent that they were able.

In the northern ports, the British proceeded to take action at once. In May, the British sent to Archangel such few additional soldiers as they were able to spare, commanded by a general who was eventually to command the entire northern expedition. Because this force was wholly inadequate for an extensive expedition, the British requested that an American contingent also be made available for service at the northern Russian ports.

Nothing was said to Wilson at this time about the plan for penetrating into the interior and linking up with the Siberian intervention. The plan was put to him as merely an arrangement for the defense of the northern ports, particularly Murmansk, against the Germans and that American troops were needed to protect great quantities of Allied war supplies. Despite these arguments in favor of sending troops to northern Russia, Wilson remained at all times skeptical of the merits of this proposed expedition. But he felt obliged to send troops because the British and French were pressing so hard, and he had refused so many of their requests that they were beginning to feel that he was not a good ally. His opposition was made more difficult by the pro-Allied attitude of the local Soviet at Murmansk and by reports from Allied representatives in Russia that the Soviet government was not really as adverse as it pretended to be to the idea of an Allied landing in the north.

In June 1918, Wilson therefore finally replied to the British government that, while he had no enthusiasm for the scheme, he would abide in this instance by the opinion of Marshal Foch, the Allied commander-in-chief on the western front. If Foch really thought the requested American battalions would be of more use in Murmansk than in France, they would be sent. Foch, at British urging, approved the diversion of this force.[9] In July, American units were placed under British command to be used in the Russian north. This was the origin of America's participation in the northern intervention.

Meanwhile, the situation in Siberia had been drastically altered. At the end of May, a conflict broke out between the Czecho-Slovak corps and the Bolsheviks, resulting in Czech control of much of the Trans-Siberian Railway. The Czech force, composed largely of men who had been taken prisoner or had deserted from the Austro-Hungarian army, had fought courageously against the Central Powers alongside the Russians. They were eager to continue to fight on the Allied side in the hope of liberating their country from Austro-Hungarian domination, and of securing Allied support for the establishment of an independent Czechoslovakia. With the signing of the Treaty of Brest-Litovsk, the Czechs found themselves in a desperate situation. If captured by the Germans, they would all be executed as traitors. Their only hope was to go westward via Vladivostok to the western front. Though the corps was strung out in trainloads along the Trans-Siberian Railway from the Ukraine to Vladivostok, this force was now the strongest single army in Russia. It was to play a vital role in Wilson's decisions about Russia.

The outbreak of hostilities was largely a product of the chaotic conditions then existing in Siberia and the frictions and misunderstandings that occurred when the Czechs encountered parties of Austrian or Hungarian war prisoners who were, after the conclusion of the Brest-Litovsk peace, due for repatriation and were trying to make their way westward along the railway. The uprising actually came as a setback to Allied military planners, who had just made arrangements with the Soviet authorities to have this portion of the corps routed to northern Russia. The outbreak of the conflict between the Czechs and the Bolsheviks made this impossible. Within a few days, the Czechs seized most of the Trans-Siberian Railway from the Volga to Irkutsk. Another body of some 18,000 Czechs had already arrived safely in Vladivostok, but at the time of the uprising there were no Czech trains in the area between Vladivostok and Irkutsk. This territory remained initially in Soviet hands.

This was the situation that confronted Colonel George B. Emerson, head of the Russian Railway Service Corps, who had been sent to Russia at the request of the Russian provisional government to help in the reorganization of the Trans-Siberian Railway. In accordance with Trotsky's request, Secretary of State Robert Lansing had instructed Emerson to go from Vladivostok to Vologda on May 19 to confer with Ambassador David R. Francis and Trotsky about the best means of aiding in the rehabilitation of the Russian railways in Europe. John F. Stevens, head of the Advisory Commission of Railway Experts to Russia, had already arrived in northern Manchuria with 100 American engineers, where he was seeking to organize and operate the Chinese Eastern Railway in the face of continuous harassment from the Japanese. Stevens reported that the Japanese opposed him constantly, "undoubtedly with the view of controlling the entire transportation system of Manchuria." To make matters worse, the Russian Governor General of the Chinese Eastern Railway, Dmitri L. Horvath, with Japanese assistance, had reorganized the Chinese Eastern Railway as a government for all of Siberia.[10]

It was not surprising, then, that the State Department had been more than willing to accede to Trotsky's request for railway assistance. In informing Ambassador Francis of Emerson's impending arrival, Lansing suggested that "any reasonable and proper suggestions or requests by the Soviet authorities be favorably considered by the Embassy and the Railway corps with the distinct proviso and *quid pro quo* that railway assistance in European Russia should be accompanied by permission for the corps to extend its activities in Siberia." If the Soviets were agreeable, "this program might immediately be commenced with the advantage of the tacit acquiescence of such authorities."[11]

So it was that as Colonel Emerson sought to make his way via the Trans-Siberian Railway to European Russia to negotiate with Trotsky for the operation of the Russian railways, the Czechs had seized most of the Trans-Siberian Railway from the Volga to Irkutsk. Although Emerson continued his efforts to reach his destination and even to mediate the conflict, Czech-Bolshevik differences soon made his mediation impossible. The Czechs refused to allow him and his party to pass through Soviet lines. Thus his efforts to cooperate with the Bolsheviks ended in failure.[12]

By the end of June 1918, Allied pressure on Wilson for intervention in Siberia was intense. Virtually all the American representatives in Russia, Siberia, and China were also united in supporting immediate intervention. The Allies were in the process of inviting Japan to intervene alone, a course of action fraught with hazard for the future of eastern Siberia and Manchuria. To complicate matters further, the threat of independent Japanese action loomed on the horizon. Yet Wilson was still opposed to both Japanese intervention and Allied intervention on the grounds that the latter would be the same thing, since the Japanese would supply the major part of the military force. He was convinced that such a policy would simply throw the Russians into the hands of the Germans. Moreover, just as in the case of northern Russia, he still desired an invitation to enter Russia from the Bolsheviks or from somebody who really represented Russian opinion.[13]

Wilson's position was fully supported by his own military advisors and by Thomas G. Masaryk, president of the Czecho-Slovak National Council, who advocated the *de facto* recognition of the Bolsheviks.[14] For the president's military advisors, the essential issue was whether the Japanese should have a "free hand in Siberia." They regarded as "wholly inadmissible solving the Russian problem by giving Japan a portion of Siberia." Moreover, they fully supported Wilson's policy of self-determination for the Russians. They believed "none of the schemes looking to the restoration of the Romanoffs or a government of that country without the consent of the governed [should] be permitted for a moment." Secretary of War Newton D. Baker would have liked "to take everybody out of Russia except the Russians . . . and let the Russians settle down and settle their own affairs."[15] Wilson agreed.

Yet in July 1918, Wilson was forced to change his mind. He not only agreed to intervention, but also took the lead in inviting the Japanese to a limited, joint intervention in Siberia. What, then, were the circumstances that brought about this complete reversal? His first reason was to "rescue" some 70,000 Czecho-Slovaks who had allegedly been attacked in Siberia by German and Austro-Hungarian prisoners of war. In late June, the Vladivostok Czechs, after seizing the city, appealed to the Allied governments, and particularly to the United States and Japan, for military support. For the British Foreign Office, which had exhausted virtually all of its arguments in the effort to win Wilson's agreement to Japanese intervention, the plight of the Czecho-Slovaks provided a new and powerful lever. Foreign Minister Arthur J. Balfour called for "immediate Allied action" as a "matter of urgent necessity." Lansing supported the British argument.[16] The Supreme War council also cabled Wilson, urging both support to the Czechs and the reestablishment of the Eastern Front.

The plight of the Czecho-Slovaks represented an entirely new development to Wilson. Here was an Allied force, allegedly attacked by German and Austro-Hungarian former prisoners of war in their efforts to remove themselves from Siberia, who were now fighting, it appeared, to keep Siberia out of German hands. Wilson could not resist their appeals for assistance. He had already issued a public declaration of "earnest sympathy" for "Czecho-Slovak nationalistic aspirations" for freedom on May 29.[17] Yet the problem was how to act without associating himself with the political schemes of the Allies or opening the door to full-scale Japanese intervention in eastern Siberia and northern Manchuria.

Wilson arrived at a decision on July 6, 1918, after consultation with his cabinet. He agreed to help the Czecho-Slovaks at Vladivostok to establish contact with their compatriots farther west and assist them in their efforts to reach the western front. At the same time, he rejected emphatically the whole Allied notion of restoring the eastern front. He proposed that the United States and Japan each send 7,000 troops to guard the line of communication of the Vladivostok Czechs as they advanced westward along the Trans-Siberian Railway to "rescue" their brethren at Irkutsk. Both governments would issue a public announcement that the purpose of sending troops was specifically to aid the Czecho-Slovaks against German and Austro-Hungarian prisoners of war, that there was "no purpose" to interfere in the internal affairs of Russia, and that the United States and Japan would guarantee not to impair the political or territorial sovereignty of Russia.[18]

It must be emphasized that Wilson's initial decision was a unilateral one. It was in no way a part of the general Allied decision for intervention in Siberia. Wilson rejected virtually every proposal that the British and French governments and the Supreme War Council had urged upon him. He surely did not consider the action that he was authorizing an intervention against the Bolsheviks; and in communicating his decision to the Allied governments, he condemned the whole notion of intervention in the bluntest terms. The British and French were furious. Yet they continued to hope that, with appropriate pressure, Wilson would expand his original plan, particularly after American troops had arrived in Siberia.[19] Ironically, while Wilson was seeking to negotiate an appropriate agreement with the Japanese to rescue the Czechs, both the British and the French had sent instructions to their respective military missions in Russia to embark on a plan for Allied intervention using the Czechs as a nucleus for the intervention force with the purpose of reestablishing the Eastern Front.

Wilson's problem was how to "rescue" the Czechs in cooperation with the Japanese government whose motives he deeply distrusted. He was clearly concerned that, once Japanese forces had arrived in Siberia, it would be difficult to induce them to leave. For the Japanese military leaders, there was little value in intervention unless it resulted in Japanese control of eastern Siberia and northern Manchuria. Wilson negotiated to limit the size of the Japanese expedition, restrict the geographical area in which it would operate, define its specific objectives, and provide the conditions for its withdrawal. Simultaneously, he sought to provide for exclusive Chinese control of the Chinese Eastern Railway, informing the Japanese that "a military occupation in Manchuria would arouse deep resentment in Russia."[20]

Throughout the month of July, Wilson tried to win Japanese agreement to the principle of "joint, equal military action." He failed. The Japanese ambassador made clear that, in the event of an emergency, Japan might be forced to send additional troops "without consultation." "Very much put out" by the Japanese reply, Wilson thought that because Japan's plan was so different from his won that it might be best not to act at all. He believed their plan would give the natural impression to the Russian people that the expedition "had more in view than merely assisting the Czechs." Wilson warned that if Japan and the other Allies concluded that a large expedition was a military necessity, then the United States "would be compelled to withdraw as that was not our plan."[21]

Wilson wrote the public announcement of his decision to rescue the Czechs (usually referred to as the *aide-mémoire*) on his personal typewriter and released it to the press on the afternoon of August 3. Once again he made clear that the United States would take no part in military intervention or sanction it in principle. It "would add to the present sad confusion in Russia rather than cure it, injure her rather than help her, and . . . would be of no advantage in the prosecution or main design to win the war against Germany." Military action was admissible in Russia only to help the Czecho-Slovaks, to steady any efforts at self-government or self-defense in which the Russians themselves might be willing to accept assistance, and to guard military stores, which Russian forces might subsequently need. Wilson also announced his approval of the use of American troops at Murmansk and Archangel for the same objectives.[22]

General William S. Graves, commander of the American expedition, received his orders for the Siberian command directly from Secretary of War Newton D. Baker. After handing him a copy of Wilson's *aide-mémoire* of August 3, Baker cautioned him that the Japanese intended to expand on the Asiatic mainland. Graves's instructions forbade any interference in the internal affairs of the Russian people; his army was not to engage in hostile action against anyone. Baker warned him that he would be "walking on eggs loaded with dynamite."[23]

Allied requests for both a military and political expansion of the expeditions soon led Wilson to fear that there was some "influence . . . at work to pull absolutely away" from the proposed American plan, which he believed the other governments had accepted, and "proceed to do what we said we would not do, namely form a new Eastern Front."[24] Although Wilson was concerned over the plight of the Czechs, his "clear judgment" was to "insist that the Czecho-Slovaks be brought out eastward to Vladivostok and conveyed to the Western Front in Europe . . . according to the original agreement made with them."[25] Once again Wilson emphasized to the British that American policy was clear, unaltered, and in entire accord with the policy submitted to the Japanese government originally, that is "to rescue the Czechs," after which the Japanese and American forces would retire and both forces would evacuate Russian territory.[26]

The British Foreign Office responded that the American decision to hold its troops in eastern Siberia would not affect the British determination to aid the Czechs in holding their position west of the Urals. They feared that if the Czechs withdrew to the east, the "loyal" Russians would be left to the mercy of their enemies. Moreover, the British government indicated its intention to request the French and Japanese government to follow British policy in standing by the "loyal" Russians against the Bolsheviks. The British added that, if the United States was unable to "assist us beyond the point indicated, we hope they will not discourage our other Allies from helping us."[27]

By this time, Wilson was also clashing head-on with the Japanese. Tokyo informed Washington of its decision to send an independent Japanese force under the terms of a Sino-Japanese Military Agreement of May 16, 1918, to protect the Manchurian border from invasion by the Bolsheviks. This action was taken despite the fact that the Chinese government denied repeatedly and emphatically that its borders had been violated either by the Bolsheviks or former German prisoners of war. The Japanese claimed that their expedition into the zone of the Chinese Eastern Railway was "entirely different in nature from the present joint intervention in Vladivostok or from military action in Russian territory, and the only nations that had interests involved are Japan and China."[28] "Very much disturbed" by these reports, which had resulted in the transfer of 12,000 Japanese troops along the line of the Chinese Eastern Railway, Wilson sent a strong protest to the Japanese government. At the same time, John F. Stevens reported that Japan was making every effort to control the operation of the railways, and that without quick action American railroad men would be "out of business completely."[29] The State Department urged Stevens to use his best efforts to forward the movement of the Czecho-Slovaks and warned him "to avoid alliance with or support to any political group or faction in Russia." Concurrently, plans were initiated for placing the general direction of the Trans-Siberian and Chinese Eastern Railways in the hands of Stevens and the Russian Railway Service Corps.[30]

Because the Allies had accepted Japanese command over the Siberian expedition, Wilson was concerned about turning over military control of the railways to the Japanese—even if under the technical direction of Stevens. Therefore, he began negotiations to secure the consent of Thomas G. Masaryk, the acknowledged political leader of the Czechs, to use the Czech military forces in the implementation of an international railway plan to control both the Trans-Siberian and the Chinese Eastern Railways.[31] At the same time, Wilson, who had absolutely forbidden General Graves to establish himself at any point along the Trans-Siberian Railway beyond Vladivostok, now agreed to request permission from China to station Graves in northern Manchuria, both in order to expedite the eastward movement of the Czechs and to curb Japanese action along the line of the Chinese Eastern Railway.[32] The Chinese government immediately granted the necessary permission and added informally that it "heartily welcomed" the presence of American troops and railway assistance, although the Chinese feared that Japan might resent any expression of that sort.[33] Wilson at once sent Roland S. Morris, the U.S. Ambassador to Japan as well as his former student and someone in whom he had complete confidence, to negotiate a railway agreement with the Allied and Russian representatives on the spot.[34]

Japan continued to pour troops into Siberia and northern Manchuria. By the time the armistice was signed on November 11, 1918, Japan had sent 72,400 men, all of them under the direct control of the General Staff in Tokyo. The United States continued to protest vigorously against Japanese action. At the same time it sought to place the railways under international military control and to operate them through the Russian Railway Service Corps. After months of patient negotiation and an internal struggle within the government, Japan finally signed the Inter-Allied Railway Agreement. Wilson regarded this plan as of "inestimable value to the people of Russia and the United States, as well as the world in general." He advised Congress that "it is felt that this matter can be treated entirely apart from the general Russian problem, as irrespective of what our policy may be toward Russia, and irrespective of further Russian developments, it is essential that we maintain the policy of the Open Door with reference to the Siberian and particularly the Chinese Eastern Railway."[35]

On February 15, 1919, the day before Wilson left the Paris Peace Conference for a trip to the United States, Winston S. Churchill came over from England specifically to get Wilson's views on the Russian problem. What was to be the policy, peace or war? Surely Wilson would not leave Paris without answering so important a question. Wilson had very clear answers on two points. First, he believed that Allied intervention in Russia was ineffectual and deleterious; he advocated the withdrawal of Allied and American troops from all parts of Russian territory. Second, he was not opposed to an informal meeting between American and Bolshevik representatives for the purpose of securing information. He would meet them alone, if necessary. He pointed to the conflicting sources of information in both official and unofficial reports indicating that it was impossible to obtain a coherent picture of Russian affairs. Churchill averred that the withdrawal of allied troops would place some 500,000 non-Bolshevik troops at the mercy of the Bolsheviks and leave "an undeterminable vista of violence and misery." Wilson replied that, because none of the Allies could reinforce its armies there, withdrawal seemed the best solution. Moreover, he added, even when the Allies supplied non-Bolsheviks with arms, they "made very little use of them."[36]

After Wilson had left Paris, Churchill distorted Wilson's concluding remarks to indicate a willingness to participate with other Allies in anything necessary and practicable to help the non-Bolshevik Russian armies then in the field. Churchill immediately initiated efforts for joint military action to aid the White Russian armies in maintaining themselves against the Bolsheviks; at the same time Churchill sought measures to safeguard Finland, Estonia, Livonia, Poland, and Rumania.[37]

Wilson was outraged by Churchill's actions, and immediately instructed the American peace commissioners to oppose any policies that did not mean the "earliest practicable withdrawal of military forces." He instructed Colonel Edward M. House to make it plain to the Allied statesmen that "we are not at war with Russia and will in no circumstances that we can now foresee, take part in military operations there against the Russians."[38] General Tasker H. Bliss immediately explained Wilson's views to Churchill, and the project was dropped.[39]

As we look back on the American expeditions to northern Russia and Siberia today, they appear pathetic and ill-conceived ventures. Woodrow Wilson, harried with wartime burdens, and torn between his own instincts and his feelings of obligation to his allies, did his best at all times to keep the American action from assuming the form of an interference in Russian internal affairs. His policy can be best understood within the context of his own moral and ethical principles. He faced the classic dilemma of the moral man seeking to implement a principled policy.

An examination of that policy leaves no doubt that President Wilson sought in every possible way within the limits of coalition diplomacy to preserve

Russian territorial integrity, to support the right of the Russian people for self-determination, and to restrain his own allies from turning the entire enterprise into an anti-Bolshevik crusade to overthrow the Soviet government. The Bolsheviks themselves conceded that the United States had been justified in following such a policy when, in 1933, after being shown certain documents concerning American policy, they agreed to drop all claims against the United States for its part in the Siberian intervention. As Secretary of State Cordell Hull pointed out, "These latter documents made clear to [Soviet Commissar of Foreign Affairs] Litvinov that American forces had not been in Siberia to wrest territory from Russia but to insure the withdrawal of the Japanese who had a far larger force in Siberia with the intent to occupy it permanently."[40] For the Russians to say that these expeditions represented imperialistic motives and constituted a serious injury to the Russian people is a figment of the imagination of Soviet propagandists, useful to their political purpose, but not to the development of historical truth. Their allegations that Woodrow Wilson took the lead in promoting hostile action against the Soviet Union in an effort to destroy the Soviet state at birth simply cannot be substantiated by an examination of the documentary record.

Now that the Cold War is over and the Soviet state has dissolved, it remains to be seen how the new leaders of Russia will interpret the 1918–20 American expedition to Russia. But one thing is clear with the opening of the British, French, and Czech archives on the Allied interventions. They reveal that the original intent of the Allies was to recreate an eastern front. When that objective could not be realized, Allied interventions did indeed become efforts to overthrow the Soviet state. Those records also make clear the extent to which Woodrow Wilson successfully resisted every effort to sanction or participate in these undertakings and consistently opposed the dismemberment of the Russian empire not only by the Japanese but also by the British and the French.[41]

NOTES

1. David S. Foglesong sees U.S. intervention as *America's Secret War Against Bolshevism* (Chapel Hill, N.C., 1995), while both Lloyd Ambrosius and Henry Kissinger see Wilson's policies as providing the pattern for other anticommunist interventions such as Vietnam. See Ambrosius, *Woodrow Wilson and the American Diplomatic Traditions* (Cambridge, 1987), 294–95, and Kissinger, *Diplomacy* (New York, 1994) 653–54, 658, 698.

2. Notes of an interview with the president at the White House, Oct. 16, 1918, Papers of Sir Eric Geddes, Add. MSS. 116/1809, Public Record Office, KEW; also reproduced in Wilton B. Fowler, *British-American Relations, 1917–1918: The Role of Sir William Wiseman* (Princeton, N.J., 1969), pp. 283–90.

3. Lansing to David R. Francis, April 3, 1917, *Foreign Relations of the United States,*

1918, Russia, 3 vols. (Washington, 1931–32), 1: 17, hereafter cited as *Foreign Relations, 1918, Russia.*

4. Arthur S. Link, David W. Hirst, John E. Little et al., eds., *The Papers of Woodrow Wilson,* 68 vols. (Princeton, N.J., 1966–1992), 45:534–39, hereafter cited as PWW.

5. Ibid., 45:537.

6. Ibid., 46:35.

7. Ibid., 46:545.

8. Betty Miller Unterberger, *The United States, Revolutionary Russia, and the Rise of Czechoslovakia* (Chapel Hill, N.C., 1998), pp. 159–69.

9. Betty Miller Unterberger, *America's Siberian Expedition 1918–1920: A Study in National Policy* (New York, 1969), pp. 68, 72.

10. Lansing to Wilson, May 10, 1918; Wilson to Lansing, May 20, 1918; Memorandum for Secretary of State by Basil Miles, May 21, 1918, handed to Wilson by Lansing, May 21, 1918, PWW, 47:591–95; 48:73, 104–6; Stevens to Lansing, April 10 and 29, 1918, *Foreign Relations, 1918, Russia,* 3: 229, 231.

11. Lansing to Francis, May 29, 1918, State Department Records, 861.00/2079½ National Archives, hereafter cited as SDR.

12. Emerson to Francis, June 21, 1918, SDR, 861.77/541. For a description of the efforts of both Consul General Ernest L. Harris at Irkutsk and Emerson to negotiate the conflict, see Betty Miller Unterberger, "The United States and the Czech-Bolshevik Conflict, 1918," *Proceedings of Conference on War and Diplomacy* (Charleston, S.C., 1976), pp. 145–53, and George F. Kennan, *The Decision to Intervene* (Princeton, N.J., 1958), pp. 282–91.

13. Diary of Breckinridge Long, May 31, 1918; Papers of Breckinridge Long, Library of Congress, hereafter cited as Long Diary and Long Papers. See also Unterberger, *America's Siberian Expedition,* pp. 48–49, 60; The Diary of Robert Lansing, June 11, 1918, Papers of Robert Lansing, Library of Congress, hereafter cited as Lansing Diary; Wiseman to Drummond, June 14, 1918, Papers of Sir William Wiseman, Yale University Library, hereafter cited as Wiseman Papers; PWW, 48:315–16; Reading to Balfour, June 16, 1918, Papers of Arthur J. Balfour in Public Record Office, hereafter cited as Balfour Papers.

14. Answers given by Masaryk to direct questions of United States Ambassador in Tokyo, April 11, 1918 in *Vznik Československa 1918: Dokumenty Československé zahraniení Politiky* (Praha, 1994), 81–83.

15. Masaryk to Charles R. Crane, April 10, 1918, SDR, 861.00/2721; Richard Crane to Wilson, May 7, 1918, with Masaryk enclosure, Woodrow Wilson Papers Library of Congress; PWW, 47:548–52; White House Appointment Book, June 19, 1918; Chicago *Denní Hlasatel,* June 21, 1918; Thomas G. Masaryk, *The Making of a State: Memories and Observations* (New York, 1927), pp. 299–300; Bliss to Baker, June 18, 1918, Wilson Papers; Baker to Wilson, June 19, 1918, Papers of Newton D. Baker, Library of Congress, hereafter cited as Baker Papers; Wilson to Baker, June 19, 1918, Baker Papers; March to Baker, June 24, 1918, Wilson Papers; PWW, 48:418–21; Bliss to March, June 24, 1918, Papers of Tasker H. Bliss, Library of Congress, hereafter cited as Bliss Papers; March to Wilson, June 24, 1918, in Peyton C. March, *Nation at War* (New York, 1932), pp. 116–20; Frederick Palmer, *Newton D. Baker: America at War* (New York, 1931), 2: 321.

16. Balfour to Reading, June 21, 1918, Foreign Office Papers, 371/3324, No. 110145, p. 16; Lansing to Wilson, June 23, 1918, enclosing paraphrase of a telegram from Lockhart to the Foreign Office, June 20, 1918, SDR, 861.00/2164½; PWW, 48:398–99.

17. Phillips to Lansing, May 25, 1918, SDR, 763.72/10294½; Lansing, Circular Telegram, May 29, 1918, Foreign Relations, 1918, Russia, 2:183.

18. Memorandum of the Secretary of State of a conference at the White House in reference to the Siberian situation, July 6, 1918, PWW, 48:542–43. The American proposals were issued to the Allied governments in an aide mémoire on July 17, 1918; PWW, 48:639–43.

19. Lansing to Wilson, July 9, 1918, ibid., 48:574–75; Diary of William Phillips, July 9, 1918, Papers of William Phillips, Harvard University Library, hereafter cited as Phillips Diary; Diary of Gordon Auchincloss, July 9, 1918, Yale University Library, hereafter cited as Auchincloss Diary; Reading to Lloyd George and Balfour, July 9 and 10, 1918, Wiseman Papers; PWW, 48:586–87; Chicago Denní Hlasatel, July 11, 1918.

20. Wilson to Long, July 26, 1918, Long Papers; Auchincloss Diary, July 24 and 25, 1918; Wilson to Josephus Daniels, Aug. 1, 1918, Wilson Papers; Charles Seymour, ed., Intimate Papers of Colonel House (Boston, 1928), 3:415; Foreign Relations, 1918, Russia, 2:297–98, 301–2, 304–5, 314; Unterberger, America's Siberian Expedition, pp. 82–86; Thomas E. La Fargue, China and the World War (Stanford, 1937), p. 169.

21. Frank L. Polk Diary, July 16 and Aug. 3, 1918, in Papers of Frank L. Polk, Yale University Library, hereafter cited as Polk Diary; Foreign Relations, 1918, Russia, 2:292, 306–7, 324–26; Auchincloss Diary, July 25, 1918; PWW, 49:91–97.

22. Polk to Morris, Aug 3, 1918, Foreign Relations, 1918, Russia, 2:328–29; PWW, 49:170–72.

23. "Major General William S. Graves," United States Army Recruiting News; tribute by Frank H. King, Associated Press correspondent with the A. E. F. Siberia, both in Papers of William S. Graves, United States Military Academy; Graves, America's Siberian Adventure, 1918–1920 (New York, 1931), pp. 2–4.

24. Wilson to Lansing, Sept. 5, 1918, SDR, 861.00/7381; PWW, 49:448; John Van A. MacMurray, Chargé in China, to Lansing, Aug. 30, 1918, SDR, 861.00/2617. See also Wilson to Lansing, Sept. 17, 1918, SDR, 861.00/3009; PWW, 51:25–26; and John W. Long, "American Intervention in Russia: The North Russian Expedition, 1918–19," Diplomatic History 6 (Winter 1982), 57.

25. Wilson to Lansing, Sept. 17, 1918, SDR, 861.00/3009; PWW, 51:25–26.

26. Wiseman to Reading and Drummond, Sept. 21, 1918, Papers of Lord Reading, Public Record Office; Wilson to Lansing, Sept. 23, 1918, SDR, 861.00/3013; PWW, 51:91.

27. Barclay to Lansing, Oct. 3, 1918, Foreign Relations, 1918, Russia, 2:403–4.

28. CAB 23/7; War Cabinet 475/32, meeting held Sept. 23, 1918, War Cabinet Papers Public Records Office; Fowler, British-American Relations, p. 195; Polk Diary, Aug. 10, 1918; Foreign Relations, 1918, Russia, 2:330–31, 334, 335, 343–46, 348–49, 378; Tatsuji Takeuchi, War and Diplomacy in the Japanese Empire (New York, 1935), p. 209; see also New York Times, Aug. 18, 1918.

29. Lansing to Morris, Sept. 6, 1918, Foreign Relations, 1918, Russia, 3:242–43; V. K. Wellington Koo, Chinese Minister at Washington, to Lansing, Sept. 13, 1918,

Foreign Relations, 1918, Russia, 2:378; Caldwell to Lansing, *Foreign Relations, 1918, Russia,* 3:239, Lansing Diary, Aug. 21, 1918; Polk to Moser, Aug. 10, 1918, *Foreign Relations, 1918, Russia,* 3:237.

30. Willing Spencer, Chargé in Japan, to Lansing, Sept, 18, 1918; Morris to Lansing, Sept. 18 and 20, 1918; MacMurray to Lansing, Sept. 19, 1918, *Foreign Relations, 1918, Russia,* 3:257–62.

31. Long Diary, Sept. 19 and 23, 1918; Memorandum of conversation with Dr. Masaryk, Sept. 23, 1918; Long to American Legation at Peking, Sept. 23, 1918, Long Papers; *Vznik Československa 1918,* 273.

32. Wilson to Lansing, Sept. 26, 1918, Long Papers; PWW, 51:121–22; Lansing to Morris, Sept. 26, 1918, MacMurray to Lansing, Sept. 28, 1918, *Foreign Relations, 1918, Russia,* 2:392–96; Lansing to Barclay, Sept. 27, 1918, Foreign Office Papers, 115/2450, pp. 141, 143–47; Lansing to MacMurray, Sept. 26, 1918, SDR, 861.00/2791a.

33. MacMurray to Lansing, Sept. 28, 1918, *Foreign Relations, 1918, Russia,* 2:396.

34. Unterberger, *America's Siberian Expedition,* p. 110; Diary of Cary T. Grayson, Dec. 9, 1918, in possession of Cary T. Grayson, Jr.; hereafter cited as Grayson Diary; PWW, 53:343.

35. Admiral Austin M. Knight to Daniels, Nov. 4, 1918, WA6, Russian situation, Naval Records Collection; Ingersoll to F. Leonard, Nov. 17, 1918, SDR, 861A.01/131; Memorandum on the Japanese role in the intervention in Siberia, Oct. 15, 1918, Wiseman Papers; Polk Diary, Dec. 23, 1918; *Foreign Relations, 1919, Russia* (Washington, 1937), pp. 239, 246–48, 244, 250–51.

36. Winston S. Churchill, *The Aftermath* (New York, 1929), pp. 173–74; Minutes of the Fourteenth Session of the Supreme War Council held in M. Pichon's Room at the Quai d'Orsay, Paris, Feb. 14, 1919, *Foreign Relations, 1919, Russia,* pp. 57–59; Major General Sir C. E. Callwell, *Field-Marshal Sir Henry Wilson: His Life and Diaries,* 2 vols. (London, 1927), 2:170.

37. Churchill, *The Aftermath,* p. 174; Lansing to Polk, Feb. 14, 1919, *Foreign Relations, 1919, Russia,* pp. 68–69; David Lloyd George, *Memoirs of the Peace Conference,* 2 vols. (New Haven, 1939), 1:242. The American representatives opposed the adoption of this resolution.

38. Wilson to Commission to Negotiate Peace, Feb. 19, 1919, PWW, 55:208; Seymour, *Intimate Papers,* 4:348. Lloyd George also protested against Churchill's project. Lloyd George, *Memoirs of the Peace Conference,* 1:243–44.

39. Commission to Negotiate Peace to Polk, Feb. 23, 1919, PWW, 55:232; Seymour, *Intimate Papers,* 4:348; Bliss to House, Feb. 17, 1919, Bliss Papers, not sent.

40. Cordell Hull, *Memoirs* (New York, 1948), 2:299; Maxim Litvinov to President Roosevelt, Nov. 16, 1933, *Foreign Relations, 1933,* 2:814; Press release, Nov. 22, 1933, Stanley Hornbeck Papers, Hoover Institution.

41. See Unterberger, *The United States, Revolutionary Russia, and the Rise of Czechoslovakia,* pp. 159–283; Michael Kettle, *The Road to Intervention: March-November 1918* (London and New York, 1988), and *Churchill and the Archangel Fiasco: November 1918–July 1919* (London and New York, 1993).

Chapter 15

AMERICA AFTER THE COLD WAR: GLOBAL ORDER, DEMOCRACY, AND DOMESTIC CONSENT

RONALD STEEL

FOR MOST OF the past half century the relationships of both great nations and small have been governed by the power structure of the Cold War. Hardly a nation on earth was too small or too remote to be unaffected by the Cold War system. Some were dragged into it against their will because the great powers considered them to be of strategic importance; others sought to join one alliance or the other to seek protection or extract benefits. Many intellectuals also felt the need to take sides, and some, such as Arthur Schlesinger, Jr., did so even before the term "Cold War" came into being.

While the Cold War was a contest for influence between two "superpowers," the United States and the Soviet Union, these nations could hardly be considered as equal, except perhaps by the crudest measure of nuclear destructive power. From every aspect—military, economic, political—the United States was incontestably the stronger power. Its air and naval bases circled the globe, it dominated its alliances with Western Europe and Japan, it exercised a protectorship over Latin America and much of the Middle East, it maintained a network of client states in strategic areas, and it enjoyed a surplus of power enabling it to pursue the contest at ever-higher levels of engagement for as long as might be necessary.

With its incomparable natural resources, advanced industrial base, skilled labor force, and technological prowess it was indisputably, as it has been for much of this century, the world's leading economic power. As the world's oldest constitutional democracy, its government was freely chosen by its citizens and enjoyed the strength of that allegiance. Its customs and political system ensured individual freedoms that were widely emulated elsewhere. And its cultural reach was global. Throughout the world, America's influence was felt profoundly, and particularly upon the young who equated exports of American culture—whether as clothing, entertainment, leisure, generational identities, or the rationalization of time itself—with the very concept of modernization. To be a person of the mid-twentieth century was, to some extent, to have made an accommodation to American culture.

Coupled with these factors was an expansive energy that impelled Americans to export to the world the qualities and conditions they so valued for themselves. Americans have always been, to some extent, salesmen, and the Cold War gave them an opportunity to provide what so much of the world seemed to want: economic help, military protection, and political solidarity. And then there was democracy, the export product that Americans cared about most, for its adoption by others was an endorsement of America itself as the model towards which others aspired.

The Soviet Union also had its global export. Communism was a powerful ideology that offered to millions an explanation of the inequitable conditions of an otherwise inexplicable world. It was particularly appealing to the aspiring leaders of third world states newly aroused to the tremors of self-assertion and nationalism. However, the Soviet Union was not itself an inspiring example of utopian communism, having from its very inception adopted a perverted version of Marxism that was utilized to justify the most abject tyranny against its own people.

Although the corruptions of Soviet communism were soon enough revealed in the purges and *gulags* of the 1930s, the Czech coup of 1948 and the invasion of Budapest in 1956, the ideology itself—and the verbal, if hypocritical, allegiance of Soviet leaders to it—was appealing enough to many as an alternative to American style democratic capitalism that American leaders were roused to a global contest fought for the highest stakes. Communism provided the counter-ideology that activated the inherent and always powerful American sense of mission. The Cold War became a contest for the mind no less than for the body of the entire world.

This is what gave that competition its special vehemence. To American leaders the Soviet Union was not only an aggressive state that exerted its control by force over subject peoples; it promulgated a false and oppressive doctrine that further enslaved them. This is what Ronald Reagan meant when he called that country an "evil empire." Few Americans were disturbed by this phrase, for that is how they saw Moscow's domain: an empire held in thrall by military force and a pernicious ideology. The ideological, not the nationalistic, contest was all.

While the United States was unquestionably an interventionist power during the Cold War, both its actions and its inspirations were different from that of the Soviet Union. Communism is by its very nature a proselytizing ideology. It claims to be a culminating development in history and to bring about the full liberation of mankind. By definition it is universalist and not the instrument of any single power. The very notion of "socialism in one country" was a betrayal of communism, as was the claim that the Soviet version of communism should take precedence over any other.

"Socialist internationalism" served as a pretext for great power expansion by the Soviet Union. The ideology was employed in the service of the Soviet state.

This does not mean, however, that it was done entirely cynically. Political leaders, too, are governed by their intellectual assumptions, and for many the glorification of the Soviet state was not incompatible with the expansion of communism. Indeed, for them the former was the instrument of the latter.

To pursue the comparison of the Soviet and American states, the United States also pursued a path of great power expansion during the Cold War. It did so with enormous gusto, and with the conviction that it was serving a larger purpose: that purpose being both the containment of a threat and the promulgation of a liberating idea. There is unquestionably a missionary aspect to American idealism. But it is dominant only at certain times: usually when it is challenged, as was the case following World War II. However, the United States was not expansionist following World War I. Indeed, it was isolationist. Thus it seems safe to say that while at times the United States has engaged in great power expansion, Americanism is not defined by it. The pursuit of Americanism sometimes takes an interventionist, sometimes an isolationist, mode.

The United States dominated the international system in the Cold War period not only because of its great power and its expansive sense of mission, but because of the temporary demise of other powers that normally would have challenged and contained it. During the forty-odd years following World War II, Western Europe was preoccupied by reconstruction and unification, Japan by enrichment, and China by the traumas of civil war, consolidation, and modernization. None of these nations enjoyed the strength nor marshaled the will to challenge seriously either of the contending superpowers.

Europe as it was known from 1945 to 1990 was the quintessential creation of the Cold War. Divided by armies and ideology, one side under Soviet occupation, the other dependent on the United States for its ultimate protection; one side mired in a parody of early twentieth-century Marxism, the other rushing pell-mell into late twentieth-century consumerism and mass democracy; one turning deeper inward into an escapist pursuit of *heimat,* the other excitedly declaring its universalism; the two Europes assumed strikingly different identities.

The centerpiece of this divided Europe was a vacuum. Where once was positioned Europe's greatest military and economic power, Germany, there were now twin protectorates. The eastern part was a drab and compliant Soviet satellite, the western part was a prosperous but politically mute entity which looked to Washington for its defense and to Paris and Brussels for reassurance of its new identity. A divided Germany was both a consequence and a symbol of the division of Europe. It was, in other words, a central part of the Cold War system.

As such, for all its unnaturalness, it provided certain advantages for many Europeans, and even for many Germans. It meant that the greater part of Germany could be at last endowed with a firm democratic structure. Because it was now roughly the same size as its western neighbors, France, Britain, and Italy, it did not dominate the new entity known as Western Europe. Finally, after three-quarters of a century since Bismarck's unification, a place had been found for Germany in which it did not threaten its neighbors.

From the division of Germany came the great construction of post-war Europe: the Common Market and ultimately the European Community. It is highly problematical whether this would have occurred without the division of Germany and of Europe, which is to say, without the Cold War. Nor could it have come about without encouragement from the United States, and without the protection that the Atlantic Alliance provided. America was in this sense the midwife of Western Europe. The European Community, like NATO, fit neatly into a configuration of power centered upon the United States.

Yet the Cold War structure did not define the post–World War II world. It touched only tangentially three great movements which it could not control and which will long outlast it. They are, first, the reorganization of Asia. This means not only the rise of Japan as an economic colossus, but the emergence of China from generations of feudalism and civil war, and the creation of new centers of economic power along the littoral of Asia.

Second is the collapse of European colonialism and the independence of peoples previously under the control of distant imperial powers. Some of these new nations, such as India, and older ones, such as Brazil, are becoming significant powers in their own right. Others, in what we might call the "fourth world," are doomed to semi-permanent immiserization. Still others, like the oil-producing states, have become major actors because the world needs what they provide. What is euphemistically known as the South is the scene of great possibilities and great disasters. But what is important is that it can no longer be taken for granted.

The third movement, which has taken place only after the collapse of the Cold War world, is the drama of European nationalities. Once again the "national question," which had been put to rest during the long years of the Cold War, has emerged like some repressed but never extirpated specter. This struggle for national identity, which seems to have been resolved in Western Europe, though probably not fully settled, haunts the countries of the East, which are still in a stage of arrested political development. It is likely to trouble Europe for a long time to come.

World War II and the Cold War that followed stimulated the United States to an unprecedented intervention in the affairs of other nations. Yet for much of this time Americans have been highly ambivalent about the scope and even the justification for such sweeping involvements. American foreign policy during the Cold War was marked by a tension between two powerful forces: isolationism and expansionism.

The isolationist force is deeply rooted in the notion of American exceptionalism. This decrees that the United States, created as an alternative to the tyranny and corruption of the European dynasties from which its settlers first came, could retain its republican and humanistic values only by the most scrupulous separation from the affairs of the old world. Independence meant full control over the nation's destiny. America could be an exemplar to the world by not mingling too deeply in its sordid affairs. Its mission would be as a "City on the Hill" whose beacon would inspire the quest for liberty in other nations.

However, intermingled with this belief in purity through separation was the equally powerful one that America had an obligation not only to preserve, but to spread the blessings of freedom. This missionary impulse, which drove church ministers to convert the "heathens" of China and other unfortunate lands to the blessings of Christianity and capitalism, also took a political form. Salvation would be found not merely through protecting and improving the nation, but by spreading democracy throughout the world. The export of the American national product, democracy, became the means of national self-fulfillment. It also served as the justification for the most profound intervention in the internal affairs of nations everywhere.

Although a well-known saying declares that the "business of America is business," it is at least equally true that the ideology of America is democracy. Whether liberal or conservative, Americans share a profound belief that their system of government is not only best for them, but best for peoples everywhere. Indeed, it is almost as though they had to validate their system to themselves by converting the entire world to it. Although to many foreigners the promulgation of democracy is perceived as a justification for American expansion, to Americans it is seen as an onerous but necessary duty. As President Woodrow Wilson stated in his war message of April 1917, the United States made the decision to enter the European conflict "for democracy, for the right of those who submit to authority to have a voice in their own government, for the right and liberties of small nations . . . and to make the world itself free."

To the outside world this may seem hypocritical, with idealism, as General de Gaulle once commented, serving as the mask behind which the will to power exerted itself. Or, as Graham Greene has tried to demonstrate in his powerful novel, *The Quiet American,* it can be self-deceptively naive. The effort to force others to accept what is presumably good for them, even by the most violent means, is not one of the most widely admired aspects of the American character. But as President Lyndon Johnson once said to his critics during the Vietnam War: "Let no one doubt the well springs of American idealism." But such statements cannot be easily dismissed as either hypocritical or naive. This is because they are deeply felt and serve an important purpose. They affirm the concerns of a nation that, though settled as a European colony, had to create its own identity. Beyond that, it had also to justify actions taken by settlers to secure that identity. This means that it had to come to terms with the virtual extermination by white settlers of the native peoples of North America, and with the commercial traffic in human beings that was slavery.

That uniquely American art form—the Western—deals precisely with the great issue of the subduing of the continent and of its inhabitants. The "winning of the West" was defined as a struggle for civilization against the forces of savagery. The morality of Westerns lies in the utilization of terrible force as the means to the attainment of a higher purpose. Force cannot be condoned in itself; it can be justified only as the instrument of a greater end. In this sense the American film hero is a lonely fighter for virtue and the rights of the downtrodden. He is Superman, Shane, or the Terminator, using force not for its own sake, but for the way in which it can help others. Contrast this to the British hero of spy and action dramas, James Bond. Rather than an idealist, Bond is a hired cynic. Ostensibly on "her Majesty's secret service," his only values are those of power and prestige, and his only interests those of pleasure. He is the sensualist, while Superman is the puritan.

Despite this powerful missionary impulse of Americans, they have often been reluctant to go abroad, in the celebrated phrase of John Quincy Adams, "in search of monsters to destroy." The American public is essentially inward-looking. It is preoccupied by the internal issues of American society, and has been accustomed to do so by a long history of detachment from foreign quarrels. The great geographical distance of the United States from both Europe and Asia, as well as from the continent of South America, has spared it from invasion, conquest, and even from extensive cultural interaction with dangerous rivals. For the United States, during much of its history, foreign affairs was a choice, not a necessity; a danger, not an opportunity.

No wonder that to this day, even in a time of instant communications, so many Americans feel ambivalent about an activist American role on the world stage, or why they often view this as a distraction from the primary issue of the domestic society. In order for Americans to be persuaded to expend their lives, their fortunes, and, in the phrase, their sacred honor, abroad, they need to be given a compelling reason. One reason that is often presented is that other countries need their help. Extending the dictum that help to one person from another is usually received with gratitude, Americans expect to be thanked for what they perceive as their assistance. From this stems what many foreigners describe as the celebrated need of Americans to be liked. It is not an unreasonable expectation, given that Americans see their actions as bestowing a favor. The fact that others may see U.S. involvement in their affairs differently results in considerable puzzlement. Thus it is that largesse, when thwarted, turns to disillusion, or even to anger and punishment. One has only to look at the frustrations of the hunger relief operation in Somalia in 1993 to see the principle in operation.

Because Americans have traditionally been quite content to let other nations tear themselves apart as they will, the professional elites whose job it is to orchestrate as extensive a foreign policy as possible must first of all persuade the domestic constituency. Unlike most other countries, where foreign policy is viewed as the prerogative of a privileged class, every American feels that his views must be taken into account. For this reason the foreign policy professionals must produce elaborate justifications, based on self-interest or altruism, for American involvement in foreign quarrels. Even when these involvements are quite limited or seemingly reasonable, they are promoted with all the subtlety of the launching of a new detergent. A democracy like the United States does not enjoy the luxury of an unobtrusive foreign policy.

When foreign entanglements are considered to be an intrusion or an indulgence, it is not surprising that detachment—which is often disparagingly referred to by activists as isolationism—should have a significant appeal. At times of perceived danger, as during much of the contest with the Soviet Union, this appeal wanes and there is general support for an interventionist foreign policy. Yet if the interventionist actions seem out of proportion to the danger, as they did to many during the Vietnam War, support for intervention deteriorates.

As a general rule the liberal left tends to be interventionist and the right isolationist. This is because liberals believe that America has a duty to reform the world, while conservatives believe that Americans have their hands full taking care of themselves. The Cold War confused this dichotomy because the adversary seemed not only menacing, but espoused communism. Thus the right, by definition anti-communist, tended to be more interventionist than the left, particularly from the Vietnam War onwards. Now that the Cold War is over, the traditional categories have reasserted themselves: the left is no longer isolationist, neo- or otherwise, and the right no longer interventionist.

All of the above would suggest that American foreign policy is less a calculation of interest than it is an elaborate morality tale. There is much to support such an interpretation. Americans are rarely content to discuss whether or not a given policy is effective. The crucial question is whether it is right or wrong. For this reason it can be understood only in terms of its moral component, whether it be real or imagined. Because no foreign policy can survive without the support of a majority, Americans on balance believe that their relations with the rest of the world are predominantly virtuous. For this reason they are quite impervious to accusations of foreign, or even isolated domestic, critics. Thus, for example, the derogation (particularly during the Vietnam War period) of American diplomacy as "imperialistic" had virtually no effect on American thinking: this for the simple reason that a great power acting altruistically to help a besieged small nation to be democratic could not, by definition, behave in an imperialistic manner.

Foreign critics on the left, and particularly those of a Marxist persuasion, never showed an understanding of this tension in American thinking. When denouncing imperialism they would employ economic categories such as cheap labor, exploitation of natural resources, and the like. But whatever the economic component, it was far less significant than the psychological and historical ones that govern the American political character. It is simply not possible to explain American foreign policy in essentially economic terms. The oscillation between isolation and intervention, the persistent emphasis on morality, the obsession with freedom and democracy, the relentless proselytization cannot be stuffed into an economic straitjacket. American foreign policy may often be naive or hypocritical, but it can never be confined to a balance sheet.

Forty years ago an American secretary of state noted, to considerable consternation in London, that Britain had lost an empire but not yet found a role. To most Americans this was nothing more than a factual observation of the shifting tides of power that had placed the United States in the role once enjoyed by Britain as global hegemon. To many Britons, however, unaccustomed to their sharply diminished ability to determine the course of events, this was akin to *lèsemajesté*.

As a result of the usual turning of the wheel of fortune, Americans now find themselves grappling with some of the same problems Britons did two generations ago. To be sure, the decline of power has not been nearly so great or so abrupt. The United States is still the world's leading industrial and military power and, given responsible leadership, is likely to remain so well into the foreseeable future. The collapse of the Soviet Union as a great imperial power has removed from the scene its only military rival and left it in lonely splendor as the world's only surviving superpower.

However, the title means less than it once did. The arena for the actual exercise of such power is sharply limited. The deterrent effect of nuclear weapons works only against other nuclear powers. It is irrelevant against what is becoming the most pervasive type of violence in today's world: state and group terrorism. Even conventional force, however overwhelming, can be applied only in limited situations. Although highly effective on the ground in Kuwait and Iraq, its use did not bring about the desired political objective: Saddam Hussein remained in power. Nor is it likely that the United States would mount a similar operation in the future unless a vital interest seemed to be at stake. While vital interests are not always easy to decide, as the fierce debates among elites over Bosnia revealed, intervention in European ethnic wars was strongly resisted.

The end of the Cold War has left the United States not only without an enemy, but without an overriding sense of political purpose. Over the past forty years that purpose was a redemptive and, if you will, imperial one:

guarding the domain of the "free world" from communism and extending the scope of American power. But the extension of power was always justified by the containment of communism. Without that it would have seemed, as its critics often charged, indeed imperialistic.

Yet even granting some validity to the critics, American policy was less driven by ambitions of imperial aggrandizement than was often charged. Were this not the case, there would not now be a clamor—even among parts of the elite—for a withdrawal from extensive overseas commitments. Great empires normally find reasons to justify themselves, even in the absence of a threat to physical security. Although this goal is expressed in appeals for U.S. command of a "new world order" we also find a powerful impetus to focus on domestic problems, even at the expense of traditional foreign involvements. The urge to reform and redeem is no less powerful than it was, but its objective has switched.

For the first time since the eve of World War II the United States is confronted with the choice between two very different approaches to foreign policy. To describe these two alternatives as isolationism and interventionism would be inaccurately reductionist. But such extreme formulations also contain a modicum of truth, for they raise the question of whether the nation shall pursue its interests by looking primarily inward or outward.

To a degree unlike that of any other nation, the United States has declared the promulgation of democracy to be a major foreign policy objective. Indeed, one might even argue that Americans see their advocacy of democracy as a global crusade justifying both sacrifice and extreme measures of coercion. This self-declared crusade for democracy has two quite different aspects.

The first is an affirmation of the political ideology of the United States. The nation "conceived in liberty" affirms its qualities by seeking to extend them to others no less than, for example, republican France did by fostering revolutionary movements across Europe. Yet, as with the young French republic, this goes beyond mere affirmation to express an inner compulsion to justify and extend. Liberty is thus perceived not merely as a blessing to be savored, but as an obligation that involves spreading it to others. To hoard it oneself is not only avaricious, but dilutes, or even betrays, its very essence, which is universalism. Thus the exportation of democracy, particularly in its capitalistic free market version, is an integral part of America's sense of mission.

The second aspect of the crusade for democracy is its utility as the justification for actions that might otherwise seem unduly meddlesome, or self-aggrandizing, or belligerent. During the Cold War this function was served by dictatorial communism, and intervention took the form of altruistic liberation. Even in a post-communist world, however, great powers have interests abroad that they seek to ensure by force. But such intervention, even for a major interest like access to a vital raw material, cannot easily be justified to Americans on such crass terms. George Bush attempted this briefly during the Persian Gulf crisis of 1990–91 when he momentarily tried to justify the liberation of Kuwait in terms of access to a cheap and available source of oil. This did not go down well with a public that sought more noble reasons for intervention. The punishment of an aggressor and the defense of democracy was once again invoked, even though it meant restoring to power an odiously self-indulgent and repressive dictatorship in Kuwait.

If this seems hypocritical, consider by contrast the behavior of French leaders who, with the approval of their citizens, periodically send troops to recalcitrant former colonies to ensure their economic and political cooperation in the greater prosperity of the French Republic. Avowedly *Realpolitik* diplomacy, of the kind practiced by the Europeans, and attempted during the Nixon administration by Henry Kissinger, makes Americans uncomfortable. It is too explicitly cynical and self-serving. What others may condemn as hypocrisy, Americans view as a necessary, but uneasy, compromise between morality and realism.

American Cold War internationalism, or, if you will, interventionism, stabilized the terrible political and economic turmoil in Western Europe following World War II and financed its economic reconstruction. A prosperous and democratic Western Europe, indeed the European Community itself, is in large degree a product of American intervention. Without American assistance these nations would have found it far more difficult to regain their economic prosperity. And without such prosperity the prospects for democracy would, in some of these nations, have been less favorable.

Nor can one justifiably ignore the benefits of American military protection, which defended Western Europe from a possible extension of the fate that befell the nations to the east, and did so while assuming the greatest burden of the cost itself. If these nations had had to assume the full cost of their own defense, they might not have become so prosperous or politically stable. These would have been different societies than they are today. The extraordinary political and economic success of Western Europe is in significant part a result of the American Cold War intervention, from which Europe benefited enormously and for which it paid very little.

Among the European nations none benefited so greatly as Germany. From the disgrace and destruction incurred as a result of its own criminal behavior, the former Third Reich, or at least the greater part of it, found protection, prosperity, and even democracy. How deep Germany's newfound democratic values really are remains to be seen, for they have never seriously been tested. Indeed, they have hardly been tested at all until the current upheavals caused by the unification of the westernized Federal Republic with the stalinized remnant of the old Reich in 1990. The greatest problem of this marriage is not economic, severe though that is, but political, and the effects that unification with a totalitarian state will have on democracy itself in the old Federal Republic. Germany's reconciliation with its western neighbors, which resulted precisely from its division and its eagerness to be accepted into the wider European Community, is a product of its division. As the passage of the Cold War ended that division, so it also ended the American guardianship that eased anxieties about the course that a strong Germany might take.

It was not in Europe, oddly enough, that the competition between the United States and the Soviet Union focused. The lines of demarcation there were too firmly drawn, the contending armies too powerfully matched, and the stakes too high to inspire adventurism. Rather it was in the nether regions of the Third World that the Americans and the Russians struggled for influence through the acquisition of client states and the fighting of proxy wars. Places like Korea, Vietnam, Cuba, Nicaragua, Angola, Afghanistan, all of little intrinsic importance in themselves, became significant because Washington and Moscow transformed them into symbols of their own influence. What was trivial became critical precisely because one or the other of the superpowers chose to lay down a stake there to test the other.

The passing of the Cold War has changed that as well. So long as it lasted a number of Third World nations benefited enormously. They in effect became privileged wards. Their politicians were generously bribed, their economies heavily subsidized, their armed forces equipped with the latest military gadgetry, their brutal treatment of their own people justified so long as it served the larger purposes of their benefactor. Now, with the disappearance of one superpower, the contest is over. The subsidies have dried up and the struggles of local warlords has gone unnoticed as interest has shifted elsewhere. With rare exceptions the fledgling states of the Third World, whose fate was once deemed so crucial, will sink into the political backwaters from which the superpowers momentarily snatched them.

As we have seen in even the short time since the end of the Cold War, there is not yet a new international order, and no source of power with the political will formerly exercised by the United States and the Soviet Union. The sorry spectacle of Europe's abdication from the war in divided Yugoslavia indicated not only that there is not yet, in a political sense, any Europe, but also no will on the part of any European nation to take a leadership role. Left to its own devices, Europe floundered, made excuses, and acquiesced. Since, in the case of Bosnia, the United States chose not to act alone, the European nations found an excuse not to act at all. What this demonstrated is that, for the foreseeable future, there is unlikely to be an international order of any sort without active American involvement and leadership.

This does not fit the current American mood, which is to concentrate on neglected domestic problems. But neither "Europe," whatever it is, nor Japan, not any other nation or combination of nations is capable or willing to take a leadership role. None has the power base, the public support, or the international following to do so. None has even the desire. The European nations, themselves so shielded from war for two generations by their protectors, refuse to intervene in a barbaric civil war in the very heart of the continent. There is little reason to expect anything other than a continued political caution and even disengagement by the European nations and Japan. Eventually that will change in unforeseen ways. But at this juncture that moment remains distant.

Thus we are confronted with the depressing but inescapable fact that the perilous but ordered world of rival twin hegemons has, with the end of the Cold War, brought us to a world with no hegemons and no order. Even if Americans wanted to play the role of the single hegemon, it would be difficult to do so, given the nation's economic troubles and mounting domestic needs. But there is, among Americans, no will to dominate, and no enthusiasm for the presumed glories (which have so seduced other countries in the past) it might bring.

While the passing of the Cold War has deprived the United States of its old role as the world's guardian against communism, the search for a compensatory role continues. Some find this in a restructured NATO, which will allow the United States to play a major part in the creation of a post–Cold War European identity. Others seek it in a revitalized United Nations, which would be transformed from an international debating society to a world court and police force.

Behind these schemes and others lies the assumption that a new structure for order must be found to replace that shattered by the collapse of the Soviet empire and the bipolar balance. George Bush, seeking to pin a label on it, called it the "new world order." Although its parameters are vague, the concept rests on the Wilsonian premise that justice rather than force shall be used to resolve international grievances. Powerful nations should be restrained in their behavior by a rule of law imposed by international consensus. In such a formulation the United Nations plays a major role as a sanctifying force, if not yet as prime enforcer.

For George Bush the war against Iraq for the liberation of Kuwait was the link between the Cold War and the new world order. During the former the United States, as leader of the Western alliance, blocked the expansion of communism. In the latter, it stepped forward as the enforcer of the rules of order endorsed by the international community of nations.

The new world order, as conceived by Bush, was an attempt to establish a post–Cold War consensus that had been shattered by the collapse of communism. Such a consensus would require both American leadership of the international community and an agreed-upon system of norms to which all nations could, at least verbally, subscribe. As such it promised to provide a continuing leadership role for the United States despite the disappearance of the threat that had originally inspired and justified such a role.

On what principles would such a post-communist structure rest? At least two were required: one that would correspond to American values, and the other that would win the support of other nations. They were not identical. The U.S. interventions in the two European wars of this century and the more recent interventions of the Cold War were justified on the premise that they were in defense of liberty. Indeed, it was asserted, and to some extent believed, that the survival of American freedoms hinged on the extension of freedom to other peoples: that the world, like a nation, could not exist "half slave and half free." Thus there would be an idealistic component to American global activism.

The notion of order, with its implied protection of the status quo, is not so highly valued among Americans. In any competition it normally takes second place to the exercise of freedom. In this regard one has only to consider the refusal of Americans to restrict the private ownership of guns even at the cost of a high level of violence in public life. Yet the concept of order, if an ambivalent value for individuals, is highly valued by states in the international system. It is normally the condition of their integrity and survival. Violent challengers to order are normally aggressor states. Thus the principle of order, which is in effect the preservation of the status quo, is one to which all territorially satisfied states can pay allegiance.

Liberty and order were the foundation for Bush's post–Cold War foreign policy. American security would be redefined as synonymous with world order—that is, with the maintenance of the international status quo. While this was appropriate for an avowedly status quo power, it was more troublesome for one, like the United States, pledged to the extension of liberty. Bush tried to bridge the gap by equating order with freedom: by stating that only in a world where all peoples were free would there be a stable order, and only in a world governed by the rule of law could there be true freedom.

This rhetorical formulation left much to be desired as the base for a new U.S. foreign policy. It ignored the fact that freedom is divisible: some peoples may enjoy its blessings while others suffer under tyranny or in servitude. Order is similarly sporadic: places that languish quietly for decades can suddenly erupt into the most terrible violence, as in post–Cold War Yugoslavia. The attempt to impose order from the outside does not necessarily result in the extension of liberty, as the United States learned in the case of Kuwait; just as the expansion of freedom often provokes disorder, as is evidenced throughout much of the former Soviet empire or in South Africa.

For these reasons the notion of a new world order has proved to be exceedingly troublesome to explain and difficult to apply. Where attempted against the expansionist drives of Iraq, it has resulted in military victory and political defeat. The rhetoric has far outpaced the results, causing considerable disillusionment among the American public. Other nations that participated in the military action against Iraq found that they were expected to pay the costs of the operation without being able to control its strategy. This undermined future support for such operations, as soon became apparent in the case of Bosnia. Further, as the Bosnian case dramatized, there was far less support in the United States or in Europe for military actions for either freedom or order where economic interests were not at stake. The new world order, which seemed so triumphantly affirmed at Kuwait in 1991, broke down ignominiously at Sarajevo two years later.

The search for a post-Cold War order rests on a triangular conundrum. No one can define what it should be, who should decide, or how it should be enforced. Is it order, freedom, or simply the containment of violent conflict? Should decisions be made by the great powers, by the regional states most involved, or by transient majorities in the United Nations? Even assuming a political consensus, should enforcement be left to the great powers or should an international constabulary be formed?

The dilemma that these questions pose is that there is no international society to make the rules of the post–Cold War world or to enforce them. In a world without superpowers there is little reason to fear a cataclysmic war, but there is also none of the order that the superpowers were able to exert upon weaker states. We are reverting to an earlier pattern of wars among smaller nations or even within such nations. These small wars, many of them of ethnic origin, are likely to be widespread and frequent. There is not yet an international society to contain or settle them, nor is one presently foreseeable. The challenge facing neighboring states will be to avoid being sucked into such conflicts.

The quest for a new world order rests on the assumption that the international society (presumably the United Nations) will act as a unified body to condemn aggression and force reasonable settlements. Yet, aside from the problem of enforcement, there is the fact that states have reason to be ambivalent about the forcible resolution of conflicts by an international entity. While they might support such intervention against states they deem to be outlaws, they resist setting a precedent that might one day be used against them. To grant law-enforcing powers to an international assembly when there is no international society is to tread on grounds that many states would consider dangerous.

For this reason American enthusiasm for a greatly strengthened UN is filled with ambiguities. There is a desire to see malefactors punished, but not at the expense of inhibiting America's own freedom of action. Other major powers display a similar attitude. American support for the UN has been high because the UN has, in the case of the Gulf War, ratified American decisions. In other areas the UN has not impeded America's ability to intervene unilaterally. Part of the UN's appeal has been its very powerlessness. If, however, it should acquire powers of compliance, it could well lose the measure of support it currently enjoys. Americans are not likely to allow vital issues of national interest to be decided by transient majorities in a UN dominated by unstable and repressive third world nations. Nor, for that matter, are other major nations.

During most of the Cold War the foreign policy elite and the American public shared a common perception of the nation's global interests. The one great exception were the latter stages of the Vietnam War, when significant sections of the public rejected elite leadership. The common denominator was the perceived threat of communism. So long as it could be portrayed as a direct threat to American security, the public supported the government's policies of containment and intervention. The demise of communism has once again led to a similar dissonance.

The term "foreign policy elite" covers not only government officials dealing directly with international issues, but also those in foundations, journalism, academia, research institutes, and business with a professional interest in foreign affairs. This elite is generally well-informed and positioned in places of influence. A significant portion of this elite has a direct professional interest in the widest possible engagement of the United States in the affairs of other nations. For many their livelihood depends on it. Others have a more indirect or intellectual interest, but nonetheless share the view that the United States has both a need and a responsibility to intervene actively in the world's affairs.

The end of the Cold War has not, for the most part, affected this predilection. Yet while this elite still views foreign policy as preeminent, the public at large has moved sharply in the other direction. The evaporation of fears about the nation's physical security has sharply reduced public support for extensive overseas military involvements. The Gulf War of 1991 was not an exception because it was portrayed as essential to the security of American oil supplies. Unlike foreign policy elites, the public is largely unconcerned with such issues as political "presence" or the exertion of "leadership"—particularly if any serious cost is required.

For the general public, the nation's fifty-year preoccupation with foreign affairs was seen as an onerous and exceptional measure dictated by threats from aggressive adversaries. For foreign policy elites it was, by contrast, simply the assumption by the United States of its global responsibilities. Today the gulf between these two perceptions has become significant. The wider public, concerned with such domestic issues as unemployment, crime, violence, and declining competitiveness, favors retrenchment from extensive overseas commitments.

The belief is widespread that disorder at home is a far greater threat to American interests than any problems abroad. This attitude was confirmed by the 1992 presidential elections, in which Bill Clinton won his victory by concentrating almost exclusively on domestic themes. Indeed, George Bush's much-noted interest in foreign affairs was treated as a handicap. To label this shift in public attitudes as isolationist would be a mistake. The public does not favor withdrawal from the world, and in fact accepts the high degree of economic and political interdependence that has taken place over the past decades. Rather it simply believes that the disappearance of a serious foreign military threat requires a major reallocation of priorities. To call this isolationist is to misunderstand both its cause and its extent.

Given this change in both the nation's condition and the public mood, grandiose ambitions for an American-orchestrated "new world order" seem misplaced and ill-fated. Such a scheme lacks not only the security anxieties of the Cold War to give it flesh, but also the emotional drive of Wilsonian moralism. Foreign policy elites are no longer accorded the public trust that allows them to indulge in sweeping conceptions of national interest. They are constrained by the belief that interests must be limited to areas where security is seriously threatened or else where intervention is unassailably promised to be cheap. The Gulf War was presented in such a way that it passed the first test. The Somalia operation passed the second test; the struggle over Bosnia did not.

For the past half-century much of the world has looked to the United States for protection against tyrannical dictatorships and has grown accustomed to a dominant American role in the affairs of other nations. This situation endured for such a long time that it was easy to ignore how greatly it had been dictated by particular events: notably the threat posed by Soviet power and the relative weakness of other major nations.

The demise of the Soviet threat has made the recovery of the rest of the world even more significant. Today the majority of Americans, and Europeans as well, believe that the greatest dangers to their well-being are economic, and that their most serious competitors are their Cold War allies. Time and evolving conditions will no doubt change that. But for now, the Cold War paradigms of military danger and American protection are no longer relevant either to the United States or its former Cold War allies.

During the long decades of the Cold War, America's allies and dependencies came to take for granted its energetic involvement in their affairs. Although they were dependent on American protection, they complained often enough about the scope, the pretensions, and even the arrogance of what was sometimes called the *pax americana*. It was easy to criticize this situation because it seemed so immutable. And it was known that even criticism would not induce an American abandonment. But today the criticism is muted, precisely because the involvement can no longer be taken for granted. Even such Cold War contraptions as NATO remain in place as much from European anxieties as American ambitions. The old cries of "Yankee Go Home" have suddenly stilled now that it has become a reality. After so many complaints about American interference, many nations will have reason to regret its demise.

They will regret not only because the United States was, on balance, a benign hegemon, but also because no power or institution presently exists to replace it. NATO is receiving artificial respiration, the European Community is frantically treading water, and the United Nations has not yet either the power or the authority to be an international enforcer.

For the foreseeable future, in what is likely to be a long transitional period after the end of the Cold War, we will be living in a world lacking an organizing principle; one dominated by a ferocious ethnic and religious nationalism, by an unbridgeable gap between the industrial north and the impoverished south, and, compared to the solid, if dangerous, structure of the Cold War, conditions that can only be described as that of international anarchy. This is a situation which the United States, even if it had the will, lacks the power to correct. This is the reality to which both Americans and those who once took its power over their affairs for granted must adjust.

PART FIVE

IDEOLOGICAL CONTROVERSIES

Chapter 16

CHRISTOPHER LASCH'S QUARREL WITH LIBERALISM

Louis Menand

M ODERN LIFE, to some of its critics, looks like a giant wrecking yard of traditions, with no one around to straighten up the mess. In the middle of the yard there is a small tin shed, and inside the shed the apologists of fragmentation sit. These are the liberals. They explain how it is that we are better off without guides to conduct that are any more substantive than the right of each of us to pick up whatever pieces catch his fancy, and why it is that life inside the yard counts as liberation. People who take this view of modernity have two alternatives: they can gather together bits of the failed traditions and construct from them a philosophy of conduct that might supplant liberalism's emptiness, or they can choose, intellectually, at least, to live outside the yard altogether. The first way is the perilous way, since it runs the risk of producing simply another trophy of liberalism's sterile value of "inclusivity," another sign that the system is working for everybody, even for the people who pretend to hate it. This is why it is not enough for the opponents of liberalism simply to construct alternative models; they must never cease to insist that liberalism is actively the enemy—that it is not the consequence of modernity, but its original mad inventor.

Christopher Lasch began his career as a historian and critic of American liberalism. His analysis of liberalism led him to an analysis of some of the alternatives to liberalism in American political thought and, eventually, to a long excursion to social history and cultural criticism. It was clear from this work that he was unhappy with the dominant political and intellectual traditions in American life, and distressed by the mess he thought those traditions had gotten us into. But it was not clear what he thought we might do to organize our lives more propitiously until the publication of *The True and Only Heaven* (1991), in which he returned to the criticism of liberalism with which he started, but this time offered a prescription.

What did Lasch mean by "liberalism"? Beyond the broad idea that liberalism is the philosophical foundation of the modern condition, the term has been used to describe such a variety of specific views that it has become a vexing one to define. Some people we call liberals—those associated with the War on Poverty in the 1960s, say, or with George McGovern's 1972 presidential campaign—believe that the government should provide, in some measure, for the basic welfare of its citizens. Others—Michael Dukakis or Bill Clinton, for instance—think that a vigorous and expanding free-market economy is more likely to produce prosperity. Some liberals want foreign policy to be dictated by a concern for human rights and democratic values, as Jimmy Carter did, others, like Richard Nixon—in this respect a traditionally liberal president—believe that our relations with other nations should be governed by an unsentimental assessment of our own interests.

These disagreements among liberals are not a recent development, a splitting up of what was once a unified core of beliefs. Liberal thought has been divided along similar lines since at least the early years of the century, when liberals argued about America's entry into the First World War, about the growing dominance of large corporations in the American economy, and about the nature of Soviet communism. But in Lasch's view, all liberals, whether they dislike corporate capitalism or welcome it, whether they approve of American intervention in foreign conflicts or deplore it, share a common attitude: they are all optimists, believers in moral and material progress. Liberals believe that as civilization advances (by which, Lasch thought, liberals usually mean "as people become more liberal"), more wants and desires are satisfied, and fewer prejudices and superstitions inhibit us. Once life was made miserable by bad kings and bad teeth; now we have democracy and dentists, political freedom and physical comfort, and thus, liberals believe, we can say that people have become happier, and that life is improving.

It was this faith in progress, Lasch argued in his first book, *The American Liberals and the Russian Revolution* (1962), that made it so difficult for many liberals in 1917 to understand the Communist revolution in Russia as the malign event it was. For to do so would have meant calling into question this central tenet of liberal faith: that history is a continuous progression from tyranny toward freedom, whose advance is marked by a series of democratic revolutions. Liberals are themselves the heirs of a revolutionary tradition, Lasch pointed out; how were they to accept the fact of a revolution that rejected the liberal ideal? And even if Soviet communism proved to be antiliberal and antidemocratic (as, of course, it did), liberals insisted on regarding its emergence as only a temporary setback in the advance of progress; in the end, liberalism must triumph even in Russia, because the triumph of liberalism was destined to be universal.

The American Liberals and the Russian Revolution is a detailed study of the political debate during the years of the First World War—from 1914 to 1919. But the argument was clearly addressed to the liberals of Lasch's own day. When Lasch wrote that "liberalism in America, no less than communism in Russia, has always been a messianic creed, which staked everything on the ultimate triumph of liberalism throughout the world,"[1] he was describing, he thought, not only the liberalism of 1919—of Woodrow Wilson and Walter Lippmann—but the liberalism of the Kennedy administration as well.

This was an ingenious and antithetical point to make. For to describe liberalism as a messianic creed in 1962 was to call the vampire killer a vampire—as the titles of two standard expositions of liberal political theory in the early Cold War era suggest: Arthur M. Schlesinger, Jr.'s *The Vital Center* (1949) and Daniel Bell's *The End of Ideology* (1960). Contemporary liberalism, for those writers, was precisely not an absolutist, world-transforming politics. It was a problem-solving, consensus-reaching politics, one that "dedicates itself," as Schlesinger suggested, "to problems as they come."[2] Such pragmatism could only be impeded by prior ideological convictions, which Bell analyzed specifically as displaced religious and messianic impulses. "Ideology, which once was a road to action, has come to be a dead end," he claimed. "Few serious minds believe any longer that one can set down 'blueprints' and through 'social engineering' bring about a new utopia of social harmony."[3] "People who know they alone are right find it hard to compromise," was the way Schlesinger put it; "and compromise is the strategy of democracy."[4] A little utopianism might be fine as a spur to political engagement, but the business of politics lay in fine-tuning the machinery that makes social and economic freedoms possible, and in resisting ideology and messianism wherever they threaten those freedoms. Liberals were not supposed to become obsessed with the ends (or "the end") of history.

It is possible to be messianic in the effort to root out messianism, though. Even pragmatism can suffer from hubris; and Lasch's detection of a self-aggrandizing impulse, a secret determination to convert the world to its own "anti-ideological" ideology, in the ostensibly instrumentalist politics of mid-century liberalism, was an insight whose accuracy was confirmed, for many people, by America's subsequent entanglement, under a series of liberal administrations, in Vietnam. Lasch's accusation was also, of course, one that any liberal disenchanted with the self-righteous certainty of some of his fellow liberals might have made.[5] It need not have led anyone to abandon liberalism. After all, a liberal might reasonably ask, so long as we don't force people to become like us, why *shouldn't* we hope that liberal institutions—democratic societies and free markets—become universal?

For Lasch, however, the point had a different consequence. He began to see not only liberalism, but the whole march of "progress" itself as a creeping tyranny of centralized social and political control. Though liberalism was the ascendant political theory of this historical process, even many of the adversaries of liberalism, Lasch concluded, shared its optimism and its passion for transforming people's lives. In *The New Radicalism in America* (1965) and *The Agony of the American Left* (1969), he considered some of these adversaries: the "cultural radicals," such as Mabel Dodge Luhan and Randolph Bourne; the turn-of-the-century populists and socialists; and the leaders of the progressive movement, which, during the first two decades of the century, sought to restore a (somewhat ill-defined) sense of "civic virtue" to American political and economic life. Among these, only populism and socialism—"two broad patterns of opposition to corporate capitalism, occasionally converging but ideologically distinct"[6]—seemed to Lasch to have offered a genuine alternative to the corporate economy and the liberal state; their failure, early in the century, marked for him the death of all real dissent.

For the reformers and cultural radicals, he decided, were in the end only participating in the general effort to "enlighten"—and thus remold—the citizenry from the top down, through public education and artistic and literary culture; and this was an enterprise so congenial to the liberal mentality that liberals found it easy to adopt the radical style, and to patronize intellectual culture, in a way that rendered those traditions powerless. The Kennedy administration, with its indulgence of artists and intellectuals enthralled by the illusion that they were having an influence on the exercise of political power, represented, as Lasch saw it, the culmination of this process. As for the progressive movement, associated with the followers of Theodore Roosevelt and with liberal militants such as Herbert Croly, Walter Lippmann, and William Weyl, it was progressive "chiefly in attacking the archaic entrepreneurial capitalism the existence of which impeded the rationalization of American industry," and thus "actually served the needs of the industrial system."[7] In seeking to reform the system rather than to resist it—to discover ways for more people to partake of the material prosperity capitalism provided rather than ways to prevent big business from turning people into well-fed "wage slaves"—the progressives only smoothed capitalism's path. So that by mid-century, Lasch concluded, it had become "almost impossible for criticism of existing policies to become part of political discourse. The language of American politics increasingly resembles an Orwellian monologue."[8]

Having come to the bottom of the political barrel, Lasch turned first to social history and then to jeremiad. *Haven in a Heartless World* (1977) proposed that the history of modern society can be described as "the socialization of production, followed by the socialization of reproduction."[9] By the first phrase, Lasch meant the division of labor that accompanied the emergence of industrial capitalism, and that, by depriving people of control over their work, deprived them as well of the virtues unalienated labor instills. A day on an assembly line spent fixing the heads on pins, to use Adam Smith's famous example of specialization in *The Wealth of Nations,* is not likely to lead a person to an elevated conception of life, or to give him a sense of independence and self-confidence. (This was a warning about the moral effects of specialization that Smith himself recorded elsewhere in his writings.) By "the socialization of reproduction," Lasch meant the proliferation, beginning in the nineteenth century, of the so-called helping professions: the doctors, psychologists, teachers, child guidance experts, juvenile court officers, and so forth, who, by their constant intervention in people's private lives, "eroded the capacity for self-help and social invention."[10]

This second development constitutes, in Lasch's view, liberalism's worst betrayal. For liberalism, he argued, had struck a deal: in return for transforming the worker from an independent producer of goods into a fixer of heads on pins, it was agreed that people would be free to pursue happiness and virtue in their private lives in whatever manner they chose. The workplace was thus severed from the home, and the family became the "haven in a heartless world." But no sooner was the deal made, Lasch argued, than liberalism reneged. Private life was immediately made prey to the quasi-official helping professions and to the "forces of organized virtue," led by "feminists, temperance advocates, educational reformers, liberal ministers, penologists, doctors, and bureaucrats."[11] "From the moment the conception of the family as a refuge made its historical appearance, the same forces that gave rise to the new privacy began to erode it. . . . The hope that private transactions could make up for the collapse of communal traditions and civic order"[12] was killed by organized kindness.

Modern life, in Lasch's conception, is thus predicated on one basic transaction: the exchange of genuine independence for pseudo-liberation. Liberals and reformers will free us from the repressiveness of the patriarchal family, of the closed ethnic community—even of our own unhappiness. All we have to do is to surrender ourselves to the benevolent paternalism of the sociologists, psychiatrists, educators, and corporate and welfare bureaucrats. But those "helpers" have effectively destroyed the very institutions, such as the nuclear family, through which character and independence were traditionally instilled. The responsibility for raising children has been lifted from the shoulders of parents (thus discrediting their authority) and been placed in the offices of medical and educational professionals and experts; a pattern of "normal" development is now enforced by the public schools, whose purpose has been reconceived as socialization—turning people into good citizens on the liberal model, rather than simply introducing them to knowledge. "Liberating" people has meant, in short, converting them into permanent dependents of the modern state and its "human science" apparatchiks.

Lasch's argument, at this point in his work, had begun to show some similarity to that of Michel Foucault, whose analysis of modern institutional benevolence as a tyrannical system of social controls Lasch wrote about approvingly.[13] Perhaps a stronger, or more immediate, influence was Philip Rieff's notion of "the triumph of the therapeutic"—the idea that the twentieth-century belief in personal liberation has created a new culture organized around a new type of human being, whom Rieff called "psychological man." It was Lasch's development of this argument of Rieff's that yielded the work for which he is famous.

The Culture of Narcissism (1979) was a book of its moment. It appeared at the close of a depressing decade and near the close of an unpopular presidency. Lasch was, in fact, one of the luminaries invited to Camp David to help

Jimmy Carter organize his thoughts for the speech proposing that Americans were suffering a "crisis of confidence," and this well-publicized distinction no doubt helped put the book on the best-seller list. Its argument is a little more complicated than many people whose knowledge of it came largely at second hand may have assumed. Lasch proposed that the modern developments he had examined in his earlier work—the demise of the family and the erosion of private life generally—had produced "a new form of personality organization."[14] If (as he thought) people were behaving and feeling differently, it was because a fundamental change had taken place not only in beliefs and values—in what people thought moral, or permissible, or desirable—but in the structure of the mind itself. Our "social arrangements live on," he proposed, "in the individual, buried in the mind below the level of consciousness."[15]

The principal evidence for this assertion—beyond sociological observations about a "sense of inner emptiness," the "decline of the play spirit," and so forth—were psychiatric reports on contemporary personality disorders, which were (Lasch claimed) increasingly assuming a "narcissistic" pattern. Lasch was not, as some of his more casual readers may have assumed, using "narcissism" in the everyday sense of "self-centered" or "hedonistic." He was using the term in a clinical sense that had been developed in a psychoanalytic tradition arising out of Freudian theory—in the work of Heinz Kohut, Otto Kernberg, and the object-relations psychologist Melanie Klein. In this literature, a "narcissist" is not someone with an overweening sense of self, but, on the contrary, someone with a very weak sense of self.

In order to make the psychoanalytic data he had assembled fit the case he was making about the emergence of a new personality type in society at large, Lasch made one further assumption: that "pathology represents a heightened version of normality"[16]—that is, that a clinically disordered personality, of the kind reported in psychoanalytic studies, is representative of the current "normal" personality type. This made for a rather elaborate theoretical contraption. The reader was being called upon to make the following assumptions, any one of which is clearly vulnerable to challenge: that changes in education, the role of the family, the nature of work, and so on are capable of producing fundamental changes, "below the level of consciousness," in people's psychological makeup; that the changes in American life over the last hundred years have been extensive and monolithic enough to create an entire population dominated by this new personality type; that the pathological personality does indeed present a version of the normal personality; and that the particular examples of narcissistic behavior adduced by Lasch in 1979—among them the Manson Family killings, the kidnapping of Patty Hearst, the attack on theatrical illusion in contemporary drama, "the fascination with oral sex,"[17] and the streaker craze—are evidence of long-term personality disintegration, rather than isolated responses to a confusing but transitory historical moment.

(There was also the problem that a writer who had elsewhere suggested that psychiatry was, in the hands of some of its practitioners, at least, one of the corrupting forces in modern life was relying rather heavily on a psychiatric conception of the "normal.") *The Culture of Narcissism* was thus an easy book to misunderstand. Lasch was not saying that things were better in the 1950s, as conservatives offended by countercultural permissiveness probably took him to be saying. He was not saying that things were better in the 1960s, as former activists disgusted by the "me-ism" of the 1970s are likely to have imagined. He was diagnosing a condition that originated, he believed, in the nineteenth century.

The Minimal Self (1984) was written to correct the misapprehensions of the earlier book's admirers. The "narcissistic" self, Lasch explained, was really a type of what he was now calling the "minimal" self—"a self uncertain of its own outlines, [yet] longing either to remake the world in its own image" (as in the case of technocratic reformers and other acolytes of "progress") "or to merge into its environment in a blissful union"[18] (as in the case of counterculturalists, feminists, and ecological utopians). Authentic selfhood lies between these extremes, he wrote—in an acceptance of limits without despair. But the conditions in which such a self might be forged were being destroyed.

What is distinctive about Lasch's criticism of modern life, besides its unusually broad scope, is its moral and personal intensity. For it is one thing—and not an uncommon thing among academic intellectuals—to analyze modern democratic society as a system of social controls masquerading as personal freedoms, without concluding anything more radical (or less banal) than that all societies must hold themselves together somehow, and that an officially "open" society will find means for doing so that are designed to appear as uncoercive as possible. But Lasch showed no interest in this kind of analytic detachment, which he regarded as just the kind of superior sociological "expertise" he associated with the bureaucratic and professionalist mentality he abhorred.[19] He was (or he gave, in his work, the impression of being) a man who believed he had caught "the modern project"[20]—his phrase for the group of social and political tendencies he analyzed—in an enormous lie, and who cannot rest until the lie has been exposed. There is an invasion-of-the-body-snatchers urgency to his writing; and this gave to it, over the years, an increasingly aggrieved, and sometimes paranoid, tone. It also drew him to a style of relentless and contentious assertion which can be, to put it gently, extremely off-putting. It was an unusual style for a scholar to resort to, and I think he meant it, quite deliberately, to be offensive: an affront to the modern taste for cool and logically seamless forms of persuasion. If he did mean it this way, it works.

The True and Only Heaven was the first place in which Lasch tried to suggest, with some degree of comprehensiveness, a way out of the regrettable condition he thought the modern liberal view had left us in. It is much the longest of his books, and it suffers from many of the faults one has come to associate with his work: it lingers pedantically on minor matters and dashes through major ones; it makes much of points almost everyone would concede and ignores obvious objections to its more controversial assertions; and it is written from a position that had hardened into something like dogmatism. Lasch was, after all, a writer who had argued that "all medical technology has done is to increase patients' dependence on machines and the medical experts who operate [them]";[21] that "new ideas of sexual liberation—the celebration of oral sex, masturbation, and homosexuality—spring from the prevailing fear of heterosexual passion, even of sexual intercourse itself";[22] that the reliance on medical intervention during pregnancy "helped women in their campaign for voluntary motherhood by raising the cost of pregnancy to their husbands— not only the financial cost but the emotional cost of the doctor's intrusion into the bedroom, his usurpation of the husband's sexual prerogatives";[23] that the imposition of child labor laws "obscured the positive possibility of children working alongside their parents at jobs of recognized importance";[24] and that "the prison life of the past looks in our time like liberation itself."[25]

Like all of Lasch's books, *The True and Only Heaven* was clearly designed to be responsive to contemporary anxieties—in this case, to concern about the ecological dangers that are bound, it seems, to accompany the spread of capitalist economies across the globe. Lasch argued in the book that if we continue to believe, as the religion of progress encourages us to believe, that somehow everyone in the world can be given the standard of living of a middle-class American, the planet will be used up long before we ever arrive at the dubious utopia. He was not the first person to sound this warning, but he did, as usual, sound it in a provocative manner.

By the time of *The True and Only Heaven,* Lasch had come to regard the belief in progress not as simply an interesting paradox in twentieth-century liberal thought, but as the dominant ideology of modern history. It is in the name of progress, he thought, that traditional sources of happiness and virtue—work, faith, the family, even an independent sense of self—are being destroyed; and he began his book with an analysis of the false values of the modern liberal outlook, proposing, for each value or attitude to be rejected, an alternative. This discussion is filled with references to various thinkers and ideas, as is the case throughout *The True and Only Heaven;* but references to specific policies or social arrangements are scarce, so that the analysis has a theoretical or abstract cast. Lasch's purpose, evidently, was to establish a vocabulary.

Lasch argued, as he had in his first book nearly thirty years earlier, that liberals are optimists: they believe in an unlimited ability to provide for an ever-expanding array of human wants. A worthier sentiment, he felt, is "hope"—an acceptance of limits without despair (as he had described it in *The Minimal Self*). Liberals espouse a kind of Enlightenment universalism; they regard their truths as self-evident to all reasonable people, and therefore as applicable to everyone. He recommended instead an emphasis on particularism—a recognition of the persistence of national and ethnic loyalties. Nostalgia, he argued, is progress's "ideological twin,"[26] since it is a way of thinking about the past that makes it seem irrecoverable, and makes change seem inevitable. He proposed "memory" as an alternative, a way of seeing the past and present as continuous. Instead of the modern conception of people as consumers, working only to provide themselves with the means to satisfy material wants, he suggested a conception of people as producers, working in order to acquire the virtues labor instills—among them independence, responsibility, and self-sufficiency. And in place of "self-interest," which defines the economic man of liberal individualism, he proposed "virtue," which defines the citizen ready to take an active part in community life.

This much of Lasch's argument, directed at the mentality, certainly recognizable, that sees no limits to economic growth, and that understands the ends of social and economic policy to be simply the creation and satisfaction of more consumers, still has a timely appeal. The collapse of the Communist economies was greeted in some quarters, as Lasch in 1962 suggested it would, as evidence of the inevitable global triumph of liberalism—the theoretically predicted "end of history," in the catchphrase made popular by Francis Fukuyama. And on these matters, as Lasch quite rightly pointed out, there is no longer an appreciable difference in mainstream American political thought between "liberals" and "conservatives." The "New Right," in this respect, proved a sham: Ronald Reagan was no less a worshipper of progress—no less an optimist, a nostalgist, and a global crusader for the American way—than any classic liberal one might name.

Much of the attention Lasch's book received when it appeared was therefore, as might have been expected, preoccupied with its attack on the "progressive" worldview; and the general terms that define the substitute worldview the book proposed are plainly attractive. Who would want to defend "optimism" against "hope," "nostalgia" against "memory," "self-interest" against "virtue"? So long as the discussion remains at this level of abstraction, there is very little to argue. But Lasch had a broader purpose: he had undertaken to reconstruct a political and moral tradition in which his "alternative" values are rooted. This tradition he called "populism," and it is not possible to engage his argument in a serious way without confronting the challenges this tradition makes (or Lasch understood it to make) to modern liberal assumptions.

Lasch meant by "populism" something more than the late-nineteenth-century political movement the term ordinarily denotes; indeed, the book contains very little discussion of William Jennings Bryan, for instance, or of the southern populist leader Tom Watson.[27] The populist tradition Lasch described has been transmitted through an oddly assorted sequence of thinkers.

These thinkers all share one attitude, of course: an antagonism to the modern liberal outlook as Lasch had defined it. This may express itself in an appreciation for the "civic virtues"—the virtues derived from personal independence, political participation, and genuinely productive labor; in an acceptance of "fate" (one of the book's key terms) and of the idea of limits; or in an admiration for a set of characteristics Lasch identified with lower-middle-class, or "petty-bourgeois," culture: moral conservatism, egalitarianism, loyalty, and the struggle against the moral temptation of resentment (that is, the capacity for forgiveness).

Among the social and political critics Lasch regarded as populists are writers who defend small-scale producers (farmers, artisans, and so forth), who despise creditors, and who oppose the culture of uplift and universal philanthropy because of its disruptive intervention in personal and family life. These sentiments are, he thought, particularly strongly expressed in the writings of Tom Paine; the English radical William Cobbett; the nineteenth-century editor, transcendentalist, and controversialist Orestes Brownson; and the author of the classic of populist political economy, *Progress and Poverty* (1879), Henry George. Two labor-movement theorists from the turn of the century are important to Lasch's tradition as champions of small-scale producers: the French syndicalist Georges Sorel, whose *Reflections on Violence* (1908) was admired by critics of the Third Republic in France and of liberalism in England, and the British guild socialist G.D.H. Cole. By proposing to restore control over production to the worker, Lasch argued, syndicalism and guild socialism represented genuine alternatives to corporate capitalism. What socialists and the labor movement generally ended up settling for, he felt (and Cole is his example), was a top-down welfare system that turned the worker into a consumer, and left him, though more secure in his job, even more dependent.

This tradition of political and economic criticism is complemented, Lasch argued, by a parallel tradition of moral criticism—and this proposal is the chief novelty of the book, and the key to its creation of an alternative to liberal fragmentation. The major figure is Emerson, whose recognition, in the late essay on "Fate" (1860), that "freedom lies in the acceptance of necessity" Lasch regarded as the philosophical centerpiece of populist thought. Emerson's fatalism is ignored, he thought, by the Emersonians—"those professional Pollyannas"—and he proposed to restore us to a proper understanding, principally by reading Emerson by the lights of the Puritan divine Jonathan Edwards. Two other writers, both readily associated with Emerson, are said to share the populist moral vision: Thomas Carlyle, in *Sartor Resartus* (1834) and the essays on heroes and hero worship published in 1841, and William James, in the discussion of the "twice-born" in *The Varieties of Religious Experience* (1902) and in the essay "The Moral Equivalent of War" (1910).

Lasch traced the course of populist ideals in a group of twentieth-century American writers: Josiah Royce, Randolph Bourne, Herbert Croly, Waldo

Frank, John Dewey, the New Dealer Thurman Arnold, and Reinhold Niebuhr. In some of these cases, he was reconsidering writers whose ideas he had once criticized. Croly, for instance, whose *The Promise of American Life* (1910) Lasch once regarded as a typical example of the progressive's naive understanding of the nature of corporate power,[28] was praised for recognizing, in a later book, *Progressive Democracy* (1914), the importance of endowing the worker with a sense of responsibility—and for perceiving that the specialization required by big business and mass production would destroy the possibilities for meaningful work. Niebuhr (one of the heroes of Schlesinger's *The Vital Center*) was attacked by Lasch in *The New Radicalism in America* for taking an uncritical and Manichean view of the struggle between American liberal democracy and Soviet totalitarianism—for assuming too readily the inherent virtue of the American way and the monolithic evil of Soviet communism.[29] In *The True and Only Heaven,* though, Niebuhr appears as a critic of liberalism. His defense of "particularism"—of the innate desire of groups to protect their difference and autonomy against the liberal inclination to force compromises on competing interests—now seemed to Lasch to make him a misunderstood antagonist of liberal ideology.

Niebuhr is also important to the populist tradition, as Lasch interpreted it, because of his insistence on the desirability of forgiveness, and the futility of resentment, in struggles for social justice; and Lasch's consideration of this aspect of Niebuhr's thought leads directly to the only political success story in the book: Martin Luther King, Jr.'s leadership of the southern civil rights movement. King succeeded, Lasch believed, by appealing to the populist virtues of lower-middle-class communities in the South—both black and white—and by preaching the doctrine of "a spiritual discipline against resentment." Blacks in King's movement did not seek revenge for the injustices they had suffered, since they understood (or King, who had studied Niebuhr as a divinity student, understood) Niebuhr's teaching that to combat injustice and coercion with more injustice and coercion is only to perpetuate a cycle of conflict. But, Lasch argued, when King and his associates attempted to mobilize victims of poverty in the inner cities of the North, they could no longer appeal, as they had in the South, to communities of people who understood the value of forgiveness. Resentment against the powerful became instead the motivating emotion of the struggle, with disastrous results.

Lower-middle-class virtues persist, Lasch thought, but as an endangered moral species, preyed upon by the social-engineering schemes of the liberal professional classes. The controversy between suburban liberals and working-class city residents over the busing of school children to achieve racial integration and the struggle over abortion rights are, he suggested, recent instances of liberal imperialism. In the Boston busing wars, and in the struggles for open housing in the suburbs of Chicago, lower-middle-class white communities were reviled, and even demonized, by liberals; yet their "only crime," Lasch said, "so far as anyone could see, was their sense of ethnic solidarity."[30] The populist solution, apparently, would have entailed an attempt to transform the inner city into a "real community," rather than to compel people to ignore their ethnic and racial differences—though Lasch was vague about how this transformation would take place.

In the case of abortion rights, one might imagine that pro-choice advocates, because of their insistence that the decision to have an abortion should be left to the individual woman rather than foreclosed by the state, would have had the stronger case for Lasch. But Lasch regarded the procedure of abortion itself as an instance of technological intrusion into the natural process of reproduction, and he accused the proponents of abortion rights of advocating social engineering—of trying to use medical advances to eliminate the "unwanted" in the name of social improvement. (This view of the pro-choice mentality derives mainly from a single sociological study, Kristin Luker's *Abortion and the Politics of Motherhood* [1984].)

And yet in these cases there is at least some engagement between the classes. In general, Lasch thought, "neither left- nor right-wing intellectuals . . . seem to have much interest in the rest of American society."[31] A revived populist tradition, he concluded, would challenge the ideologues of progress, and help to answer "the great question of twentieth-century politics":[32] how we are to restore a spirited civic virtue to our lives.

This does not mean that Lasch was proposing a resurrection of the populist political and economic program (thought his lengthy and often quarrelsome elaboration of that program sometimes made it appear otherwise). As he conceded, much of populist economic theory—with its hatred of creditors and landlords, its monetary gimmicks and paper money schemes, its call for a return to small-scale production—was anachronistic even in the nineteenth century. Many populist political convictions are similarly outdated: the belief that armed conflict breeds virtue in the citizenry, for example, surely died in the Battle of the Somme. Lasch was not suggesting that all the facts of modern history could be repealed, or that someday we might all become yeoman farmers, with our ancestral rifles hanging next to the fireplace—though he would perhaps have liked us to think more respectfully of yeoman farmers.

The real argument of his book was a more philosophical one, having to do with the juxtaposition of populist economic theory, such as it is, with the tradition of moral criticism Lasch found in Edwards, Emerson, Carlyle, James, Niebuhr, and others. His point seemed to be that we need a political economy that matches the moral economy (as Lasch believed those writers understood it) of the universe. The universe, in this conception, is a place in which we earn our way, and do so in part by recognizing that there are limits to how far we can go, and forces militating against us that we cannot control. Character is built by striving to perform the role fate has assigned us, and a society that recognized this truth would be one which understood that conditions a modern person finds oppressive—obedience to family discipline, acceptance of the restrictions of place and class, military conscription, demeaning or unre-munerative work—are really the conditions that make a full and independent life possible.

The reason populists give for agitating against capitalists, creditors, and landlords is that those are classes of people who profit without producing. In doing so, they violate the principles of an economics based on a labor theory of value—the foundation if not only populist and Marxist but even liberal economic theory in the nineteenth century. More than that, though, they violate the universe's moral principle of just compensation. You must give something to get something back. Only if we are producers will we deserve to consume. And to be a "producer" in the larger, moral sense means to feel oneself responsible for all of what one does in one's life.

This is not an unattractive philosophical conception. But what happens when it touches ground in the thought and practice of a particular "populist" writer? Consider the case of Georges Sorel, whose militant version of socialist syndicalism appealed to Lasch because of its rejection of both liberal and Marxist utopianism. Among the less attractive features of Sorel's thought, Lasch noted in passing, is "probably" anti-Semitism.[33] But a man who compared France's struggle against the Jews to America's against the "Yellow Peril," who wrote that "the French should defend their state, their customs, and their ideas against the Jewish invaders" and that "the so-called excesses of the Bolsheviks were due to the Jewish elements that had penetrated the movement," and who referred, in two of the works Lasch cited, *Reflections on Violence* and *The Illusion of Progress,* to "big Jew bankers" is not only "probably" an anti-Semite.[34] Nor was Sorel's anti-Semitism simply a detachable element of his general outlook. It was the obvious, if not the unavoidable, consequence of an economic theory that demonized financiers and creditors.

And this side of populist thought is of a paranoid piece throughout: the dislike of professional armies, as an instance of specialization that deprives citizens of the virtue-making activity of war; the dislike of those who lend the state the money to pay its armies, and who therefore supposedly find it in their interest to foment war; the defense of local religious and ethnic communities—these are all classic sources of anti-Semitism. They are also among the sources of fascism, particularly in France. "The intellectual father of fascism," one French admirer called Sorel in the 1920s;[35] and although Lasch noted Sorel's close association with the Action Française and his enthusiastically reciprocated admiration for Mussolini (later complemented by an equally fervent admiration for Lenin), he did not explain why this aspect of Sorel's thought, of which he plainly did not approve, should be regarded as irrelevant to the aspects he had praised. And the same is true of the racism, jingoism, and demagoguery associated with populist political movements generally; Lasch acknowledged these tendencies, but asked us to ignore them—

occasionally by the discreditable tactic of throwing our suspicions back in our faces. He addressed the question of Sorel's connections to fascism, for instance, simply by remarking that "liberals' obsession with fascism . . . leads them to see 'fascist tendencies' or 'proto-fascism' in all opinions unsympathetic to liberalism."[36] This may or may not be true, but it is not an argument.

The True and Only Heaven was, one assumes, intended to provoke many such arguments about the selective readings and unorthodox interpretations of various figures. But there are two larger criticisms I think Lasch invited, and they have application not only to that book, but to his work generally. Of the many peculiarities about the moral tradition Lasch constructed in *The True and Only Heaven*, the most astonishing is the omission of Freud—a writer who had played an important part in Lasch's earlier thinking. For surely the Freudian notion of psychic economy involves exactly the principle of compensation, and exactly the tragic sense of life, that Lasch so passionately admired in thinkers of far smaller intellectual stature. But a writer like Freud could not figure in Lasch's account, because Freud has already been accepted as one of the heroes of modern culture. And this is also, it seems to me, why the writers who do have a prominent place in Lasch's tradition are either minor and eccentric figures, like Brownson and Sorel, or major ones who are supposed to have been misread by everyone else, like Emerson or Niebuhr. For to have conceded that the "populist" moral conception is simply a limited and somewhat cranky version of a moral conception we find everywhere in modern culture would mean conceding that values modern society is supposed to have made obsolete are actually to be found at the very heart of modern life.

If, as Lasch suggested in his work on the family, there is a "deal" on which modern liberal society was founded, it is that we shall have the freedom to criticize the conditions in which we live. This bargain has given us an enormous body of literary and intellectual work, fiercely protected by liberal institutions, whose moral intention is to complicate all the issues that traditional liberal theory makes too simple. Lionel Trilling wrote a famous book to make this point; but *The Liberal Imagination* was not mentioned by Lasch. He seemed, and not only on the evidence of *The True and Only Heaven,* simply deaf to literature. "Misgivings were destined to be confined to a shadowy half-life on the fringes of debate,"[37] he wrote of the spread of specialization and the division of labor in the early years of the Industrial Revolution. It is as though Wordsworth, Dickens, and Thoreau had never written, or their books never read.

At the core of Lasch's condemnation of liberalism is the familiar charge that liberalism is effectively without content—that "liberal man" is a wind-up contraption that chases its own short-term interests, and the liberal state a night watchman that only keeps the streets clean and the fights fair (or, at least, "efficient"). But liberalism does have a moral conception of the self, which is expressed in the political doctrine of rights. There is virtually no mention of rights in Lasch's attack on the elements of the modern liberal outlook, or in his analysis, in *The True and Only Heaven,* of particular political events, such as the disputes about busing and abortion. Elsewhere, he linked modern feminism's attachment to medical technology to the eighteenth-century idea of individual rights: the progressive mentality, he thought, regards access to reproductive technology as an enhancement of the woman's right to choose whether to bear children.[38] And it is clear that, like many other critics of liberalism, he wanted to replace talk of rights in our political vocabulary with talk of duties—talk of what we owe to our society and to each other, rather than what is owed to us. "Rights-bearers," he claimed near the end of his life, in a symposium on the subject, "are regarded as autonomous individuals, and that is precisely the style of thinking we are trying to avoid."[39]

This seems to me to be an insufficient account of rights. It is insufficient historically because the recognition of individual rights figures crucially in the liberal idea of what counts as progress. And it is insufficient morally, as well, since our notion of exactly what a right entails—to speak freely, or to bear arms, or to travel or own property—and under what circumstances it must give way to other claims, is the subject of continual debate. The history of United States Supreme Court decisions alone is ample evidence of the intellectual and moral complexity of the idea of rights. It is true that from one perspective rights appear to uphold private interests against public goods—to protect my desire to publish obscene material, for example, against the community's desire to maintain standards of good taste. But from another perspective, a system of enumerated rights against the state, such as the Bill of Rights provides, is precisely an acknowledgment of the *general* claim of society as a whole against the individual. This was the view taken by liberal contemporaries of Lasch's turn-of-the-century populists, such as the younger Oliver Wendell Holmes: that it is only because we recognize the legitimacy of society's claims generally that we undertake to respect the desire of people to be exempted from those claims in specified kinds of behavior.

Because the subject is dismissed altogether from *The True and Only Heaven,* rights have no place in the book's account of the southern civil rights movement, and this seems to me to be a telling omission. For what saves Lasch's populist tradition from being merely a bouquet of the values left strewn in the wake of progress is his contention that the populist spirit continues to have a life in real communities. Since the South has been the breeding ground for many populist politicians in this century, and since the South was itself a classic example of antiliberal "particularism"—"the preindustrial society par excellence," as Lasch once called it[40]—one would have expected him to give special attention to the character of southern life. But prominent southern populists go almost unmentioned in *The True and Only Heaven.* Huey Long's name, for example, appears only twice, in lists of the sort of people liberals unfairly associate with populism. George Wallace turns up more often; but although Lasch seemed to disapprove of the politics of resentment Wallace practiced during his days as a segregationist, his remarks on Wallace were otherwise not unkind, and he noted Wallace's eventual acceptance of racial integration approvingly as testimony to the ability to one local ethnic constituency—lower-middle-class southern whites—to respond to a moral appeal from another.

It is true that the Montgomery bus boycott of 1955, which is where the modern civil rights movement began, is one of the noblest political events in our history, and that it was made possible by the religious faith of a lower-class ethnic community—southern blacks—essentially untouched by legalistic ways of thinking. But it is not true, as Lasch suggested it is, that the boycotters' victory, or the victories in other civil rights campaigns in the South, came about because lower-middle-class southern whites understood the justice of the blacks' moral appeal. Southern whites did not take a notable part in the Montgomery protest, except to oppose it and to humiliate and harass its participants. The protest succeeded because on the day a local judge issued the injunction that would have broken the boycott, the Supreme Court ruled that the black citizens of Montgomery had the right to sit where they chose on city buses. There was no "local solution" to the problem of racial segregation in the South because the principle at stake was not a local principle.

Lasch was always at his most acerbic in his criticism of middle-class liberals who impose the values of their culture on lower-middle-class communities and families, and he had much to say in his discussion of subjects like the busing controversy and the abortion debate about the attitude of moral superiority some liberals assume toward the less educated people who oppose them. There is indeed some ugliness in the middle-class attitudes he described; but to take note of the ugliness does not dispose of the matter.

Back in the 1960s, a group of filmmakers, Drew Associates, was invited by the Kennedy administration to film its enforcement of the court-ordered desegregation of the University of Alabama—the incident that culminated in George Wallace's famous "stand in the schoolhouse door." The film that was produced, *Crisis: Behind a Presidential Commitment*, covers events both at the White House and in Alabama. It is sometimes shown on public television, and it dramatizes the cultural friction Lasch writes about. Robert Kennedy, in the White House, and his deputy, Nicholas DeB. Katzenbach, in Alabama—Ivy League liberals, supremely assured of their virtue—are seen discussing their strategy for handling Wallace as though Wallace were an inconvenient road hazard, a man, in their calculus, of no moral account whatever. And Wallace is seen arriving at the university and accepting expressions of support from the people waiting to greet him with the easy familiarity of a man who knows them and is part of a genuine community.

Wallace was as successful a populist as the postwar era produced, and the Kennedy administration was undoubtedly the incarnation of the modern liberal mentality as Lasch conceives it. There is something slightly chilling about the confrontation, as there is when you watch any ancient and deeply rooted thing smoothly and expertly obliterated by the forces of "progress." But Kennedy and Katzenbach were right, and Wallace was wrong.

NOTES

1. Lasch, *The American Liberals and the Russian Revolution* (New York: Columbia University Press, 1962), p. xvi.

2. Schlesinger, *The Vital Center: The Politics of Freedom* (Boston: Houghton Mifflin, 1949), p. 256.

3. Bell, *The End of Ideology: On the Exhaustion of Political Ideas in the Fifties* (New York: Free Press, 1960), pp. 370, 373.

4. Schlesinger, *The Vital Center*, p. 174.

5. Bell himself, in fact, criticized the messianic character of liberal anticommunism in the 1950s; see *The End of Ideology*, pp. 108–112.

6. Lasch, *The Agony of the American Left* (New York: Knopf, 1969), p. 5.

7. Ibid., p. 10

8. Ibid., p. 29.

9. Lasch, *Haven in a Heartless World: The Family Beseiged* (New York: Basic Books, 1977), p. xv.

10. Ibid., p. xxi.

11. Ibid., p. 169.

12. Ibid., p. 168.

13. See Lasch, "Life in the Therapeutic State," *The New York Review of Books*, June 12, 1980, pp. 24–32.

14. Lasch, *The Culture of Narcissism: American Life in an Age of Diminishing Expectations* (New York: Norton, 1979), p. 94.

15. Ibid., p. 51.

16. Ibid., p. 175.

17. Ibid., p. 50.

18. Lasch, *The Minimal Self: Psychic Survival in Troubled Times* (New York: Norton, 1984), p. 19.

19. See Lasch's remarks on professional historians in "Consensus: An Academic Question?" *Journal of American History* 76 (1989), pp. 457–459.

20. Lasch, "The Saving Remnant," *The New Republic*, November 19, 1990, p. 33.

21. Lasch, *The Culture of Narcissism*, p. 42.

22. Lasch, *Haven in a Heartless World*, p. 183.

23. Lasch, "Life in the Therapeutic State," p. 27.

24. Lasch, "The Crime of Quality Time" (an interview), *New Perspectives Quarterly* 7 (Winter 1990), p. 48.

25. Lasch, *The Culture of Narcissism*, p. 99.

26. Lasch, *The True and Only Heaven: Progress and Its Critics* (New York: Norton, 1991), p. 82.

27. Lasch had written sympathetically about populist political movements before; see *The Agony of the American Left*, pp. 3–31, and "Populism, Socialism, and McGovern-

ism," in *The World of Nations: Reflections on American History, Politics, and Culture* (New York: Knopf, 1973), pp. 160–182.

28. See Lasch, "Herbert Croly's America," *The New York Review of Books*, July 1, 1965, pp. 18–19.

29. See Lasch, *The New Radicalism in America, 1889–1963: The Intellectual as a Social Type* (New York: Knopf, 1965), pp. 299–303.

30. Lasch, *The True and Only Heaven*, p. 402.

31. Ibid., p. 526.

32. Ibid., p. 531.

33. Ibid., p. 305.

34. See Eugen Weber, *Action Française: Royalism and Reaction in Twentieth-Century France* (Stanford: Stanford University Press, 1962), p. 74, and Michael Curtis, *Three Against the Republic: Sorel, Barrès, and Maurras* (Princeton: Princeton University Press, 1959), pp. 211–212.

35. Georges Valois, in *Le fascisme* (1927); quoted in Zeev Sternhell, *Neither Right nor Left: Fascist Ideology in France* (Berkeley: University of California Press, 1986), p. 9.

36. Lasch, *The True and Only Heaven*, p. 305.

37. Ibid., pp. 56–57.

38. See Lasch, "Birth, Death, and Technology: The Limits of Cultural Laissez-Faire," in *The World of Nations*, pp. 294–307.

39. Lasch, "Who Owes What to Whom?" *Harper's*, February 1991, p. 49.

40. Lasch, *The New Radicalism in America*, p. xii.

Chapter 17

BLACK STUDIES AS ACADEMIC DISCIPLINE

AND POLITICAL STRUGGLE

Eugene D. Genovese

W ITHIN THE last quarter century, academia has gone through a series of struggles, usually painful, often bitter, sometimes violent, over racial segregation, exclusion, and discrimination. Until well after the Second World War the record of our universities, professional associations, and scholarly journals constituted a racist outrage, the extent of which has not yet been properly assessed. It should be enough to recall that even the great W.E.B. Du Bois could not teach at a "white" university despite his Harvard degrees and outstanding academic record; that his work and that of numerous other black scholars now recognized as of high quality went unnoticed or was denigrated; that the professional associations went to great lengths to exclude blacks from participation and promoted flagrant racist propaganda under the guise of science; that black authors and work in Black Studies were unwelcome in the leading professional journals. In short, the professions disgraced themselves, perhaps none worse than the historical profession.

Much has changed for the better, but some of the deepest problems remain not merely unresolved but undiscussed. Here I wish to focus on a problem that arose during the 1960s and 1970s and remains with us: Black Studies as an intellectual discipline and the programs instituted to promote it. Black Studies programs may not rank as the most important racially charged problem on our campuses, but it may well be the most revealing. For unless the stagnation and ghettoization of Black Studies programs are arrested, we shall, however inadvertently, condemn our universities and professions to many years of shame-faced complicity in an increasingly ominous resurgence of white racism and black despair.

In focusing on Black Studies programs I intend a criticism of one feature of Arthur Schlesinger's analysis in *The Disuniting of America*, in which he staunchly defends the principle of an American nation, however much ethnically varied and nuanced, and vigorously combats the ominous attempt to deny the very existence of an American nationality. I heartily agree with its principal thesis, and much admire the historical and political argumentation arrayed in its support. But I take issue with its implicit assimilation of the black experience to that of other ethnic groups and minorities.

The black experience in the United States has been unique, not in the trivial sense in which all historical experience may be judged unique, but in the special sense that it has no analogue in the Caribbean, Brazil, South Africa, or anywhere else. A caveat: I shall argue that "black nationalism" is a historically legitimate expression of that unique experience, but I shall invoke that problematic term only because it is widely accepted as a kind of shorthand for a complex reality that cannot accurately be labeled. If the argument of this paper is sound, the term is a misnomer. It nonetheless remains unavoidable because our grossly inadequate political language propels us toward analogies and reference points that generate much more confusion than illumination.

Not until recently were white students in any numbers made aware of the grim realities of slavery, of the achievement of an Afro-American culture forged under conditions of extreme adversity, and of the richness of an African heritage previously and ignorantly dismissed as barbarous and without lasting value. Not until recently could black students in any numbers study their own heritage in a positive atmosphere outside the black colleges.

These hard-won gains are once more at risk. Despite the vast changes of the last quarter century, the typical white student cannot avoid imbibing heavy doses of racism. America's history, culture, traditions, socioeconomic realities—just about everything—conspires to that effect. If the universities do not accept a social responsibility to educate our young to reject racism, what social responsibility would they accept? Simultaneously, if black students are to be welcomed on predominantly white campuses, they must be offered a stable environment in which they are not patronized as perpetual victims whose every weakness is someone else's fault and may be excused as the result of vast if vague objective forces. That environment must include, among other things, academically competent black professors and a curriculum that takes account of their heritage.

Black Studies programs are today being undermined by self-proclaimed supporters, white even more readily than black. Notwithstanding the honorable record of some campuses, most Black Studies programs have been condemned to ghettoization. Three reasons or, better, excuses are advanced for treating Black Studies programs as an intellectually worthless political plaything or for absorbing them into jerry-built programs in "Ethnic Studies," "Urban Studies," or something else.

First, we hear complaints about a decline in student interest. One must suppose that if our students decide not to enroll in mathematics or physics, to say nothing of art history or classics, those subjects should be abolished or reduced to a skeleton existence. Educators generally recognize that certain subjects are a necessary part of the curriculum and must be allowed to remain viable despite the vicissitudes of enrollments. The argument from enrollments reduces to a polite way of saying that the subject matter of Black Studies programs need not be taken seriously.

Except for those who wish to become teachers, professional scholars, and perhaps ministers, black students sensibly prefer to major in law, medicine, the sciences, business administration, engineering, or some other subject. Many readily cite potential income, but even the most militant and politically committed will acknowledge that their communities need doctors, lawyers, and businessmen. In 1968 a gifted black student at Yale, an English major with a special interest in Shakespeare, explained: "We have a big job to do in our communities to educate black people, and whites too, about our heritage and problems. Even if it only comes to participation in a local PTA, black professionals, businessmen, and workers have to know black history and the specifics of the black condition in America. We have to be able to respond to the needs of the people in our communities and be able to convince whites to respond."

Second, it is widely assumed if less widely expressed that Black Studies is just not a proper academic subject—not an intellectual discipline with a manageable subject matter and discrete methods. This argument was leveled at many other programs now accepted as legitimate, for almost every interdisciplinary program, most notably American Studies, had to face the same charge when first launched. In its most benign aspect, it represents merely the institutional—not necessarily the ideological—conservatism of those who constantly struggle to keep maximum resources and prestige attached to their particular departments. Yet the best of the older interdisciplinary programs have demonstrated the advantages of combining the methods of discrete disciplines. The strength of American Studies programs, for example, has always lain in their combination of traditional methods of historical inquiry, sometimes fortified by mathematics and economic theory, with the methods of literary criticism and art history as well as, increasingly, folklore, archeology, and other branches of the humanities and social sciences.

The charge against Black Studies, therefore, concerns the intellectual content. Is there a legitimate subject with appropriate data? This question immediately reveals itself as ideological projection—a charge that Black Studies is merely a political enterprise designed to develop and disseminate Afrocentric and black-nationalist ideology and propaganda. The argument that Black Studies is not a proper subject reveals a breathtaking ignorance of an enormous body of excellent scholarship. A long list of our country's most respected scholars, to say nothing of outstanding scholars in Africa, the Caribbean, Latin America, Israel, and Europe, have created, by all reasonable criteria, a distinct subject. Even the sourest of critics do not deny the high level of much of the work on the black experience. Let that much be duly registered.

The argument has nonetheless become more subtle. It denies the validity of anything that might be called the black experience. More precisely, it seeks to assimilate that experience to the experiences of European, Asian, and Latin American immigrants and thereby to deny its claims to being unique.

Hence, the argument concedes only that the activities of black people should command attention in such traditional disciplines as history, economics, sociology, and literature or should be included in Urban Studies or Ethnic Studies programs. In this view, the demand to study the black experience only makes sense on allegedly discredited black-nationalist assumptions and is therefore merely a political stratagem. It never seems to occur to those who make this argument that their own position only makes sense on integrationist assumptions and is therefore not one whit less ideological and open to the charge of being a political stratagem.

Academia normally defines as political that which lies beyond its liberal consensus, which is generally if not always accurately perceived as "liberal." And academia defines as objective and scientific that which expresses its own prejudices and viewpoint. At least rhetorically, integrationism is "in." Indeed, in discussions of Black Studies, integrationism is "in" even for those who show little enthusiasm for it in their own communities. Black nationalism is "out"— and that is that, with "that" defined as objective, scientific truth.

To speak of a black experience implies that the African diaspora offers a body of subject matter worthy of discrete study. It does not imply any particular concept of Negritude or Panafrican or the assertion that black peoples everywhere in the world have more in common with each other than they have with the whites of their particular countries. Such ideological constructs should not be rejected out of hand, for they do lend themselves to respectable intellectual defense. But within the universities they ought to be seen as hypotheses to be investigated along with alternate hypotheses and subjected to rigorous empirical investigation in an atmosphere of mutually respectful intellectual discourse. Any serious Black Studies program ought to be viewed as a terrain of ideological as well as scientific contention. But then the same might be said of the humanities and social sciences in general.

Consider for example the vigorous and salutary storm over *Time on the Cross* by Robert W. Fogel and Stanley L. Engerman. The debates over econometric methods and scientific calculations of economic growth and labor productivity accompanied harsher debates over their bold attempts to analyze black culture in slavery. Basically, they argued that the slaves absorbed bourgeois values, especially a bourgeois work ethic. Their opponents challenged these theses and insisted that a growing body of work on black work habits, religion, family life, and folklore pointed in an opposite direction—that a distinctly black culture had arisen from the slave quarters to resist not only slavery but the attempt to impose white culture and values.

Fogel and Engerman, whatever else they had in mind, knew that they were writing an integrationist tract, and, indeed, they said as much in response to criticism. Yet most of their critics have maintained an embarrassed silence over the implications of their counterargument, which emphatically provided aid and comfort to those who build on the premises of black nationalism. These questions cannot be fudged without a plunge into rank intellectual dishonesty and political irresponsibility. But there is virtually no place in the traditional curriculum and departmental structure for a full-scale airing of such urgent problems. They can only be taken up in a program that simultaneously studies black history, religion, folklore, and family life together with the more familiar problems of political economy, anthropology, political theory, and social psychology.

To put it another way, Black Studies has emerged as quintessentially interdisciplinary. And it is wonderfully funny to notice how, at one and the same time, so many educators are pleading for increased interdisciplinary studies while frowning upon a body of subject matter that has proven especially amenable to the combination of methods and data across a wide spectrum of discrete disciplines. It may be doubted that any other subject has so successfully lent itself to the highest quality of work in such "hard" disciplines as econometrics and such "soft" disciplines as folklore.

Black Studies has emerged on the cutting edge of the long sought integration of the humanities and social sciences. For a quarter century it has flourished on the frontier of creative scholarship, as exemplified by Fogel's Nobel Prize in 1993, to say nothing of no few Pulitzer, Bancroft, and other prizes. Specifically, no longer does the historical profession satisfy itself with the study of elites and politics, narrowly defined. A broad consensus has proclaimed the need to study "popular" as well as "high" culture and the relation between the two. But nowhere, not even in the burgeoning studies of working-class and women's history, have the achievement in Black Studies been matched.

The study of religion may serve as an illustration. Building on the pioneering work of W.E.B. Du Bois, Carter Woodson, Melville Herskovits, Roger Bastide, and others, black and white scholars in the United States, Latin America, Africa, and Europe have been unraveling the religious experiences of slaves throughout the Americas. Among other accomplishments, they have demonstrated the links between traditional African religions and Afro-American variants of Christianity and have been exploring the relation of religious values and movements to economic performance, resistance and accommodation to slavery, family life, and other subjects. In so doing, they have made methodological advances in the history and sociology of religion. What knowledgeable scholar would today deny these achievements?

Comparative history offers another example. American historians have finally recognized that the history of their country cannot be understood in isolation; that its economic development, political institutions, constitutional history, class structure, and national culture must be studied in relation to those of other nations and peoples; that in no other way can specific theses, broad interpretations, or claims to uniqueness be tested. Again, no subject has taken longer strides in the application of the comparative method than Black Studies has.

American history has itself been enormously enriched by the creative work in Black Studies. Yet somehow we are expected to believe that this work deserves prizes when done outside the structure of Black Studies programs but poses a threat to the Republic when done inside. Indeed, we face the absurd situation in which as Black Studies takes great strides forward, Black Studies programs are increasingly scorned.

The problem is political, the facade academic. The problem concerns professional and institutional politics, which largely reduce to struggles for turf, but, more ominously, national politics. To be blunt: more than a few universities either designed their Black Studies programs to fail or caved into political pressures of a kind everyone knew could only lead to failure. To meet political demands, administrations and faculties allowed hastily constructed Black Studies programs to appoint many professors who could command little respect on campus, and then they crippled the programs on grounds that they did not measure up to standards that were not applied in the first place. Some universities have established quality programs, and there is no reason other than political maneuvering that others cannot follow suit even at this late date. But to do so would require that universities educate their faculties on the intrinsic intellectual value of Black Studies.

It may be objected that blacks brought the worst on themselves. It was, after all, they who called for separation in autonomous all-black departments, often with separate recreational as well as professional facilities. And in truth, much might be said about the scenarios that in the worst cases have resulted in cadre-training schools for those committed to the irrationalities of "Afrocentrists," to say nothing of quasi-Hitlerian demagogues. It was apparent in 1968, when the political agitation for Black Studies programs burst upon us, that our leading universities were caving in to preposterous demands in order to ride out the storm. Whether deliberately or no, they effected a ghettoization that rendered the programs worthless or worse. In precious few cases, if indeed any, was a good-faith effort made to separate the reasonable and just demands of black students from the irrational and self-defeating.

The rage over Afrocentrism is merely the latest version of this decades-old story. No time need be wasted on blather that aims to denigrate the great civilization of the West while it presents a child's version of Africa as well as Asia and precolonial Latin America. But once again the unwillingness of universities to promote full, open, honest debate has had ironical results. For not only are integrationists, black and white, being silenced. It is by no means clear that Afrocentrism, as normally preached, contributes to a serious black-nationalist interpretation of the black experience in the United States. Arguably, it encourages a black racism that would assimilate the black experience in the United States to a transnational racial myth and thereby render incoherent all attempts to construct a rational black-nationalist perspective on American history.

How far separate facilities for black faculty and students may legitimately and wisely be extended in state universities and predominantly white private universities is another question. Let us be frank: Without a strong dose of separatism, even the best Black Studies programs would have been swallowed whole by entrenched white faculty members, who would certainly have imposed an integrationist ideology on them in the guise of promoting non-ideological and value-free social science. To correct centuries of injustice on campuses that were dominated by ideologically biased, if sometimes well-meaning whites, a new generation of black intellectuals had to take possession of their heritage and of the training of black youth. Black Studies could never have advanced without the emergence of fresh black voices, as well as the willingness of whites to hear any black voices at all. That intellectual project was necessarily political, and the disorder, mistakes, and tactical extremism that went into the making proved a necessary if disquieting price to pay for the results.

The implications for university structure and governance await sober discussion. But when we have worked through the hesitations, excuses, and confusion and have made due allowances for honest doubts, we come to the heart of the matter: the unwillingness of the white academy even to consider the possibility that black nationalism represents an authentic tendency within black America, rather than a pathological response to oppression. To the best of my knowledge, no university that has set up a Black Studies program or that has refused to do so has even openly and frankly debated the issue. And now some universities have retreated before the bluffs mounted by a handful of black racists who spout virtually national-socialist doctrine thinly disguised as Afrocentrism. Accordingly, the initial refusal to treat Black Studies with respect is turning into a self-fulfilling prophecy and a marvelous excuse to pander to campus bullies while ignoring the responsibility to create academically viable programs with high intellectual standards.

The question remains: Why do the powers-that-be refuse to do their simple duty—refuse, that is, to carry through a thorough depoliticization of Black Studies programs that would provide a forum for respectful debate between integrationist, black-nationalist, and other ideologies, demanding only that all hypotheses and theses be subject, so far as possible, to proven methods of empirical investigation? Why, that is, do not our universities strengthen the academic performance of existing programs by adequate financing and an insistence upon professional standards as high as are demanded for any other subject? The answer, I fear, lies in the ultimate scandal in a generally scandalous story. Black Studies programs will remain sources of black-nationalist sensibility and ideological formation because the content of Black Studies as an intellectual discipline is increasingly revealing itself as containing a strong black-nationalist component.

It does so not only or primarily in response to the political strong-arm tactics and brutal psychological warfare that are in evidence and must be combatted, but also in response to the findings of the most respected, painstaking, and disinterested scholarly work. For the hidden truth of the matter, which the white academy pretends not to notice, is that such recent works as the much-praised studies of slavery overwhelmingly support a generally black-nationalist interpretation of the black experience in the United States. Consider such important general books on the masterly work on black history by John Hope Franklin, such general studies of slavery as those of John Blassingame, Leslie Owens, George Rawick, and Sterling Stuckey, and add some of the more widely praised books on specific aspects of the black experience in slavery—Lawrence Levine and Charles Joyner on black culture, Amiri Baraka on music, Douglas Dillard on language, Herbert Gutman on the family, Vincent Harding on political struggles, Leon Litwack on the onset of emancipation, Albert Raboteau on religion. When taken together, these books and no few others in essence reveal an overwhelming consensus on the emergence of a distinct black culture in slavery. Some of the authors are black, others white. Some sympathize with the integrationists, others with the black nationalists. Yet all, in one way or the other, have documented the emergence of a black community that lived in intimate contact with whites, contributed to a general southern and American culture, absorbed much from whites and Indians too, and, withal, forged a black culture significantly distinct, significantly autonomous, significantly African-influenced, and nonetheless specifically American.

The black-nationalist interpretation of the black experience is by no means "proven," much less sanctified, by this scholarship. No such work in itself could prove the general superiority of black-nationalist over integrationist interpretation. What it does do is to bury the "pathology" interpretation of black nationalism and establish beyond reasonable doubt the claims of the black-nationalist interpretation to a fair hearing. At issue here is historical authenticity, not political correctness. Nationalism is a political process, not an intellectual abstraction. Blacks could take full account of the duality of their national development and its black-nationalist component and yet reject separatism in favor of integrationist politics. Or vice versa: they could take full account of their "Americanness" and strongly prefer integration and yet decide that only some form of separatist politics is necessary to protect the interests of the great majority of their people. All such questions they can and will decide for themselves, and whites would do well to withhold gratuitous advice.

Black Studies programs are no place to settle such political matters, any more than, say American Studies programs are the place to settle disputes between liberals and conservatives. Rather, they are the place to do the scholarship and conduct the debates that can lay the foundation for rational political decisions made in an appropriate arena. Academic freedom, not political correctness in the service of one ideology or another, must become the order of the day in Black Studies programs as in all other programs. And note the irony: the cowardly administrations that have in many places permitted black nationalists or Afrocentrists or other ideologues to harangue students and hire faculty according to political criteria have thereby expressed their utter contempt for the legitimate claims to a measure of autonomy for black Americans. For what else are they doing except using the power of white-dominated institutions to determine the outcome of political struggles in the black community?

Recognition of the legitimacy of black claims to a measure of autonomy in the larger society can be served within the universities only in one way: by a firm commitment to the highest academic standards in an atmosphere of maximum academic freedom. But to achieve that goal the universities would have to adhere to their own endlessly professed principles—the one thing they once again seem incapable of doing.

PART SIX

INTELLECTUAL HEROES

Chapter 18

WILLIAM JAMES AND THE STRENUOUS RESPONSIBILITY

OF THE LIBERAL INTELLECTUAL

GEORGE COTKIN

F OR THE LAST half century, John Dewey has been heralded as the crucial participant in the conversation of American liberalism and pragmatism. As Henry Steele Commager remarked famously at mid-century, "It
is scarcely an exaggeration to say that for a generation no major issue was
clarified until Dewey had spoken." More recently, Robert Westbrook's sweeping intellectual biography of Dewey has reemphasized Dewey's import, albeit
now as the apostle of liberalism as participatory democracy rather than as
elitist social engineering. And in philosophy, Richard Rorty's claims for Dewey
as the foundational anti-foundationalist thinker have made him come alive
once again in present debates about post-modernism, its possibilities and
promise.[1]

In the shuffle of interpretation and emphasis, William James's importance
to both liberalism and pragmatism is often ignored. To be sure, a sustained
fascination remains with James as individual and philosopher. With few exceptions, his philosophy has been viewed as peripheral to the concerns of
modern liberalism.[2] Arthur M. Schlesinger, Jr., has been one of the lonely
voices asserting James's centrality to a liberal perspective. In the essay, "The
One Against the Many," written just prior to the assassination of John F. Kennedy and in the midst of the Cold War, Schlesinger celebrated Jamesian pragmatism in the political realm. He invoked James's pluralism, openness to the
diversity of experience, and vision of a universe "marked by growth, variety,
ambiguity, mystery, and contingency." The Jamesian universe of philosophy
and politics stood in stark contrast to Communism's reliance on absolutism,
determinism, and intolerance. In his struggle to develop a "vital center," a
chastened yet exuberant liberalism, Schlesinger turned with ardor to the example of William James.[3]

Whether or not one agrees fully with Schlesinger on James, he did hit the
bull's-eye about the importance of James's general philosophical perspective to
understanding and resuscitating liberalism. While Dewey's brand of liberalism
will maintain its influence, it is possible that James's beacon of thought will

better illuminate the possibilities of a strenuous, responsible, and tolerant liberal perspective as we enter a new century. The map of modern liberalism, like that of all traditions, is conflicted. All liberals have accepted that government must offer direction to the economy, although opinions vary as to the optimal degree of planning. But the pendulum of what might be called the liberal temper or imagination has often swung back and forth between extremes of heady optimism and dour pessimism about the possibility and even desirability of large-scale social and personal reformation. While some liberals, such as Dewey, have exulted in the play of participatory democracy, the promise of education, and the logic of instrumental reason to transform society, other liberals have championed the tragic sense of life, the limitations inherent in human nature and dangers of utopian schemes of social engineering. These apparent differences have often coexisted within the liberal tradition, forming the conversation that has defined the movement.

Many of the key thinkers in the liberal tradition of the twentieth century, who helped to define the essential contours of the tragic sense of life, of the necessity of a strenuous, non-utopian engagement with domestic and foreign problems, defined themselves against Dewey and aspects of pragmatism. Often overlooked is the extent to which they worked consciously or unconsciously under the sign of William James. After all, even when Randolph Bourne pilloried Dewey for supporting the First World War and defamed pragmatism as devoid of values, he still upheld James as an exemplar.[4] Other thinkers central to the history of modern American liberalism, such as Reinhold Niebuhr, Horace Kallen, Irwin Edman, Charles Frankel, and Schlesinger, may also be seen as thinking from Jamesian premises.[5] Finally, even Richard Rorty may some day be considered as less a Deweyan than as a devoted tiller of the soil that James made fecund a century ago.

Jamesian liberalism, as well as Jamesian pragmatism, has two essential aspects. In James, certainly more than in Dewey, there is respect for tradition and the necessity of habit, and an enduring recognition of the tragic elements, of the limitations that are inherent in the nature of human existence. In the fashion of later liberals, James never allows these insights to drench the parade of possibility, but they do help to define the route that the parade will take. And James persists—at times trying to convince himself and his public—that we must allow a role for faith, for a finite God, that we must in a world of uncertainty take responsibility for the amelioration of problems, and that when faced with evil, such as the imperialism of the Spanish-American War, then we must act to oppose it. Opposition to evils does not take the form of the weak tea of high but impotent idealism, but begins with a recognition of how human nature functions and of why war cries and the will to power operate so strongly. Only by facing these realities squarely can the party of peace be triumphant over the party of war. Within all of this, James seasons the meat of his philosophy with an emphasis on tolerance, openness, and empathy. While these imperatives sometimes make his overall liberalism appear to run aground in the shallow waters of pure tolerance, James avoids disaster when he recognizes that decisions must be made and enthusiastically pursued given the realities of moral necessity and forced options. Despite all of the problems that have been associated with the intellectual in the public sphere, James never felt comfortable ceding leadership to the masses, or to reifying democracy as an absolute value. His fabled openness was nicely balanced by his recognition of the responsibilities of the intellectual, and by his calls for "*les intellectuels*" to provide moral leadership in times of trouble.

James's political liberalism was Mugwump in its outlines, but tolerant in its specifics: civil service and governmental reform, anti-imperialism, apprehension about the excesses of both business and labor, and Anglophilia. Thankfully, James did not share with his fellow Mugwumps a paranoid sense of isolation that occasionally issued forth in a pure distaste for democracy, in xenophobia, and in wails of despair about the absolute decline of standards and elite rule in America.[6]

James's politics were flavored by his early bouts with the demons of philosophical doubt and neurasthenic invalidism. The outline of James's early life problems are quite familiar: depression, uncertainty, and physical pain.[7] James, like many of his generation, faced not only vocational indecision, but also philosophical anxiety. Drawing on insights from modern science, oftentimes in the language if not the logic of Darwinism, young men and women like James shivered in the face of a world that might have no meaning—mere "cosmic weather" was how Chauncey Wright phrased it. Even if instilled with meaning, the universe then appeared to be fully determined, a naturalist purgatory rendering individual action meaningless. In an age when the older religious certitudes and responsibilities seemed to have waned or at least taken on an air of weakness, James could barely find solace in religion. Faced with a phalanx of anxieties, James retreated into the numbingly comfortable world of the neurasthenic.[8]

Escape from the "pessimism and the nightmare or suicidal view of life," as he phrased it in "Is Life Worth Living?" (1895), finally came with marriage and maturity, with the offer of a teaching position at Harvard, and with some degree of philosophical reflection.[9] James's famous resolution of the early 1870s to declare the reality of free will by first believing in it did not lift him immediately from the slough of depression. A sense of the tragic—as it had played itself out in James's own early years—would always remain just below the surface of both philosophy and politics. Well into his fifties, James still realized that "I am a victim of neurasthenia and of the sense of hollowness and unreality that goes with it."[10]

Out of this furnace James forged his philosophical and political outlook. This does not negate James's sustained and serious involvement with the implications of the Darwinian revolution in science, nor does it suggest that in his professional philosophy that James was anything but deeply engaging the questions that had been brought center stage by Kant and Hegel, as well as by British associationists. It was as a psychologist and philosopher of genius that James made his mark. But he never limited his audience or concerns solely to the *fach* of philosophical debate. He wanted his life and work to breathe the open air of intellectual life; he aspired to be a public philosopher.

In his first book, *The Principles of Psychology* (1890), James intended to make psychology into an empirical science, to move it away from metaphysical speculation down to the *terra firma* of physiology.[11] His failures in this endeavor were as notable as his successes. What makes parts of the *Psychology* particularly revealing of James's general perspective, and its continuing relevance in regard to liberalism, was his rejection of Spencerian passive adaptation to the environment. For James, human beings had developed the power of selective attention, will, and habit. Such powers did not absolve them from dealing with the realities of the environment, to be sure, but it meant, as he would later phrase it in *Pragmatism* (1907), that "in our cognitive as well as in our active life we are creative. We *add*, both to the subject and to the predicative part of reality. . . . Man *engenders* truths upon it."[12] For all the emphasis on the will associated with this perspective—one that was shared in even more Promethean and optimistic fashion in Dewey's "New Psychology"—a harder edge coexisted in James's psychology that suggested limitations and constrained possibilities.

Consider the seminal and popular chapter on "Habit" where James speaks in the tones of Victorian moralism. Alas, certain congenital habits—such as James's hesitation about making decisions—can be debilitating. The only way to escape is to form, ever so slowly and with ever so much resolution, new habits to replace old ones. In the reconstruction of the self, James suggests, a battle is consistently being waged. The process remains the same: only by force of will, by "*gratuitous exercise*" of the desired action, and the eventual transformation of the action into habit, can the individual become someone else.[13] As James wrote, "Sow an action and reap a habit; sow a habit and you reap a character; sow a character and you reap a destiny."[14]

For all of the hearty Victorian optimism that can be read into this almost Horatio Alger narration of self-refashioning, there remains a subtext of difficulty and indeed perhaps of self-delusion about the entire process. In words that remain relevant today—especially in the face of various therapeutics promising immediate reconstructions and renewals of the self, and in the buoyant optimism in Richard Rorty's work about the private individual managing to spin off new narratives that will create a new self—James emphasizes that habit is a conservative force, one that allows the individual to deal with the flux of reality, with the constant barrage of stimuli.[15] "By the age of thirty," as James knowingly wrote, "the character has set like plaster, and will never soften again."[16]

James never resolved the tension between effort of will and hardening of character. Unresolved dichotomies in James actually make him a more interesting and instructive thinker for our times; such tensions prevent him from wallowing in despair or insipidly proclaiming the absolute necessity of personal and social progress. If, in the end, James invariably alights upon the branch of a strenuous engagement with life, it is only because he wills—out of the depths of despair—to opt for the pragmatic value of such a belief.

No less than Dewey, James drank from the fountain of Darwinian science. Each held to the scientific approach of hypothesis formation, experimentation, and warranted assertibility. And each of them refused to accept that science and philosophy were engaged, or should delude themselves, about any "quest for certainty." But Dewey seemed to rest comfortably in the certainty of the scientific method as a way of resolving nearly all dilemmas. James, in contrast, while defending pragmatism and respecting science greatly, never hypostatized the scientific frame of mind. More importantly, for James, philosophical and scientific ideals still needed to be fitted to the sensibilities and sensitivities of religion and tradition.[17]

Here James's philosophy comports well with the tragic sense of life that entered into American liberalism in the 1920s.[18] Evil and tragedy were inherent in the human experience. James spent little time worrying about why evil existed. It did, and it needed to be confronted. Opposition to evil was made easier when the individual, or society, acted with the sense that heroic actions were somehow in accord with the best wishes of a finite God. This might seem like a tepid formula for heroic action, but James believed that it would help human beings to overcome a debilitating sense of the tragic. Similarly, as he elaborated in *The Varieties of Religious Experience* (1902), Jamesian moralism rejected the sentimentalism of the once-born soul who rested assured that he or she was saved and allowed to take as many "moral holidays" as they so desired. Such a religious perspective, all too common in our society today, while fascinating to James, seemed in the end too shallow, unable to withstand adversity and to open one up to the realities of other individuals.

Rather than the once-born religious perspective, James identified with the "twice-born sick soul." Such an individual—and here James wrote autobiographically—had touched the depths of despair, had faced squarely the reality of tragedy. Out of this moral confrontation, a newborn soul emerged, capable of accepting that "the world is all the richer for having a devil in it, *so long as we keep our foot upon his neck.*"[19] More importantly, for James's politics of liberalism, this strenuous individual gained a sense of perspective, an openness to the problems and struggles of others that allowed him or her to attempt to understand, rather than to condemn, other perspectives. This did not mean for James that all religious or moral perspectives were equally useful. He made his preferences apparent for the twice born over the once born soul. He also realized that religious certitude could be a problem.

When hardened into the certitude that one had achieved all the answers, the road to inquiry, in the personal, social, and political realm, became dangerously closed.[20]

When James published *Pragmatism* he was attacked for jettisoning fixed notions of truth and for negating the possibility of achieving truths in both a future and a collective sense. In a world where ideas were to be considered by their "cash-value" and where traditional philosophical puzzles were dismissed as not amenable to solution, Jamesian pragmatism was seen as dangerously anarchistic and wild. As Bertrand Russell remarked, pragmatism seemed to require "iron clads and Maxim guns" as the "ultimate arbiters of metaphysical truth."[21] Certainly, James helped to bring forth this distaste, thanks to his jaunty language and wonderful characterization of the "radical pragmatist" as rejecting the tight "belly band" of the rationalistic universe in favor of a "happy-go-lucky anarchistic" attitude to the universe.[22]

And yet, deeply fixed within the text of *Pragmatism* is a sense of high seriousness that respects continuity and values tradition. While James refuses to speak of truth in the singular or of truth with a capital "T" and while he emphasizes the flux and openness of the universe, he does not leave the individual staring into the abyss. In the often neglected passages of the chapter "What Pragmatism Means," James's pragmatism does more than resolve the arid metaphysical disputes; he tries to move the conversation of philosophy "away from abstraction and insufficiency, from verbal solutions, from bad *a priori* reasons, from fixed principles, closed systems, and pretended absolutes and origins."[23] James concludes that it is a necessary part of human nature to value tradition and common sense. Without the solid mass of past ideas, concepts proven in the marketplace of ideas and action, the individual and society would waste too much time reinventing the wheel. Truth, in a world of novelty and change, was defined by James by how well new ideas assimilated with previous truths. Learning is a process of combining the old with the new: "New truth is always a go-between, a smoother-over of transitions. It marries old opinion to new fact so as ever to show a minimum of jolt, a maximum of continuity."[24] To sober up those who might take the Jamesian critique of foundationalism down into the dark alleys of solipsism or irrationality, James further warned: "Woe to him whose beliefs play fast and loose with the order which realities follow in his experience: they will lead him nowhere or else make false connections."[25]

If James is only read as a philosopher of limitations and respect for the past, his import for a chastened liberalism would be apparent but hardly compelling. Joined to this perspective is a willed belief to openness, tolerance, and pluralism. The origins of this emphasis were inscribed out of his own personal history, out of his identification with the expansiveness that he read into the twice-born saints and with his own metaphysical views of a universe marked by chance, novelty, and above all else by a variety of perspectives.

James was not a moral philosopher, and he did not attempt with the comprehensiveness of a Henry Sedgwick or the earnestness of a John Dewey to develop a systematic ethical or moral system.[26] In his only attempt to develop a moral philosophy explicitly, "The Moral Philosopher and the Moral Life" (1891), James recognized that in a world populated by more than one consciousness, by more than one person's desires, there was certain to be a "pinch" between desire and possibility. James could imagine a dystopia where reconciliation was possible, but it would cost those desires that made for the zest and excitement in life. Nor did he hold out any hope that the elite held the answers: "Better chaos forever than an order based on any closet-philosopher's rule," concluded James.[27]

The context for the widening emphasis on tolerance, openness, and pluralism is to be found in the heady decade of the 1890s, as labor conflict, social dislocation, and incipient imperialist adventures impinged heavily on James's consciousness. He began to worry about how one might strenuously engage the world without becoming intolerant of others. The need for a strenuous engagement on the side of good versus evil grew out of James's own history of indecisiveness; he recognized that many from his own class suffered from a type of Hamletism, that prevented them from employing their talents within the hurly-burly world of everyday experience, political and otherwise. Jamesian energy, heroism, and commitment were designed to not only remind his compatriots of their social and intellectual responsibility to fight for decent government, but to do so with a sense that such battles were heroic. He managed, in a speech paying homage to the courage of Colonel Robert Gould Shaw and the Negro soldiers who perished in the attack on Fort Wagner during the Civil War, to suggest that intellectuals in 1897 exhibit a renewed form of "civic courage," a fighting kind of liberalism or mugwumpery, lest the republic fall to new insidious forces led by "rabid partisans or empty quacks."[28]

In essay after essay in the 1890s James begged those of his class to make life worth living by a strenuous reformism and commitment to fighting evil. Perhaps his most apt and problematic student was Theodore Roosevelt. Roosevelt, no less than James, was concerned with energizing the collective will and potentialities of the elite to confront the problems of modern society, to steer a middle ground between what Roosevelt viewed as the dangers of revolution and the inertia of standpatism. James and Roosevelt parted company most instructively in their different relations to the question of America as an imperial power. James found Roosevelt's position to be philosophically fraudulent, disrespectful of American traditions of fair play, and dangerously celebratory of abstractionism and violence. He berated Roosevelt as a Hegelian (the worst epithet in James's philosophical lexicon), because he preached "abstract war worship" predicated on "aesthetic abstractness." In sum, Roosevelt had succumbed to the "big, hollow, resounding, corrupting, sophisticating torrent of mere brutal momentum and irrationality."[29]

This presented James with a problem that hit hard in a deeply personal and professional manner. The heart of James's developing pragmatism, as expressed in "The Will to Believe" (1897) and in "Philosophical Conceptions and Practical Results" (1898), had been his appeal for the reinvigoration of the American ruling class, for renewed displays of strenuosity and energy. Roosevelt employed the vocabulary and excitement of James, but directed them to aims quite at variance with the values that James held dear. James wanted a strenuous, fighting liberalism capable of defeating the enthusiasms of imperial conquest or cheap politics.

James proceeded along two fronts in developing his strenuous liberalism. First, he valorized the themes of tolerance and openness. In his own favorite essay, "On a Certain Blindness in Human Beings" (c. 1898), James evoked the inner realities of each and every individual. He naively extolled the "primitive" virtues of the working class. In a more productive manner, James preached an ethics of openness to the variety of the human condition. He achieved this most effectively in the form of a parable about a trip that he had made through the magnificent mountains of North Carolina. In the midst of astonishing beauty, James encountered a squatter's shack—"a mere ugly picture on the retina"—a pitiful monument to man's disrespect for nature. As James reflected on his first impression, he recognized that another perspective existed. For the squatter, the clearing in the woods represented "a symbol redolent with moral memories and sang a very paean of duty, struggle, and success." James failed to weigh the relative rights (an especially important issue in today's landscape of environmental concerns) of the individual versus nature; that was not the point of the parable. Instead James wanted to show that no one individual, especially Teddy Roosevelt, had a lock on justice, reason, or truth.[30]

In a series of impassioned editorials to the *Boston Evening Transcript* and in his capacity as an active member of the New England Anti-Imperialist League, James attacked the Spanish-American War as violating American principles of freedom and self-determination. The war was a philosophically monstrous exercise, and another example of how the modern state controlled and manipulated the masses and public opinion with dire consequences. Within this context James penned what summed up his wariness about the iron cage of modern existence in 1899:

> I am against bigness and greatness in all their forms, and with the invisible molecular moral forces that work from individual to individual, stealing in through the crannies of the world like so many soft rootlets, or like the capillary oozing of water, and yet rending the hardest monuments of man's pride, if you give them time. The bigger the unit you deal with, the hollower, the more brutal, the more mendacious the life displayed. So I am against all big organizations as such, national ones first and foremost; against all big successes and big results; and in favor of the eternal forces of truth which always work in the individual and immediately unsuccessful way,

under-dogs always, till history comes, after they are long dead, and puts them on top.—You need take no notice of these ebullitions of spleen, which are probably quite unintelligible to anyone but myself.[31]

Unintelligible perhaps; consistent with all aspects of a modern liberalism, certainly not. But with this venting of his spleen against the forces of bigness and abstraction in the form of imperialism, James uttered truths that remain compelling. James realized, as did Kafka in his own manner, and as a later generation of chastened liberals like Reinhold Niebuhr and others later grasped, that surcease from the problems of modernity would not be found in utopian solutions or moral evasions. James placed his faith in the protection of the private realm in the face of an encroaching sphere that rationalized and oppressed with the confidence and efficiency of instrumental logic, clothed in the benign language of science and progress.

James's analysis of the dilemma of the individual in modern society, as already stated, was not politically deep; he never—as Dewey attempted in *The Public and Its Problems* (1927) and *Individualism, Old and New* (1929)—fully comprehended how the traditional American notion of individualism was, if not bereft of meaning, at least badly in need of revision given the complexities of modern society. James understood little of the economic and geopolitical forces that produced imperialism; he often regarded imperialism as a form of hysteria, of individual psychology compounded into social pathology. Whatever the interpretive *aporia* in James's response to the problem of imperialism, his essay "The Moral Equivalent of War" remains a model of both the style and the substance of James's strenuous liberalism.

"The Moral Equivalent," first presented as a talk in 1906 and later revised and published in 1910, begins with James identifying more with the war party than with anti-imperialists. The blood of his anti-imperialist audience must have curdled when James ejaculated that "War is the *strong* life; it is life *in extremis*. . . . History is a bath of blood."[32] The warriors and their allies were heartier souls, responding to deeply ingrained instincts. They were also, in James's view, capable of great acts of individual and collective heroism. In contrast, anti-imperialists appeared as desiccated and abstract. This is a strange argument coming from an anti-imperialist. But James wanted to retain the heroism and hardihood of the war party without succumbing to what he considered the *tedium vitae* of the elite classes. His solution, already suggested back in 1890 in *The Principles of Psychology*, was to have the cake of strenuosity without the deadly frosting of imperialist bloodshed, through an outlet that allowed for conscious sublimation of the war instincts into better modes of expression.

The lust for blood could not be wished away in the name of religious sentiment or moral abnegation. The propensity for battle must be acknowledged and respected before it could be redirected through a "moral equivalent."

James wanted to retain the instinctual desires for hardihood and toil, for sacrifice and rigor, without having to resort to violence. Thus he suggested that the government might conscript young men—note the gendered differences between James and his friend Jane Addams—to work together with civic courage as an "army enlisted against *nature*."[33] James called for the pampered young men of the middle and upper class to become attuned (literally and figuratively) to the hard labor of working-class life so that they would have "their childishness knocked out of them, and come back into society with healthier sympathies and soberer ideas."[34]

James believed that "the martial type of character can be bred without war": naive, but also insightful in a way that later generations of chastened liberals might appreciate for its stirring recognition of struggle and sacrifice. In contrast, Dewey, in a private communication, ridiculed James's "moral equivalent of war" solution for its aristocratic blindness to the strenuosity of the everyday existence of workers.[35] But James would maintain that the sympathy and empathy gained by the "aristocrats" might help them to understand better the working class and also vitiate some of their own abstract and concrete zealotry for war. The upper classes, the ruling elite, were James's intended audience. Central to James's prescription are the ethical imperatives that form the core of his strenuous liberalism—recognition that habits such as blood lust may be deeply integrated into the human stock and thus not easily wished away by kindly sentiments; that the individual and the unit must work together to wrestle beneficial meaning out of existence; in all of these endeavors (as he stressed in his writings on religion) even when our chances of success were limited, the struggle in and of itself against evil and for higher ideals was valid and necessary. To shirk from responsibility was unacceptable.

How to be "responsible" has been one of the most perplexing issues for intellectuals in this century.[36] Elitism has easily attached itself to calls for responsibility, as intellectuals have appointed themselves the natural guardians of truth and wisdom. With a development of a technical intelligentsia, the doyens of planning and administration have sometimes tended to push to the side as antiquated certain ideals of democratic participation. While James never succumbed to the elitism of technocratic idealism, he did in "The Social Value of the College-Bred" (1907) attempt to forge a critical role for the intellectual in a democracy—the responsibility to lead, as well as to educate, the masses in an expansive and positive fashion.

At first glance, "The Social Value of the College-Bred" seems very un-Jamesian, somehow outside the pluralistic moral compass of pragmatism, and certainly far removed from the progressive educational ideals that Dewey was actively developing at the time. Although James refused to condemn democracy as an abstract or utopian ideal, he admitted that democracy suffered from "[v]ulgarity enthroned and institutionalized. . . . Uncle Sam with the hog instead of the eagle for his heraldic emblem."[37] Unlike Dewey, who later argued that the cure for democracy was more democracy, James called upon university graduates to exert leadership marked by wideness of sympathy and cultivated "critical sensibilities [that] grow both more acute and less fanatical." The responsibility of "*les intellectuels*" as James had earlier claimed should be endemic within the culture. College-trained individuals must distinguish, by dint of their humanistic learning, "a general sense of what under various disguises, *superiority* has always signified and may still signify." James is still too much of the pluralist, the perspectivist to freeze superiority into a narrow, cold container. But distinctions must be made between good and bad ideas, and that, at the same time, those able to make such discriminations remain open to new additions that are valuable, while tossing aside "cheap and trashy" ideas or faddish concepts.[38]

Education in the humanities is not foolproof; it falters when young men and women enter college as either "a blind pig or vulgarian" and graduate without improved sensibilities. Thankfully, many do learn the power of good judgment, secure standards, and widen their understanding. These students gain the invaluable ability "*to know a good man when you see him.* This is as true of women's as of men's colleges," and James does not intend this ideal to be seen as either "a joke" or as "a one-sided abstraction." Once the humanistically trained male or female graduates, he or she must assume responsibility as an intellectual elite, and seriously attempt to become a public intellectual, by raising the level of public discourse, helping to "show the way" by the force of their reason and presence. In some cases, "individuals of genius show the way, and set the patterns, which common people then adopt and follow" (109). In the end, whether the leader is the superior genius or the intelligent humanist, the value of the college-bred is exhibited in the tone that he or she brings to public discourse. Proper tone and manner are not mere "dislikes and disdains" but, with responsibility, "are to be the yeast-cake for democracy's dough." Salvation, or at least survival, is to be exemplified by the college graduate's "spreading power" of wisdom, expressed in a tone at once "higher, healthier," and more robust than that normally found in the public arena.[39]

Of course, in the wake of Foucauldian-inspired critiques against the very notion of the "universal intellectual" and the now common dismissal of the possibility of any consensus about what should constitute the canon of great books, liberal education, or even wisdom, James's pleading might seem anachronistic. But when "The Social Value of the College-Bred" is read within the context of James's overall corpus, his importance for helping to set the agenda of liberalism in the United States takes on a significance that transcends the context of his time and the lack of depth of some of his political thinking.

James is telling us in all of his work to remember that while limitation and tragedy are never distant from our lives, we must strenuously engage ourselves openly and tolerantly with life. Openness and tolerance are not ends in and of themselves, although it certainly doesn't hurt to always attempt to approach them as such. There are no absolutes. All decisions and policies require discriminations, based on sometimes inadequate evidence, sometimes with a nod toward the power of tradition but decided always in the shadow of the chastening ground of human limitation. Only with these intellectual and moral imperatives in mind—for James and his spiritual and intellectual descendants such as Niebuhr, Lionel Trilling, and Arthur Schlesinger, Jr.—can a viable liberalism be created, capable of withstanding the terrors of both the arrogant left and the fanatical right. As Schlesinger recognized, in Jamesian terms, in the concluding words of *The Vital Center* (1949):

> The commitment [against the forces of the right and left] is complex and rigorous. When has it not been so? If democracy cannot produce the large resolute breed of men capable of the climactic effort it will founder. Out of the effort, out of the struggle alone, can come the high courage and faith which will preserve freedom.[40]

NOTES

1. Henry Steele Commager, *The American Mind* (New Haven: Yale University Press, 1950), 100; Robert Westbrook, *John Dewey and American Democracy* (Ithaca: Cornell University Press, 1991); Richard Rorty, "Overcoming the Tradition: Heidegger and Dewey," in *Consequences of Pragmatism* (Minneapolis: University of Minnesota Press, 1982), 37–59.

2. I attempt to connect James's philosophy with the cultural and political problems of his era, without making the claim that he is a sophisticated political thinker, in my *William James, Public Philosopher* (Baltimore: Johns Hopkins University Press, 1990). Also, Deborah Coon, "'One Moment in the World's Salvation': Anarchism and the Radicalization of Williams James," *Journal of American History* 83 (June, 1996), 70–99. Less appreciative of James's political acumen are Bruce Kuklick, *The Rise of American Philosophy: Cambridge, Massachusetts, 1860–1930* (New Haven: Yale University Press, 1977), 309–14; and Ross Posnock, *The Trial of Curiosity: Henry James, William James, and the Challenge of Modernity* (New York: Oxford University Press, 1991).

3. Arthur M. Schlesinger, Jr., "The One Against the Many," in *Paths of American Thought*, ed. Arthur M. Schlesinger, Jr., and Morton White (Boston: Houghton Mifflin, 1963), 535. Two decades later Schlesinger continued to invoke James, chiding American intellectual historians for not being "sufficiently acquainted" with the thought and relevance of James. See Schlesinger, "Intellectual History: A Time for Despair?" *Journal of American History* 66 (March, 1980), 891.

4. Randolph Bourne, "Twilight of Idols" (1917), in Bourne, *War and the Intellectuals*, ed. Carl Resek (New York: Harper Torchbooks, 1964), 53–55, 64. Excellent, albeit different, interpretations of the Bourne and Dewey controversy will be found in Westbrook, *John Dewey*, 195–212, and Casey Nelson Blake, *Beloved Community: The Cultural Criticism of Randolph Bourne, Van Wyck Brooks, Waldo Frank, & Lewis Mumford* (Chapel Hill: University of North Carolina Press, 1990), 157–180.

5. George Cotkin, "Middle-Ground Pragmatists: The Popularization of Philosophy in American Culture," *The Journal of the History of Ideas* 55 (April, 1994), 283–302.

6. On James's politics, see Cotkin, *William James*, 127–30.

7. On James's depression and its implications, see Howard M. Feinstein, *Becoming William James* (Ithaca: Cornell University Press, 1984); Ralph Barton Perry, *The Thought and Character of William James* (Boston: Little, Brown, 1935); R.W.B. Lewis, *The Jameses* (New York: Farrar, Strauss and Giroux, 1991); Cotkin, *William James*, 19–72.

8. On the context for James and his generation, see Jackson Lears, *No Place of Grace* (New York: Pantheon Books, 1981); James Turner, *Without God, Without Creed: The Origins of Unbelief in America* (Baltimore: Johns Hopkins University Press, 1985); George Cotkin, *Reluctant Modernism: American Thought and Culture, 1880–1900* (New York: Twayne, 1992).

9. William James, "Is Life Worth Living?" in *The Will to Believe* (Cambridge: Harvard University Press, 1979), 39–40.

10. William James to G. W. Howison, 17 July 1895, in *The Letter of William James*, ed. Henry James (Boston: Atlantic Monthly Press, 1920), 2:23.

11. On this endeavor, see the impressive study by Gerald E. Myers, *William James: His Life and Thought* (New Haven: Yale University Press, 1986). Also, Daniel W. Bjork, *William James, The Center of His Vision* (New York: Columbia University Press, 1988).

12. William James, *Pragmatism* (Cambridge: Harvard University Press, 1975), 123.

13. William James, *The Principles of Psychology* (Cambridge: Harvard University Press, 1981), 122–31.

14. Quoted in Perry, *Thought and Character*, 2:90.

15. On this theme, see Philip Rieff, *The Triumph of the Therapeutic* (New York: Harper Torchbook, 1968). Richard Rorty presents his ideal of individual refashioning through the creation of narratives in *Contingency, Irony and Solidarity* (Cambridge: Cambridge University Press, 1989), 23–43.

16. James, *Principles*, 1:126.

17. On James's relationship to scientific currents, see David A. Hollinger, "William James and the Culture of Inquiry" and "The Problem of Pragmatism in American History," both in Hollinger, *In the American Province* (Bloomington: Indiana University Press, 1985), 3–43.

18. Richard Wightman Fox, "Tragedy, Responsibility, and the American Intellectual, 1925–1950," in *Lewis Mumford: Public Intellectual*, Thomas P. and Agatha C. Hughes (New York: Oxford University Press, 1990), 323–37.

19. William James, *The Varieties of Religious Experience* (Cambridge: Harvard University Press, 1985), 48.

20. James, *Varieties*, note 2, 385.

21. Quoted in Cotkin, *William James*, 158.

22. James, *Pragmatism*, 124.

23. Ibid., 31.

24. Ibid., 35.

25. Ibid., 99, 101.

26. For an impressive reading of ethical philosophy and politics in this era, see James T. Kloppenberg, *Uncertain Victory: Social Democracy and Progressivism in European and American Thought, 1870–1920* (New York: Oxford University Press, 1986).

27. James, "The Moral Philosopher and the Moral Life," in *The Will to Believe*, 155.

28. James, *Essays in Religion and Morality* (Cambridge: Harvard University Press, 1982), 73.

29. On James, Roosevelt, and the problem of imperialism, see Cotkin, *William James*, 139.

30. James, "On a Certain Blindness in Human Beings," in *Talks to Teachers on Psychology* (Cambridge: Harvard University Press, 1983), 133–134. For a critique of James's understanding for others, see M. C. Otto, "On a Certain Blindness in William James," *Ethnics: International Journal of Social, Political and Legal Philosophy* 53 (April, 1943), 184–191.

31. James to Mrs. Henry Whitman, 7 June 1899, in *Letters*, 2:90.

32. James, "The Moral Equivalent of War," in *Essays in Religion and Morality*, 163.

33. For the gendered aspects of James's essay, see Jane Roland Martin, "Martial Virtues or Capital Vices? William James' Moral Equivalent of War Revisited," *Journal of Thought* 22 (Fall, 1987), 32–44; Linda Schott, "Jane Addams and Williams James on Alternatives to War," *The Journal of the History of Ideas* 54 (April, 1993), 241–54.

34. James, "The Moral Equivalent of War," 172.

35. Quoted in Myers, *William James*, n. 151, 602.

36. Criticisms are readily found. A particularly insightful account of the problems of intellectuals in relation to Communism will be found in Tony Judt, *Past Imperfect: French Intellectuals, 1944–1956* (Berkeley: University of California Press, 1992). On the shifting politics of an interesting group of American thinkers, see John P. Diggins, *Up From Communism: Conservative Odysseys in American Intellectual History* (New York: Harper and Row, 1975).

37. James, "The Social Value of the College-Bred," in James, *Essays, Comments, and Reviews* (Cambridge: Harvard University Press, 1987), 109.

38. James, "The Social Value," 108, 110.

39. Ibid.; quotations at 106–111 *passim*.

40. Schlesinger, *The Vital Center* (Boston: Houghton Mifflin, 1949), 256.

Chapter 19

HENRY STEELE COMMAGER'S ACTIVIST HISTORY

Neil Jumonville

W HEN ALLAN NEVINS died in 1971, his best friend Henry Steele Commager wrote a note to Nevins's wife. Commager reminded Mary Nevins that her husband had not only been one of the leading and most prolific historians in America, but had also led an astonishing public career. "There is no one who can take his place," Commager told her, "for his kind of scholar is pretty well a thing of the past; modern scholars are technicians who are afraid of big projects, or public enthusiasms; what is really at stake here is the attitude towards history, and modern historians have lost faith in history—as Allan never did."[1]

Part of what Commager meant is that Nevins functioned as an intellectual as well as a scholar. The distinction has been made frequently in the recent past. An intellectual is one who writes for the general educated public instead of experts, addresses issues of contemporary social or political importance as an activist, and is partisan rather than neutral. A scholar, by contrast, writes for his or her professional peers and usually in books instead of essays, avoids contemporary issues in favor of less immediately contentious archival research, and aims for objectivity or neutrality rather than partisanship.[2] The intellectual and scholarly roles are not mutually exclusive, of course, and a person might function as one in the morning and the other in the afternoon. Naturally, for professional reasons many prefer to keep the roles separate and wear only one hat at a time.

But our histories and accounts of American intellectual life seldom include consideration of historians. We are likely to hear about the political and cultural activism of journalists, lawyers, literary critics, and sociologists, but rarely historians. And historians have no one to blame but themselves—not only because they write many of the accounts and could well include those from their own discipline, but also because historians as a rule have shied away from contemporary public enthusiasms and have had less impact on political life than they could have.

More than other scholars, historians have been threatened by partisanship and the present because they have been afraid that they would be mistaken for journalists and lose their special responsibility to interpret the past. Unlike historians, sociologists and literary critics have no need to fear losing their scholarly identities by addressing matters of contemporary debate since the present is part of their professional assignment.

Still, over the course of the twentieth century there have been a handful of historians who have resisted the pressure to remain exclusively within the scholarly corral. Charles Beard, Allan Nevins, Henry Steele Commager, C. Vann Woodward, and Arthur Schlesinger, Jr., among others, have all been activist intellectuals in addition to producing prolific professional scholarship. Yet, with a few notable exceptions, their intellectual contributions have been ignored as though their scholarly output is all that is fair to assess.[3] These historians have added to the record of our intellectual life as much as sociologists like Daniel Bell or Nathan Glazer, literary critics like Alfred Kazin or Edmund Wilson, or economists like Robert Heilbroner or Robert Lekachman. The activist identities of American historians should not be ignored. Overlooking their activism will make them no better historians, but it will prevent us from adding the necessary complexity to our intellectual record.

A natural candidate for this process of reevaluation is Henry Steele Commager. Because he was born in 1902, accepted his first teaching job at the age of 24, and was active into the 1980s, his career spanned the twentieth century as that of few historians have. A self-acknowledged Jeffersonian liberal and Deweyean pragmatist, Commager wrote or edited several shelves of books, was an unusually prolific author of articles for the general press, and lectured around the country as if an itinerant. McCarthyism had no more energetic public opponent than Commager, who became known after World War II as a champion of civil liberties. Because he was so prominently identified as a liberal, many of the strengths and contradictions of liberalism in this period are especially apparent in his own example.

Happy to admit that he was a New Deal Jeffersonian liberal in his early years, Commager shared none of the socialist background or left-wing liturgy of those in his generation such as the New York intellectuals (Lionel Trilling, Daniel Bell, Irving Howe, Harold Rosenberg, Sidney Hook, and others in the orbit of *Partisan Review, Commentary,* and *Dissent*). Yet, in an intriguing political turnabout, as those formerly socialist *Partisan* writers became increasingly conservative in the decades after World War II, the "merely" liberal Commager became increasing radical and vocal in his opposition to American policy. By the 1960s an observer might have been excused for assuming that it was Commager instead of the New York intellectuals who had socialist roots.

Although he was a leader against McCarthyism and opposed the excesses of the Cold War outlook, at midcentury Commager was not an unremitting critic of American foreign policy. Yes, he thought that the United States was too militaristic and was expected to treat other countries as we would not allow them to treat us. But he also endorsed at least some of the State Department view of foreign policy. In passing remarks in the *New York Times Magazine,* he defended the U.S. alliance with the "reactionary" Chiang Kai-shek during World War II for strategic purposes, and he justified U.S. support for the right-wing Perón regime in Argentina because we were pursuing Pan American unity. Sounding like a pragmatic diplomat, he reported that "great principles of foreign policy. . . . are formulated in response to national needs—above all to the needs of collective security."[4]

Yet he became more radical in the application of his liberal beliefs over the course of the next decade, perhaps because of his disillusionment with American policies during the McCarthy era. And while he became a recognized critic of American domestic policy on such matters as civil liberties in the early 1950s, his increasingly prominent disapproval of U.S. foreign policy didn't appear until a decade later. Evidence of his mounting critical liberalism can be found in his protest in 1960 in the New York Times about Eisenhower's use of NATO bases for air surveillance of the Soviet Union, and his repeated complaints to his colleague Allan Nevins beginning in 1960 about aggressive U.S. policies regarding China, Berlin, and Cuba. Then in October 1963, a month before Kennedy was assassinated, and while the attention of others was turned elsewhere, he asked Nevins: "Are we being as stupid in Vietnam as it seems?"[5]

When Lyndon Johnson took office Commager found his Great Society plans a reason for optimism but thought his foreign policy was frightening.[6] Increasingly upset by American involvement in Vietnam, Commager launched an active campaign in 1965 to bring his opinions to government leaders and the public. In telegrams to Secretary of Defense Robert McNamara, Undersecretary of State George Ball, and Senator J. William Fulbright, chairman of the Senate Foreign Relations Committee, Commager suggested that the Vietcong attack in February 1965 on the American airfield at Pleiku was only the same kind of challenge as the Bay of Pigs operation was against Cuba. "Would we have tolerated retaliatory action from Russia or China," he asked them, "or even from Cuba?"[7]

Less than a week later, a Commager letter to the New York Times accused the United States of using double-talk, a "two-level vocabulary" like that used by the Communists or characters in George Orwell's 1984. McNamara, he charged, spoke of North Vietnamese sneak attacks of murder and terror. But were American attacks announced in advance and did they avoid death and terror? Surely, he noted, U.S. bombing created more terror to civilians than did guerrilla attacks on military installations.[8] His letter prompted some readers to reply to him personally. A senior in political science at Temple University encouraged him to continue the historic obligation of individuals in Commager's profession "to guide the public and prod the government." Similarly, a woman recommended that he keep up his actions since citizens had "a small voice" while he and his fellow professors could "beat a louder drum."[9]

Continuing his spring 1965 campaign in the Times, he reproached Secretary of State Dean Rusk for distinguishing between the U.S. invasion of Cuba and the Vietcong invasion of South Vietnam because, as Rusk said, there had been no regular elections in Cuba. There had been no regular elections in South Vietnam either, Commager noted, and it was the Diem government and the United States that opposed them. Castro's government, he told Rusk, had more popular support than South Vietnam's. Besides, he asked the secretary of state, since there had been no popular elections in Taiwan, would that justify Chinese attacks? Throughout the year he continued his protests in national newspapers.[10] Commager wasn't just being a crank or an obstructionist in 1965, responding idiosyncratically to various reports as he read them. There was a pattern in his complaints about the war: that the United States could not operate by a double standard. The United States could not act as the aggressor yet portray itself as the passive victim.

Like Theodore Parker, about whom he had written his first book in 1936, Commager was unwilling merely to issue angry denunciations from his study. Unable to resist mounting a platform, he crisscrossed the country speaking against the war at graduations, before historical societies, to interested organizations, seeming to leave only the occasional church picnic unaddressed.

Enjoying his public notoriety, he debated Deputy Assistant Secretary of Defense for International Security Affairs Alvin Friedman before an audience at his home institution, Amherst College, in December 1965.[11] With Dr. Martin Luther King, Jr., he addressed an overflow crowd of more than 3,000 people at Riverside Church near Columbia University in New York in April 1967. While outside the church on Riverside Drive about thirty-five marching protesters picketed King's remarks, Commager rose to the platform inside and spoke to the gathering that had been put together by the Clergy and Laymen Concerned About Vietnam. Our involvement in the Vietnam War, he instructed them, "is the product of an obsession with Communism—we call it a conspiracy just as the Communists used to talk about capitalist conspiracies—something that is, therefore, not nearly a rival system, but an eradicable moral evil."[12] A month later Commager was one of several principals who took part in a nationally broadcast peace teach-in that was formally called the "national day of inquiry." From Harvard, John Kenneth Galbraith, John K. Fairbank, Stanley Hoffman, and Jerome Cohen were heard. In the midwest, Hans J. Morgenthau and Cassius Clay were the speakers, and from Amherst Commager broadcast his remarks.[13]

Campaigning against the war so publicly was sure to make Commager the target of hostile fire. He became a favorite topic at the conservative *National Review* where William F. Buckley, Jr., and his colleagues wrote with disgust about Commager's public comments and actions.[14] Although he ignored most of the criticism of his war position, the disagreement on Vietnam that Commager found most painful was with his old friend Allan Nevins. Nevins was a liberal who supported Woodrow Wilson and the New Deal, organized a Columbia faculty group for Adlai Stevenson while Eisenhower was still president there, and backed John Kennedy. Yet he had always been more conservative than Commager. When Nevins attended the University of Illinois his mentor, Professor Stuart Sherman, remarked that he had the "temper to make a good Tory writer," and since then Nevins had written respectful accounts of business leaders such as John D. Rockefeller and Henry Ford and had helped promote the field of business history as a worthy pursuit.[15] "He wasn't a crusader," Commager once noted of Nevins. "He wasn't passionate about wrongdoing. He was aware of it, and when the votes were counted, he was on the right side," as in his support of Adlai Stevenson.[16] But Nevins didn't have the soul of a dissenter.

In 1965 Commager told Nevins that "your infatuation with LBJ has blinded you to most of his failings." He warned Nevins, "We are making terrible mistakes in Vietnam and elsewhere; I think Rusk weak and McNamara and Bundy dangerous; they have the Acheson get tough philosophy. I am terribly disturbed at what it may all lead to." Johnson's domestic policy, Commager admitted, was quite admirable, but his foreign policy was dangerously reminiscent of Goldwater's.[17]

Nevins was unconvinced. "Why is it," he asked Commager, "you hate Johnson as you once hated Hoover, and later hated Eisenhower?—three good men, who wrought patriotically for the republic? I see no fault in Johnson's home policy, and on the whole support his foreign moves."[18] Early in 1966, he wrote his most direct and thoughtful response to Commager's unending letters and articles against the war. Nevins compared the Vietnam engagement to the Civil War, about which he was currently writing. "I do not see eye to eye with you on Vietnam," he acknowledged. "Of course everybody is unhappy about the mess, and I heartily wish we could get an agreement on a decent peace; but what alternative do we have for our present course? Peace at any price sounds attractive now as it did to Horace Greeley and Horatio Seymour and other highminded men in 1864. But the price, and a steep one, would be paid at once by Siam and Laos and Malaysia; and a few years hence by India and Australia; and in time by ourselves." Nevins's friend Mort Lewis later recalled that "Allan would say he couldn't understand all the 'fuss' about our 'high' casualties in Vietnam. He was writing about a war in which more than 600,000 Americans had died."[19]

Even the usually conservative Samuel Eliot Morison eventually opposed the war and was no comfort to Nevins. Although Morison had been the official historian of U.S. Naval Operations during World War II, he refused to support Naval policy off the coast of Vietnam. By 1967 Morison had lost confidence in "the military-industrial complex," and he wrote to Lyndon Johnson that "I am not a peace demonstrator, signer of petitions, writer of angry letters to newspapers, but as a senior citizen who loves his country . . . I beg you freshly to ponder the situation."[20]

Unfortunately, Nevins became alienated from many of his friends during the last few years of his life because of their views on the war. He broke relations with his oldest friend, Walter Lippmann, because he thought Lippmann was too critical of Johnson on the war. "He thought that patriotism required that we win the war," Commager noted about Nevins. "He wrote the famous letter to Johnson, saying, don't listen to all these critics. Lincoln, too, had his critics." Commager was sorry to see his friend plagued by these issues in old age. "It's very sad at the end of his life that the Vietnam War should have come between himself and so many of his friends," he said of Nevins. But he "never allowed it to come between us, except perhaps in a kind of aura, when I saw him from time to time, of reluctance and aloofness, but his letters remained as ebullient as ever."[21]

Yet with Commager's increasingly critical tone in comparison to many liberals of his generation came the burden of having to live with some of the contradictions of his outlook. For example, certainly his was not the only position a Jeffersonian liberal could take about the war in Vietnam, as surely he must have known. With equal validity a Jeffersonian could support American involvement in the war—since the United States represented a liberal, market-oriented society characterized by civil liberties and free expression (Jeffersonian virtues) fighting against a totalitarian worldview that represented its greatest threat. Nor did Commager's pragmatism provide him an easy rationale against the war, since pragmatists such as the New York intellectuals argued that Communism was an absolutism that threatened pragmatic views and so it had to be opposed vigorously.[22]

Sidney Hook, for example, was a self-described Jeffersonian liberal and pragmatist who felt differently than Commager about the war.[23] The U.S. military involvement in Southeast Asia, he admitted, wasn't necessary for our own security. But once we became involved, he believed, "we incurred obligations that we could not honorably disregard, if only to make credible our reliability as an ally in a common cause elsewhere." So Hook supported the gradual withdrawal of American troops and the Vietnamization of the war that constituted the core of Nixon's program.[24]

Commager was too impatient to support a withdrawal in small increments and felt that we should simply get out since we didn't belong there. But, while morally admirable, Commager's position on Vietnam also left him open to charges that echoed from his past: that he failed to weigh the consequences of his proposals sufficiently. When in the early 1950s Commager and Hook had disagreed about McCarthyism, each claiming to be the true pragmatist, Hook had found weak Commager's suggestion that the nation should simply stop fretting about domestic Communism. As a fellow pragmatist, Hook had reminded him that "the consequences of one proposal are never decisive unless we weigh them against the consequences of other proposals including the proposal to do nothing."[25]

Similarly, critics of Commager's stand on Vietnam could ask him if he had weighed the consequences of immediate withdrawal and doing nothing for the South Vietnamese or the cause of freedom. When, in the pages of *Saturday Review* in 1965, an article of Commager's appeared next to a piece by Leo Cherne, chairman of the executive committee of Freedom House in New York, the distinction was highlighted. Cherne pointed out that an individual could make a moral and conscientious plea for a simple American withdrawal. "But there should be no illusion about the consequences," Cherne warned. "There will be a bloody purge of the non-Communist leaders and intellectuals, such as has occurred in every other Communist takeover,"[26] In the article following Cherne's in the magazine, Commager spoke of the principles and ethics that were violated by fighting in Vietnam, but he never seriously addressed Cherne's (and Hook's) problem of consequences—the consequences of doing nothing.

A similar disagreement arose between Mary McCarthy and Diana Trilling in the *New York Review of Books* in January 1968. McCarthy recommended that intellectuals not sully themselves with the details of an incremental pullout from Vietnam but instead appeal to morality and demand an immediate withdrawal. Intellectuals deal with principles, not consequences, she suggested. But Trilling asked her what would happen to those left behind? McCarthy responded that, like all those on the wrong side of a revolution, they would likely "be left to face the music; that is the tough luck of being a camp follower."

Yet is morality so easy, Trilling wondered? "If South Vietnam falls to the Communists, who stifle opposition and kill their enemies," she asked, "is this not of moral concern to intellectuals?" McCarthy replied that all of us condemn thousands to death daily by not responding to charities, but we live with it. "When Mrs. Trilling reproaches me as an intellectual for my lack of moral concern," McCarthy retorted, "she makes me think of the Polish proverb about the wolf who eats lamb while choking with sobs and the wolf who just eats lamb."[27]

Perhaps Sidney Hook and Leo Cherne were wolves who sobbed when they ate lamb, while Commager simply ate lamb. But some thought the issue more serious than that, and subscribed to Max Weber's contrast between the "ethnic of ultimate ends" and the "ethic of responsibility." Those involved in politics, Weber advised, need to be strong enough to make difficult choices in light of the consequences of their actions. It is impossible to say when a leader should follow the ethic of absolute ends and when the ethic of responsibility, Weber admitted, since the two "are not absolute contrasts but rather supplements," which only together constitute a whole person. Still, Weber found it "genuinely human" and "immensely moving" when a person evaluated the consequences of a proposal and then announced, "Here I stand; I can do no other."

Those with a weak will should not apply for political leadership, since distasteful policies must be enacted. "He who seeks the salvation of the soul, of his own and others," Weber warned, "should not seek it along the avenue of politics, for the quite different tasks of politics can only be solved by violence."[28]

Like Mary McCarthy's proposals, Commager's opposition to Vietnam stressed the moral necessities at the expense of the practical consequences of withdrawal. It was a courageous and principled posture, but it was strongly resented by those who felt that intellectuals did not have the luxury of ignoring the consequences of their proposals. Again, Commager's position on Vietnam was reminiscent of his stand on McCarthyism twenty years earlier that had earned him such disapproval from Hook, Roger Baldwin, and others.[29]

Yet Commager's was an early, principled, and courageous public commitment against American involvement in Vietnam. Because he had always been less actively anticommunist than other liberals such as the New York intellectuals, Commager was able to function as an earlier, more vigorous, and more useful critic of the Vietnam War—a war which was, after all, the result of decades of anticommunist ideology and policy produced by the intellectual community.

But, despite his early complaints about the war, perhaps even Commager's brand of liberalism contributed to America's involvement in Vietnam. In the liberal community broadly defined, in the forties and fifties, it was mainly those around the *Nation*, *PM*, and related publications who opposed the Cold War assumptions that led to Vietnam.[30] Although Commager contested strident anticommunism, was a leader in the fight against McCarthyism, and was a friend of the *Nation*, he was during these years a more enthusiastic supporter of U.S. internationalism than others in the *Nation* orbit. And while socialist New York intellectuals like Irving Howe were converted slowly to interventionism during the 1940s, Commager had been a Wilsonian since the 1920s.

It was Woodrow Wilson who Commager quoted in 1942 and 1943 about the need to win the peace as well as the war. Sounding much like Henry Luce's *Life* editorial "The American Century," Commager counseled that the United States must abandon not only political isolationism, but also "economic and social, cultural and moral isolation." If we were to adopt the leadership role in the world community for which nature had cast us we had to "prepare for it psychologically as well as politically." The United States could never again allow itself to be weak. "War came," he reported, "because we were inadequately prepared for it." Never again should the United States follow the lead of isolationists like Senator Borah who had a misguided fear of "foreign entanglements." A decade later in the *New York Times Magazine* he was still warning against isolationism, and two years later, in 1954, he was holding up the example of Winston Churchill as a fellow critic of "isolationist pressures."[31]

Perhaps we would expect Commager to have been an interventionist during World War II and so we find it unsurprising that he also maintained that position during the dark years of the Cold War in the 1950s. But what are we to make of his criticism, as late as 1964, that the Republican Party should be ashamed that it was isolationist and had abandoned its earlier internationalism of Theodore Roosevelt and Elihu Root?[32] How can we reconcile that with his complaints to Nevins and the *Times*, from 1960 onward, about American intervention in Cuba and Vietnam, and his disgust at Kennedy's enthusiasm or meddling?[33]

Indeed, how can we harmonize his criticism of isolationism with his rise, during the mid-1960s, to a position as one of the most articulate public critics of American intervention? On Monday, February 20, 1967, Commager appeared before the Senate Foreign Relations Committee to discuss foreign policy. The headline on the front page of the *New York Times* the next day reported, "Commager Declares U.S. Overextends World Role," and was followed by a lengthy article wrapped around his photo. The *Times* described him as "a dean of American historians" who, when he appeared before the Fulbright hearings, "spent most of the three hours in what often sounded like a graduate seminar."[34]

The assembled senators heard from Commager that great powers have to use their power lightly. Because nationalism effectively had countered the powerful nations, which weren't able to employ their force absolutely, the strong nations had to exercise their might sparingly. Wasn't our complaint against Britain in 1776 that they used more power than they needed? America is a nation, he told them, whose Constitution and traditions were founded on a limitation of strength. It must continue to be so.

Did the committee believe that the United States had the resources and will to be an Asian power, as our excursion in Vietnam seemed to forecast? Trained initially as a Europeanist, Commager insisted that we had none of the same responsibility for Asia that we did for Europe. The United States, he regretted, was driven by a fear of Communism, which he saw as a replay of our long-standing fear of a corrupt European Old World. That fear of the Old World was the flip side of what Commager viewed as the unique American sense of mission in the global community. But in that community, he complained, the United States had a double standard. We needed to admit that we mounted our own aggressions against other countries and that the Communists didn't invent aggression. After all, the eighteenth-century American ideology of democracy was as subversive to Europe as Communism is to America in the twentieth century. So, he told the senators, we need to take the long view and cultivate patience with the revolutions and ideologies of other nations.[35]

Those who continued to support Lyndon Johnson's foreign policy objected to Commager's statement. As David Rudgers reminded Commager in the *New York Times*, "Whether the United States is overextended or not depends entirely upon how much power the nation desires to put forth." American military forces went from nearly nothing to encircling the world in the five years following 1940. Neither did the United States choose its opposition to Communism from a "missionary impulse," as Commager had suggested, but instead from a practical self-interest. "Finally," Rudgers pointed out, "if the threat of monolithic world Communism had dissipated, it is largely because both the Soviet Union and Red China have been faced with the fact of American military power placed against them."[36]

Further, despite Alfred Kazin's congratulatory letter assuring him that he "was very happy to see your noble mug so prominently displayed in a part of the Times usually reserved for the Mafia and Arthur M. Schlesinger," most of Kazin's fellow New York intellectuals would have blanched at Commager's suggestion that Americans had to be patient with other ideologies.[37] Much of the liberal intellectual community—from Sidney Hook and Irving Kristol on the neoconservative end to Harold Rosenberg and Lewis Coser on the more radical side—thought that the very function of the intellectual was to struggle against rival ideologies in order to produce the best result. After all, didn't even Commager's Jefferson believe in the active competition and struggle of contending ideas?

And again, how can we explain his earlier hostility to isolationism in light of his strong opposition to Vietnam? Did Commager change from interventionist to isolationist? No. Despite the appearance, he never was an *interventionist*. Instead he was an *internationalist*. Nurtured on Wilsonianism, he saw a sharp distinction between the two terms. The United States needed to maintain an international role by joining an organization like the League of Nations or the United Nations, he thought, because nationalism was a great danger. But he felt that a One World outlook, in which only an international body should settle problems, was not interventionist. So his criticisms of American isolationism were quite consistent with his opposition to American intervention in Vietnam.

This concurrent internationalism and hostility to interventionism was apparent in his writing throughout his career. In 1946, for example, while advising the United States against starting an arms race, he warned that our very reliance on atomic warfare "means that though we have abandoned isolationism intellectually, we have not yet abandoned it emotionally, or adjusted ourselves to the reality of One World." At the dawn of the Cold War, that is, he cautioned that "though we have formally committed ourselves to the United Nations Organization and are active in its deliberations, we prefer to conduct our security policy as if that organization did not exist or were condemned in advance to impotence. It means that we are using our position as the leading nation in the world to inspire fear rather than confidence."[38] That is, the United States was acting as an interventionist instead of an internationalist power.

Twenty years later he used that same argument against the Johnson administration's Vietnam policy. Late in 1964 he wrote Senator Fulbright and told him that the United States should submit the Vietnam problem to the Security Council of the United Nations. In addition, the United States should ask China to help with the solution, since the United States couldn't impose its solution unilaterally on Vietnam any more than China or the Soviets could impose a solution on Cuba or Guatemala. If the United States tried to act alone, he told Fulbright, it would create a disaster.[39]

Others of Commager's professional friends, such as Schlesinger, were content to be known as interventionists. In *The Vital Center* (1949) Schlesinger pondered the most "effective means of overthrowing an established government," wondered how to stop "the loss of Asia and Africa to the Soviet Union," and concluded that while One World government was a noble ambition for the future, in the present it would only "serve to distract men of good will from the urgent tasks of the moment."[40]

Because many liberals, such as Schlesinger or members of the New York intellectuals, were committed interventionists, they had a more difficult time than Commager extricating themselves from the outlook that produced American involvement in Vietnam. Consequently they ended up with a more ambivalent opposition to the war or a later and more muted resistance to it. Commager's internationalism is part of what accounted for his greater foreign policy radicalism in the 1960s than many others in the liberal community.

A more genuine contradiction, shared by many liberals of his generation, confronted Commager with respect to the power of the presidency. Not surprising for the Hamiltonian ethic interlaced with his Jeffersonianism, so characteristic of early twentieth-century progressivism, Commager admired a strong presidency. As a New Dealer he had promoted Roosevelt's active leadership style. In 1941 Commager, then under the spell of war, declared enthusiastically that "all the 'strong' Presidents were 'great' Presidents, and all the 'great' Presidents were 'strong' Presidents." Nor had any weak president ever been permanently cherished by the nation.

Further, when the power of the presidency declined and Congress transgressed the Constitution during Reconstruction, it showed that a strong legislature and not a strong executive was the greatest danger. So "the only dictatorship in our history that seriously threatened the foundations of our constitutional system and of our liberties was Congressional dictatorship," and, conversely, "without exception periods of democratic advance have coincided with periods of Executive power."[41]

Then in early 1951, when there was a national debate about whether President Truman or Congress had the right to decide if and how many U.S. troops would be committed to Korea and to NATO forces bound for Western Europe, Commager supported the presidential prerogative. Sending troops to Korea without congressional authorization wasn't a usurpation of power, he announced, and he ridiculed a resolution to require congressional approval before military forces could be sent out of the country in the future. The Constitution declared that the president was to make sure the laws were faithfully executed, and Commager maintained that "laws" meant treaties as well as statutes.

The U.S. Constitution, he reported, was not only a document but also a tradition of precedents, and presidents had ordered troops to a variety of places. These acts had "involved the danger of war" abroad, so in effect presidents were able to encourage wars if they so wished. Congress or the courts had never repudiated those presidential powers nor failed to fund them. When Congress approved U.S. involvement in NATO and the UN, it fit the president with the defense and security obligations membership entailed. If the Congress now denied the president "the right to use troops or arms abroad," then the charters of those organizations to which we belonged would be meaningless.[42]

Angered, conservative Senator Robert A. Taft, Republican of Ohio, accused Commager of believing that the president "has the right to start a war whenever he sees fit to do so." Taft pointed out that Commager confused the president's valid right to direct a war that was already being waged with an alleged right to make whatever peacetime troop maneuvers he wished. Until war is declared, Taft asserted, the right of Congress "to restrain warlike actions is fully justified." In response, Commager admitted that he supported "the Presidential system of government" but denied that he defended a president's right to start a war whenever he chose. Standing with Commager on this issue, Schlesinger called Taft's opinions "demonstrably irresponsible."[43]

When the Bricker amendment was proposed in 1953 in order to limit the president's power to make agreements with foreign governments, Commager denounced it. The Founders, after all, had given the president the "amplest authority" in foreign relations. It was conservative conspiracy theorists and McCarthy's isolationist paranoiacs who supported the amendment at just that time "when our international responsibilities imperatively demand the strengthening, not the weakening, of the executive branch." Unfortunately, Commager noted, the Bricker amendment was "inspired by an unwillingness to assume the great role which the United States is now required to play in world affairs."[44]

During the thirty years following Franklin Roosevelt's assumption of power, Commager was an enthusiastic proponent of strong presidential power. In the pursuit of an appropriate domestic and foreign policy, he and many liberals fought for great power for FDR against a conservative Congress, and supported extra terms for him. Even Truman, except for an occasional loyalty oath, had been considered by liberals to be fighting popular struggles abroad and was not at war with citizens at home. Congress during the 1930s and 1940s was more conservative than the executive branch, and so in Commager's view less trust-worthy. But by the mid-1960s this had changed. Commager and many other liberals now began to denounce the enlarged presidential power assumed by Lyndon Johnson and Richard Nixon when it was employed to stage unpopular military excursions abroad, assault a liberal Congress at home, and combat citizens on issues of civil rights, war protest, dissent, and drugs. In Commager's perception it was now Congress instead of the executive branch that housed figures who questioned the established orthodoxies.

In this reversal of opinion, Commager was in good company. While Sena-tors Fulbright and Wayne Morse in 1951 had, like Commager, supported Truman's presidential power with respect to military commitments, by the 1960s those senators were among the most notable opponents of presidential prerogative in the Vietnam War. Schlesinger was another who had changed his mind. Initially standing with Commager against Taft's support of Con-gress, by the time Nixon was in office Schlesinger wanted limits on the presi-dency and admitted that "Senator Taft had a much more substantial point than [I] supposed twenty years ago." Commager, meanwhile, never acknowledged that he had altered his position. But liberals didn't have to worry about mo-nopolizing the backflips. Nixon and other conservatives who had supported the increased power of the conservative Congress at midcentury magically had come to realize, by the time he assumed the executive office, the national importance of increasing the strength of the presidency.[45]

In 1968, during the Johnson administration, when the Senate was consider-ing a resolution to limit the presidential use of armed force outside the United States, Commager turned from his earlier position and supported the resolu-tion vigorously. Now he found in the history of past administrations, from Monroe to the present, a tradition that would caution us against trusting the president's war powers instead of encouraging executive leadership as he for-merly suggested.

Why should we restrict presidents when we hadn't in the past? Because now they were motivated by ideological instead of practical concerns, an interest-ing distinction that would be so impossible to demonstrate that Commager didn't even try. Further, now we were part of an international body that was responsible for keeping the peace. Yet he didn't bother to mention that the United States was already a member of the United Nations several years prior to his arguing the opposite side of the issue in his debate with Taft and his criticism of the Bricker amendment.

The misuse of presidential power, he determined, was driven by our obses-sion with Communism and would not end until we had regained our sobriety. The abuse of executive power was a reflection "of abuse of power by the American people and nation" which had characterized the preceding two de-cades. We were destroying not only our moral authority in the world but also our political institutions at home.[46]

Then on March 8, 1971, Commager was the first person to give testimony before the Senate Foreign Relations Committee when it began considering whether to create a War Powers Act that would limit the president's authority. The *New York Times* reported that he gave "a 45-minute history lecture followed by a 90-minute seminar" before "his new senatorial students." As he had suggested in earlier decades, he told the senators that a judgment of the war powers had to be rooted in history instead of theory, precedence rather than the written Constitutional document. But now Commager believed that the unambiguous intention of the Constitutional framers was "to make it impossible for a 'ruler' to plunge the nation into war."

Further, the committee heard that presidential war powers were now being used for a new kind of intervention. Recent military excursions were global instead of domestic or hemispheric, and they were motivated by the new doctrine that the United States had vital interests in distant locations. Interventions were no longer justified as emergency moves but instead were assumed to be a routine use of presidential power. All of this was part of the Cold War disease, a psychology obsessed with power, and the American belief that it could solve uncomfortable problems quickly with force.[47]

When he realized in the early 1970s that the deceptive and underhanded Nixon was emblematic of the worst aspects of the Cold War, Commager was spurred to an even greater worry about presidential power. In the *New York Times* in 1971 he accused Nixon of distrusting free speech and the press more than any other president since John Adams. Nixon was trying to ride "roughshod" over constitutional liberties by wiretapping, using police force, and trying to silence journalists, and his administration was eager to use censorship and coercion instead of reason and persuasion.[48]

The handling of the Pentagon Papers case by Nixon's lieutenants was typical. Not only had they tried to intimidate the television networks and then filed suit against the *New York Times*. Now at the end of 1971 they had subpoenaed a legislative assistant to Senator Gravel, who had read some of the papers into the Congressional Record. Nixon's officials at the Justice Department, claiming that Gravel's action threatened national security, were, according to Commager, threatening "the constitutional privileges of a co-ordinate branch of the Government." Nixon's executive branch was trying to subordinate the other branches under its dominance, in violation of constitutional principles.[49]

Because of his outspoken public criticism of the Nixon administration, Commager was asked to join the Committee for Public Justice, a liberal group that was formed to battle the erosion of constitutional liberties. The group began in the spring of 1970 with a handful of individuals associated with the *Nation* and the *New York Review of Books*, and then broadened to take in a mix of Hollywood stars and various academic notables—including historians such as C. Vann Woodward, Schlesinger, and Commager.[50] "Now we are to have, God help us, four more years of what is surely the most constitutionally insensitive administration of this century," Schlesinger lamented to Commager when Nixon was reelected in November 1972. "And what a ghastly irony that Nixon should be President at the time of the Bicentennial of the Declaration."[51]

His writing, activity, and associations didn't earn Commager friends in the executive branch, and it was reported that he was on an FBI "no-contact list" of individuals whom agents should avoid unless given special permission. This meant that Commager and others on the list were considered to be antagonistic enough to the Bureau that unfavorable contact by the FBI could result in bad publicity.[52] And indeed Commager was troubled by the FBI. Secrecy and deceit, he warned, were "now fundamental not only to the conduct of the war but to the conduct of foreign and even domestic affairs." While totalitarian countries lived by deceit, the Nixon presidency was hardly better, since it operated by "lies so innumerable that no one can keep up with them, so insolent that they confound refutation, and so shameless that in time they benumb the moral sensibilities of the American people."[53]

His friend Schlesinger ended up on a different enemies list. Late in June 1973, Schlesinger and several hundred others found that they were included in a White House file, several inches thick, entitled "Opponents List and Political Enemies Project." Apparently Schlesinger was considered to be one of Nixon's antagonists whom the administration, as John Dean so thoughtfully phrased it, would attempt to "screw" with "the available Federal machinery," such as the Internal Revenue Service. Among those sharing space on the list with Schlesinger were such dangerous enemies of the republic as Barbra Streisand, Paul Newman, Joe Namath, and *Baltimore Sun* writer Thomas O'Neill, who had died three months before the list was constructed. "I suppose Hitler and Stalin may have had such lists," Schlesinger remarked, "but no American President. Nixon saw himself as being above the law, and those under him acted accordingly."[54]

While Commager was not alone in his concern about a presidency out of control, he was recognized as a leading voice on the issue. In a front-page article in the *New York Times* in the spring of 1973, Commager was quoted prominently as saying that Nixon had used powers that had no precedents. In what the *Times* called "an extreme but not uncommon view," Commager explained that Nixon had "usurped or aggrandized authority in almost every field," and, by his attacks on Congress and the Supreme Court, had assaulted the constitutional system as no earlier president had done even in wartime—Lincoln not excepted. Others clearly thought that Commager was wrong, and that Nixon merely had expanded the power of the presidency in degree but not in kind. The real expansion of presidential power, many observers thought, had occurred under Kennedy and Johnson.[55]

In October 1973, the *New York Times* ran a headline announcing "Commager Urges Nixon Impeachment," under which it reported a speech in which he claimed that Nixon had violated the law thirteen times, and that he should be dismissed from office for his "long, unparalleled record of corruption and illegal actions." Although Commager's friend Barbara Tuchman had earlier called only for Nixon's voluntary resignation, less than a week after Commager's challenge she supported his position and declared that it was now up to Congress not to set "a precedent of acquiescence" that could destroy our political system near its two-hundredth birthday.[56]

As the problems of impeachment began to be discussed by national leaders, Commager took to the newspapers on two occasions to outline Nixon's five specific crimes that justified the action. First, by lying to Congress and the American people about the conflict in Cambodia, he circumvented the Constitutional right of Congress to declare war. Second, that action also prevented Congress from exercising its right to appropriate funds for war. Third, Nixon's impoundment of funds for domestic programs denied Congress its Constitutional independence. Fourth, he transgressed the Bill of Rights by applying prior censorship over the press. Fifth, he undermined the democratic political process by resorting to dirty tricks.[57]

Yet, as Melvin Grayson pointed out in the *New York Times*, "each of the five putative grounds for the impeachment of President Nixon" in Commager's articles "could have been applied with equal validity to John F. Kennedy." JFK, after all, usurped war powers in the Bay of Pigs invasion, used electronic surveillance against the Reverend Dr. Martin Luther King, Jr., and performed what the press referred to as "pranks" against opponents. These five charges could have been leveled against many other presidents as well. "Mr. Commager's failure to point this out," Grayson concluded, "leads me to suspect that, despite his credentials, he is not so much a historian as he is a pamphleteer."[58]

That was not the only problem with Commager's position, of course. Equally uncomfortable was the contradiction, as in the case of the War Powers testimony, that he had been for much of his early career a supporter of a strong presidency. If his earlier endorsement of presidential power hadn't envisioned a Nixonian misuse of the office, it promoted the changes that led to it. Still, despite the dramatic evolution on this issue by Commager and other liberals, he was one of the principled voices attempting to recreate a tolerant democratic ethic during the sixties and their immediate aftermath by reining in arbitrary and unconstitutional actions. Although some might have thought his liberalism weak and naive, others found it a useful antidote to the arrogance and misuse of power poisoning America in this period.

And perhaps contradictions may be forgiven. A political life, even for the most principled, is often a confusing journey. For even if one holds tight to principle, inflexibly and rigidly, the background and surrounding context in which that principle must be applied are constantly changing. Not only do the terms themselves change, so that individualists are called liberals at one point in history and then libertarian conservatives at another. Even more uncomfortable is the necessity for a person to change principle in order to pursue a consistent goal over time.

Who would suggest that historians such as Commager or Schlesinger should never change their minds on an issue of such importance, or that they were wrong to do so in this case? Arguing against a position they formerly supported took courage and could not have been comfortable. In order to produce what they considered to be a more liberal, humane, and democratic political culture, they changed their opinions on the balance of power between Congress and the president. If, by fear of contradiction, they had failed to pursue their vision of the proper democratic process, it would only have suggested arid and inflexible minds.

While there are important affinities between Commager's beliefs and some other sections of the liberal intellectual community, as have been suggested here, there are significant differences that should not be overlooked. Because most liberals shared at least some commitment to civil liberties, free expression, and competition, their differences are what most clearly defined them. Among other important tribes of liberal political intellectuals in the decades after World War II, it is useful to measure the ideas of Commager against the beliefs of those associated with the *Nation* magazine and those who subscribed to the values of the New York intellectuals.

Although Commager was fond of the *Nation*, shared its hostility to McCarthyism, and respected its defense of civil liberties, he was never as sympathetic to the Soviet Union, with which he had neither imaginative nor ideological connection. The magazine's dissenting posture he found admirable, but its editorial voice was never sufficiently internationalist. If other magazines too strongly supported the United States, the *Nation* too firmly backed the Soviets. Neither side deposited its trust in a One World view built around the United Nations.

With the New York intellectuals Commager shared few traits but Schlesinger shared many. Sure, Schlesinger was raised in Cambridge rather than New York, amid affluence instead of poverty, and missed the socialist background and subsequent disillusionment of the New York group. Yet he shared their enthusiastic anticommunism in the 1940s and 1950s, joined them in fighting philosophical and political absolutism, wrote for their publications, was an active member of New York intellectual organizations such as the American Committee for Cultural Freedom, and attended their conferences from New York to Milan. Perhaps most importantly Schlesinger was keenly influenced by the work of Reinhold Niebuhr, so he held in common with members of the New York group such as Lionel Trilling, Richard Hofstadter, and Daniel Bell their emphasis on tragedy, ambiguity, and irony. It was a chastened postwar sensibility that many of the New York intellectuals had learned either from Niebuhr or from their experience, during the Cold War and the rise of mass society, of having to abandon their earlier socialist optimism and many of their former ideals.[59]

While Commager, who was no friend of totalitarianism, would have agreed with much of what Schlesinger wrote in *The Vital Center*, it never would have occurred to him to adopt its apocalyptic tone nor to write a book promoting Cold War policies—partly because Commager never considered domestic Communism a greater threat than the infringement of civil liberties. Schlesinger was one who, like Sidney Hook and the other New York intellectuals, took ideological issues very seriously and realized that the future of freedom might hang in the outcome of intellectual battles. So when the fellow-travelling Waldorf Conference was staged in New York in 1949, for example, Schlesinger was drawn to oppose it publicly by addressing the anticommunist Americans for Intellectual Freedom conference at the Freedom House in New York.

Commager, meanwhile, was nowhere to be found. Not only did he avoid ideological polemics such as the Waldorf affair represented, but he might have been on the other side of the issue from Schlesinger and the New York group. Commager's political outlook was dangerously close to what in *The Vital Center* Schlesinger had contemptuously called "doughface" liberalism: liberalism that he considered too soft on Communism. In his book Schlesinger was disdainful of the doughface Independent Citizens Committee for the Arts, Sciences, and Professions, and its outgrowth the Progressive Citizens of America. Because Commager was chairman of the ICC's Westchester chapter, Schlesinger in 1947 warned him of its dangers. "In other words," he advised Commager, "I don't think you belong in the ICC, and I hope to hell you stay out of the PCA."[60]

When *The Vital Center* appeared in 1949 Commager reviewed it sympathetically but cautiously for the *New York Herald-Tribune*. The book was useful in its criticism of totalitarianism, Commager found, and valuable in its promotion of moderation instead of extremism. But he also discovered that Schlesinger waged an uncomfortably narrow argument against the left and was "pretty hard on the Progressives," to whom Commager had far closer ties than Schlesinger. Many of those criticized in the book as irresponsible leftists Commager considered merely well-intentioned dissenters. He reminded Schlesinger that "a complacent society has need of fanatics" and "a wholesome society has room for all shades of opinion."

Their difference of opinion resulted from their slightly different vantages. So while Schlesinger warned that the United States was fatally slow to recognize the totalitarian threat, Commager responded that "fatal is a strong word, and we are still alive. The number of intellectuals who were ever taken in by Communism is certainly negligible." Commager felt that, because Schlesinger associated with those such as the New York intellectuals who were acutely aware of the Communist presence in the intellectual community, perhaps the author of *The Vital Center* had overreacted to the situation. "Mr. Schlesinger's investigations of Communism in New York and Washington," Commager suggested simply, "may have persuaded him of a danger which he might not have observed had he worked in Chicago or Minneapolis or Kansas City."[61]

Further, Commager would not have thought to disparage the *Nation*'s record on Communism, as was done by Schlesinger and the New York group.[62] Still no one, least of all Schlesinger, thought that Commager was in any way sympathetic to Soviet Communism. Instead it was felt that he was insufficiently enthusiastic in his anticommunism. Being a civil libertarian and Jeffersonian, Commager wanted no element of speech or thought repressed, including unpopular Soviet ideas. In fact, as his writings reveal, he considered anticommunism to be a greater danger than Communism to the United States. In the rhetoric of the period, while Schlesinger and the New York intellectuals were anticommunists, Commager would have been considered by many to be an anti-anticommunist.

Much of the difference between the liberalism of Schlesinger and Commager results from their dissimilar philosophical alignments. Commager was never a theoretical writer. On several occasions he acknowledged that he followed Trevelyan's advice that a theory was something that you should take from instead of bring to your work.[63] What theory he did employ was of a concrete sort: a Jeffersonianism, a Deweyan pragmatism, a vision of democratic process derived from his study of constitutional law and the works of figures such as Tocqueville. Like the New York intellectuals, Schlesinger was quite different. As *The Vital Center* demonstrates, he was comfortable citing Marx or Trotsky, Schumpeter or Rosa Luxemburg, Keynes or Spencer, Kierkegaard or Fromm, Koestler or Niebuhr.

Like others of his generation who were sensitive to the passing winds of theory, in the wake of World War II Schlesinger felt the impact of the darker philosophical conceptions articulated by Niebuhr and others. Schlesinger's work revealed a tragic and ironic sense of history, a respect for ambiguity, complexity, and unpredictability, and this Niebuhrian vision separated him from Commager, whose liberalism continued to bear the optimistic tone of unfallen Jeffersonianism. Consequently, in the decades after World War II Commager focused most of his activist energies on preserving civil liberties, a Jeffersonian concern, while Schlesinger (until the Nixon presidency) aimed his initiatives at opposing totalitarianism, a more Niebuhrian preoccupation.

Even in the early 1970s, when Commager lamented signs of moral declension in America, his work had an optimistic scent, whereas Schlesinger, decades earlier, had decided that the threat of the Soviet Union had burst "the bubble of the false optimism of the nineteenth century." But while Schlesinger's detractors considered his fervent anticommunism a weakness, it reflected that Niebuhrian side of him that was tough enough to face the uncomfortable choices that Commager's critics accused him of avoiding. If not every-one embraced the solutions Schlesinger offered in *The Vital Center*, at least his readers found him addressing such problems as whether or not a citizen had a right to work for the government, what constituted the relevant details of political loyalty, and other related questions.[64] These were the kinds of di-lemmas that Sidney Hook, Irving Kristol, Roger Baldwin, and others thought Commager left untouched.

Yet Commager's reputation has suffered during the past generation not so much because of his politics but rather his scholarship. Because he was part of that group of intellectual historians at midcentury who searched for an Ameri-can character, rendering his writing not immediately employable by our cur-rent multicultural ethic, his American studies orientation no longer seems interesting to younger scholars. Looking back on his noted *The American Mind* (1950), many now find it disappointing.

But perhaps the current generation is looking in the wrong place for Com-mager's contribution. From the compilation of his activist intellectual speeches and essays from the 1950s through the early 1970s came his two best books: *Freedom and Order* (1966) and *The Defeat of America* (1974). There, in his history and advice about how to protect dissent, individual rights, constitutional powers, and democratic liberties, his analytical and polemical powers are most evident. His mind and rhetoric were always sharpest when operating as an intellectual activist instead of an Olympian scholar, and his brief journalistic pieces in these two books gave him the proper vehicle to show his strengths.

The past generation has incorrectly supposed that Commager's reputation should rise or fall entirely on the scholarly merits of *The American Mind* and similar histories. We should realize that Commager and many other similar historians share a trait in common with those figures in related fields such as Daniel Bell, Lionel Trilling, or Sidney Hook: their contributions to culture will only be properly assessed when both their intellectual and scholarly efforts are taken into account.

NOTES

1. Commager to Mary Nevins, March 16, 1971, Allan Nevins file, Henry Steele Commager papers (HSCP), Amherst College.

2. For representative discussion of the distinction between intellectuals and scholars see Russell Jacoby, *The Last Intellectuals* (New York: Basic Books, 1987); Neil Jumon-ville, *Critical Crossings* (Berkeley: University of California Press, 1991); Theodore Ham-erow, *Reflections on History and Historians* (Madison: University of Wisconsin Press, 1987); and Christopher Jencks and David Riesman, quoted Peter Novick, *That Noble Dream* (New York: Cambridge University Press, 1988), pp. 52–53.

3. For recent accounts of the intellectual activities of historians see Michael Wreszin, "Arthur Schlesinger, Jr., Scholar-Activist in Cold War America: 1946–1956," *Salmagundi* 63–64: 255–85, Spring-Summer 1984; Roy Rosenzweig, "Marketing the Past: *American Heritage* and Popular History in the United States, 1954–1984," *Radical History Review* 32: 7–29, March 1985; Novick, *That Noble Dream*; Jonathan Wiener, "Radical Historians and the Crisis in American History, 1959–1980," *Journal of American History* 76 (2): 399–434, September 1989; and Michael D. Bess, "E. P. Thompson: The Historian as Activist," *American Historical Review* 98 (1): 18–38, February 1993.

4. Henry Steele Commager, "An Inquiry into 'Appeasement,'" *New York Times Magazine*, February 11, 1951, pp. 39–40.

5. Henry Steele Commager, letter to the editor, *New York Times*, May 17, 1960, p. 36. Commager to Allan Nevins, September 23, 1961, October 15, 1961, October 23, 1962, and October 29, 1963; box 76, Allan Nevins papers, Rare Book and Manuscript Library, Columbia University.

6. Commager to Allan Nevins, April 20, 1965; box 81, Allan Nevins papers.

7. Drafts of telegrams from Commager to Lyndon Johnson, Robert McNamara, George Ball, and J. William Fulbright, February 7, 1965, Vietnam War file, HSCP.

8. Henry Steele Commager, draft of letter to the editor of the *New York Times*, February 12, 1965; Vietnam War file, HSCP.

9. William J. King, Jr., to Commager, February 17, 1965; Edith Titon to Commager, February 17, 1965; Vietnam War file, HSCP.

10. Henry Steele Commager, draft of letter to the editor of the *New York Times*, March 7, 1965; drafts of letters to the editor of the New York *Herald-Tribune*, March 31, 1965, July 29, 1965, and December 1, 1965; Vietnam War file, HSCP.

11. *New York Times*, December 5, 1965, p. 13.

12. *New York Times*, April 5, 1967, pp. 1–2.

13. *New York Times*, May 11, 1967, p. 9.

14. "The Week," *National Review* 19 (31): 832, August 8, 1967; "For the Record," *National Review* 19 (19): 542, May 16, 1967.

15. Donald F. Tingley, "Allan Nevins: A Reminiscence," *Journal of the Illinois State Historical Society* 66 (2): 177–86, Summer 1973, pp. 183–85. Nevins suggested that business history "is far more important to the development of the republic, and to an understanding of our civilization, than our political or intellectual history." Allan Nevins, "Business and the Historian," in Ray Allen Billington, ed., *Allan Nevins on History* (New York: Scribner's, 1975), p. 81. For his sympathy toward business history see also pp. 70–73, 112, and Harvey Wish, *The American Historian* (New York: Oxford University Press, 1960), p. 326.

16. Henry Steele Commager, "The Reminiscences of Henry Steele Commager [1979]," Columbia University Oral History Research Office, New York, 1983, p. 51.

17. Commager to Allan Nevins, November 17 (no year), February 23, 1965, and April 20, 1965; box 81, Allan Nevins papers.

18. Allan Nevins to Commager, April 26, 1965, and April 30, 1965; Allan Nevins file, HSCP.

19. Allan Nevins to Commager, January 22, 1966; Allan Nevins file, HSCP. Mort R. Lewis, "Allan Nevins' Triumph of Will," *American History Illustrated* 11 (9): 26–33, January 1977, p. 32.

20. Gregory Pfitzer, *Samuel Eliot Morison's Historical World* (Boston: Northeastern University Press, 1991), pp. 270–71.

21. Commager, "Reminiscences," pp. 52–53.

22. Jumonville, *Critical Crossings*, chapters 1, 3.

23. For most of his life Hook thought of himself as a Jeffersonian, and in fact shortly before his death he claimed he was more of a Jeffersonian than Commager. (Hook to the author, December 19, 1988.) While some might object to Hook's description of himself as a Jeffersonian, the term does underscore basic values shared by Hook and Commager about the benefits of intellectual freedom, open debate, and a marketplace of ideas. True, Hook wasn't a pure Jeffersonian, in the original conception of that term, but then neither was Commager.

24. Sidney Hook, "America Now: A Failure of Nerve?" *Commentary* 60 (1): 41–43, July 1975, p. 42.

25. Sidney Hook, "Unpragmatic Liberalism," *New Republic* 130: 18–21, May 24, 1954, p. 19.

26. Leo Cherne, "Why We Can't Withdraw," *Saturday Review*, December 18, 1965, p. 17.

27. Mary McCarthy, *The Seventeenth Degree* (New York: Harcourt Brace Jovanovich, 1974), pp. 149–55, 171–87. Reprinted from Diana Trilling and Mary McCarthy, "On Withdrawing from Vietnam: An Exchange," *New York Review of Books* 10 (1): 5–10, January 18, 1968.

28. Max Weber, "Politics as a Vocation," in H. H. Gerth and C. Wright Mills, eds., *From Max Weber: Essays in Sociology* (New York: Oxford University Press, 1946), pp. 120, 126–27.

29. Hook, "Unpragmatic Liberalism." Irving Kristol, "'Civil Liberties,' 1952—A Study in Confusion," *Commentary* 13 (3): 228–36, March 1952. Roger Baldwin, letter to the editor, *Harper's*, November 1947 (no page number).

30. For the split in the liberal intellectual community, see Jumonville, *Critical Crossings*, chapter 1–3; and William L. O'Neill, *A Better World* (New York: Simon and Schuster, 1982).

31. Henry Steele Commager, "The Last Best Hope of Earth," *Senior Scholastic* January 5–10, 1942, p. 13; "Why the War Came," *Senior Scholastic*, February 2, 1942, p. 8; "The Senators and the Peace," *Senior Scholastic*, April 5–10, 1943, p. 9; "The Lessons of April 6, 1917," *New York Times Magazine*, April 6, 1952, p. 13; and "Maker of History, Writer of History," *Reporter* 10: 34–38, January 19, 1954, p. 38.

32. Henry Steele Commager, "The Republican Party 'Is a Mess,'" *New York Times Magazine*, January 12, 1964, p. 9.

33. Henry Steele Commager, letters to the editor, *New York Times*, May 17, 1960, p. 36; April 17, 1963, p. 40. Commager to Allan Nevins, September 23, 1961, October 15, 1961, October 23, 1962; box 76, Allan Nevins papers.

34. *New York Times*, February 21, 1967, pp. 1, 16.

35. Henry Steele Commager, "Statement by Henry Steele Commager at the Hearings Before the Committee on Foreign Relations of the United States Senate, February 20, 1967," Commager's own manuscript of his talk; copy in the Senator J. W. Fulbright and Fulbright Hearings file, HSCP.

36. David F. Rudgers, letter to the editor, *New York Times*, March 5, 1967, section 4, p. 9.

37. Alfred Kazin to Commager, February 21, 1967; J. W. Fulbright and Fulbright Hearings file, HSCP.

38. Henry Steele Commager, "Where Are We Headed?" *Atlantic* 177: 54–59, February 1946, pp. 57–58.

39. J. William Fulbright to Commager, December 15, 1964; Commager to Fulbright, December 20, 1964; Vietnam War file, HSCP.

40. Arthur Schlesinger, Jr., *The Vital Center* (Boston: Houghton Mifflin, 1949), pp. 221, 230, 240–41.

41. Henry Steele Commager, "Are We Creating a Dictator?" *New York Times Magazine*, March 2, 1941, pp. 3, 23–24.

42. Henry Steele Commager, "Presidential Power: The Issue Analyzed," *New York Times Magazine*, January 14, 1951, pp. 11, 23–24.

43. *New York Times*, January 16, 1951, p. 10; January 22, 1951, p. 16; Arthur Schlesinger, Jr., *The Imperial Presidency* (Boston: Houghton Mifflin, 1973), p. 139.

44. Henry Steele Commager, "The Perilous Folly of Senator Bricker," *Reporter* 9: 12–17, October 13, 1953, pp. 12, 17.

45. Schlesinger, *The Imperial Presidency*, pp. 138, 285–86.

46. Henry Steele Commager, "Can We Limit Presidential Power?" *Defeat of America*, pp. 48–58; first printed in the *New Republic*, April 6, 1968.

47. Henry Steele Commager, "Determining on Peace and War" (reprint of Commager's Senate testimony), *Defeat of America*, pp. 59–81.

48. Henry Steele Commager, *New York Times*, June 18, 1971, p. 38.

49. Henry Steele Commager, "A Senator's Immunity," *New York Times*, October 15, 1971, p. 41.

50. Norman Dorsen (Chairman of CPJ) to Commager, October 10, 1972; Committee for Public Justice file, HSCP.

51. Arthur Schlesinger, Jr., to Commager, November 9, 1972; Arthur Schlesinger, Jr., file, HSCP.

52. *New York Times*, January 14, 1972, p. 21.

53. Commager, *Defeat of America*, pp. 96–97.

54. *New York Times*, June 28, 1973, pp. 1, 38. "Creating a New Who's Who," *Time* 102 (2): 19, July 9, 1973.

55. *New York Times*, March 4, 1973, pp. 1, 47.

56. *New York Times*, October 23, 1973, p. 32; Barbara Tuchman, *Practicing History* (New York: Ballantine, 1982), pp. 297–301.

57. Henry Steele Commager, "The Real Bases for Impeachment," *The Defeat of America*, pp. 141–49 (reprinted from *Newsday*, May 12, 1974); "Five Grounds for Impeaching the President," *New York Times*, June 28, 1974, p. 33.

58. *New York Times*, July 13, 1974, p. 22.

59. On Schlesinger's anticommunist ties to the New York intellectuals, see Wreszin, "Arthur Schlesinger, Jr., Scholar-Activist," pp. 268–69. For his anticommunism generally see Schlesinger, *The Vital Center*. On his anti-absolutist connections to the New York group, see Neil Jumonville, "The New York Intellectuals' Defence of the Intellect," *Queen's Quarterly* 97 (2): 290–304, Summer 1990; and Schlesinger, "The Opening of the American Mind," *New York Times Book Review*, July 23, 1989, pp. 1, 23–24. For his debt to Niebuhr see Marcus Cunliffe, "Arthur M. Schlesinger, Jr.," in Marcus Cunliffe

and Robin Winks, eds., *Pastmasters* (New York: Harper and Row, 1969), pp. 363–64, 373–74. Daniel Bell noted that he, Niebuhr, Lionel Trilling, and Richard Hofstadter were all influenced by the winds of irony, complexity, tragedy, ambiguity, capriciousness, and limitation at midcentury. "The thing which put together Niebuhr, Trilling, and Hofstadter," Bell reported, ". . . is the emphasis on the tragic sense of life." Interview with Daniel Bell, May 20, 1985; and Jumonville, *Critical Crossings*, pp. 124–26.

60. Schlesinger, *The Vital Center*, pp. 115, 136, 150. Hannah Dorner (executive director of the ICCASP) to Commager, August 2, 1946; Schlesinger to Commager, January 3, 1947; Arthur Schlesinger, Jr., file, HSCP.

61. Henry Steele Commager, "The Survival of Liberalism in Our World," *New York Herald-Tribune Weekly Book Review* 26 (4): 1, 17, September 11, 1949, p. 1.

62. Schlesinger, *The Vital Center*, p. 37; Jumonville, *Critical Crossings*, chapter 1.

63. Henry Steele Commager, *The Study of History* (Columbus, Ohio: Merrill, 1966), p. viii.

64. Schlesinger, *The Vital Center*, pp. 212–17.

Chapter 20

EDMUND WILSON AT OXFORD

IsaIah Berlin

I MET EDMUND WILSON, I think, sometime in the early spring of 1946, after I had come back from Moscow to finish the job I was doing at the British Embassy in Washington. I had been in Washington during the war years, and my friend the Russian composer Nicolas Nabokov, who, like his cousin Vladimir, was a friend of Wilson's, thought that he might like to meet me (I had expressed my intense admiration for *Axel's Castle* and *The Triple Thinkers*) and talk about Russian literature and other topics. Wilson refused. He was convinced that any British official could want to meet him only in order to rope him into the British propaganda machine. He was acutely isolationist: his Anglophobia, which in any case had been fairly acute, was increased by the reflection that England had once again managed to drag America into a dreadful and totally unnecessary war, and he had no wish to meet any representative of that country. However, once the war was over he evidently decided that he was no longer in any danger of being inveigled into pro-British activities, and asked me to lunch at the Princeton Club in New York.

I was, I own, rather taken aback by his appearance. I do not know what I had imagined a distinguished literary critic to look like, but there stood before me a thickset, red-faced, pot-bellied figure, not unlike President Hoover in appearance; but once he began to talk, almost before we had sat down, I forgot everything save his conversation. He spoke in a curiously strangled voice, with gaps between his sentences, as if ideas jostled and thrashed about inside him, getting in each other's way as they struggled to emerge, which made for short bursts, emitted staccato, interspersed with gentle, low-voiced, legato passages. He spoke in a moving and imaginative fashion about the American writers of his generation, about Dante, and about what the Russian poet Pushkin had meant to him. He described his visit to the Soviet Union in 1935 and the appalling effect which this had had upon him, for, like many other members of the American intelligentsia, he had once tended to idealize the Communist regime.

The climax of his visit was a meeting with Prince D. S. Mirsky. Mirsky was a brilliant, highly original émigré writer in English on Russian literature who had become a convert to Marxism in England; he then returned to Russia and soon after this published a book denouncing British writers and intellectuals, some of whom had befriended him. Wilson found him in Moscow in a very low and wretched state (two years later he was arrested and sent to a camp, where he died). Mirsky's downfall and pathetic condition had made an indelible impression on Wilson, and he spoke long and bitterly about the passing of his own political infatuation. He then talked about Russian literature in general, and particularly about Chekhov and Gogol, as well as I have ever heard anyone talk on any literary topic. I was completely fascinated; I felt honored to have met this greatly gifted and morally impressive man. We became friends. I did not return to the United States until 1949, when I went to teach at Harvard, and stayed a night with Wilson at Wellfleet, where he was living with his wife Elena. I went to see them both on subsequent visits in the 1950s.

In 1954 he came to England and telephoned virtually from the airport to tell me that he wished to come to Oxford and stay with me for a day or two. I welcomed this. Since I was not married then, I was living in All Souls College. Wilson did stay two nights with me in a not very attractive college room (which he describes with characteristic acerbity in his diary).[1] He was in a splendidly Anglophobic mood. On the first morning, before lunch, we went for a walk to look at the colleges. When we passed Christ Church, he looked at the decaying library (not then yet refaced, as it would be later, with the assistance of the Rockefeller Foundation) and said, "Oh, most of these buildings look in very poor shape—I think they're actually falling down," and looked delighted. "I think that's the case with a lot of England," he went on; "I think your country deserves a bit of this."

He then launched into a sweeping attack on academic life and academics in general as murderers of all that was living and real in literature and art—classical, medieval, modern. I asked him whether there were no academics he liked or admired. He said that there were indeed a few: one was Christian Gauss, his teacher at Princeton, whose lectures he had greatly admired and whom he had liked and deeply respected as a man; another was Norman Kemp Smith, who had been a professor of philosophy at Princeton in his day and was now living in retirement in Scotland. (Wilson had gone to see him during a visit to England in 1945, the visit on which the pages about England in *Europe Without Baedeker* were founded.) Apart from these he could for the moment think of no one.

The diatribe continued (I had no idea whether this was a passing mood, induced by Oxford, or a permanent attitude): he could wish for no worse fate for anyone than to hold a job at a university, particularly if it were connected with literary studies; he had heard that Archibald MacLeish contemplated becoming, or had become, a professor somewhere; was it Harvard? It was a fate that that ass deserved (I had read Wilson's devastating parody, "The Omelet of A. MacLeish," and had realized that this poet was not one of his favorites). Then there had been the ridiculous Ted Spencer at Harvard, who tried to seek him out but had died before any relationship could be attempted; and there was also Spencer's protégé, Harry Levin—a clever man, and widely read, with interesting things to say, who had had it in him to become something if only he had not chosen to make a career at Harvard, which had turned him into a pedantic schoolmaster, buried in trivial detail, a Dryasdust, who turned everything into dust, a kind of colored dust. "Oh, but I can't explain it," he said. "I talked to him about Howells—he doesn't think Howells is any good at all." He went on to say that Harry Levin was, in spite of all this, not a bad fellow; he could be highly perceptive and interesting, but he was ridiculous about Howells. I was under the impression that they were friends (as I feel sure in fact they were), and was taken aback by these remarks about Levin, whom I admired and whose essay on Stendhal I thought a remarkable piece of work. But he would not relent. His next target was Perry Miller; then C. S. Lewis; he went on and on in a ferocious fashion. Perhaps Tennyson talked about Churton Collins in this way when he called him a louse in the locks of literature. I saw no reason to doubt that he spoke of me in similar fashion; it was obviously part of him; I loved him as he was.

He asked me whether it was to be his fate to meet more academics at lunch or dinner. I relieved his fears about lunch by saying the guests would be Stephen Spender and another man of letters (I cannot remember who); in the evening, however, if he wished to dine in All Souls as he had suggested, he might well meet some academics. Would he prefer to dine in a restaurant? No, he said, he wished to plumb the depths of old, decayed, conservative English academic life in its death-throes. I remember his words: "It can't be long now," he said ominously. "I think we're in at the kill." I did not ask him to develop this theme, but tried to divert him on to other subjects. No good. He said that in England—London—writers and the like formed little cliques, jealous coteries engaged in keeping each other out; there was no real literary world; Evelyn Waugh could not be in a room with Peter Quennell, a perfectly decent man of letters; both had spoken ill of Cyril Connolly; Auden was ostracized; nobody had a kind word to say about MacNeice or Angus Wilson; and so on and so on. Most of this seemed absurdly misconceived to me. To get him off this topic I asked him—unwisely, as it turned out—what his last visit to England had been like. But by then it was time for lunch. He seemed to enjoy the company, denounced the writers of the *Partisan Review*, said that Philip Rahv was able enough but, like the rest of them, used literature to make political points, and praised V. S. Pritchett as one of the few critics whose thought was free and who had something to say.

After lunch he reminded me of my earlier question and told me what had occurred during his previous London visit. He had arrived as a kind of war correspondent, and the wartime British Ministry of Information had detached the well-known publisher Hamish Hamilton, who was then a member of that ministry and was half American, to look after him. Hamilton had organized a party of eminent members of the British literary establishment. According to Wilson, he saw at the party, among others, T. S. Eliot, one or two Sitwells, Cyril Connolly, Siegfried Sassoon, Harold Nicolson, Peter Quennell, and, I think, Rosamond Lehmann. He wished to talk to none of these. "T. S. Eliot," he said, "is a gifted poet, but somewhere inside him there is a scoundrel. When I see him, which is not often, I just cannot take him. I do not wish to meet him, although I think some of his poetry is wonderful—it repels me, but it is poetry." The Sitwells he dismissed as being of no interest. The only person there that he was able to speak to was Compton Mackenzie—they swapped stories about life before and during the First World War, and he found the appearance, manner, and conversation of the old buccaneer quite entrancing.

I gradually realized that there is a sense in which Wilson belonged to an earlier generation than the literary intelligentsia of England at that time; that the kind of people he preferred were the Edwardians—full-blooded, masculine men of letters, with sometimes coarse (and even to some degree philistine) but vital personalities—and that this was the world to which Compton Mackenzie truly belonged. Desmond MacCarthy had once described to David Cecil and myself a typical dinner he had attended some years before the First World War in a London club—the Reform, or it may have been the Travellers'. Present were Rudyard Kipling, H. G. Wells, Max Beerbohm, Hilaire Belloc, G. K. Chesterton, Arnold Bennett, and Bernard Shaw, as well as Henry James and the young Hugh Walpole. There was no talk about literature or the arts, or friendship or nature or morality or personal relations or the ends of life—the kinds of things that were discussed in Bloomsbury. There was not a touch of anything faintly aesthetic—the talk was hearty, concerned with royalties, publishers, love affairs, absurd adventures, society scandals, and anecdotes about famous persons, accompanied by gusts of laughter, puns, limericks, a great deal of mutual banter, jokes about money, women, and foreigners, and a great deal of drink. The atmosphere was that of a male dining club of vigorous, amusing, sometimes rather vulgar friends. These were the best-known authors of the time, the "blind leaders of the blind" so much disliked and disapproved of by Bloomsbury. It seemed to me that Edmund Wilson, for all his unerring sense of quality and his moral preoccupations, had an affinity with these masters. I do not think that he would have greatly enjoyed tea with Virginia Woolf or an evening with Lytton Strachey.

Hence the literary party in London did not suit him at all, and, after a few perfunctory words with E. M. Forster about Jane Austen, he told Hamish Hamilton that he wanted to get away from it as soon as possible. After the conversation with Compton Mackenzie he swiftly withdrew, to the disappointment, so Hamilton told me, of some of those invited. All he wished to do was to go to Scotland and see his mentor, Kemp Smith. Hamish Hamilton, who had probably never heard of this Kantian scholar, did his best to arrange for the journey to Scotland. Wilson did manage to see him—he told me that he had had a good time with him, that they had talked about the old times with great pleasure and had discussed the decline in the standards of European scholarship. Then he came back to London to be met at the station by the courteous and indefatigable Hamilton, who tried to persuade him to get into a taxi to go to his hotel. It was evening; Wilson had become convinced (so he told me) that what Hamilton was mainly anxious to do was to prevent him from seeing the prostitutes who then walked the streets of London in exceptional numbers (so he had been told). He did his best to evade Hamilton, for whom he had by then conceived one of his violent, irrational dislikes (by this time reciprocated by Hamilton, who told me on a later occasion that Wilson was one of the most unpleasant and difficult people he had ever encountered). Wilson did get into a taxi, but, by God, he got out of it after five minutes, and he *did* walk the streets, particularly Park Lane, and he *did* see prostitutes, and he felt that he had scored off the officials who had been sent to escort him, almost, he thought, in the manner of the Russian secret police.

I tried to persuade him that all that Hamish Hamilton had attempted to do was to extend the kind of courtesies which cultural institutions thought to be his due. Wilson would have none of that: he was certain that an attempt was being made to bear-lead him in London, to prevent him from meeting unsuitable people whom in fact he might have liked to meet. This conviction—that there was a general conspiracy in England, of a Soviet type, not to let him meet unsuitable people—obsessed him, and was to surface later in Oxford. I asked him if he had disliked every literary person he had met in London. He said, "No, I like Evelyn Waugh and Cyril Connolly best." Why? "Because I thought they were so nasty." Perhaps this referred to later meetings, because I do not know if Evelyn Waugh was in London during the war, in which he served as a soldier. He had also taken to Angus Wilson because he reminded him of the heartfelt human feelings of the kind of Americans with whom he felt at home. It was the aestheticism, the prissiness, the superciliousness, the cliquishness, the thin, piping voices, the bloodlessness, the preoccupation with one's own emotions both in life and in literature—all of which he (no less than D. H. Lawrence) attributed to Bloomsbury—that irritated him. He thought the whole of English literary life was infected by this. I don't know what he would have said about J. B. Priestley—I think that he was, perhaps, below his angle of vision. He could not bear the thought of the Huxleys, Aldous or Julian.

Evening fell, and it was time for dinner in the Common Room of All Souls College. He had me dining on one side and the senior fellow, the historian A. L. Rowse, on the other. He hardly spoke to Rowse, although Rowse tried to speak to him. He turned to me brusquely and engaged in conversation about mutual friends in America—Justice Felix Frankfurter and his wife, Nicolas Nabokov and his wives, the playwright Sam Behrman, Mary McCarthy (to whom Wilson had been married), Conrad Aiken, Arthur Schlesinger, Judge Learned Hand, and others. Reluctantly he turned to his other side and allowed himself to be addressed by Rowse. He answered in monosyllables. After coffee, when we came back to my rooms, he complained that a flood of British nationalist propaganda had been poured over him by Rowse at dinner, that he had not come to Oxford to be made a victim of cultural chauvinists. I think that on a later occasion, when Rowse went to see him in the United States, they may have got on a little better—but on this occasion he was in a grumpy mood and would not let up.

He said that he realized why the All Souls College servants removed the plates so rapidly, hardly letting him finish a single dish—he spoke of a Barmecide feast—it was because they were acutely class-conscious, hated their masters, wanted to serve them as gracelessly as possible and get away from their hated presence as quickly as they could. He had noticed, he said, that class consciousness was clearly rampant in this ancient establishment. I did not argue with him—he was, I think, past convincing on this and most other points. What he said was characteristic wonderful nonsense, of course. The majority of scouts (servants) in Oxford were certainly then, and perhaps are still, among the most conservative of its inhabitants; they were conscious carriers of ancient college traditions, old retainers if ever there were such, who for the most part—certainly at that time—refused to be unionized, on the ground that this was an insult to what they conceived to be their status and very special function. The servants at All Souls exemplified this type almost to the point of caricature.

It was plain that Wilson on that day—as on many others—lived in a world of angry fantasy, particularly in the case of anything British, and although I was devoted to him, felt deep admiration and respect for him to his dying day, and remain intensely proud of the friendship that bound us, I knew that it was useless to argue with him once he got the bit between his teeth. This was certainly the case during his stay with me in Oxford. After dinner I had invited my colleague David Cecil, the novelist Iris Murdoch and her husband, the critic John Bayley, and the philosopher Stuart Hampshire to meet him. It was not a happy evening. He took against everyone in the room. He mistook Bayley for the critic Humphry House (with whom he might well have got on) and virtually ignored him and everyone else. He became listless, answered in monosyllables, gurgled, drank a great deal of whisky, and looked with hateful eyes at everyone. Although Iris, who is the soul of courtesy and kindness, tried to make things go, and John Bayley, a beguiling talker, did his best, the old bear remained in his lair, glaring balefully from time to time and trying to drown his boredom in drink. The evening came to an early end. At the end of it he burst out about these feeble creatures—aristocrats who dabbled in literature were useless; the dons were all bloodless monks, cut off from all that mattered. Why could I not have invited one of the few academics with guts, like A. J. P. Taylor, whom he wanted to meet because he liked his radical polemics? I said that I knew and liked Taylor, despite a slight *froideur* caused by a somewhat disparaging review he had written of a small book I had just published, but that I would gladly arrange a meeting between them—and did so on the following day.

Taylor was most amiable to us both. Wilson said that he had quite enjoyed his visit to Taylor's rooms in Magdalen College. But then Taylor had taken him to a lecture by Steven Runciman on a Byzantine subject, which bored him stiff; once again he heard the overrefined and, to him, deeply depressing accents of Bloomsbury, those high, thin voices which he could not bear. (I do not know how many of these voices he had ever actually heard.) I also arranged for him to see the Jewish historian Cecil Roth, because at this time he took an increasing interest in Jewish history and was learning Hebrew—it was not long before the publication of his book on the Dead Sea Scrolls. That visit also went well, particularly as I had warned him that Roth was something of a bore, though a worthy and learned antiquary; those mildly disparaging words were enough to make Wilson like him. He muttered something about being kept from people he admired by persons (myself) who for some reason decided to "blackball" them—more fantasy, more mild paranoia.

Once he had formed a sociological and psychological hypothesis, he held onto it grimly with a kind of pleased deliberate perversity, against all evidence. He told me that the only persons he had truly enjoyed meeting in England, apart from his old friend Sylvester Gates, whom he had known at Harvard many years before, were Connolly (again because what he said was so malicious), Taylor, Roth, and Angus Wilson. The rest seemed to him repellent. "And Compton Mackenzie? And Kemp Smith?" Yes, indeed, these too, but that was all. The most hateful figure to him in England, he said, was Winston Churchill, who was nothing but a typical low-grade American journalist. If it were not for Sylvester Gates and myself he would not have come to England. Did Oxford still contain a ridiculous puffed-up fellow called Maurice Bowra, whom he had met with Gates and who, for all his knowledge of languages, had no understanding whatever of literature? He loved literature—that was evident—a pity that he had nothing of interest to say about it; he gathered that he was a friend of mine: how could this be? His conversation was banal and empty to a degree, just a lot of shouting. He could not understand how such writers as Cyril Connolly and Evelyn Waugh could be said to owe so much to this inflated philistine—they were at least gifted, he was a caricature John Bull. The diatribes went on. By this time he had drunk a great deal and his eyes were almost closed. I managed to get him to his bedroom, not without some difficulty.

Next day he was serene and gentle. We talked about Russian writers, about his life in Talcottville, which he pressed me to visit with him, about Hebrew tenses and the structure of the Hungarian language (which he contemplated acquiring), about his intense admiration for the poetry of W. H. Auden, about the interesting position of the *New Yorker* in American cultural life, about the monstrously patronizing attitude of Europeans, not only the despicable English but the French and even the Italians, toward American culture, toward such great poets as Walt Whitman and such prose writers as Herman Melville and Henry James—they were recognized, but the fact that they were Americans had always, it seemed to him, to be explained away or apologized for. But America would show them. There was a wonderful generation of young technologists and engineers coming up in America, confident, gifted, clear-headed, uncluttered men in thin drill suits (I remember this odd description), inventors of excellent new gadgets; these men were building a new, fresh, highly practical civilization that would respond to new human needs and would open prospects of wonderful new comforts of life, and this would supersede the decay and self-conceit and squalor of a fast-declining, petty-minded European culture. Nevertheless, these *boutades* of his were less violent than on the day before and rarer. Wilson was in a calmer and happier mood, quite relaxed. He explained that his life was, and always had been, literature and writers, that music[2] and even painting meant less, even though they did mean a great deal: Malraux was marvelous on sculpture. Nothing had contributed so much to his ideas about life and art—to what seemed to him to matter, politics and all—as the great Russian masters. Pushkin had begun to move him more than Shakespeare, but not more than Dante; what terrible nonsense Orwell had written about Tolstoy and *Lear*. He said that his distaste for the English had been increased by the knock-kneed creatures he met in London and Oxford. Did I know his friend Jason Epstein? He was, he thought, himself misanthropic enough, but Epstein outdid him—his dislike of mankind was phenomenal. He liked Epstein, and liked that in him.

After which he left. It could not be regarded as a successful visit. In spite of this, he did come back to Oxford with his wife Elena to stay for a couple of days with me and my wife—by that time we were living in a house of our own—and I took care not to invite Oxford academics to meet him, however great their eagerness and admiration. I preferred to meet him in Boston, London, and New York.

He was, in my eyes, a great critic, and a noble and moving human being, whom I loved and respected and wanted to have a good opinion of me; I was deeply touched when, not long before he died, he made me inscribe a line from the Bible with a diamond upon the windowpane of his house in Wellfleet, a privilege reserved for friends. The line was a verse from Isaiah, with whom, he insisted, I had obviously identified myself—another ineradicable fantasy, like his obstinate insistence that I had written as I did about Tolstoy only because I, too, was a fox, longing to be, indeed believing myself to be, a hedgehog. Nothing said to deny this absurdity made the faintest impression on him. He knew that "like all Jews" I sought unity and a metaphysically integrated organic world; in fact, I believe the exact opposite. The constructions of his inner world withstood all external evidence. He was prey to wild fantasies, to absurd conjectures, to irrational hatreds and loves. The fact that my prejudices largely coincided with his own was, of course, an immense source of sympathy and endearment. It was perhaps this more than anything else that brought us together.

His judgments were often erratic, and he was prey to delusions, but his humanity and integrity were total. When we went off on a tangent it might end anywhere. His review in the *New Yorker* of Pasternak's *Doctor Zhivago* was the best and most understanding, I think, in any language; but his speculation in a later article on the meaning of various names and symbols in the novel was crazy to a degree.[3] He managed to combine profound insight and extraordinary vision into cultures not his own with turbulent prejudices, hatreds, and a great deal of pure nonsense; he sometimes misfired totally and missed the target by miles; yet most of his denunciations were deserved. He was the last major critic in the tradition of Johnson, Sainte-Beuve, Belinsky, and Matthew Arnold; his aim and practice were to consider works of literature within a larger social and cultural frame—one which included an absorbed, acutely penetrating, direct, wonderfully illuminating view of the author's personality, goals, and social and personal origins, the surrounding moral, intellectual, and political worlds, and the nature of the author's vision—and to present the writer, the work, and its complex setting as interrelated, integrated wholes. He told me during his visit that the modern tendency toward purely literary scholarship, toward an often deliberate ignoring of the texture of the writer's life and society, for him lacked all genuine content. I agreed with him, fervently. Art shone for him, but not by its own light alone. He is gone, and has not left his peer.

NOTES

1. Edmund Wilson, *The Fifties*, ed. Leon Edel (New York, 1986), p. 135 (entry for 20–21 January 1954).

2. I once asked him, I cannot think why, whether he liked Wagner. He said, I think, "Yes, yes, I did, yes, when I was much younger, but it is not the kind of stuff I can listen to now."

3. The two articles are "Doctor Life and His Guardian Angel," *New Yorker*, 15 November 1958, 201–26, and (with Barbara Deming and Evgenia Lehovich) "Legend and Symbol in *Doctor Zhivago*," *Nation*, 18 April 1959, 363–73, also in *Encounter* 12, 6 (June 1959), 5–16; both were reprinted in Wilson's *The Bit Between My Teeth: A Literary Chronicle of 1950–1965* (London, 1966).

SELECTED BIBLIOGRAPHY OF WORKS BY SCHLESINGER

BOOKS

Orestes A. Brownson (1939)
The Age of Jackson (1945)
The Vital Center (1949)
The Politics of Freedom (1950)
The General and the President (with Richard Rovere) (1951)
The Age of Roosevelt, 3 volumes
　　The Crisis of the Old Order (1957)
　　The Coming of the New Deal (1959)
　　The Politics of Upheaval (1960)
The Politics of Hope (1963)
A Thousand Days: John F. Kennedy in the White House (1965)
Ideas and Responsibility: The Intellectual and Society (1966)
Herbert H. Lehman (1967)
The Bitter Heritage (1967)
Congress and the Presidency (with Alfred De Grazia) (1967)
Violence: America in the Sixties (1968)
The Crisis of Confidence (1969)
The Imperial Presidency (1973)
Robert Kennedy and His Times (1978)
The Cycles of American History (1986)
The Disuniting of America (1992)

EDITED COLLECTIONS

Paths of American Thought (1963)
History of American Presidential Elections, 1789–1968 (1971)
　　Supplemental Volume, 1972–1984 (1986)
The Coming to Power: Critical Presidential Elections in American History (1972)
History of United States Political Parties (1973)
The Dynamics of World Power (1973)
Congress Investigates: A Documented History 1792–1974 (with Roger Bruns) (1975)
Almanac of American History (1983)
Running for President: The Candidates and Their Images (1994)

CONTRIBUTORS

SIR ISAIAH BERLIN is Professor (Emeritus) at Oxford University and has had a long interest in the Counter-Enlightenment and Russian intellectual history. Among his many publications are *Karl Marx* and *Against the Grain*.

JOHN MORTON BLUM, Professor (Emeritus) of History at Yale University, is author of, among other works, *The Republican Roosevelt* and *Years of Discord*.

ALAN BRINKLEY is Professor of History at Columbia University and author of *Voices of Protest* and *The End of Reform*.

GEORGE COTKIN, Professor of History at California Polytechnic University at San Luis Obispo, has written *William James: Public Philosopher* and *Reluctant Modernism*.

JOHN PATRICK DIGGINS is Professor of History at the Graduate Center of the City University of New York. His recent books include *The Promise of Pragmatism* and *Max Weber*.

JOHN KENNETH GALBRAITH is Professor (Emeritus) of Economics at Harvard University and former U.S. Ambassador to India. Among his many works are *The Affluent Society* and *The Great Depression*.

EUGENE D. GENOVESE is a retired Distinguished Scholar in Residence at the University Center in Georgia. Among his publications are *Roll Jordan Roll* and *The Southern Tradition*.

NEIL JUMONVILLE is Professor of History at Florida State University. He has written *Crooked Crossings: The New York Intellectuals* and is currently working on a biography of Henry Steele Commager.

GEORGE F. KENNAN is a Fellow at the Institute for Advanced Study in Princeton and former U.S. Ambassador to the Soviet Union. His vast body of scholarship includes *American Diplomacy* and *Russia and the West*.

WILLIAM E. LEUCHTENBURG is Professor of History at the University of North Carolina, Chapel Hill, and former president of the American Historical Association. He is the author of, among other works, *Franklin D. Roosevelt and the New Deal* and *The Supreme Court Reborn*.

MICHAEL LIND is an editor at the *New Yorker* and author of *The Next American Nation*, *Up From Conservatism*, and the novel *Power Town*.

JEAN V. MATTHEWS, Professor of History at the University of Western Ontario, has written *Rufus Choate* and *Toward a New Society*.

KATHLEEN D. MCCARTHY is Professor of History at the Graduate Center of the City University of New York and Director of the Center for the Study of Philanthropy. She is the author of *Women's Culture* and *Noblesse Oblige*.

LOUIS MENAND is Professor of English at the Graduate Center of the City University of New York and a contributing editor to the *New York Review of Books*. He has written

Discovering Modernism and is editor of the forthcoming *The Future of Academic Freedom.*

ROBERT REMINI is Professor (Emeritus) of History at the University of Illinois at Chicago and author of *Andrew Jackson* and *Henry Clay.*

LEO P. RIBUFFO, Professor of History at George Washington University, is the author of *The Old Christian Right* and *Right, Left, Center.*

FRED SIEGEL, Professor of History at Cooper Union College, has written *Troubled Journey* and is working on a study of modern urban liberalism.

RONALD STEEL is Professor of International Relations at the University of Southern California. His works include *Walter Lippmann and the American Century* and *Pax Americana.*

HUGH THOMAS, a member of the House of Lords, taught at Oxford University and served as an advisor to Prime Minister Margaret Thatcher. His books include *The Spanish Civil War* and *Conquest: Montezuma, Cortez, and the Fall of Old Mexico.*

BETTY MILLER UNTERBERGER, Professor of History at Texas A&M University, is author of *America's Siberian Expedition* and *The United States, Revolutionary Russia, and the Rise of Czechoslovakia.*

RICHARD C. WADE, Professor (Emeritus) of History at the Graduate Center of the City University of New York, is author of *The Urban Frontier* and is currently working on a project to address the problem of illiteracy in America.

SEAN WILENTZ, Professor of History at Princeton University, has written *Chants Democratic* and, with Paul Johnson, *The Kingdom of Matthias.*

ACKNOWLEDGMENTS

Chapter 1, "The Historian and the Public Realm," by William E. Leuchtenburg, was first published in the *American Historical Review* 97, no. 1 (Februrary 1992): 1–18.

Chapter 3, "The Historian and the Cycles of History," by George F. Kennan, was first published in the *New York Review of Books* (November 6, 1986).

Chapter 8, "Race, Sex, and the Dimensions of Liberty in Antebellum America," by Jean V. Matthews, was first published in a different version in *Journal of the Early Republic* 6 (Fall 1986): 275–291.

Chapter 14, "Woodrow Wilson and the Cold War," by Betty Miller Unterberger, was delivered in a different version as an address at Texas A & M University in 1986.

Chapter 15, "America after the Cold War: Global Order, Democracy, and Domestic Consent," by Ronald Steel, was reproduced by permission of the author. Copyright © 1994 Ronald Steel. First published in *The International System after the Collapse of the East-West Order* (Netherlands: Martinus Nijhoff Publishers, 1994).

Chapter 20, "Edmund Wilson at Oxford," was reproduced with permission of the author. Copyright © Isaiah Berlin 1987. First published in the *Yale Review*.

DATE DUE